Beyond Foundationalism

BEYOND FOUNDATIONALISM

Shaping Theology in a Postmodern Context

Stanley J. Grenz and John R. Franke

Westminster John Knox Press
LOUISVILLE
LONDON · LEIDEN

Unless indicated otherwise, all scripture quotations in the publication are from the Holy Bible, New International Version. Copyright © 1973, 1978, 1984 International Bible Society. Used by permission of Zondervan Bible Publishers. Scripture quotations marked NIV ILE are from New International Version, Inclusive Language Edition, Hodder & Stoughton. Scripture quota-tions marked NRSV are from the New Revised Standard Version of the Bible, copyright © 1989 by the Division of Christian Education of the National Council of the Churches of Christ in the U.S.A., and are used by permission.

Book design by Sharon Adams
Cover design by Mark Abrams

First edition
Published by Westminster John Knox Press
Louisville, Kentucky

This book is printed on acid-free paper that meets the American National Standards Institute Z39.48 standard. ⊗

PRINTED IN THE UNITED STATES OF AMERICA

02 03 04 05 06 07 08 09 10 — 10 9 8 7 6 5 4 3 2

Library of Congress Cataloging-in-Publication Data

Grenz, Stanley, 1950–
    Beyond foundationalism: shaping theology in a postmodern context / Stanley J. Grenz and John R. Franke.— 1st ed.
        p. cm.
    Includes bibliographical references and index.
    ISBN 0-664-25769-0 (pbk.: alk. paper)
    1. Theology, Doctrinal—History—19th century. 2. Theology, Doctrinal—History—20th century. I. Franke, John R. II. Title.

BT28 .G747 2001
230'.01—dc21

00-040419

To Gordon R. Lewis
and Robert A. Peterson
who instilled in us the importance
of a sound theological method

Contents

Preface

At the conclusion of the 1995 Wheaton Theology Conference on the possibilities and challenges of dialogue between "evangelical" and "postliberal" theologians, George Lindbeck startled many in attendance with his closing remark. After expressing his appreciation for the conversation that had occurred at the conference, he boldly asserted that "if the sort of research program represented by postliberalism has a real future as a communal enterprise of the church, it's more likely to be carried on by evangelicals than anyone else."[1] In a previous gathering at Wheaton, this time a meeting of the Society of Christian Philosophers in 1994, Nancey Murphy mused about the possibility of conservatives consciously adopting an approach to method that could facilitate the reformulation of theology in a postmodern framework. She suggested that such an endeavor might lead to a lessening of the stark left-right division that has characterized theology in the modern era.[2] Admonitions and observations such as these suggest that the time is ripe for evangelicals to enter into the broader methodological conversation, which in many respects has been dominated in the last hundred years by thinkers standing in the mainline and liberal theological traditions. What follows in this volume is an attempt by two theologians representing the conservative trajectory in theology to provide a theological framework in which the kind of ecclesiologically focused, evangelically tuned, communally directed research program envisioned and called for by Lindbeck might flourish. It is offered with the goal of fostering the type of postmodern and post-divisive theological endeavor anticipated by Murphy.

The genesis of this project lies in John's preparation in the summer of 1993 to begin teaching theology at Biblical Theological Seminary in the fall after

---

1. "A Panel Discussion: Lindbeck, Hunsinger, McGrath and Fackre," in *The Nature of Confession: Evangelicals and Postliberals in Conversation,* ed. Timothy R. Phillips and Dennis L. Okholm (Downers Grove, Ill.: InterVarsity Press, 1996), 253.

2. Nancey Murphy, "Philosophical Resources for Postmodern Evangelical Theology," *Christian Scholar's Review* 26, no. 2 (Winter 1996): 184–205.

spending three years in England. In the process of developing lectures for an introductory course on theology and theological method he read Stan's then recently published book *Revisioning Evangelical Theology*,[3] which called for an approach to theology that more effectively addressed the postmodern context. This work provided an initial framework for John's rethinking of questions relating to the nature, task, and method of theology in the contemporary setting. Over the next two years he became convinced that the proposal sketched out by Stan in *Revisioning*, while essentially sound, needed to be developed more fully, and he set himself to that task. In the spring of 1996, Stan's visit to Biblical Seminary to deliver a series of lectures provided the occasion for our discussion of John's plan to write a full-scale work on theological method that developed and extended Stan's proposal. In that context, Stan suggested that we consider writing the book together, and after further conversation over the next several months we decided to follow this course of action. Thus, *Beyond Foundationalism* represents our joint attempt to extend and more fully delineate Stan's earlier work on the shape of theology.

Our conversations throughout the envisioning and writing process have resulted in a truly coauthored book. In order to expedite this project we agreed that Stan would take responsibility for composing the initial drafts of chapters 3, 5, 7, and 8 while John would produce the first drafts of chapters 1, 2, 4, and 6. During and after the production of the drafts we were continually engaged in further reflection, conversation, editing, and refinement with respect to the content of each individual chapter as well as the shape of the work as a whole. The result of this process is a book that represents in its entirety the work and theological position of both its authors. In the case of chapter 2, John reworked and augmented an essay that Stan originally composed as a presentation to the 1998 annual meeting of the Christian Theological Research Fellowship. A longer form of this paper appeared as "Beyond Foundationalism: Is a Nonfoundationalist Evangelical Theology Possible?" in *Christian Scholar's Review* 30/1 (Fall 2000). Moreover, a shorter version of the argument presented in chapter 3 was published as "The Spirit and the Word: The World-Creating Function of the Text" in *Theology Today* 57/3 (2000). And finally, a highly compressed form of the main proposal delineated in this volume appeared in chapter 6 of Stan's book *Renewing the Center: Evangelical Theology in a Post-Theological Era* (Grand Rapids: Baker, 2000). We express our appreciation to the publishers for graciously granting us permission to use materials from these essays in this volume.

The writing of *Beyond Foundationalism* was facilitated by a sabbatical leave from Biblical Seminary for John during the 1998–99 academic year and his appointment as a scholar-in-residence at Regent College. This allowed the two of us to spend the year together in Vancouver conversing about methodological

---

3. Stanley J. Grenz, *Revisioning Evangelical Theology: A Fresh Agenda for the 21st Century* (Downers Grove, Ill.: InterVarsity Press, 1993).

issues and honing our proposal for an approach to method that we believed could move theology beyond the crisis and into the opportunity that the demise of foundationalism occasions. We therefore thank the board and administration of Biblical Theological Seminary in Hatfield, Pennsylvania, for granting John the year-long sabbatical leave, as well as Carey Theological College and Regent College in Vancouver, British Columbia, for providing an institutional context for us to carry on our efforts. We also acknowledge our debt to our research/teaching assistants, Marcus Tso and Linda Dietch, for their work in support of this project as well as to Michael Roberts, who helped produce the list of works cited, and Laura Habecker, who compiled the index. We thank as well the staff at Westminster John Knox Press for their work on the editorial side of this project, especially Stephanie Egnotovich who not only shepherded the manuscript through the publication procedure but also offered constant encouragement to us along the way.

During our formative years as college and seminary students, we were the recipients of input from many people who poured themselves into our lives and sought to shape us as scholars in and for the church. Yet for each of us one particular person stands out as central in the development of our initial understanding concerning the importance of a sound theological method. For me (Stan), that first theological mentor was Gordon Lewis at Denver Seminary, who initiated me into what I would call the grand tradition of theological rationalism that reigned in many evangelical circles throughout the modern era. Moreover, immediately after my seminary graduation, Professor Lewis graciously delivered a memorable "charge to the candidate" at my ordination, the spirit of which I have sought throughout my career to honor and uphold. In my case (John), I look to Robert Peterson who now teaches at Covenant Theological Seminary in St. Louis but was on the faculty at Biblical Seminary while I was a student there. In addition to shaping my understanding of what it means to be a theologian for the people of God, Professor Peterson became a trusted friend and guide. He served as a model of committed Christian scholarship and encouraged me to confront the difficult questions of faith. For these reasons, we gladly dedicate this volume to Professors Gordon R. Lewis and Robert A. Peterson.

PART ONE
THEOLOGY IN THE POSTMODERN SITUATION

Chapter One

Beyond Fragmentation: Theology and the Contemporary Setting

Pneumatology is the principle of an ecclesiology of a communion which assumes local cultures and initiatives into a unity, not of mere uniformity but of a coherent harmony.
—Mariasusai Dhavamony[1]

Let anyone who has an ear listen to what the Spirit is saying to the churches.
—Revelation 2:7, 11, 17, 29; 3:6, 13, 22

Theology is in a time of transition and ferment, partly as a result of the collapse of the categories and paradigms of the modern world as spawned by the Enlightenment. Transition and ferment are not new to the theological enterprise, however. In one sense, the current situation bears similarity to other periods in history when cultural upheaval led to the rethinking of accepted norms of Christian theological discourse. The expression of Christian thought has taken shape and has been revised in the context of numerous cultural transitions: from an initially Hebraic setting to the Hellenistic world; from the thought forms of Greco-Roman culture to those of Franco-Germanic; from the world of medieval feudalism to the Renaissance; from the Renaissance to the Enlightenment; from the developed world to the third world; and currently, from a modern to a postmodern context.

Throughout this history Christian theology has shown itself to be remarkably adaptable in its task of assisting the church in extending and establishing the message of the gospel in a wide variety of contexts. At the same time,

---

1. Mariasusai Dhavamony, "The Christian Theology of Inculturation," *Studia Missionalia* 44 (1995): 42.

theological history also provides numerous examples of the inappropriate accommodation of Christian faith to various ideologies and cultural norms. This checkered past confirms the vitality of Christian theology while warning of the dangers of too closely associating it with any particular form of cultural expression.

Although the current situation is not unlike other contexts in the history of theology, it also bears the distinctive mark of fragmentation.[2] We are living in the midst of a widespread fragmentation and perhaps even disintegration that appears to be affecting all dimensions of Western culture, including the theological enterprise. Consequently, fragmentation has become perhaps the most obvious characteristic of the theological landscape today. Princeton theologian J. Wentzel van Huyssteen notes both this characteristic and its apparent source: "Even the briefest overview of our contemporary theological landscape reveals the startling fragmentation caused by what is often called 'the postmodern challenge' of our times."[3] As van Huyssteen indicates, the almost bewildering fragmentation characteristic of our day is linked to the postmodern context in which we are living.

Fragmentation need not spell the demise of theology, however. In fact, the contemporary situation might even provide the occasion for a renaissance of theology itself. But for such a renewal to occur, theologians must come to understand the nature of the transition that has been transpiring in Western culture and its significance for the theological discipline. They must set themselves to the task of grappling with the implications of our setting, lying as it does "after modernity,"[4] for the shaping of theology.

Theology in the Midst of Fragmentation

The theological fragmentation that seems to be the order of the day extends well beyond the division between liberal and conservative theology that typified the theological discussion throughout much of the twentieth century. Today we find significant differences not only between these groups but also *within* them, differences regarding a host of theological issues, including basic questions about the nature of theology and the theological task.

Fragmentation—Mainline and Conservative

At one time it was commonplace to view the theological discussion as a debate involving two sparring partners and to see the theological landscape as neatly divided between the liberals and the conservatives, each of whom, it was

---

2. For one account of this fragmentation, see Paul Lakeland, *Postmodernity: Christian Identity in a Fragmented Age* (Minneapolis: Fortress Press, 1997).

3. J. Wentzel van Huyssteen, "Tradition and the Task of Theology," *Theology Today* 55/2 (July, 1998): 213.

4. For this designation, see Thomas C. Oden, *After Modernity . . . What? Agenda for Theology* (Grand Rapids: Zondervan, 1990).

thought, sported a united front. Today division—even fragmentation—has invaded both camps.

Fragmentation in Mainline Theology

Fragmentation now characterizes the heirs of the liberal theological program, for the once seemingly monolithic mainline theology seems to be beset with a deep rift. On one side of this fracture stands a group of thinkers who desire to maintain the theological trajectory that finds its roots in the program pioneered by nineteenth century liberalism. David Tracy uses the term "revisionist" to describe this group of contemporary theologians who continue, in some sense, to pursue the goals and concerns of nineteenth-century "liberal" theology.[5] These theologians continue to uphold the primacy of universal human experience as providing the foundation for the theological task.[6]

For example, Tracy maintains that Christian theology "can best be described as philosophical reflection upon the meanings present in common human experience and language and upon the meanings present in the Christian fact."[7] Moreover, he asserts that scriptural claims must be scrutinized and critiqued according to the criteria of common human experience[8] to correlate Christian faith with the common concerns and experiences shared by all people and with the development of an objective and universally accessible approach to religion. In short, according to Tracy, theology must speak in ways that are "disclosive and transformative for any intelligent, reasonable, responsible human being."[9] Theologians must not conceive of their task as that of speaking only to religious adherents but rather as that of developing patterns of discourse and argument that seek to persuade all people of the truths they profess.

In recent years, the contemporary embodiment of the liberal program has come under sharp critique from another group of mainline theologians, who are often associated with the designation "postliberal."[10] From the standpoint of these theologians, Tracy's proposal is a classic example of allowing the world to "absorb the text." Building from the pioneering work of Hans Frei,[11] especially

---

5. David Tracy, *Blessed Rage for Order: The New Pluralism in Theology* (New York: Seabury Press, 1975).

6. Prominent theologians who have been associated with the "revisionist" paradigm include Paul Tillich, Karl Rahner, Hans Kung, Edward Schillebeeckx, Langdon Gilkey, Peter Hodgson, and Schubert Ogden. Francis Schüssler Fiorenza, *Foundational Theology: Jesus and the Church* (New York: Crossroad, 1984), 276–7.

7. Tracy, *Blessed Rage for Order*, 43.

8. Ibid., 44.

9. David Tracy, "Defending the Public Character of Theology," *The Christian Century* 98 (April 1981): 351–2.

10. The term "postliberal" is used by George Lindbeck to describe an approach to theology based on a "cultural-linguistic model" of religion. George Lindbeck, *The Nature of Doctrine: Religion and Theology in a Postliberal Age* (Philadelphia: Westminster Press, 1984). Other "postliberal" theologians include Hans Frei, Paul Holmer, David Kelsey, Ronald Thiemann, William Werpehowski, William Placher, Kathryn Tanner, and George Hunsinger.

11. George W. Stroup, *The Promise of Narrative Theology* (Atlanta: John Knox Press, 1981), 36.

his influential book *The Eclipse of Biblical Narrative* (1974),[12] and following the lead of Karl Barth's earlier call for a wholesale break with the liberalism of his day, postliberals advocate a move beyond the latent liberal program they find within much of the theology of the twentieth century.

George Lindbeck, who is arguably the most widely discussed postliberal theologian, offers a program that reverses the direction of conformity he thinks characterizes the revisionist paradigm.[13] Instead of seeking to contextualize the biblical message in such a way as to conform it to the conceptualities of the modern world, as in the revisionist program, Lindbeck calls for an approach to theology that seeks to redescribe and contextualize the modern world using the stories, symbols, and categories of the Bible. From his perspective this allows Christian scripture to play the lead role in the process of Christian culture formation, rather than the secular world, whose thought forms are alien to those of the Bible. He calls this program "intratextual theology" and defines its task as follows: "Intratextual theology redescribes reality within the scriptural framework rather than translating Scripture into extrascriptural categories. It is the text, so to speak, which absorbs the world, rather than the world the text."[14]

Postliberal theology takes as its starting point the shared language and practices of a particular religious community and understands its primary task as that of self-description rather than correlation with universal human experience and reason. It is concerned with reflection on the intrasystemic relationship of beliefs within the Christian faith and the constructive and coherent articulation of these beliefs or doctrines. As William Placher puts it, this approach to theology attempts to provide a coherent explanation of "how the world looks from a Christian perspective, with whatever persuasive force that account musters and whatever connections it may happen to make with other perspectives, but it does not systematically ground or defend or explicate that picture in terms of universal criteria of meaningfulness or truth."[15]

At the same time, postliberals remain solidly within the liberal tradition, insofar as they do not, as George Lindbeck notes, advocate "abandoning modern developments and returning to some form of preliberal orthodoxy."[16] Yet, from the perspective of those who work out of the revisionist paradigm, such an approach to theology amounts to a retreat into a sort of Christian "ghetto" that insulates Christianity, or for that matter any other religion, from critical scrutiny and cuts off any relevance for theology in the arena of public dis-

---

12. Hans Frei, *The Eclipse of Biblical Narrative: A Study in Eighteenth and Nineteenth Century Hermeneutics* (New Haven, Conn.: Yale University Press, 1974).

13. Nicholas Wolterstorff has suggested that this reversal of conformity constitutes the deepest "guiding metaphor" for Lindbeck and "postliberal" theologians. Nicholas Wolterstorff, *What New Haven and Grand Rapids Have to Say to Each Other*, (Grand Rapids: Calvin College, 1993), 2.

14. Lindbeck, *Nature of Doctrine*, 118.

15. William C. Placher, *Unapologetic Theology: A Christian Voice in a Pluralistic Conversation* (Louisville, Ky.: Westminster/John Knox Press, 1989), 19.

16. Lindbeck, *Nature of Doctrine*, 7.

course.[17] Revisionist theologian James Gustafson has attacked Lindbeck's position as a destructive "sectarian" inducement that legitimates the withdrawal of Christianity from its cultural surroundings. He asserts that if theology follows such a "perilous" path its voice will be silenced and its message eclipsed.[18]

Fragmentation in Conservative Theology

A parallel division is evident within the conservative theological house as well. In fact, in recent years an increasing number of commentators have sounded warnings that ominous storm clouds are rising on the evangelical theological horizon and suggested that the possibility of outright schism threatens the evangelical coalition. In their attempts to bring to light the growing fissure, concerned observers devise a variety of grids by which to gauge the exact nature of the imminent breach in the evangelical ranks. Evangelical theologian Millard Erickson has identified what he sees as the dangerous tendencies of a group of thinkers he lumps together somewhat superficially as comprising "the evangelical left."[19]

Timothy Phillips and Dennis Okholm offer a quite different appraisal. Rather than suggesting that evangelicals are fragmenting over whether or not they should appropriate a reigning theological outlook of a past generation as Erickson does, the two Wheaton College theologians look to a current theological development, postliberalism, for the source of the current parting of ways, which according to Phillips and Okholm divides evangelical theologians into not two, but three, distinct groups. On the right are those who follow Carl Henry's earlier wholesale rejection of the new movement. The "postconservatives" on the left, according to the authors' somewhat misleading portrayal, "have linked their proposals with the postliberals." Phillips and Okholm themselves prefer the group of "moderates" who purportedly establish a common cause with the postliberals while sharply questioning the postliberal agenda.[20]

Another provocative characterization of the fragmentation among evangelical theologians is offered by Roger Olson, who sees the emergence of two loose coalitions among evangelical theologians.[21] On one side are the "traditionalists," who uphold "traditional interpretations and formulations as binding and normative" and tend "to look with suspicion upon any doctrinal revisions and

---

17. David Kelsey, "Church Discourse and Public Realm," *Theology and Dialogue: Essays in Conversation with George Lindbeck*, ed. Bruce D. Marshall (Notre Dame, Ind.: University of Notre Dame Press, 1990), 7–34.

18. James M. Gustafson, "The Sectarian Temptation: Reflections on Theology, the Church, and the University," *Proceedings of the Catholic Theological Society of America* 40 (1985): 93–4.

19. Millard J. Erickson, *The Evangelical Left* (Grand Rapids: Baker, 1997); Idem, *Postmodernizing the Faith* (Grand Rapids: Baker, 1998).

20. Timothy R. Phillips and Dennis L. Okholm, "The Nature of Confession: Evangelicals and Postliberals," in *The Nature of Confession: Evangelicals and Postliberals in Conversation*, ed. Timothy R. Phillips and Dennis L. Okholm (Downers Grove, Ill.: InterVarsity Press, 1996),14–15.

21. Roger E. Olson, "The Future of Evangelical Theology," *Christianity Today* 42 (February 9, 1998): 40–48.

new proposals arising out of theological reflection." On the other side are the "reformists," who value "the continuing process of constructive theology seeking new light breaking forth from God's word."[22] Olson offers a perceptive, yet controversial, description of the attitudes of these two constituencies toward three significant issues: theological boundaries, the nature and progress of doctrine, and interaction with nonevangelical theologies and culture in general.

Olson describes evangelical traditionalists as responding to the question of theological boundaries by viewing evangelicalism as a "bounded set" category and seeking to determine those who are "inside" the community and those who are on the "outside." They believe that the only way to "avoid the slide into debilitating relativism and pluralism" is to develop firm boundaries. One way of achieving this is to "look to the past and acknowledge some outstanding signposts and landmarks in the history of theology as irreversible and unquestionable achievements in interpreting Scripture." As an example, many evangelical traditionalists turn to the writings and confessions of the sixteenth-century magisterial Reformation as providing the "touchstone of doctrinal truth for authentic evangelicalism."[23]

As to the nature and progress of doctrine, according to Olson's characterization traditionalists emphasize the close identification of central doctrinal affirmations with what is "directly taught in Scripture." Therefore, they tend to see doctrine as lying at the heart of the enduring essence of Christianity. For traditionalists it is not "experience or liturgy or forms of community but belief in a set of doctrinal affirmations that can be translated without substantial loss across cultures and languages throughout the centuries and across continents." In this way doctrine is the "enduring essence" of Christianity and thus traditionally accepted doctrinal formulations constitute a first-order language of revelation. Given this understanding of doctrine as a first-order language of revelation, traditionalists view doctrinal progress as "digging deeper into the historic sources and translating them for contemporary people." Thus, progress is viewed as the "effective spelling out of past achievements in theology."[24]

Because evangelical traditionalists understand the doctrinal products of their theologizing as communicating the essence of Christianity and providing norms for Christian faith, they tend to view the theology produced by those who do not share their evangelical convictions as being of little positive value. Rather, such theologies must be exposed as false and heretical in order to safeguard the theological boundaries of the church. Likewise, traditionalists tend to be resistant to the incorporation of culture as an integral part of the theological enterprise, believing that doing so will lead to the sort of cultural accommodation they see in liberal theology.

Evangelical reformists differ strongly with traditionalists on these issues. Reformists understand evangelicalism as a "centered-set" category rather than

22. Ibid., 41.
23. Ibid.
24. Ibid., 44.

the "bounded-set" of the traditionalists. They insist that the boundaries remain "open and relatively undefined" and look to the broad, central evangelical commitments as providing coherence for their approach to theology.[25] While nurturing a respect for the rich theological tradition of the past, reformists "recognize the fallibility of every human tradition and the need for ongoing reformulation of human perceptions of truth." Therefore, reformists look to the future and seek legitimate change within the continuity of the past as the basis for the continuing vitality of evangelical theology.[26]

In contrast to traditionalists, reformists draw a sharp distinction between doctrinal and theological formulations and the language of the biblical text. They view theological constructions as the church's later interpretations of the stories and teachings of canonical scripture. As such, they are continually subject to the judgment of scripture and must therefore be "held more lightly than the first-order language of the Bible and worship." The enduring essence of Christianity is not to be found in the fallible doctrines of the church but rather in the work of God in the lives of human beings. Doctrinal and theological progress for the reformist involves the discovery of "new light" flowing from the biblical narratives. Reformists maintain that by reflecting on the meanings of revelation "in the light of contemporary problems, theology can discover new solutions that may have even seemed heretical to earlier generations steeped in philosophies and cultures alien to the biblical thought world."[27]

This conception of the provisional, ongoing nature of theology means that reformist evangelicals tend to view nonevangelical theologies as "ambiguous and flawed quests for truth" from which they can learn. Such belief systems can raise appropriate theological questions overlooked by more conservative theologians and stimulate fresh thinking on the part of evangelicals. In the same way, reformists believe that they can learn from the study and examination of the thought forms and insights of contemporary culture. "Reformists live by the motto that 'all truth is God's truth—wherever it is found' and attempt to remain open to the contributions of any and all serious thinkers who seek honestly after truth." Reformists emphasize dialogue as the proper approach to the ideas of the broader theological community and contemporary culture.[28]

Fragmentation and the Postmodern Context

Reflecting on the state of the discipline, Jeffrey Stout recently quipped that contemporary theology, "like an empty pile in solitaire, is waiting for a new king

---

25. Olson defines this central evangelical core as a commitment to the Bible as the supreme norm of truth for Christian belief and practice; a supernatural worldview that is centered in a transcendent, personal God; a focus on the forgiving and transforming grace of God through Jesus Christ in the experience of conversion; and the notion that the primary task of theology is to serve the church in its mission to make the grace of God known to the whole world. Ibid., 40.

26. Ibid., 42.

27. Ibid., 44.

28. Ibid., 47.

to come along and get things started again."[29] Stout's observation is astute. Yet as Nancey Murphy notes, he fails to consider the possibility that in the meantime the rules of the game might have changed.[30]

The advent of the postmodern situation brings to light the realization that although for a hundred years conservative and liberal theologians have seemingly been going their separate ways, both have actually been responding, albeit in different ways, to the same agenda, the agenda of modernity.[31] Rather than evidencing a progression from preliberal to liberal to postliberal, as George Lindbeck proposes,[32] recent theological history suggests a different trajectory. Modernity, and not liberalism, was the focal point of the theological conversation from Schleiermacher to the present. In this conversation, the liberal and conservative theological traditions offered their own particular response to a problematic framed by the modernist cultural milieu they both shared.

The rules, however, have indeed changed. Theology, which earlier moved from the premodern to the modern and in the process spawned both liberalism and conservativism, now finds itself confronted with the postmodern situation. And the current fragmentation of theological discourse, which has emerged even within traditionally liberal and conservative circles, is in part the fallout from this change in the rules for theological discourse. Given the long-standing entrenchment of modernist assumptions, we should not be surprised to find that the postmodern challenge engenders suspicion and hostility among persons on both sides of the older theological divide. Commenting on the significance of this cultural transition, Murphy states that although the relationship between liberals and conservatives has generally been acrimonious, the differences between the two "are less significant than those between modern thinkers of all sorts and those who have adopted the standpoint of a new intellectual world in the making."[33]

In the cultural setting "after modernity," many theologians continue to pursue the modernist theological agenda. They routinely either discount the significance of the intellectual and cultural changes transpiring in our society or view such changes as largely negative. These thinkers, whether liberal or conservative, advocate that theologians maintain the course their forebears charted in response to the questions that arose out of the Enlightenment. Yet a growing number of theologians are convinced that Christians ought to take seriously the church's context within the contemporary postmodern cultural milieu. In keeping with this assumption, these thinkers draw insight for their theological work from certain impulses within postmodern writers and their precursors. Moreover, some

---

29. Jeffrey Stout, *Flight from Authority: Religion, Morality, and the Quest for Autonomy* (Notre Dame, Ind.: University of Notre Dame Press, 1981), 148.

30. Nancey Murphy, *Beyond Liberalism and Fundamentalism: How Modern and Postmodern Philosophy Set the Theological Agenda* (Valley Forge, Penn.: Trinity Press International, 1996), 85.

31. For a detailed comparison of the ways in which the both the conservative and the liberal theological agendas have been shaped by modernity, see ibid., 11–82.

32. Lindbeck, *Nature of Doctrine*, 15–19.

33. Murphy, *Beyond Liberalism and Fundamentalism*, x.

of them, both "conservative" and "liberal," have started to engage in unexpectedly fruitful conversations with those from across the older divide who have likewise begun to appropriate postmodern insights for their work.[34] Ironically, the desire to take the postmodern context seriously has not only been the catalyst making such dialogue possible but has also aroused the suspicions of those who believe that such a posture threatens to compromise fundamental commitments, whether those commitments be classically liberal or conservative.

Theological Method and the Discipline of Theology

The current situation, in the light of the history of theology, poses a set of related questions: How should theology respond to the collapse of the modern worldview? How can Christian scripture that emerged in particular ancient contexts exercise a normative function for culturally diverse incarnations of Christian theology? What is the value of past theological formulations? What is the role of culture in theological reflection? Each of these questions points to the broader issue of theological method.

Theological Method in Recent Thought

The quest for a proper method to guide the theological enterprise is, of course, not a new phenomenon. Instead, the questions we posed in the preceding paragraph have occupied theologians from the beginning of the Christian era. Nevertheless, we believe that theologians today engage in the conversation about method at a crucial moment in the history of theological thought. The contemporary context is characterized simultaneously by both a heightened interest in method as well as by a broad disinterest regarding the questions it raises.

Method and Mainline Theology

In recent years theological method has become the subject of an extensive and ongoing discussion in mainline Protestantism. Jeffrey Stout has suggested that this is due to the failure of theology in its attempt to play a meaningful role as a "distinctive contributor" to the public discourse of our culture.[35] Due in part to their inability to gain a hearing, theologians in the mainline churches have increasingly gravitated to the issue of method in the hope that greater intradisciplinary clarification with respect to the plausibility and intelligibility of theological discourse will serve to attract the interest of a culture whose attention is fixed in other directions. The problem with this approach is that it has served,

---

34. See, for example, Timothy R. Phillips and Dennis Okholm, eds., *The Nature of Confession: Evangelicals and Postliberals in Conversation* (Downers Grove, Ill.: InterVarsity Press, 1996). Also see Roger E. Olson, "Whales and Elephants: Both God's Creatures But Can They Meet? Evangelicals and Liberals in Dialogue," *Pro Ecclesia* 4, no. 2 (Spring 1995): 165–89.

35. Jeffrey Stout, *Ethics After Babel: The Languages of Morals and Their Discontents* (Boston: Beacon Press, 1988), 163.

if possible, to marginalize theology even further in the public perception, as well as to alienate those few who were attending to what was being said.

As worrisome as theologians find this situation, the relative lack of interest in theology in the church is a much greater concern. Miroslav Volf observes that while scholars address other scholars and students, the church is listening to other voices. He candidly declares, "Theologians are on the sidelines. Like the streetcorner preachers of yesterday, they find themselves talking to a crowd too hurried to honor them with more than a fleeting glance."[36] Stout reiterates the point in poignant terms: "Preoccupation with method is like clearing your throat: it can go on for only so long before you lose your audience."[37] This concern over the loss of audience, even in the church, has led an increasing number of voices in the mainline to urge that contemporary theologians "abandon their preoccupation with methodology and get on with the business of really doing theology," to cite William Placher's plea.[38]

The implied distinction between theological method and "really doing theology," however, is misleading. It suggests that various approaches to method stand in isolation from the content of theology, serving merely as prolegomena to various theological systems. It assumes that a response to methodological questions can be formulated from a position of neutrality, that is, apart from other theological, hermeneutical, or philosophical commitments. In contrast to this latent modernist assumption, conceptions of method emerge only in the context of an interrelated web of beliefs. Method is not simply a self-sufficient programmatic enterprise that can be readily abstracted from the rest of theology. Rather, decisions made about the method of theology both *inform* the entire conceptualization of a theological model and are themselves *informed by* the theological conclusions that emerge from that model.

As Miroslav Volf asserts, "method is message" in that "all major methodological decisions have implications for the whole of the theological edifice and, inversely, all major theological decisions (such as the questions of faith and reason, grace and works, church and society) shape theological method."[39] Thus, while Jeffrey Stout's poignant and oft-repeated phrase about methodological throat clearing serves as an important warning against fixating on questions of method to the exclusion of others, it is nevertheless important not to lose sight of the significance of method and its inextricable connection to the whole of theology.

Formulating a theological method is a matter of "message" and, as such, is itself an engagement in constructive theology. At the same time, the point of constructive reflection on theological method is to facilitate more fully the process of "doing theology." In short, although consideration of method is itself

---

36. Miroslav Volf, "Theology, Meaning & Power: A Conversation with George Lindbeck on Theology & the Nature of Christian Difference," in *The Nature of Confession: Evangelicals and Postliberals in Conversation*, ed. Timothy R. Phillips and Dennis L. Okholm (Downers Grove, Ill.: InterVarsity Press), 45.

37. Stout, *Ethics After Babel*, 163.

38. Placher, *Unapologetic Theology*, 7.

39. Volf, "Theology, Meaning & Power," 46.

a matter of constructive theology, the articulation of a methodological approach to theology differs in significant ways from the task of setting forth coherent conceptions of Christian doctrines and thereby dealing with such matters as theology proper, Christology, ecclesiology, or eschatology.

Method in Evangelical Theology

If theologians in mainline theological circles have been in need of a reminder that theology involves more than simply reflecting on method, their evangelical counterparts require other counsel. If mainliners have labored extensively over questions of method to the neglect of actually putting methodological constructions to work in the task of doing theology, the situation in evangelical Protestantism is nearly the reverse. Evangelical theologians have produced numerous works concerned with the content and exposition of theology. Yet they have given little attention to methodological concerns. Nor have they applied themselves to the careful examination of philosophical presuppositions or to theological hermeneutics.

Evangelicals have long bypassed the questions raised by theological method and moved directly to the task of making theological assertions and constructing theological systems, as though the process of moving from the ancient biblical text to the contemporary affirmation of doctrine and theology was self-evident. In his recent work on theological method, evangelical theologian Richard Lints flatly states, "The evangelical tradition has not been nurtured to think methodologically."[40]

As accurate as this observation appears at first glance, it may in fact fail to do justice to a subtlety of evangelical thought. After all, many of the recent efforts in evangelical systematics begin with some discussion of theological method.[41] Why then the paucity of significant engagement with methodological issues in evangelical theology? A careful reading of various evangelical systematic theologies provides a clue. Although they are written from a variety of different theological perspectives (Reformed, Wesleyan, Baptist, dispensationalist, charismatic, etc.) and arrive at strikingly different conclusions about issues of central importance in theology, on the question of method they are remarkably similar. For the most part these evangelical systematic theologies all make use of a decidedly rationalist approach to theological method.

The rationalist approach that typifies evangelical theology is characterized by a commitment to the Bible as the source book of information for systematic theology. As such, it is viewed as a rather loose and disorganized collection of factual, propositional statements. The task of theology in turn becomes that of collecting and arranging these varied statements in such a way as to bring their underlying unity into relief and reveal the eternal system of timeless truths to

---

40. Richard Lints, *The Fabric of Theology: A Prolegomenon to Evangelical Theology* (Grand Rapids: Wm. B. Eerdmans Publishing Co., 1993), 259.

41. For a survey of recent works in evangelical systematic theology, see Gabriel Fackre, *The Christian Story: A Narrative Interpretation of Basic Christian Doctrine*, 3rd ed. (Grand Rapids: Wm. B. Eerdmans Publishing Co., 1996), 254–57.

which they point. This "concordance" or "rationalist loci" conception of theology looks back to Charles Hodge, arguably the most influential American theologian for evangelicals, and his view that the task of theology "is to systematize the facts of the Bible, and ascertain the principles or general truths which those facts involve."[42] Hodge's own understanding of theology is generally derived from the scholasticism characteristic of post-Reformation Protestant orthodoxy and its emphasis on rationalism.[43] Evangelicals in the twentieth century, buoyed by the assumptions of modernity, have continued, with some modifications, to follow the theological paradigm of scholasticism as exemplified in the work of Charles Hodge (as well as that of others from the "Old" Princeton tradition such as B. B. Warfield and J. Gresham Machen).[44]

In the mid-twentieth century, the classic Protestant scholastic approach to theology found an able advocate in the renowned evangelical theologian Carl F. H. Henry. Henry asserts that the sole foundation of theology rests on the presupposition that the Bible, as the self-disclosure of God, is entirely truthful in all that it teaches and that the truth of God that it contains is presented in propositional form.[45] Therefore, the task of theology is simply "to exhibit the content of biblical revelation as an orderly whole."[46] More recently, Wayne Grudem has reasserted this basic approach by defining systematic theology as the effort to determine what the whole Bible teaches about any given topic.[47]

By limiting the scope of theological reflection to the exposition of the biblical text, evangelicals have been able to sidestep the thorny issues surrounding the roles of tradition and culture in theology. Without sensing the need to deal with these concerns, due to their exclusive focus on the text of scripture, evangelicals have generally seen little reason to participate in the contemporary methodological discussion that has so captivated the rest of the theological community. What is important here is to note that this lack of reflection on and engagement with contemporary methodological/theological issues has not been because of the lack of an approach to method, but because of the particular understanding of method that evangelicals have for the most part taken for granted.

Although the scholastic theological program of Hodge and Henry is clearly still the dominant paradigm in evangelical circles, there are signs that the situation is beginning to change. Recently a number of theologians from within

---

42. Charles Hodge, *Systematic Theology*, 3 vols. (New York: Scribner, Armstrong, & Co., 1872), 1:18.

43. For a detailed discussion of theological method in the Reformed scholastic tradition, see Richard A. Muller, *Post-Reformation Reformed Dogmatics, Vol. 1: Prolegomena* (Grand Rapids: Baker, 1987).

44. For an assessment of the influence of the "Old" Princeton tradition on American Evangelicalism, see George Marsden, *Fundamentalism and American Culture: The Shaping of Twentieth-Century Evangelicalism, 1870–1925* (New York: Oxford University Press, 1980).

45. For Henry's exposition of the thesis that the Bible is the sole foundation for theology, see Carl F. H. Henry, *God, Revelation and Authority*, vol. 1 (Waco, Tex.: Word Publishing, 1976), 181–409.

46. Ibid., 244.

47. Wayne Grudem, *Systematic Theology: An Introduction to Biblical Doctrine* (Grand Rapids: Zondervan, 1994), 21.

evangelicalism have called this paradigm into question. John Jefferson Davis, for example, critiques the concordance model of theology with the observation that it "does not take adequate account of the social context of the theological task and the historicity of all theological reflection. The method tends to promote a repetition of traditional formulations of biblical doctrine, rather than appropriate recontextualizations of the doctrines in response to changing cultural and historical conditions."[48] Similarly, Stanley N. Gundry raises the question as to whether or not evangelicals "really recognize that all theology represents a contextualization," including evangelical theology.[49] Both Davis and Gundry urge evangelicals to adopt a contextual approach to theology that takes seriously the role of culture in theological formulation.

This concern is evident in the work of leading evangelical theologian Millard Erickson, who defines theology as "that discipline which strives to give a coherent statement of the doctrines of the Christian faith, based primarily upon the Scriptures, placed in the context of culture in general, worded in contemporary idiom, and related to issues of life."[50] Although this concern for contextualization is welcome, the traditional evangelical commitment to objectivism and rational propositionalism has worked against an adequate understanding of the relationship between theology and culture even among those, such as Erickson, who have called for contextualization as a part of the theological process. One of the significant results of this failure has been the relatively uncritical acceptance of modernist assumptions by most evangelical theologians.

The Nature, Task, and Purpose of Theology

In the following chapters, we seek to develop a methodological proposal that provides a framework for shaping Christian theology in such a way as to rescue the discipline from its destructive accommodation to modernity while fostering the vitality and relevance of Christian theology for the church in its various social and cultural incarnations. Before turning our attention specifically to various questions of theological method, however, it is appropriate to set forth our conception of theology itself, for our understanding of theological method is closely related to the nature of theology.

Defining Theology

What exactly is theology? What task is theology attempting to accomplish? What is the purpose of theology? The way in which these questions are answered plays a significant role in the approach and method of theological formulation, which in turn shape the entire content of theology. Yet the way in which these questions

48. John Jefferson Davis, *Foundations of Evangelical Theology* (Grand Rapids: Baker, 1984), 67.

49. Stanley N. Gundry, "Evangelical Theology: Where Should We Be Going?," *Journal of the Evangelical Theological Society* 22 (March 1979): 11.

50. Millard Erickson, *Christian Theology*, vol. 1 (Grand Rapids: Baker, 1983), 21.

are addressed and answered are themselves the products of theological constructions that emerge and take shape only in the context of broader theological convictions. The definition of the nature and task of theology is itself a matter of
theological construction that will have implications for the entire conception of
theology and vice versa. In the same way that there are no neutral methodological starting points from which to engage in the task of theology, neither are there
any neutral definitions of theology's nature and task. No theological tradition has
a privileged position with respect to the question of theology's nature and task,
yet so many crucial theological commitments are at stake in the defining act.
Thus, in the very act of defining theology, we find ourselves engaged in the
process of theologizing. Quite simply, to *define* theology is to *do* theology.

Given this understanding of defining theology as part of the process of doing
theology, we offer the following "working" definition of theology's nature, task,
and purpose:

> Christian theology is an ongoing, second-order, contextual
> discipline that engages in critical and constructive reflection
> on the faith, life, and practices of the Christian community.
> Its task is the articulation of biblically normed, historically
> informed, and culturally relevant models of the Christian
> belief-mosaic for the purpose of assisting the community of
> Christ's followers in their vocation to live as the people of
> God in the particular social-historical context in which they
> are situated.

Let us briefly examine the main components of this conception of theology.

Pilgrim Theology

Theology is a contextual discipline. It is not the intent of theology simply to set
forth, amplify, refine, and defend a timelessly fixed orthodoxy. Instead, theology is formulated in the context of the community of faith and seeks to describe
the nature of faith, the God to whom faith is directed, and the implications of
Christian faith commitment within the specific historical and cultural context
in which it is lived. Although the essential commitment of the believing
community to the God revealed in Jesus does not change, the context in which
this confession and its implications are lived out is in constant flux. Theology
attempts to assist the church in articulating the confession of Jesus as the Christ,
together with the mosaic of beliefs to which it is intricately connected, in the
appropriate thought forms of the culture in which the church is situated. In
addition, theology seeks to explicate the implications, relevance, and application of the Christian faith to life in that particular social, cultural setting.

The contextual nature of the discipline points to its ongoing nature. Because
theology draws from contemporary thought forms in theological reflection, the
categories it uses are culturally and historically conditioned. Moreover, because
the context into which the church speaks the message of the gospel is constantly

changing, the task of theology in assisting the church in the formulation and application of its faith commitments in the varied and shifting context of human life and thought never comes to an end. As Garrett Green states, "Like all interpretive activity, theology will therefore be historically and culturally grounded, not speaking from some neutral vantage point but in and for its human context. One corollary is that the theological task will never be completed this side of the Eschaton, since human beings are by nature historical and changing."[51] Thus, the task of theology is ongoing and is best characterized by the metaphor of pilgrimage. Christian theology is pilgrim theology.[52]

The contextual nature of theology points to its second-order nature. And the idea of theology as a "second-order" discipline, in turn, indicates the character of theology as an *interpretive* enterprise. The doctrinal and theological formulations of theologians are the products of human reflection on the stories, symbols, and practices of the Christian community. As such, theological statements must be sharply distinguished from these "first-order" commitments of the Christian community. For example, theological constructions and doctrines are always subservient to the narrative and teachings of canonical scripture and therefore must be held more lightly.

Servant Theology

Theology may also be viewed as a second-order discipline in its relationship to faith. Theological discourse is developed in response to faith and arises in the context of reflection on faith and the attempt to articulate its content. The purpose of theology is to serve the church by assisting in the process of coherently articulating the content and implications of the Christian faith. But the product of this reflection is always secondary; it can never replace the narrative and teachings of scripture or the Christian practice of worship and prayer. Theology serves these first-order commitments and always points to their primacy. Moreover, doctrines are not the "meaning" of the biblical stories. Instead, they function as heuristic constructions that bear witness to, and help illuminate, the formative narratives of the community. As Clark Pinnock puts it, theology needs to be viewed "as a secondary language that reflects on the meaning of the primary story" rather than as "a rational, doctrinal system that encourages people pretty well to dispense with the story."[53] The relationship of theology to the Christian story is that of servant rather than master.

The task of theology involves both critical and constructive reflection on the faith, life and practice of the Christian community. Its goal in this process is to

---

51. Garrett Green, *Imagining God: Theology & the Religious Imagination* (San Francisco: Harper & Row, 1989), 186.

52. For an account of theology as a discipline characterized by the metaphor of pilgrimage, see Michael Bauman, *Pilgrim Theology: Taking the Path of Theological Discovery* (Grand Rapids: Zondervan, 1992).

53. Clark Pinnock, *Tracking the Maze: Finding Our Way through Modern Theology from an Evangelical Perspective* (San Francisco: Harper & Row, 1990), 182.

articulate biblically normed, historically informed, and culturally relevant models of the Christian belief-mosaic. The critical task of theology involves the careful examination and scrutiny of Christian beliefs and teachings for the sake of coherence with the biblical narratives and the first-order commitments of the community, as well as to systemize these beliefs into a whole. The constructive task involves the ordering of the diverse biblical teachings and the practice of the Christian community into unified and coherent models of Christian belief that are related and applied to the contemporary historical-social context. These models should be faithful to the biblical narratives and teachings, informed by and in continuity with the historic position of the church, and relevant to the contemporary setting. Hence, the sources for such a theology are the canonical scriptures, the tradition of the church, and the thought forms of the contemporary social, cultural context.

The construction of such models does not, however, constitute the end of the theological enterprise. Rather, the purpose of theology is to serve the believing community by assisting it in its calling to live as the people of God in a particular setting. Theology does not simply serve itself but should make a difference in Christian life. Christian doctrine ought to help clarify the ways in which Christian faith should be lived and provide motivation and encouragement for Christians, individually and corporately, to live in accordance with their commitment. Theology must be related to life and ethics. Good theology ought to promote the love of God and nourish godly practice and living in the context of the Christian community as well as in society at large.[54] It is this conception of theology that our proposal seeks to serve.

Shaping Theology in a Postmodern Context

The context in which theologians devise a method for theology is characterized by chastened interest in the methodological quest. This context is marked as well by a particular cultural climate, namely, by the eclipse of the thought forms that dominated the modern world and a corresponding shift to categories that have come to be known as "postmodern" due to their reaction against modernity. The emergence of this postmodern ethos has affected all dimensions of Western culture, including theology.

The Postmodern Situation

A precise understanding of postmodernity is notoriously difficult to pin down. Despite the fact that there is no consensus concerning the meaning of the term, it has become almost a commonplace to refer to the contemporary cultural situation as postmodern.[55] The lack of clarity about the term has been magnified by

---

54. On this practical aspect of theology, see Ellen T. Charry, *By the Renewing of Your Minds: The Pastoral Function of Christian Doctrine* (New York: Oxford University Press, 1997).
55. Lakeland, *Postmodernity*, ix.

the vast array of interpreters who have attempted to comprehend and appropriate postmodern thought. Paul Lakeland observes that there are "probably a thousand different self-appointed commentators on the postmodern phenomenon and bewildering discrepancies between the ways many of these authors understand the term *postmodern* and its cognates."[56] In the context of this lack of clarity about the postmodern phenomenon, the term has come to signify widely divergent hopes and concerns among those who are attempting to address the emerging cultural and intellectual shift implied by the term. Two aspects of the postmodern ethos are especially important for theological method: the fundamental critique and rejection of modernity, and the attempt to live and think in a realm of chastened rationality characterized by the demise of modern epistemological foundationalism.

The Postmodern Rejection of Modernity

One common approach to the emergence of postmodernity has been of the negative variety. Many Christian theologians and thinkers have come to view postmodernity primarily as a threat to Christian faith. Catholic theologian Richard John Neuhaus summed up the reaction of many to postmodern thought by connecting it with relativism and subjectivism and calling it the enemy of basic thinking about moral truth.[57] This sort of response has been characteristic of thinkers across the theological spectrum. At the heart of this critique is the consistent identification of postmodern thought with deconstructive relativism and the rejection of it on that basis. In this conception postmodernism is viewed as fundamentally antithetical to Christian faith. This view has been particularly characteristic among evangelicals who, according to Mark McLeod, "tend to think that postmodernism opposes the truth, and in particular, the absolute truth of the gospel."[58]

The wholesale identification of the term postmodern with radical relativism, however, is simply too narrow to do justice to the actual breadth of the phenomenon. It is true that those most commonly associated with postmodern thought, namely, the French poststructuralists, such as Jacques Derrida, Michel Foucault, and Jean-Francois Lyotard, are committed to the project of deconstruction and can be interpreted as philosophical relativists. Nevertheless, the equation of postmodernity with Derrida and company is far too restrictive. Many postmodern thinkers distance themselves from the more radical forms and implications of poststructural and deconstructive thought.

Nancey Murphy draws a sharp distinction between the primarily deconstructive bent of Continental forms of postmodernism and the more

---

56. Ibid., ix–x.
57. Richard John Neuhaus, "A Voice in the Relativistic Wilderness," *Christianity Today* 38 (February 7, 1994): 34.
58. Mark McLeod, "Making God Dance: Postmodern Theorizing and the Christian College," *Christian Scholar's Review* 21:3 (March 1992): 281.

constructive concerns of Anglo-American postmodern thinkers.[59] Thus, the Reformed epistemology of Alvin Plantinga and Nicholas Wolterstorff offers a vigorous defense and affirmation of truth as well as a telling critique of modernity.[60] Moreover, postanalytical philosophers such as Cornel West,[61] Jeffery Stout[62] and Hilary Putnam[63] provide extensive critiques of modernity and move in postmodern directions. In ethics, the constructive communitarian approach of Alasdair MacIntyre may be called postmodern.[64] In addition, Thomas Kuhn[65] and Stephen Toulmin[66] develop constructive postmodern approaches in philosophy of science. The same situation is present in theology as well. To cite one example, the previously mentioned postliberal program, associated with Hans Frei and George Lindbeck, as well as David Kelsey,[67] Paul Holmer,[68] and Ronald Thiemann,[69] is indebted to aspects of postmodern theory.

Given the variety of intellectual endeavor that may be described as postmodern we must conclude that postmodern thought cannot accurately be associated solely with the intellectual program of Derrida and French deconstruction. The point of these examples is not to suggest that they all provide models for distinctively Christian approaches to the postmodern context but rather to illustrate the inadequacy of dismissing postmodern concerns based on the thought of only a limited number of proponents or one particular strand of postmodern thought. In fact, many postmodern thinkers and programs are engaged in the development of constructive projects.

The breadth of postmodern thought suggested by the few examples offered previously raises the question as to what, if anything, gives unity and cohesion to what is labeled *postmodern*. Given the diversity of postmodern thought it is hardly surprising that many assume that there is no unity to the movement. Dan Stiver, however, points out that we should not expect postmodernism to

59. Nancey Murphy, *Anglo-American Postmodernity: Philosophical Perspectives on Science, Religion, and Ethics* (Boulder, Colo.: Westview Press, 1997).

60. Alvin Plantinga and Nicholas Wolterstorff, eds., *Faith and Rationality: Reason and Belief in God* (Notre Dame, Ind.: University of Notre Dame Press, 1983).

61. Cornel West, *Prophetic Thought in Postmodern Times* (Monroe, Minn.: Common Courage, 1993).

62. Jeffrey Stout, *Flight from Authority: Religion, Morality, and the Quest for Autonomy* (Notre Dame, Ind.: University of Notre Dame Press, 1981).

63. Hilary Putnam, *Reason, Truth, and History* (Cambridge: Cambridge University Press, 1981).

64. Alasdair MacIntyre, *Whose Justice? Which Rationality?* (Notre Dame, Ind.: University of Notre Dame Press, 1988).

65. Thomas Kuhn, *The Structure of Scientific Revolutions*, 2nd ed. (Chicago: University of Chicago Press, 1970).

66. Stephen Toulmin, *The Uses of Argument* (Cambridge: Cambridge University Press, 1958); and idem, *Cosmopolis: The Hidden Agenda of Modernity* (Chicago: University of Chicago Press, 1990).

67. David H. Kelsey, *The Uses of Scripture in Recent Theology* (Philadelphia: Fortress Press, 1975).

68. Paul L. Holmer, *The Grammar of Faith* (New York: Harper & Row, 1978).

69. Ronald F. Thiemann, *Revelation and Theology: The Gospel As Narrated Promise* (Notre Dame, Ind.: University of Notre Dame Press, 1985).

be characterized by a tight conformity to particular categories and patterns of thought. He notes, "We use terms like analytic philosophy, existentialism, phenomenology, structuralism, process philosophy, and pragmatism with meaning but also with awareness that it is notoriously difficult to come up with demarcation criteria that will tell us in any and every case who is and is not in the pertinent group. Postmodernism is that kind of term."[70] This difficulty is exacerbated by the fact that in many respects postmodern thought is in its early stages and is still in process.

This situation presses the question as to whether any similarity can be found within the diversity of postmodern thought so as to make sense of the movement, while moving beyond the narrow understanding that only sees it as a synonym for deconstruction. To address this circumstance it will be helpful to see postmodernism as a label that identifies an ongoing paradigm shift in Western culture. Here Stiver provides assistance. He observes, "When one surveys the panorama of contemporary thought it is evident in field after field, in discipline after discipline, that a significant critique of modernity has arisen along with a discussion of a paradigm change. The upshot is that the kind of change under discussion is not incremental or piecemeal, but structural and thoroughgoing."[71] Almost without exception, those who are engaged in the pursuit of this paradigm shift use the term *postmodern*. Stiver suggests that this entails three dimensions. The first is the stringent criticism of modernity. A second is "the notion that modernity's ailments will not be solved by Band-Aid treatment; rather, radical surgery is required. Even more than that, something like a massive reconfiguration, namely, a paradigm switch, is unavoidable." The third dimension Stiver points out is the development of "some sketch, usually rather vague, of what such a new paradigm would look like."[72] From this description it is clear that the unity of the movement lies not in any tentative sketch of the details of a new paradigm but rather in the rejection of the program of modernity. This insight enables us to suggest a basic, minimalist understanding of postmodernism.

The term is best understood as referring primarily to the rejection of the central features of modernity. As Diogenes Allen puts it, postmodern thought is discourse in the aftermath of modernity.[73] At this level we find a remarkable congruence among those who adopt the label *postmodern* as a description of their work, a congruence that extends from Derrida to postliberals and includes even the so-called postconservative evangelicals. Broadly speaking the term *postmodern* implies the rejection of certain central features of the modern project, such as its quest for certain, objective, and universal knowledge, along with

70. Dan R. Stiver, "The Uneasy Alliance between Evangelicalism and Postmodernism: A Reply to Anthony Thiselton," in *The Challenge of Postmodernism: An Evangelical Engagement*, ed. David Dockery (Wheaton, Ill.: Bridge Point, 1995), 242.
71. Ibid., 243.
72. Ibid.
73. Diogenes Allen, "The End of the Modern World," *Christian Scholar's Review* 22/4 (June, 1993): 341.

its dualism and its assumption of the inherent goodness of knowledge. It is this critical agenda, rather than any proposed constructive paradigm to replace the modern vision, that unites postmodern thinkers.

The Protestant Reformation provides an example of a similar situation. The sixteenth-century Protestants were in agreement that the medieval Roman Catholic tradition had corrupted the Christian faith and so made the Reformation of the church necessary. Although they were united in what they were against, when it came to the task of setting forth a positive agenda they were fragmented. Consequently, they struggled without success to achieve a unified movement. In a similar manner, postmodern thinkers are united not by agreement about a particular constructive agenda but by their shared belief that the modern project is inadequate and their shared commitment to the task of developing new paradigms for intellectual pursuit.

The postmodern quest for new paradigms has significantly shaped the discipline of theology in the past twenty years, as theologians from various contexts and traditions have sought to "fill the void" left by the rejection of modernity. Terrence Tilley cites ten alternative postmodern theologies, which he divides into four categories: constructive postmodernisms, postmodern dissolutions, postliberal theology, and theologies of communal praxis.[74] Kevin Vanhoozer, in contrast, identifies eight types of postmodern theology: radical orthodoxy, postliberal theology, postconservative theology, deconstructive a/theology, reconstructive theology, postmetaphysical theology, feminist theology, and Anglo-American postmodernity: a theology of communal praxis.[75]

Each of these typologies indicates the presence today of a number of constructive postmodern theological programs. Clearly, postmodernism cannot be dismissed as nothing more than a deconstructive agenda that stands in stark opposition to Christian faith and thought. On the contrary, there is much evidence that suggests that the postmodern context has actually been responsible for the renewal of theology as an intellectual discipline after a period of stagnation under the weight of modernist demands concerning the acquisition of knowledge. Freed from the constraints of modernity, postmodern concerns have spawned numerous new theological programs.

The broad construal of postmodern thought as a critique and rejection of modernity leads to one central dimension of the postmodern ethos that is especially important for theological method. At the heart of the postmodern ethos is the attempt in the aftermath of modern hubris to rethink the nature of rationality. And the result of this attempt is what might be termed *chastened rationality.*

---

74. Terrence W. Tilley, *Postmodern Theologies: The Challenge of Religious Diversity* (Maryknoll, N.Y.: Orbis Books, 1995).

75. Kevin J. Vanhoozer, *The Cambridge Companion to Postmodern Theology* (Cambridge: Cambridge University Press, forthcoming).

Chastened Rationality and the Demise of Foundationalism

Chastened rationality is marked by the transition from a realist to a constructionist view of truth and the world.[76] Postmodern thinkers maintain that humans do not view the world from an objective vantage point but structure their world through the concepts they bring to it, such as language. Human languages function as social conventions that describe the world in a variety of ways depending on the context of the speaker. No simple, one-to-one relationship exists between language and the world, and thus no single linguistic description can serve to provide an objective conception of the "real" world.

Chastened rationality is also manifest in the "loss of the metanarrative" and the advent of "local" stories. Postmodern thinkers assert that the all-encompassing narratives of scientific progress that shaped and legitimated modern society have lost their credibility and power. Further, they maintain that the very idea of the metanarrative is no longer credible.[77] This is not to suggest that narratives no longer function in the postmodern context. However, the narratives that give shape to the postmodern ethos are "local" rather than universal. Postmodernity embraces the narratives of *particular* peoples and celebrates the diversity and plurality of the world without attempting to discover a "grand scheme" into which all of these particular stories must fit.

Above all, however, postmodern, chastened rationality entails the rejection of epistemological foundationalism. In the modern era, the pursuit of knowledge was deeply influenced by the thought forms of the Enlightenment, with foundationalism lying at its heart. The goal of the foundationalist agenda is the discovery of an approach to knowledge that will provide rational human beings with absolute, incontestable certainty regarding the truthfulness of their beliefs. According to foundationalists, the acquisition of knowledge ought to proceed in a manner somewhat similar to the construction of a building. Knowledge must be built on a sure foundation. The Enlightenment epistemological foundation consists of a set of incontestable beliefs or unassailable first principles on the basis of which the pursuit of knowledge can proceed. These basic beliefs or first principles must be universal, objective, and discernible to any rational person.

This foundationalist conception of knowledge came to dominate the discipline of theology as theologians reshaped the theological structure in accordance with this rationalist approach. In the nineteenth and twentieth centuries, the foundationalist impulse produced a theological division in the Anglo-American context between the "left" and the "right." Liberals constructed theology on the foundation of an unassailable religious experience, whereas conservatives looked to an error-free Bible as the incontrovertible foundation of

76. See, for example, Walter Truett Anderson, *Reality Isn't What It Used to Be: Theatrical Politics, Ready-to-Wear Religion, Global Myths, Primitive Chic, and Other Wonders of the Postmodern World* (San Francisco: Harper & Row, 1990).

77. Jean-Francois Lyotard, *The Postmodern Condition: A Report on Knowledge,* trans. Geoff Bennington and Brian Massumi (Minneapolis: University of Minnesota Press, 1984), xxiv.

their theology.[78] In the postmodern context, however, foundationalism is in dramatic retreat, as its assertions about the objectivity, certainty, and universality of knowledge have come under withering critique. The demise of foundationalism carries fundamental and far-reaching implications for theological method.

Postmodern Theology As Theology beyond Foundationalism

The intellectual genesis for the following chapters lies in our sense of the importance of casting theological method anew in a manner that takes seriously the postmodern context. Consequently, in chapter 2 we examine the critique of foundationalism and propose an alternative model for theology. The purpose of this chapter is to set the stage for the methodological proposal that follows in the rest of the book by exploring the move beyond foundationalism so as to discern its implications for shaping theology in a postmodern context.

Postmodern Theology As Conversation: the Sources for Theology

A theology that seeks to take seriously postmodern sensitivities views itself as conversation. This theological construction may be characterized as an ongoing conversation we share as participants in the faith community as to the meaning of the symbols through which we express our understanding of the world we inhabit. This constructive theological conversation requires the interplay, or perichoretic dance, of three sources of insight or types of conversation partners. A discussion of these sources for theology occupies Part 2 of this volume.

In chapter 3 we suggest that the normative authority for Christian theology, life, and practice is the Spirit speaking through scripture. In this context we argue that the Bible serves as the norming norm in theology in that it functions as the instrumentality of the Spirit. Borrowing insights from contemporary speech-act theory, we suggest that the Bible is the instrumentality of the Spirit, in that the Spirit appropriates the biblical text in order to address the Christian community through the ages. This address can take several forms, in keeping with the manifold diversity of writings that constitute the Bible.

Chapter 4 considers the role of tradition as a crucial and indispensable source for theology. Like all Christians everywhere, we read the biblical text today conscious that we are part of an ongoing listening community and therefore that we are participants in a hermeneutical trajectory. For this reason, Christian tradition provides a reference point for us today, alerting us to some of the pitfalls we should avoid and pointing us in directions that hold promise as we engage in the theological calling.

---

78. On this liberal-conservative debate concerning the proper foundation for theology, see Nancey Murphy, *Beyond Liberalism and Fundamentalism*, 11–35.

In chapter 5, we explore the idea that culture forms the embedding context for the theological task. We argue that whereas the ultimate authority in the church is the Spirit speaking through scripture, the Spirit's speaking through scripture is always a contextual speaking; it always comes to its hearers within a specific historical-cultural context. The specificity of the Spirit's speaking means that the conversation with culture and cultural context is crucial to the hermeneutical task. We seek to listen to the voice of the Spirit through scripture, who speaks to us in the particularity of the historical-cultural context in which we live. This hermeneutical process occurs in part as the discoveries and insights of the various disciplines of human learning inform our theological construction. Moreover, drawing from Pannenberg's insight that because God is the ground of truth all truth ultimately comes together in God, we assert that theology engages all human knowledge in its task of articulating the Christian belief-mosaic in a relevant manner.

Postmodern Theology As Christian Theology: Theology's Focal Motifs

A nonfoundationalist theological method leads to the conclusion that ultimately all theology is—as the "postmodern condition" suggests—"local" or "specific." It is the conversation of a particular group in a particular moment of their ongoing existence in the world. Despite the specificity of all theology, these various local theologies share in common a "family resemblance" or a similar pattern, shape, or style that comprises them as authentically *Christian* theology. In Part 3 we examine the three focal motifs that give coherence to Christian theology. A theology that is truly Christian, we argue, is trinitarian in structure (or content), communitarian in focus, and eschatological in orientation.

Chapter 6 explores the trinitarian dimension of Christian theology as its content or structuring motif. By its very definition theology—the teaching about God—has as its central interest the divine reality as well as God's actions in creation. Moreover, the Christian answer to the question "Who is God?" ultimately surrounds the doctrine of the Trinity. Taking our cue from the ancient confessions of the church, we claim that Christian theology is always trinitarian theology. Because Christian theology is committed to finding its basis in the being and action of the triune God, it should be ordered and structured in a manner that reflects the primacy of this fundamental Christian confession.

Chapter 7 focuses on *community* as the integrative motif of theology and thus on the communitarian character of Christian theology. In keeping with the realization that humans are social creatures who, following the conclusions of chapter 6, image the triune God in relationships, we set forth the case that a Christian theology that is truly trinitarian will also be completely communitarian. The trinitarian content of theology leads to a theology that finds its integration through the concept of community, which theme brings together the various strands of theological reflection into a single web or mosaic. In this chapter we indicate why community lies at the heart of Christian theology and determine in what sense theology is by its very nature communitarian.

Chapter 8 brings the discussion to its conclusion by exploring eschatology as theology's orienting motif. Stated more sharply, in this chapter we argue that all theology is eschatology, insofar as eschatology serves to *orient* all theological reflection. By this we mean that theology must be at every turn directed toward and informed by a Christian understanding of creation's divinely given *telos*. In explicating theology's eschatological motif, we offer our final statement not only about theological method but about theology itself. Viewed from the eschatological perspective, the ultimate, highest, and final purpose of theology becomes that of articulating the Christian belief-mosaic in accordance with the future world God is fashioning and for the sake of the church's mission as the sign in the present, anticipatory era of the glorious age to come.

In this manner we propose a theological method that gives rise to a theology that lies beyond the demise of foundationalism. Such a theology is the product of the reflection of the Christian community in its local expressions. Despite its local nature, such a theology is in a certain sense global. It explicates the Christian belief-mosaic in accordance with the ecumenical faith of the church throughout its history and on behalf of the church throughout the world. Moreover, despite its particularity as a specifically Christian theology, such a theology is also public. It carries with it an implicit claim to be articulating a belief-mosaic that is "for all" in the only way that any claim to universality can be made, namely, as the belief-mosaic of a particular believing community. In so doing, such a theology invites wider response, just as it is offered as a contribution to the wider public conversation. As Kathryn Tanner helpfully explains,

> [T]here is no reason to think that theology's being set in a Christian cultural context rules out theological claims that are universal in scope. Because theology operates within a Christian context is not reason to think theologians are discussing matters that only concern Christians. Theologians can proclaim truths with profound ramifications for the whole of human existence; that they do so from within a Christian cultural context simply means that the claims they make are shaped by that context and are put forward from a Christian point of view. Indeed, if, as an anthropologist would insist, assertions always show the influence of some cultural context or other, following a procedure like that is the only way that universal claims are ever made.[79]

To this wider conversation, primarily within the Christian faith community but by extension directed to a wider public as well, we offer the methodological proposal that follows. We hope that our efforts will foster conversation

---

79. Kathryn Tanner, *Theories of Culture: A New Agenda for Theology* (Minneapolis: Fortress Press, 1997), 69.

about and participation in the task of theology in a manner that is responsive to the postmodern situation. Moreover, we hope that this conversation will nurture an open and flexible theology that is in keeping with the local and contextual character of the discipline, that remains thoroughly and distinctly Christian, and that fosters a renewed listening to the voice of the Spirit speaking to the churches through the scriptures. To that end, our hope and prayer is that this work will be used by God in the further realization of what Hans Frei referred to as a "generous orthodoxy."[80]

---

80. Hans Frei, "Response to 'Narrative Theology: An Evangelical Appraisal,'" *Trinity Journal* 8 (Spring 1987): 21.

Chapter Two

Beyond Foundationalism: Theology After Modernity

So this is what the Sovereign LORD says: "See, I lay a stone in Zion, a tested stone, a precious cornerstone for a sure foundation; the one who trusts will never be dismayed."

—Isaiah 28:16

For no one can lay any foundation other than the one already laid, which is Jesus Christ.

—1 Corinthians 3:11

Most human beings, of course, are not able to stand the message of the shaking of the foundations. They reject and attack the prophetic minds, not because they really disagree with them, but because they sense the truth of their words and cannot receive it.

—Paul Tillich[1]

In the previous chapter, we indicated that one aspect of the emerging postmodern ethos that is especially crucial for the task of theology in the contemporary setting is the demise of the modernist approach to knowledge. The postmodern context is characterized by the widespread rejection of the foundationalism that characterized the Enlightenment epistemology. In its place, scholars today have embarked on a quest to uncover a nonfoundationalist,[2] or,

1. Paul Tillich, *The Shaking of the Foundations* (New York: Charles Scribner's Sons, 1948), 8.
2. Stanley Hauerwas, Nancey Murphy, and Mark Nation, eds. *Theology Without Foundations: Religious Practice & the Future of Theological Truth* (Nashville: Abingdon Press, 1994); John E.

as some prefer, a postfoundationalist,[3] approach. Viewed from this perspective, we might say that the intellectual world lying "after modernity" is a realm "beyond foundationalism."

The shaking of the philosophical foundations of the modern period means not only that the rules have changed but also that the time is ripe to ask new questions about how theology ought to be pursued.[4] Indeed, the demise of foundationalism carries fundamental and far-reaching implications for theological method. The purpose of this chapter is to set the stage for the methodological proposal that follows in the rest of the book by exploring the move beyond foundationalism so as to discern its implications for the theological enterprise in the postmodern context. To this end, we begin by examining Enlightenment foundationalism and its impact on modern theology. Next we sketch the shift to a nonfoundational epistemology in philosophy and theology. Then, drawing from the observations gleaned through this discussion, we set forth the broad contours of a program that might begin to chart the way forward for contemporary theology.

How Firm a Foundation: Enlightenment Foundationalism and Modern Theology[5]

In the modern era, Protestant theologians across the theological spectrum were deeply influenced by the Enlightenment problematic as well as the solutions proposed by thinkers in the Age of Reason. At the heart of the Enlightenment outlook was a specific understanding of the nature of human knowledge. This epistemology has often been termed "foundationalism."

Modern Epistemological Foundationalism

In its broadest sense, foundationalism is merely the acknowledgment of the seemingly obvious observation that not all beliefs we hold (or assertions we formulate) are on the same level, but that some beliefs (or assertions) anchor others. Stated in the opposite manner, certain of our beliefs (or assertions) receive their support from other beliefs (or assertions) that are more "basic" or "foundational."[6] Defined in this manner, nearly every thinker is in some sense a foundationalist.

Thiel, *Nonfoundationalism* (Minneapolis: Fortress Press, 1994).

3. J. Wentzel van Huyssteen, *Essays in Postfoundationalist Theology* (Grand Rapids: Wm. B. Eerdmans Publishing Co.); F. LeRon Shults, *The Postfoundationalist Task of Theology: Wolfhart Pannenberg and the New Theological Rationality* (Grand Rapids: Wm. B. Eerdmans Pubishing Co., 1999).

4. Nancey Murphy, *Beyond Liberalism and Fundamentalism: How Modern and Postmodern Philosophy Set the Theological Agenda* (Valley Forge, Penn.: Trinity Press International, 1996), 1.

5. For the idea of using the hymn title as a symbol of the current intellectual shift, we are indebted to Rodney Clapp, "How Firm a Foundation: Can Evangelicals be Nonfoundationalists?," in *The Nature of Confession: Evangelicals and Postliberals in Conversation*, ed. Dennis L. Okholm and Timothy R. Phillips (Downers Grove, Ill.: InterVarsity Press, 1996), 81–92.

6. For this basic definition, see, for example, W. Jay Wood, *Epistemology: Becoming Intellectually Virtuous* (Downers Grove, Ill.: InterVarsity Press, 1998), 78–79.

Philosophical Foundationalism

In philosophical circles, however, "foundationalism" refers to a much stronger epistemological stance than is entailed in this observation about how beliefs intersect. At the heart of the foundationalist agenda is the desire to overcome the uncertainty generated by our human liability to error and the inevitable disagreements that follow. Foundationalists are convinced that the only way to solve this problem is to find some means of grounding the entire edifice of human knowledge on invincible certainty.[7] This quest for complete epistemological certitude is often termed "strong" or "classical foundationalism."

Foundationalist epistemological proposals routinely draw from the metaphor of a building to conceive how human knowledge arises.[8] According to foundationalists, the acquisition of knowledge ought to proceed in a manner somewhat similar to the construction of a building. Like a physical edifice, knowledge must be built on a sure foundation. This epistemological foundation consists of either a set of unquestioned beliefs or certain first principles on the basis of which the pursuit of knowledge can proceed. These basic beliefs or first principles are supposedly universal, context-free, and available—at least theoretically—to any rational person. The foundationalist's initial task, then, becomes that of establishing an epistemological foundation for the construction of the human knowing project by determining, and perhaps even demonstrating, the foundational beliefs or principles on which knowledge rests. Viewed under the foundationalist rubric, therefore, reasoning moves in only one direction—from the bottom up, that is, from basic beliefs or first principles to resultant conclusions.

Actually, there are three primary aspects to the foundationalist picture of knowledge: the basic or immediate beliefs (or first principles), which form the bedrock undergirding everything else we are justified in believing; the mediate or nonbasic beliefs we derived from these; and the basing relation, that is, the connection between our basic beliefs (or first principles) and our nonbasic beliefs that specifies how the epistemic certainty of basic beliefs can be transferred to nonbasic beliefs.[9] Strong foundationalists demand that the foundations of human knowledge be unshakably certain and assert that the only way this certitude can be transferred to nonbasic beliefs is by the ordinary logical relations of either deduction (such as deducing other truths from innate ideas [e.g., Descartes]) or induction (such as deriving truths from sense impressions caused by the material world [e.g., Locke]).

Finally, in addition to distinguishing between basic and nonbasic beliefs, foundationalists generally relegate religious beliefs to the latter status. Hence,

---

7. Wood, *Epistemology*, 84.

8. For the use of this metaphor in Descartes's writings, see René Descartes, *Selected Philosophical Writings*, trans. John Cottingham, Robert Stoothoff, and Dugald Murdoch (New York: Cambridge University Press, 1988), 23, 24, 26–27, 76, 80.

9. This is delineated in Wood, *Epistemology*, 84.

foundationalism often moves beyond description—beyond merely describing the difference between basic and nonbasic beliefs—to prescription—dictating what sorts of belief are properly basic.[10] Similarly, foundationalism becomes a prescription determining what constitutes a correct, acceptable, or rightly structured system of beliefs.[11]

Enlightenment Foundationalism

The story of the rise of modern foundationalism is well known. Yet, because this epistemological commitment is so ingrained within many theologians, even to the point of being accepted by many as self-evident, we do well to remind ourselves of the high points of that narrative.

The problem of error and the quest for epistemological certainty—the quest for a means by which we can justify our claims to knowledge—dates at least to the ancient Greek philosophers. But in Western philosophical history, this difficulty became acute in the Enlightenment. Historians routinely look to the French philosopher René Descartes as the progenitor of modern foundationalism.[12] In contrast to premodern Western philosophers who tended simply to assume the foundations for philosophical inquiry, Descartes began his philosophical work by attempting to establish that foundation.[13]

Descartes lived in troubled times. In the aftermath of the Reformation, which had divided "Christ's seamless garment" and resulted in the Thirty Years War, questions about religion and morality could no longer be settled by appeal to a commonly acknowledged tradition. Further, through his travels Descartes discovered how culturally based and culturally dependent beliefs actually are.[14] Descartes's response to this situation was to seek certitude within the mind of the knowing subject. To accomplish this task, Descartes brought all his beliefs and assumptions under scrutiny. He doubted everything until he arrived at a belief he could not doubt, namely, that he was doubting. This led to his appropriation of the dictum, "I think; therefore, I am."

In this manner, Descartes claimed to have established the foundations of knowledge by appeal to the mind's own experience of certainty. On this basis, he began to construct anew the human knowledge edifice. Descartes was convinced that this epistemological program yields knowledge that is certain, culture- and tradition-free, universal, and reflective of a reality that exists outside the mind (this latter being a central feature of a position known as "metaphysical realism" or simply "realism").

---

10. Merold Westphal, "A Reader's Guide to 'Reformed Epistemology,'" *Perspectives* 7/9 (November 1992): 10–11.

11. Alvin Plantinga, "Reason and Belief in God," in *Faith and Rationality: Faith and Belief in God*, ed. Alvin Plantinga and Nicholas Wolterstorff (Notre Dame, Ind.: University of Notre Dame Press, 1983), 48.

12. See, for example, Wood, *Epistemology*, 79.

13. See, for example, John E. Thiel, *Nonfoundationalism* (Minneapolis: Fortress Press, 1994), 4.

14. René Descartes, "Discourse on Method" in *Philosophical Works of Descartes*, trans. Elizabeth Haldane and G. R. T. Ross (New York: Dover Publications, 1955), 1:90–91.

Other philosophers took issue with specific aspects of Descartes's proposal. John Locke, for example, rejected Descartes's view that our basic beliefs consist in innate ideas from which we deduce other beliefs. Locke argued that the foundation for human knowledge lies in sense experience, that is, in observations of the world, from which we induce conclusions (a proposal known as empiricism).

Another proposed modification came from the Scottish philosopher, Thomas Reid. Reid pointed out that our psychological constitution draws us irresistibly to accept certain first principles as self-evident. Because we have no reason to suspect that these psychological processes are misleading, he added, we are epistemically entitled to accept and employ these first principles.[15] Reid's proposal (which was to play a crucial role in nineteenth-century conservative theology) led to a variant sometimes known as "soft" or "modest foundationalism." According to Jay Wood, "Modest foundationalists make no claims about the invincible certainty of one's basic beliefs or about a need to be reflectively aware of which beliefs have the status of basic. Instead of claiming that one's basic beliefs enjoy infallible certainty, modest foundationists ascribe only prima facie certainty" (that is, such beliefs can be overridden but are acceptable unless one has good reasons for thinking that they have been undermined).[16]

Despite disagreements over particulars, however, most Enlightenment thinkers readily adopted Descartes's concern to establish some type of sure foundation for the human knowing project. And with this concern, the Enlightenment project assumed a realist metaphysic and evidenced a strong preference for the correspondence theory of truth, that is, the epistemological outlook that focuses on the truth value of individual propositions and declares a proposition to be "true" if and only if—or to the extent that—it corresponds with some fact.[17]

Foundationalist Theology

The concerns of Descartes and other Enlightenment thinkers spilled over the boundaries of the philosophical guild. Indeed, the foundationalist problematic challenged traditional viewpoints and reformulated thinking in every area of Western society, including theology and religious belief. Soon theologians, swooning under the foundationalist spell, found themselves refashioning the theological edifice in accordance with the newly devised rationalist method.

Enlightenment Theology

The foundationalist impulse led thinkers to draw a sharp distinction between "natural religion" —those beliefs that were seemingly demonstrable by reason—and "revealed religion"—the more particular doctrines taught by specific

15. Wood, *Epistemology*, 100.
16. Ibid., 98.
17. Bede Rundle, "Correspondence Theory of Truth," in *The Oxford Companion to Philosophy*, ed. Ted Honderich (New York: Oxford University Press, 1995), 166.

religious communities. As the Age of Reason unfolded, the latter came increas-ingly under attack, for natural theology—with its more certain foundation in the rationalist method of inquiry—came to enjoy the exalted status of being deemed the true religion. The intellectual highway to the primacy of natural over revealed religion was paved by Locke's revolutionary thesis that when divested of its dogmatic baggage Christianity was the most reasonable form of religion. Other Enlightenment thinkers sought to reduce religion to its most basic elements, which they believed to be universal and therefore reasonable. In the process they constructed a theological alternative to orthodoxy—the deism that played such an important part in the founding of the American republic.

Despite the work of Locke and others, by the time the Age of Reason drew to a close, many intellectuals had abandoned the religion of reason for either skepticism[18] or religious relativism.[19] In the end, they concluded, reason is incompetent to answer the great metaphysical questions about God, morality, and the meaning of life. Many thinkers in the eighteenth century could see only two cogent alternatives: (1) blindly accepting classical Christian doctrine by appeal to the Bible (or the church) or (2) embracing the skeptical rationalism that seemed to be the final product of the enlightened mind.[20]

Nineteenth-century Foundationalist Theology

In the nineteenth century, however, a new breed of theologians refused to be boxed in by these two options. With the Enlightenment thinkers, they assumed that there was no going behind the quest for certainty introduced by Descartes; there was no return to a seemingly irrational appeal to external religious author-ity. Still committed to the foundationalist agenda, these thinkers sought a new bedrock on which to construct the theological house. In the end, the debate as to what might provide the proper foundation for theology netted two basic answers.

For theology's sure foundation, some thinkers looked to religious experi-ence, which, although personal in nature, is—they thought—nevertheless uni-versally human. The attempt to construct theology on the basis of human religious experience became a specific concern of classical Protestant liberal-ism. This approach to theology was first articulated by Friedrich Schleiermacher, who maintained that the essence of religion is an awareness of absolute dependence or the experience of God consciousness. In his work, Schleiermacher attempted to demonstrate that all doctrines were derivable from this experiential foundation. However, in his estimation these doctrines did not emerge in a rationalist, logical manner "but rather in the sense that

18. David Hume was the exemplar of enlightened skepticism. For a discussion of this devel-opment, see Arthur Cushman McGiffert, *Protestant Thought Before Kant* (London: Duckworth, 1911), 230–251.

19. Paradigmatic was the position of Gotthold Lessing. For a summary of Lessing's views, see William C. Placher, *A History of Christian Theology* (Philadelphia: Westminster Press, 1983), 249–50.

20. See, for example, McGiffert's conclusion. McGiffert, *Protestant Thought Before Kant*, 253.

they were apt or adequate *expressions* of that core experience," to cite Murphy's description of Schleiermacher's program.[21] Following in the wake of Schleiermacher, nineteenth-century liberal theologians portrayed the Christian faith in general and Jesus' life and teaching in particular as the fulfillment of humankind's highest religious (or moral) aspirations, aspirations that these thinkers thought they found engraved—albeit perhaps only in embryonic form—in (universal) human nature.

Like their liberal antagonists, conservative theologians also searched for a foundation for theology that could stand firm when subjected to the canons of a supposedly universal human reason. Conservatives came to conclude that this invulnerable foundation lay in an error-free Bible, which they viewed as the storehouse for divine revelation. Hence, the great Princeton theologian, Charles Hodge, asserted that the Bible is "free from all error, whether of doctrine, fact, or precept."[22] This inerrant foundation, in turn, could endow with epistemological certitude, at least in theory, the edifice the skilled theological craftsman constructed on it. For indeed, rather than offering merely a personal opinion on any matter under consideration, the adept theologian claimed that he was only restating in a more systematic form what scripture itself says. Conservatives such as Hodge grounded the error-free nature of scripture in its divinely inspired character. Nevertheless, many within their ranks boldly asserted that the Bible's special status as inspired, and hence the inerrancy of scripture, could be justified by appeal to rational argument, such as empirical evidence that the Bible contains prophecies that were subsequently fulfilled or that the various facts it presents are completely accurate.

The acceptance of the foundationalist approach, together with the presumed validity of metaphysical realism and the correspondence theory of truth, led conservative theologians to view the theological discipline as a science, understood in the modern sense of the study of "the ordered phenomena which we recognize through the senses."[23] Charles Hodge, for example, suggested that just as the natural scientist uncovers the facts pertaining to the natural world, so the theologian brings to light the theological facts found within the Bible.[24] Conservatives likewise assumed that the theological propositions they drew from the Bible stated universal—even eternal—facts and that the chief goal of theology as an intellectual, scientific discipline was to compile these various facts.

In this way, the firm foundation the hymn writer believed had been laid in God's "excellent Word" came to be equated with the words of the Bible, the veracity of which was thought to be unimpeachable when measured by the

21. Murphy, *Beyond Liberalism and Fundamentalism*, 22.
22. Charles Hodge, *Systematic Theology*, 3 vols. (New York: Scribner, Armstrong, & Co., 1872), 1:152.
23. For a discussion of this definition, formulated by Charles Hodge but indicative of other nineteenth-century conservatives, see George Marsden, "The Collapse of American Evangelical Academia," in *Faith and Rationality*, 245–47.
24. Hodge, *Systematic Theology*, 1:18.

canons of human reason. With such a firm foundation in place, conservative theologians were confident of their ability to complete the task of deducing from scripture the great, timeless theological truths about God and the world that divine revelation had placed within its pages. In so doing, they believed, they would formulate properly "the faith once delivered to the saints."

Liberal and Evangelical Modernists

The experiential foundationalism of Schleiermacher and other nineteenth-century theologians provided a paradigm for the approach to liberal theology into the twentieth century. For example, Shailer Mathews, professor of theology at the University of Chicago, emphasized the priority of religious experience over statements of doctrine. He maintained that Christian doctrine consisted of verbal expressions of the religious life that employed the patterns and thought forms current in the various periods of Christian history. These doctrines were not to be evaluated on the basis of their supposed objective truth content but on the basis of the degree to which they were effective in promoting and inspiring religious faith and conviction.[25]

Mathews spoke of the Bible as a historical record of the progressive religious experience of human beings. He was convinced that when the Bible was properly interpreted on the basis of appropriate historical-critical methods it provided "a trustworthy record of human experience of God."[26] Yet the Bible's importance did not lie in past experience, he argued, but in the continuation of that experience into the present context. Mathews asserted that living Christian faith is not about the "acceptance of a literature but a reproduction of attitudes and faith, a fellowship with those ancient men of imperfect morals whose hearts found God, whose lives were strengthened by the divine spirit, whose words point out the way of life, and who determined the inner character of the Christian religion." In his estimation, the other components of the faith that have been passed down through the generations are "secondary accretions," and these are to be properly "separated from the religion of Jesus Christ."[27]

The well-known Baptist preacher Harry Emerson Fosdick popularized the liberal viewpoint that all doctrines spring from the experiences of life. Fosdick argued that human beings have experiences involving their own souls, other individuals, and God. The chief value of these experiences is to be found in their practical value for life. Fosdick admitted that there was something typically human about the construction of doctrine, for human beings quite naturally attempt to "explain, unify, organize, and rationalize. They make systematized doctrines out of their experiences. And when the formula has been constructed, they love it because the experience for which it stands is precious." But he

---

25. For a full statement of Shailer Mathews's conception of religious faith and doctrine see his work, *The Faith of Modernism* (New York: Macmillan, 1924).

26. Mathews, *The Faith of Modernism*, 47.

27. Ibid., 49-50.

quickly added that over the course of history these doctrines often become unintelligible in the face of new thinking. It is at this point, according to Fosdick, that the liberal approach to doctrine provides the way forward. In his estimation, liberals had done the church a great service by discovering that religion does not consist in the formula but in the experience to which the formula points. The liberal approach, he asserted, retreats from the formula "into the experience behind it, by translating the formula back into the life out of which it came."[28]

Although propounded in an increasingly subtle and complex fashion, the experience-based approach to theology that is characteristic of liberalism continued to dominate mainline theology throughout the twentieth century.[29] The work of Harvard theologian Gordon Kaufman provides a case in point.[30] In his *Essay on Theological Method* (1979), Kaufman notes at the outset his dissatisfaction with current options in foundationalist theology together with his desire to think through afresh the task of theology and "to search for new and more adequate foundations."[31] At first glance Kaufman appears to break with the liberal program. He avers that the difficulty of determining what in fact counts as religious experience means that theology cannot be based on such experience. He opts instead to ground theology on broader cultural experience as captured in a common language, thereby shifting the focus from experience to language. Hence, Kaufman declares, it would be more accurate "to say the language we speak provides a principal foundation for our religious experience, than to hold that some pre-conceptual, pre-linguistic raw experience is the principal foundation of our theological language and thought."[32]

Nancey Murphy provides a telling critique of Kaufman's methodological proposal. In her estimation, theology becomes, for Kaufman, a "conceptual clarification of the religious terms found in ordinary language." She writes, "Kaufman's particular concern is with the concept *God*, which, following Kant, he understands as a regulative concept, constructed to make sense of a set of concepts drawn from experience."[33] Hence, despite his attempts to go beyond the liberal program, we continue to find in Kaufman an emphasis on experience as providing the foundation for theology, albeit in the modified form of an appeal to linguistic expressions that arise out of cultural experience. As Murphy notes, although Kaufman has replaced the earlier foundationalist focus on certitude with a new concern for the public nature of criteria for judging theology, his quest for public consensus "is the same as that which drove the seventeenth-century development of the foundationalist epistemological theory in the first place."[34]

28. Harry Emerson Fosdick, *The Modern Use of the Bible* (New York: Macmillan Co., 1924), 185–86.

29. Murphy, *Beyond Liberalism and Fundamentalism*, 22–28.

30. Gordon Kaufman, *An Essay on Theological Method*, rev. ed. (Missoula, Mont.: Scholars Press, 1979).

31. Ibid., x.

32. Ibid., 6.

33. Murphy, *Beyond Liberalism and Fundamentalism*, 26.

34. Ibid.

Just as the legacy of Schleiermacher dominates the liberal project to the present, the foundationalism of Hodge and other nineteenth-century conservatives sets the tone for what would become the theological paradigm of evangelical theology through most of the twentieth century. Above all, the legacy of the nineteenth-century project finds echo among contemporary rationalist or propositionalist theologians. Gordon Lewis and Bruce Demarest provide a lucid example. They maintain that the goal of theology is the amassing of true statements,[35] understood as a series of factual propositions.[36] According to this model, the theologian, assisted by the canons of logic, applies the scientific method to the deposit of revelation found in scripture in an ongoing quest to compile the one, complete, timeless body of right doctrines, formulated as a series of statements or theological assertions, each of which is true in its own right. Similarly, the understanding of the Bible as a compendium of truths unlocked through "scientific" induction that came to characterize American fundamentalism[37] lives on, for example, in Wayne Grudem's definition of systematic theology as the attempt to determine what the whole Bible teaches about any given topic.[38]

Standing behind the propositionalist model of systematic theology as well as the utility of logic in pursuit of this task are certain assumptions about the nature of God and humans. Lewis and Demarest articulate the common rationalist viewpoint when they claim that their theological enterprise "assumes (from the argumentation of apologetics and evidence concerning revelation) that God can reveal information to people who are created in his image to think his thoughts after him."[39] The principles of logic, in turn, facilitate the human process of thinking God's thoughts because these principles, which evangelical modernists assume to be universal, are "rooted ultimately in the mind and nature of the Creator."[40]

The results of the foundationalist approach of modern liberals and conservatives have been astounding. In different ways both groups have sought to respond to the challenge of the Enlightenment and rescue theology in the face of the secularist worldview of late modernity. Although the liberals and conservatives routinely dismiss each other's work, they share the single agenda of seeking to maintain the credibility of Christianity within a culture that glorifies reason and deifies science. This culture was perhaps the sole milieu of the Western church throughout much of the twentieth century. The intellectual context, however, is shifting dramatically. And this development has crucial implications for theology.

35. See, for example, Gordon R. Lewis and Bruce A. Demarest, *Integrative Theology*, 3 vols. (Grand Rapids: Zondervan, 1987), 1:25.
36. Ibid., 26–27.
37. See Mark A. Noll, *The Scandal of the Evangelical Mind* (Grand Rapids: Wm. B. Eerdmans Publishing Co., 1994), 98.
38. Wayne Grudem, *Systematic Theology: An Introduction to Biblical Doctrine* (Grand Rapids: Zondervan, 1994), 21.
39. Lewis and Demarest, *Integrative Theology*, 1:27.
40. Ibid., 1:33.

How Infirm the Foundation: Theology after Foundationalism

Foundationalism, allied as it was with metaphysical realism and the correspondence theory of truth, was undeniably the epistemological king of the post-Enlightenment, modern era. But it no longer commands the broad, unquestioned acceptance it once enjoyed. In fact, among philosophers today, foundationalism is in dramatic retreat.[41] Merold Westphal observes, "That it is philosophically indefensible is so widely agreed that its demise is the closest thing to a philosophical consensus in decades."[42] Wentzel van Huyssteen concurs: "Whatever notion of postmodernity we eventually opt for, all postmodern thinkers see the modernist quest for certainty, and the accompanying program of laying foundations for our knowledge, as a dream for the impossible, a contemporary version of the quest for the Holy Grail."[43] And Nicholas Wolterstorff offers this sobering conclusion: "On all fronts foundationalism is in bad shape. It seems to me there is nothing to do but give it up for mortally ill and learn to live in its absence."[44]

The Quest for an Alternative Epistemology

Modern foundationalism has been the target of criticism since its genesis. Yet as the nineteenth century gave way to the twentieth, certain philosophers, aware of the shortcomings of the Enlightenment epistemological agenda, became increasingly earnest in seeking a cogent alternative. For reasons we need not recount here,[45] these thinkers questioned both the foundationalist assumption of the necessity of establishing the first principles of philosophy prior to engaging in the construction of knowledge, and the preoccupation with the quest for unassailable basic beliefs. And they rejected the attendant understanding of truth as the correspondence of individual assertions with the world, each of which—in the words of one critic of foundationalism—is thought to be "true per se absolutely and unalterably."[46]

Two alternatives emerged almost simultaneously: coherentism and pragmatism. At the heart of coherentism is the suggestion that the justification for a belief lies in its "fit" with other held beliefs;[47] hence, justification entails "inclusion within a coherent system," to cite the words of philosopher Arthur Kenyon

41. For this judgment, see Thiel, *Nonfoundationalism*, 37.
42. Westphal, "Reader's Guide," 11.
43. van Huyssteen, "Tradition and the Task of Theology," 216.
44. Nicholas Wolterstorff, *Reason Within the Bounds of Religion* (Grand Rapids: Wm. B. Eerdmans Publishing Co., 1976), 52.
45. For a helpful summary of the arguments against foundationalism, see Wood, *Epistemology*, 88–98. For an early twentieth-century critique of the correspondence theory of truth by a sympathetic critic who does not reject the theory completely, see Charles A. Campbell, *Scepticism and Construction* (London: George Allen & Unwin, Ltd., 1931), 82–96.
46. Harold H. Joachim, *The Nature of Truth* (London: Oxford University Press, 1906, 1939), 72.
47. Wood, *Epistemology*, 114.

Rogers.[48] But what does it mean for a belief to cohere with other beliefs? Of course, noncontradiction must be an aspect of any coherence of beliefs. Coherentists, however, suggest that the "fitting together" of beliefs entails more than merely that the various assertions do not contradict each other. In addition, the corpus of beliefs must be interconnected in some way. In other words, rather than remaining a collection or aggregate of disjointed, discrete members that have nothing whatsoever to do with one another, the set of beliefs must form an integrated whole, and this whole must carry "explanatory power."

Coherentists, therefore, reject the foundationalist assumption that a justified set of beliefs necessarily comes in the form of an edifice resting on a base. In their estimation, the base/superstructure distinction is erroneous, for no beliefs are intrinsically basic and none are intrinsically superstructure.[49] Instead, beliefs are interdependent, each belief being supported by its connection to its neighbors and ultimately to the whole.[50] Rather than picturing human knowledge as a building, coherentists draw from the image of a network, in which beliefs come together to form an integrated belief system. Hence, knowledge is a "web of belief" (Quine[51]), a "nest of beliefs" (Kort[52]) or, to cite the more generic designation, a "conceptual scheme."[53]

In addition, whereas foundationalists tend to focus on the task of determining the truth value of each assertion independently of the others, coherentists find truth in the interconnectedness of beliefs. Truth is primarily a predicate of the belief system as a whole. Hence, the turn-of-the-century philosopher Harold H. Joachim criticizes the Cartesians for their preoccupation with what he describes as "the smallest and most abstracted fragment of knowledge, a mere mutilated shred torn from the living whole in which alone it possessed its significance." For him, the "ideal of knowledge . . . is a system, not of *truths*, but of *truth*."[54] Consequently, for coherentists, the quest for knowledge entails a "research program" (Lakatos), in which advances occur through "paradigm shifts" (Kuhn).

Despite this shift in emphasis, many modern coherentists remain committed to the quest for epistemological certainty. In fact, they embrace coherentism

---

48. Arthur Kenyon Rogers, *What Is Truth?* (New Haven, Conn.: Yale University Press, 1923), 12.

49. Jonathan Dancy, "Epistemology, Problems of," in *The Oxford Companion to Philosophy*, ed. Ted Honderich (New York: Oxford University Press, 1995), 246.

50. Murphy, *Beyond Liberalism and Fundamentalism*, 94.

51. See, for example, W. V. Quine and J. S. Ullian, *The Web of Belief* (New York: Random House, 1970).

52. Wesley A. Kort, *Take, Read: Scripture, Textuality, and Cultural Practice* (University Park, Penn.: Pennsylvania State University Press, 1996), 12.

53. Jack W. Meiland and Michael Krausz, "Introduction," in *Relativism: Cognitive and Moral*, ed. Jack W. Meiland and Michael Krausz (Notre Dame, Ind: University of Notre Dame Press, 1982), 7. In his critique of the concept, Donald Davidson offers the following summary of the typical definition: "Conceptual schemes, we are told, are ways of organizing experience; they are systems of categories that give form to the data of sensation; they are points of view from which individuals, cultures, or periods survey the passing scene." Donald Davidson, "On the Very Idea of a Conceptual Scheme," reprinted in *Relativism*, 66.

54. Harold H. Joachim, *The Nature of Truth* (London: Oxford University Press, 1906, 1939), 73, 72.

because they believe this approach provides a greater possibility of justifying beliefs. A. K. Rogers voices this illuminating appraisal:

> Mere logic never by any possibility can add more certainty to the conclusion than existed in the premises. Its ideal, is, therefore, to carry back proof to more and more general premises, until at last it finds something in its own right on which it can rest, and from which then a derivative certainty passes to the consequences. The idea of *system*, on the contrary, implies that certainty grows continually as new facts are added. . . . The conclusions, that is, have to be more certain than the premises. And the possibility of this depends, not on logical deduction from what is self-evident, but on a *coincidence* of evidence. In other words, when we see that two independent beliefs corroborate one another, the confidence we have in both is increased; and this is what we mean by their intellectual justification. For this to happen, logical processes are required, because to reinforce one another the two must come in contact in a connected system. But the essence of the validation lies not in the passing on of an equal measure of certainty due to the precess of inference, but to the *increase* of certainty due to the confluence of evidence.[55]

At the same time, some coherentists acknowledge that rather than a present reality, absolute justification of beliefs belongs to the realm of the ideal. Yet this does not mean that the unattainable ideal is any less real. Against those who argue that "finite experience is solid and fully real and clearly conceivable, an unshaken *datum* here and now; and that we must accept it without question," Joachim advocates a reversal in understanding: "In our view it is the ideal which is solid and substantial and fully actual. The finite experiences are rooted in the ideal. They share its actuality, and draw from it whatever being and conceivability they possess."[56] Thus, the coherentist move away from foundationalism entailed a shift not only from the part to the whole, but also from the actual to the ideal.

Turn-of-the-century coherentists were joined in their critique of foundationalism by the pragmatists. At first glance "pragmatism" may suggest nothing more than that truth is simply "what works," however the term may be understood. The modern pragmatist philosophers, especially Charles Peirce (1839–1914), however, had a specific understanding in view. In their estimation, the truth of any belief ought to be measured according to the belief's success in advancing "factual inquiry" (that is, "the activity aimed at the discovery of truth").[57] The pragmatists' innovation, according to Arthur E. Murphy's

---

55. Rogers, *What Is Truth?* 12–13 (italics in original).
56. Joachim, *Nature of Truth*, 82.
57. Arthur E. Murphy, *The Uses of Reason* (New York: Macmillan Co., 1943), 87.

judgment, was "[t]heir insistence that the meaning and worth of ideas is rightly judged, not by their conformity to a 'reality' set up in advance as the final standard of truth and reasonableness, but by the way they function in the context of responsible inquiry."[58]

Pragmatists such as Peirce did not differ significantly with the foundationalists about the goal of inquiry. Nor did Peirce reject the reigning metaphysical realism of the day. Rather, his pragmatism was largely an attempt to clarify the method of scientific advance. In his estimation, truth emerges as we engage in prediction followed by testing, observation, and experimental confirmation. And in contrast to the here-and-now individualism of the Cartesian method, this process requires both a long-term horizon and the cooperative contributions of a community of scientific investigators. Peirce offers this lucid definition: "The opinion which is fated to be ultimately agreed to by all who investigate, is what we mean by the truth, and the object represented in this opinion is the real."[59]

As this remark suggests, although Peirce held to the objectivity of truth and the existence of reality independent of our subjectivity, he nevertheless posited an important connection between that reality and the human pursuit of truth: "the reality of that which is real does depend on the real fact that investigation is destined to lead, at last, if continued long enough, to a belief in it."[60] Yet he rejected the suggestion that this conclusion makes reality dependent on thought. Peirce explains: "[T]he answer to this is that, on the one hand, reality is independent, not necessarily of thought in general, but only of what you or I or any finite number of men may think about it; and that, on the other hand, though the object of the final opinion depends on what that opinion is, yet what that opinion is does not depend on what you or I or any man thinks."[61]

William James explicitly advocated the connection between truth and the epistemological process implicit in Peirce: "Truth for us is simply a collective name for verification-processes, just as health, wealth, strength, etc. are names for other processes connected with life, and also pursued because it pays to pursue them. Truth is *made*, just as health, wealth and strength are made, in the course of experience."[62] In fact, James suggests that the pragmatists' central departure from the foundationalists lies precisely here. In his estimation, "the great assumption of the intellectualists [i.e., foundationalists] is that truth means essentially an inert static relation. When you've got your true idea of anything, there's an end of the matter. You're in possession; you *know*; you have

---

58. Ibid., 85–86.

59. Charles Sanders Peirce, "How to Make Our Ideas Clear," in Charles S. Peirce, *Selected Writings (Values in a Universe of Chance)*, ed. Philip P. Wiener (New York: Dover Publications, 1958), 133.

60. Ibid., 134.

61. Ibid., 133.

62. William James, *Pragmatism: A New Name for Some Old Ways of Thinking*, reprint ed. (New York: Longmans, Green and Co., 1928), 218.

fulfilled your thinking destiny." For the pragmatist James, in contrast, "[t]he truth of an idea is not a stagnant property inherent in it. Truth *happens* to an idea. It *becomes* true, is *made* true by events."[63]

If coherentism and pragmatism provided ways to leave behind the foundationalist preference for the correspondence of truth, the "turn to linguistics" offered the means to overcome metaphysical realism. Peirce himself was keenly interested in semiotics and language theory. But more significant for the quest for a nonfoundationalist epistemology via a turn to linguistics was the work of Ludwig Wittgenstein (1889–1951). In a sense, Wittgenstein completed the shift toward belief systems and the communal dimension of truth pioneered by the coherentists and the pragmatists.

Midway in his career, Wittgenstein came to realize that rather than having only a single purpose—to make assertions or state facts—language has many functions (e.g., to offer prayer, make requests, and convey ceremonial greetings). This discovery led to Wittgenstein's important concept of "language games." According to Wittgenstein, each use of language occurs within a separate and seemingly self-contained system complete with its own rules. Similar to playing a game, we require an awareness of the operative rules and significance of the terms within the context of the purpose for which we are using language. Each use of language, therefore, comprises a separate "language game." And each "game" may have little to do with the other "language games."[64]

Like the move to coherence or pragmatism, adopting the image of "language games" entailed abandoning the correspondence theory of truth. But unlike that earlier move it also opened the door for the questioning of metaphysical realism. For Wittgenstein, meaning and truth are not related—at least not directly or primarily—to an external world of "facts" waiting to be apprehended. Instead, they are an internal function of language. Because the meaning of any statement is dependent on the context—that is, on the "language game"—in which it appears, any sentence has as many meanings as contexts in which it is used. Rather than assertions of final truth or truth in any ultimate sense, all our utterances can only be deemed "true" within the context in which they are spoken.[65] Further, viewing language as a "game" presumes that language does not have its genesis in the individual mind grasping a truth or fact about the world and then expressing it in statements. Rather, language is a social phenomenon, and any statement acquires its meaning within the process of social interaction.

---

63. Ibid., 200, 201.
64. See, for example the discussion in Ludwig Wittgenstein, *Philosophical Investigations* 1.65, trans. G. E. M. Anscombe (Oxford: Basil Blackwell, 1953), 32. See also Robert C. Solomon, *Continental Philosophy since 1750: The Rise and Fall of the Self* (Oxford: Oxford University Press, 1988), 150.
65. See Hilary Lawson, "Stories about Stories," in *Dismantling Truth: Reality in the Post-Modern World,* ed. Hilary Lawson and Lisa Appignanesi (New York: St. Martin's Press, 1989), xxiii–xxiv.

Theology after Foundationalism

The Enlightenment quest for certitude served as a powerful molder of theology in the modern era. In recent years, however, several theologians have been looking to the insights of the nonfoundationalist philosophers in an effort to recast theology after the demise of foundationalism. Two of these theologians provide helpful models as to what a nonfoundational theological method might look like. In so doing they provide impulses for theological engagement with the postmodern context.

Pannenberg and Coherence

Perhaps no theologian has exemplified more clearly the application to theology of the noncorrespondence epistemological theories of the modern coherentists and pragmatists than Wolfhart Pannenberg.[66] At the heart of Pannenberg's theological agenda is the task of demonstrating the internal coherence of the doctrines and the external coherence of Christian doctrine with all knowledge.[67]

Pannenberg acknowledges that coherence is not a new idea in theological history. The scholastic theologians were concerned to show the truth of Christian doctrine through a presentation of its internal and external coherence. But he criticizes the tendency of the scholastic tradition—especially its Protestant form—to reduce the role of reason to that of illuminating truth already presupposed from revelation disclosed through what was assumed to be an inspired Bible.[68] Such a move, he maintains, led to several misguided tendencies. The scholastics unwittingly divided truth into autonomous spheres, attempted to shield the truth content of the Christian tradition from rational inquiry, and ended up placing the Bible in contradiction to every new discovery of truth, rather than integrating scientific discoveries into the truth claim of the Christian faith. In short, the doctrine of biblical inspiration failed to facilitate theologians in demonstrating the coherence of Christian doctrine with human knowledge.

Even more devastating, in Pannenberg's estimation, has been the proposal of what he refers to as "neo-Protestantism" (e.g., pietism and liberalism) that places the focus of revelation in the act of faith itself.[69] In his estimation, this approach leads to a subjectivist understanding of truth that too easily borders on irrational fanaticism and ultimately fosters an unbiblical independence of the believing subject. Rather than being merely subjective, Pannenberg argues that truth is universal. Any valid "personal truth" must be, at least in principle, true for all. Pannenberg's task, therefore, is to chart a pathway that carries greater promise than either of the widely held alternatives.

---

66. For a lengthier treatment of Pannenberg's theological method, see Stanley J. Grenz, *Reason for Hope: The Systematic Theology of Wolfhart Pannenberg* (New York: Oxford University Press, 1990), 11–43.

67. Wolfhart Pannenberg, *Systematic Theology*, trans. Geoffrey W. Bromiley, 3 vols. (Grand Rapids: Wm. B. Eerdmans Publishing Co., 1991–1998), 1:21–22.

68. Ibid., 1:28–38.

69. Ibid., 1:38–48.

The basis for Pannenberg's reformulation of a coherentist theological method lies in his understanding of truth. Although he shares the older theological goal of discovering universal truth, he rejects the concept of truth the medieval scholastics inherited from the Greek philosophical tradition, namely, that truth is found in the constant and unchanging essences—or the eternal presence—lying behind the flow of time.[70] Rather, reminiscent of modern coherentists and pragmatists but drawing squarely on what he sees as the biblical view, Pannenberg argues that truth is essentially historical. Truth is what shows itself throughout the movement of time climaxing in the end event.[71] This end, he adds, is anticipated in the present, a point Pannenberg finds evident in general human life, for we continually modify our understandings in the light of subsequent experience.

At this point, Pannenberg applies the classical Augustinian linking of truth with God to his own dynamic view of the nature of truth: The truth that emerges in the end is the truth of God,[72] who is "the reality that determines everything."[73] Consequently, all truth ultimately comes together in God, who is the ground of the unity of truth. This, in turn, leads to a coherentist theological method. For Pannenberg, the goal of theology is to demonstrate the unity of truth in God, that is, to bring all human knowledge together in our affirmation of God. Or stated in another way, theology seeks to show how the postulate of God illumines all human knowledge.[74]

Such an enterprise, however, is impossible to accomplish. The reality of God remains an open question in the contemporary world. And our human knowledge is never complete or absolutely certain. To respond to this problem, Pannenberg appeals to the eschatological nature of truth and to the scientific nature of theology. Because truth is historical, the focal point of certitude can only be the eschatological future. Only then will we know truth in its absolute fullness. Until the eschaton, truth will by its own nature always remain provisional and truth claims contestable.[75]

This suggests that theological statements, like all human assertions, are hypotheses to be tested.[76] And we test our theological assertions as we seek to determine their internal and external coherence. In a manner resembling the

---

70. In his early essay, "What Is Truth?" Pannenberg shows that the Hebrew and Greek conceptions of truth have certain common features, including that of constancy. At the same time the Hebrew conception includes and goes beyond the Greek. Wolfhart Pannenberg, *Basic Questions in Theology*, trans. George H. Kehm, 2 vols. (Philadelphia: Fortress Press, 1971), 2: 2–11.

71. See the essays "On Historical and Theological Hermeneutic" and "What is a Dogmatic Statement?" in Pannenberg, *Basic Questions*, 1: 137–210.

72. Pannenberg, *Systematic Theology*, 1:53. See also "What Is Truth?" in Pannenberg, *Basic Questions*, 2: 1–27.

73. For a statement of this foundational definition of God, which Pannenberg articulates repeatedly, see Wolfhart Pannenberg, "The Nature of a Theological Statement," *Zygon* 7/1 (March 1972): 11.

74. Pannenberg, *Systematic Theology*, 1:59–60.

75. Ibid., 1:54.

76. Ibid., 1:56–58.

modern pragmatists, therefore, Pannenberg maintains that the question of truth must be answered in the process of theological reflection and reconstruction. And like them, he remains optimistic about the ongoing quest to discover truth. Pannenberg is convinced that this testing process will confirm the power of the assertion of the reality of God to illumine the totality of human knowledge.

Lindbeck and Community Ground Rules

Pannenberg draws from a coherentist approach in his attempt to carve out a theological method that is nonfoundational yet committed to a realist metaphysic. What would theology look like if it not only rejected the correspondence theory of truth, but sought to follow Wittgenstein and move beyond realism as well? The program outlined by George Lindbeck provides a clue.

Similar to Pannenberg, Lindbeck's primary goal is to carve out an alternative to two rival, but, in his estimation, equally discredited conceptions of doctrine, both of which are in the end the results of the application of foundationalism to theological method. He terms these two the "cognitive-propositionalist" and the "experiential-expressive" approaches. The former erroneously assumes that theological statements (doctrines) make first-order truth claims (that is, they assert that something is objectively true or false), thereby identifying religion too closely with its cognitive dimension. The latter sees doctrines as the outward expressions of the "inner feelings, attitudes or existential orientations"[77] related to personal religious experience, but in the process erroneously assumes that there is some identifiable core experience common to all Christian traditions or even to all world religions.

Lindbeck's intent is to offer a third view, which he calls the "cultural-linguistic" approach. To this end, he not only follows the coherentist pathway but also reacquisitions Wittgenstein and gives to coherentism a Wittgensteinian twist. Lindbeck declares that doctrines are like rules of grammar. They constitute what we might call the rules of discourse of the believing community. Doctrines act as norms that instruct adherents how to think about and live in the world. Hence, like rules of grammar, church doctrine has a "regulative" function, serving as "community authoritative rules of discourse, attitude, and action."[78] They are "teachings regarding beliefs and practices that are considered essential to the identity or welfare of the group." As such "they indicate what constitutes faithful adherence to a community."[79] In short, Christian doctrines establish the ground rules for the "game" of Christian thinking, speaking, and living.

Lindbeck's use of Wittgenstein has far-reaching implications for the concept of truth. He notes that rules of grammar are routinely stated in the form of propositions; nevertheless, asking whether any one of them is objectively "true"

---

77. George A. Lindbeck, *The Nature of Doctrine: Religion and Theology in a Postliberal Age* (Philadelphia: Westminster Press, 1984), 16.
   78. Ibid., 18.
   79. Ibid., 74.

or "false" involves a fundamental misunderstanding of the type of proposition the rule in fact is. It entails ripping the assertion out of its context and treating it apart from its regulative role within the language itself. These rules are not intended to say anything true about a reality external to the language they regulate. Hence, each rule is only "true" in the context of the body of rules that govern the language to which the rules belong. Lindbeck suggests that we might view doctrinal statements in a similar manner. Seen from this perspective, such statements do not make "first-order" truth claims; they do not assert something objective about reality. Instead, like rules of grammar, they are second-order assertions. This suggests that church doctrines are primarily rules for speech about God, rather than actual assertions about God.[80] Hence, they make "intrasystematic" truth claims.[81] Doctrines are "true" primarily as "parts of a total pattern of speaking, thinking, feeling, and acting."[82]

His "third way" leads Lindbeck to call for an "intratextual theology" that "redescribes reality within the scriptural framework" and aims at "imaginatively incorporating all being into a Christ-centered world."[83] This theology draws from the text to explore what it means to articulate and live out the community's vision within a specific time and place.[84] Similar to Pannenberg, Lindbeck concludes that to this end the theologian expounds the doctrinal core or framework of the Christian faith, determines that it coheres within itself, and indicates how doctrine illumines human existence.

Affirming a (Non)Foundation:
Toward a Theology "Beyond Foundationalism"

Despite the century-old critique of foundationalism and the theological proposals of contemporary thinkers like Pannenberg and Lindbeck, foundationalist theology is not dead. On the contrary, a large cadre of theological modernists appear content to engage in theology in a manner that presupposes the older foundationalist epistemology.

At the same time, however, a growing number of theologians are becoming cognizant of the demise of foundationalism in philosophy and are increasingly concerned to explore the implications of this demise for theology. They believe that theology must take seriously the postmodern critique of Enlightenment foundationalism and must capitalize on the attempts of philosophers to formulate alternatives. Convinced that the quest to move beyond foundationalism is crucial for theology, they draw insights for their own work from the emerging nonfoundationalist theorists. But in what sense, or to what extent, can the theological task incorporate a nonfoundationalist epistemology?

80. Ibid., 69.
81. Ibid., 80.
82. Ibid., 64.
83. Ibid., 118.
84. Ibid., 113.

Reconstructing the Foundation

We noted earlier that the fundamental idea of foundationalism is that certain beliefs anchor other beliefs, that is, certain beliefs are "basic," and other beliefs arise as conclusions from them. Enlightenment foundationalism, however, took the matter a step further. "Strong" foundationalists relegated religious beliefs to a nonbasic status and sought to gain epistemological certitude by discovering an unassailable foundation of basic beliefs on which to construct the knowledge edifice.

Recently several evangelical philosophers, including Alvin Plantinga and Nicholas Wolterstorff, have questioned strong foundationalism while not rejecting completely the basic foundationalist insight. These thinkers join other nonfoundationalists in claiming—against the Enlightenment—that there is no universal human reason. There is no single, universal set of criteria by means of which we can judge definitively the epistemic status of all beliefs.[85] Further, according to Plantinga and Wolterstorff, reason is not the supposedly neutral medium in which human reflection takes place. Nor is it a purely formal and autonomous given that precedes, and gives shape to, intellectual reflection. Instead, they argue that reason is "person specific" and "situation specific"[86] and that the nature of reason is itself a disputed topic.[87]

At the same time, these thinkers, whose viewpoint is sometimes referred to as "Reformed epistemology,"[88] do not deny categorically the validity of the foundationalist search for basic beliefs. Indeed, Plantinga especially agrees that certain beliefs are basic. What they reject as arbitrary and indefensible is the Enlightenment foundationalist restriction on which beliefs can count as properly basic, a restriction that assigns religious beliefs to the realm of superstructure. The Reformed epistemologists, especially Plantinga, in contrast, claim unequivocally that belief in God ought at times to be viewed as properly basic.[89]

The work of the Reformed epistemologists raises the question as to what—if anything—might be deemed basic for Christian theology: Does theological reflection and construction build on something that we must presuppose? For the answer, these philosophers, like other nonfoundationalists, point to the believing community. (In fact, this is in part what makes Reformed epistemology's seemingly weak brand of foundationalism at the same time nonfoundationalist and decidedly postmodern.) Thinkers such as Plantinga and Wolterstorff acknowledge the inevitability of our being situated in a particular community and the indispensable role our respective communities (or traditions) play in shaping our conceptions of rationality as well as the religious

---

85. Wood, *Epistemology*, 170.

86. Nicholas Wolterstorff, "Can Belief in God Be Rational If It Has No Foundations?" in *Faith and Rationality*, 155.

87. Westphal, "Reader's Guide," 12.

88. For this designation, see, for example, Nicholas Wolterstorff, "Introduction," in *Faith and Rationality*, 7. See also Plantinga, "Reason and Belief in God," 73–74.

89. Westphal, "Reader's Guide," 11; Plantinga, "Reason and Belief in God," 73–78.

beliefs we deem basic and thus by appeal to which we test new claims. And they readily admit the attendant loss of certitude involved with this acknowledgment, for they realize that these various communities may disagree as to the relevant set of paradigm instances of basic beliefs.

The difficulty this poses for any claims to universal truth ought not to be overlooked. Nevertheless, the communitarian turn marks an important advance. This focus returns theological reflection to its proper primary location within the believing community, in contrast to the Enlightenment ideal that effectively took theology out of the church and put it in the academy. More specifically, nonfoundationalist approaches see Christian theology as an activity of the community that gathers around Jesus the Christ. This has far-reaching implications for theology and theological method.

Christians share a common vision, namely, to be the Christ-focused community. Many Christians would agree that, whatever else may be involved, at the heart of the Christian faith is an experience of being encountered redemptively in Jesus Christ by the God of the Bible. But we must take this observation a step further. Regardless of how it is thought to occur, the encounter with God in Christ is an identity-producing event. Through Christ, God constitutes us individually as believers and corporately as a community of believers. As a result, in a sense, to be a Christian is to be a storyteller; Christians recite narratives that recount their historical and ongoing personal encounter with God. And these are cast in the categories drawn from the biblical narrative as well as from its explication in the didactic sections of scripture. In short, viewed from this perspective, to be a Christian entails coming to see the story of God's action in Christ as the paradigm for our stories. As Christians, we share an identity-constituting narrative.

This elevation of the role of "experience" as cast in the form of "encounter with God in Christ" ought not to be confused with the older Protestant liberalism, however. Two aspects separate the Christian ethos as delineated here from the liberal project. First, as we noted earlier, liberalism transformed religious experience into a new foundationalism. Liberal theologians assumed—and sought to discern—a single, universal, foundational religious experience that supposedly lay beneath the plethora of religious experiences found in the various religious traditions. Rather than following liberalism in this direction, the Christian ethos as we understand it asserts that the various religions mediate religious experiences that are categorically different from each other. The encounter with the God of the Bible through Jesus, which is foundational to Christian identity, is shared only by those who participate in the Christian community (even though the experience is *potentially* universal, in that all persons might conceivably embrace the Christian faith). In fact, the commonality of this experience is the identifying feature of participation in this specific community, whereas a quite different experience would mark a person as a member of some other community.

Second (and providing the theoretical basis for the first), our understanding of the Christian ethos takes seriously the experience-forming dimension of interpretive frameworks. As Lindbeck has pointed out, the older liberal project tended to give primacy to experience and to view theological statements as expressions of religious experience. But this approach misunderstands the nature of experience. Experience does not precede interpretation. Rather, experiences are always filtered by an interpretive framework—a grid—that facilitates their occurrence.[90] Hence, religious experience is dependent on a cognitive framework that sets forth a specifically religious interpretation of the world. In this sense, Lindbeck is correct in saying that religions produce religious experience rather than merely being the expression of it.[91]

But we must push this move away from classical liberalism even further. There is no generic religious experience, only experiences endemic to specific religious traditions—experiences the occurrences of which are facilitated by an interpretive framework that is specific to that religious tradition. And any such interpretive framework is theological in nature, for it involves an understanding that sees the world in connection with the divine reality around which that tradition focuses. More specifically, Christian experience is facilitated by the proclamation of the Christian gospel, inherent in which is a specifically Christian theological interpretive framework, a "grid" that views the world in connection with the God of the Bible.

Christian theology, in turn, is an intellectual enterprise by and for the Christian community. Through theological reflection, the community of those whom the God of the Bible has encountered in Jesus Christ seeks to understand, clarify, and delineate its interpretive framework informed by the narrative of God's actions on behalf of all creation as revealed in the Bible. In this sense, we might say that the specifically Christian-experience-facilitating interpretative framework, arising as it does out of the biblical narrative, is "basic" for Christian theology. As the intellectual engagement with what is "basic," theology is a second-order enterprise, and in this sense theological statements constitute second-order language.

Re-forming the Mosaic

At first glance, the suggestion that the Christian interpretive framework is "basic" for theology might appear to be simply a return to Enlightenment foundationalism. In fact, however, it marks a radical departure from the Age of Reason, while maintaining the central concerns of foundationalism. The cognitive framework that is "basic" for theology is not a given that precedes the theological enterprise; it does not provide the sure foundation on which the theological edifice can in turn be constructed. Rather, in a sense the interpretive framework and theology are inseparably intertwined. Just as every

90. See, for example, Owen C. Thomas, "Theology and Experience," *Harvard Theological Review* 78/1–2 (January–April 1985): 192.

91. See, for example, Lindbeck, *Nature of Doctrine*, 34, where he states, "A religion is above all an external world . . . that molds and shapes the self and its world, rather than an expression or thematization of a preexisting self or of preconceptual experience."

interpretive framework is essentially theological, so also every articulation of the Christian cognitive framework comes already clothed in a specific theological understanding. In fact, every such articulation is the embodiment of a specific understanding of the Christian theological vision; each embodies a specific understanding of the world as it is connected to the God of the Bible.

The theologian's task, then, is not to work from an interpretive framework to a theological construct. Instead, the theological enterprise consists in setting forth in a systematic manner a properly Christian interpretive framework as informed by the Bible for the sake of the church's mission in the contemporary context. By its very nature, the systematic articulation of the Christian interpretive framework takes the form of an integrated statement of Christian doctrine. This leads inevitably to the kind of coherentist theological method Pannenberg has pioneered.

Commitment to the foundationalist approach takes most modernists, in contrast, in a quite different direction. Despite what we might surmise from the systems of Christian doctrine they produce, modernists—especially conservative modernists—routinely approach theological reflection in a somewhat piecemeal manner, indicative of an understanding of knowledge that sees it as the compiling of correct conclusions from a sure foundation. Indeed, once a theologian has set forth the proper foundation (which for the conservative modernist is often focused in an inerrant Bible, whereas for the liberal it is based on religious experience), he or she is free to construct the house of theological knowledge in any order. As a consequence, the systematic theologies of conservative modernists often give the appearance of being elaborate collections of loosely related facts derived from the Bible, which is understood as "a storehouse of facts," to cite Charles Hodge's description.[92] Rather than *systematic* theologies, they tend to be what we might call "encyclopedias of theological knowledge." And even though the treatment of the various topics in these exhaustive works generally follows a customary pattern—a pattern that has a certain logic to it—conservative modernists often admit that the chosen order is in fact quite arbitrary. Wayne Grudem, for example, writes,

> [T]here is nothing to prevent us from going to Scripture to look for answers to *any* doctrinal questions, considered in *any sequence*. The sequence of topics in this book is a very common one and has been adopted because it is orderly and lends itself well to learning and teaching. But the chapters could be read in any sequence one wanted and the conclusions should not be different, nor should the persuasiveness of the arguments—if they are rightly derived from Scripture—be significantly diminished. . . . I have tried to write the chapters so that they can be read as independent units.[93]

92. Hodge, *Systematic Theology*, 1:10.
93. Grudem, *Systematic Theology*, 32.

Of course, Grudem can release the reader to read the chapters in any sequence only because in the book's prolegomenon he has first set forth the proper foundation for what follows.

The demise of foundationalism, however, raises questions about the propriety of this paradigm. As we noted earlier, contemporary philosophers remind us that knowledge is not a collection of isolated factual statements arising directly from first principles. Rather, our beliefs form a system in which each belief is supported by its neighbors and, ultimately, by its presence within the whole. If this is the case, theology can no longer model itself after the foundationalist metaphor of constructing an edifice. We cannot spin our wheels constructing elaborate prolegomena, thinking thereby we have laid a sure foundation for the compilation of seemingly separable units of knowledge we then elaborate, whether that knowledge be biblical teaching or expressions of the highest human aspirations. Instead, we ought to view Christian doctrine as comprising a "belief-mosaic" and see theology, in turn, as the exploration of Christian doctrine viewed as an interrelated, unified whole. And we ought to envision our constructive work as leading to a mosaic of interlocking pieces that presents a single pattern, rather than merely to a collection of beads on a string.

Therefore, while we might view the Christian interpretive framework as in a certain sense foundational for theology, we could more properly speak of theology as the articulation of the cognitive mosaic of the Christian faith. This mosaic consists of the interlocking doctrines that together comprise the specifically Christian way of viewing the world. This worldview is truly theological and specifically Christian because it involves an understanding of the entire universe and of ourselves in connection with the God of the Bible and the biblical narrative of God bringing creation to its divinely destined goal. Not only does the theological task entail explicating this doctrinal mosaic, but, as Pannenberg has argued, it also includes demonstrating the explicative power of the Christian faith. It indicates the interconnectedness of the set of doctrines and the value of the Christian worldview for illuminating human experience as well as human understanding of our world.

Reconstructing the World

We noted earlier that the nonfoundationalist move to a communitarian theological method opens the door to a potentially devastating problem: How can we seek truth in a multicultural world in which various communities offer diverse theological paradigms? In other words, does theology speak about anything objective, or does it content itself with merely articulating the interpretive framework of a specific religious tradition?

Lindbeck's proposal provides a lucid example of how a nonfoundationalist approach can give rise to this problem. His claim that theological statements are second-order assertions and his close linking of doctrine with the construction of a coherent vision of the world seem to beg the sticky question as to whether such assertions and such a vision somehow reflect a reality beyond themselves.[94] Further, his suggestion that theological assertions are "in-house" statements potentially results in a "sectarian" church—one that no longer assumes any role in the public realm.[95] In short, Lindbeck's program raises the question, Does the move beyond foundationalism entail a move away from metaphysical realism?[96]

Formulated in this manner, the question is both improper and ultimately unhelpful. Perhaps we might better ask, How can a nonfoundationalist theological method lead us to statements about a world beyond our formulations? Although our more complete answer will be unfolded in subsequent chapters, a preliminary statement of our conclusions is appropriate here. Our answer takes its cue from contemporary sociologists who provide insight into the world-constructing role of society in general and language in particular.

Although Wittgenstein introduced the phrase "language game" into popular parlance, the Swiss linguist, Ferdinand de Saussure (1857–1913), provided the basis for the turn to linguistics. In contrast to his predecessors who viewed language as a natural phenomenon that develops according to fixed and discoverable laws, Saussure proposed that language is a social phenomenon[97] and that a linguistic system is a product of social convention.[98] Structuralists, such as the anthropologist Claude Levi-Strauss (b. 1908), built on Saussure's insight. Their efforts, as well as the work of the proponents of what has come to be known as "the sociology of knowledge," netted an awareness of the connection between culture (including language) and both personal identity formation and social cohesion.[99]

Culture generates a shared context in which people engage in the construction of meaning and in the task of making sense out of the world. In the words of Raymond Williams, culture functions as a "*signifying system* through which

94. This was a central point of contention in the encounter between Carl F. H. Henry and Hans Frei at Yale. See Carl F. H. Henry, "Narrative Theology: An Evangelical Appraisal," *Trinity Journal* 8 (Spring 1987): 19. For a similar critique, see Alister E. McGrath, "An Evangelical Evaluation of Postliberalism," in *Nature of Confession*, ed. Okholm and Phillips, 35–39. For a sympathetic treatment of this issue, see Bruce D. Marshall, "Absorbing the World: Christianity and the Universe of Truths," in *Theology and Dialogue: Essays in Conversation with George Lindbeck*, ed. Bruce D. Marshall (Notre Dame, Ind: University of Notre Dame Press, 1990), 69–102. Clark Pinnock notes this objection but then erroneously concludes that Lindbeck is not denying that doctrines make first-order truth claims. *Tracking the Maze: Finding Our Way through Modern Theology from an Evangelical Perspective* (San Francisco: Harper & Row, 1990), 59.

95. See, for example, David H. Kelsey, "Church Discourse and Public Realm," in *Theology and Dialogue*, 7–34.

96. For a reading of Lindbeck that suggests that his program is not inherently antirealist, see Jeffrey Hensley, "Are Postliberals Necessarily Antirealists? Reexamining the Metaphysics of Lindbeck's Postliberal Theology," in *Nature of Confession*, ed. Okholm and Phillips, 69–80.

97. David Holdcroft, *Saussure: Signs, System and Arbitrariness* (Cambridge: Cambridge University Press, 1991), 7–8.

98. Ibid., 10.

99. See, for example, Peter L. Berger and Thomas Luckmann, *The Social Construction of Reality: A Treatise in the Sociology of Knowledge*, (New York: Anchor Books, 1967), 99–104. For a fuller statement of Berger's views, see Peter L. Berger, *The Sacred Canopy: Elements of a Sociological Theory of Religion*, (Garden City, N.Y.: Doubleday, 1969), 3–51. For a summary and appraisal of Berger's contribution, see Robert Wuthnow, *Rediscovering the Sacred: Perspectives on Religion in Contemporary Society* (Grand Rapids: Wm. B. Eerdmans Publishing Co., 1992), 9–35.

necessarily (though among other means) a social order is communicated, reproduced, experienced and explored."[100] In this process, language plays a crucial role. Together with nonlinguistic modalities, such as metaphorical images and symbols, language—which we inherit from our social community—provides the conceptual tools through which we construct the world we inhabit, as well as the vehicles through which we communicate and thereby share meaning with others. In the words of Peter Berger and Thomas Luckmann, "Language objectivates the shared experiences and makes them available to all within the linguistic community, thus becoming both the basis and the instrument of the collective stock of knowledge."[101] Theology, we might conclude, explores the world-constructing, knowledge-forming, identity-forming "language" of the Christian community.

But how does this relate to an objective reality beyond our linguistic constructs? There is, of course, a certain undeniable givenness to the universe apart from the human linguistic-constructive task. Indeed, the universe predates the appearance of humans on the earth. To assume that this observation is sufficient to relegate all the talk of social construction to the trash heap, however, is to miss the point. The simple fact is, we do not inhabit the "world-in-itself"; instead, we live in a linguistic world of our own making. As Berger and Luckmann note, human reality is "socially constructed reality."[102]

At the same time, viewed from a Christian perspective, there is a certain "objectivity" to the world. But this objectivity is not that of a static reality existing outside of, and cotemporally with, our socially and linguistically constructed reality; it is not the objectivity of what some might call "the world as it is." Rather, seen through the lense of the gospel, this objectivity is the objectivity of the world as God wills it to be. Because what God wills is not a present but a future reality (e.g., Isa. 65:17–19; Rev. 21:5), the "objectivity of the world" about which we can truly speak is an objectivity of a *future*, eschatological world. And because this future reality is God's determined will for creation, as that which cannot be shaken (Heb. 12:26–28) it is far more real—more objectively real—than the present world, which is even now passing away (1 Cor. 7:31).

This observation has crucial implications for theology. As the community of Christ, we have a divinely given mandate: to be participants in God's work of constructing a world that reflects God's own will for creation, a world in which everything finds its connectedness in Jesus Christ (Col. 1:17) who is the *logos*, the ordering principle of the cosmos as God intends it to be. This mandate has a strongly linguistic dimension. We participate with God as we, through the constructive power of language, create a world that links our present with the divine future, or, we should say, as the Holy Spirit creates such a world in, among, and through us. In this ongoing, world-constructing process, the

---

100. Raymond Williams, *The Sociology of Culture* (New York: Schocken Books, 1982), 13.
101. Berger and Luckmann, *Social Construction of Reality*, 68.
102. Ibid., 189.

Spirit's primary tool is the biblical narrative. The Spirit's goal is to bring us to view all reality in accordance with God's program of molding creation into conformity with the divine eternal purpose through Jesus Christ, the Son, so that as the community of Christ we might inhabit a world that truly reflects God's purposes for creation. Because this program is in part linguistic, participating in it is theological work!

The fundamental question, however, still remains: Why give primacy to the world-constructing language of the Christian community? As Christians we would likely respond by asserting that we believe that the Christian theological vision is *true*. But on what basis can we make this claim? Must we now finally appeal to some court beyond the Christian faith itself, some rational "first principle" that supposedly carries universality? In the end, must we inevitably retreat to a foundationalist epistemology?

Here, we suggest, the wedding of communitarian and pragmatist insights offers assistance. Communitarians remind us that the goal of all social traditions is to construct a well-ordered society, although the various communities might well differ from each other as to what that society entails. This observation leads us to inquire as to which theological vision is able to provide the transcendent vision for the construction of the kind of world that particular theologizing community is in fact seeking? Which theological vision provides the framework for the construction of true community? We believe that Christian theology, focused as it is on God as the triunity of persons and on humankind as the *imago dei*, sets forth a helpful vision of the nature of the kind of community that all religious belief systems in their own way and according to their own understanding seek to foster. This vision, we maintain, provides the best transcendent basis for the human ideal of life-in-relationship, for it looks to the divine life as a plurality-in-unity as the basis for understanding what it means to be human persons-in-community.

The task of systematic theology is to show how the Christian mosaic of beliefs offers a transcendent vision of the glorious eschatological community that God wills for God's own creation and how this vision provides a coherent foundation for life-in-relationship in this penultimate age, life that ought to be visible in the community of Christ as the sign of the age to come. Implicit in the construction of a coherent presentation of the Christian vision is a claim to "validity," a claim that, however, does not look to a universally accessible present reality for confirmation but anticipates the eschatological completion of the universally directed program of the God of the Bible. The task of a helpful theological method, in turn, is to set forth a program for the shaping of a theology that can carry out the theological vocation in a manner that is solidly biblical and truly Christian and that takes seriously the postmodern situation.

PART TWO
THEOLOGY'S SOURCES

Chapter Three

Scripture: Theology's "Norming Norm"

In the beginning was the Word . . .

—John 1:1

Modern religion is to a very considerable extent a discursive practice. It encompasses ritual, and it mandates behavior and feeling, but it gives a privileged place to discourse: it grounds itself in the Word, whether that means a formally codified text or a broader conception of the divine spirit; it thrives on professional and popular interpretations of the Word; it requires the construction and maintenance of community through communication of shared convictions and experiences; and it mandates verbal expressions of sincerity, emotion, and commitment.

—Robert Wuthnow[1]

Crucial configurations and operative modes in our moral, philosophic, psychological condition . . . must now be understood as coming "after the Word" . . . my question is: what is the status and meaning of meaning, of communicative form, in the time of the "after-Word"?

—George Steiner[2]

Christians are a "people of the book." Our communal identity is bound up with a set of literary texts that together form canonical scripture. In addition,

1. Robert Wuthnow, *Rediscovering the Sacred: Perspectives on Religion in Contemporary Society* (Grand Rapids: Wm. B. Eerdmans Publishing Co., 1992), 58.
2. George Steiner, *Real Presences* (Chicago: University of Chicago Press, 1989), 93–94.

acknowledging the Bible as scripture lies at the heart of participating in the community of Christ. As David Kelsey aptly said, "[T]he decision to adopt these writings as 'canon' is not . . . a separate decision over and above a decision to become a Christian."[3]

All Christian traditions value the Bible as scripture, and therefore their adherents are "book people." Yet as heirs of the Reformation who hallmark *sola scriptura*, Protestants are especially cognizant of the foundational role scripture is to play in their lives. But what does it mean to give place to the Bible in the life of Christ's community? And what is the role of theology in this process? Questions such as these take us to the center of Christian theological method.

The overarching goal of this chapter is to explore these matters in the context of setting forth a method for theological reflection. More specifically, we inquire as to how the Bible ought to function in theology by pursuing the traditional assertion that the biblical message is theology's norming norm. At the same time, we realize that this affirmation is closely connected to another question—namely, What is the role of theology in fostering the centrality of scripture among those who claim allegiance to the God of the Bible? Before launching into our main topic, however, we must note one crucial characteristic of the context in which we engage in this discussion.

The Silence of the Bible in Modern Theology

One of the most consistent complaints aired by thinkers across the theological spectrum is that scripture has grown ominously silent in the church today. Already two decades ago George Stroup spoke for many in lamenting that

> the Bible no longer exercises anything like the authority it once did in many Christian communities. And in those communities where the Bible continues to exercise its traditional role there is little or no serious engagement with the problems of the twentieth century.[4]

The turning of a new millennium has done little to warrant a revision of his stark appraisal. The Bible seems to have lost its voice not only in the wider society but, more significantly, even in the community of Christ.

If the Bible has grown strangely silent in the church, we might follow the pathway suggested by commentators such as Hans Frei[5] and lay the blame for this tragedy at the feet of theologians and biblical scholars themselves. Of course, Christian thinkers did not set out to silence scripture. Rather, the Bible's

---

3. David H. Kelsey, *The Uses of Scripture in Recent Theology* (Philadelphia: Fortress Press, 1975), 165.

4. George W. Stroup, *The Promise of Narrative Theology* (Atlanta: John Knox Press, 1981), 26.

5. Hans Frei, *The Eclipse of Biblical Narrative: A Study in Eighteenth and Nineteenth Century Hermeneutics* (New Haven, Conn.: Yale University Press, 1974), 16.

loss of voice came as an unintended result of well-intentioned persons who sought to recover the Bible and save theology in the wake of the Enlightenment. The irony of this situation is that in a sense scripture caught laryngitis from its would-be physicians.

The chief culprit in the undermining of the Bible's status in the church has been modern theology itself. As we noted in chapter 2, in their attempt to find certainty for Christian faith in a world imbued with Cartesian skepticism, theologians followed the philosophers' lead and trotted after the pied piper of foundationalism. The foundationalist impulse led to a reassessment of the nature and role of the Bible in theology and, by extension, in the church.

Liberalism and the Bible

One significant attempt to place theology on firmer footing in the wake of the Enlightenment was the liberal theological project. At the heart of liberalism was an innovative relocation of the locus of theological authority away from the traditional sources such as Bible and church, and toward a supposedly universal human reality—religious experience. Liberals viewed experience as the unassailable authority that could facilitate them in determining what in the Bible is sheer custom and what constitutes abiding, universal truth.[6] As a result, religious experience became the "sure" foundation on which liberal theology was built.

This move led liberal theologians to break with the older emphasis on the Bible as divinely given revelation. Liberals, in contrast, focused on the human authorship of scripture, viewing the Bible as the product of fallible humans who were—to cite the description of L. Harold DeWolf—"conditioned and limited by their times and their individual peculiarities, though also rising frequently to great heights of expression under the illumination of God's self-disclosing presence."[7] Because they believed that the Bible itself was not the Word of God in the strict sense,[8] liberals like DeWolf suggested that "[t]he reader who would hear the true word of God in the reading of the Bible must be prepared to discriminate between the word of God and the words of men."[9]

This did not mean, however, that the Bible was unimportant for liberal theologians.[10] The turn to religious experience led to an innovative proposal as to

---

6. Roy A. Harrisville and Walter Sundberg, *The Bible in Modern Culture: Theology and Historical-Critical Method from Spinoza to Käsemann* (Grand Rapids: Wm. B. Eerdmans Publishing Co., 1995), 27.

7. L. Harold DeWolf, *The Case for Theology in Liberal Perspective* (Philadelphia: Westminster Press, 1959), 48.

8. Ibid., 17.

9. Ibid., 48.

10. Miller, for example, writes, "But one should never conclude that the Scriptures are unimportant for the liberal Christian. Quite the contrary, they are central to the Christian faith. The fact that more attention is given to them as symbolic documents than as historical documents does not distort their importance." Donald E. Miller, *The Case for Liberal Christianity* (San Francisco: Harper & Row, 1981), 36.

the nature and function of scripture. The Bible was a human book, of course, and hence a "mixed bag" of truth and error.[11] Yet it remained special, for in it godly people witnessed to their encounter with God. Although liberals knew full well that these experiences were written long ago in the thought forms and categories of ancient, foreign cultures, they remained optimistic about the ability of the Bible to speak to modern people. The connection liberals posited as linking ancients with moderns was their observation that certain, basic human experiences remain the same in every era and in each culture. The tasks of the theologian, in turn, became to seek the "abiding experiences" that stand underneath the biblical materials and reformulate their meaning in ways that are intelligible to modern persons.[12]

The goal of liberal theologians, therefore, was to gain a hearing for scripture in the modern world. Like George Stroup, they were convinced that the Bible had fallen woefully silent, a silence that they believed was due to the distance between the ancient and the modern worlds but that could be bridged by appeal to religious experience as a universally human phenomenon. Despite this heroic attempt to salvage the Bible for the modern mind-set, in the end the liberal foundationalism of religious experience undercut the well-intended goal of its architects. The Bible was no longer read as text but as record—as an inspiring chronicle of human religious experience. Hence, more important than the text itself were the religious experiences—the encounters with God—that lay behind the text and to which the biblical writings bore witness. As this shift in focus happened, any idea of the biblical *text* as such being "voice" soon became eclipsed by the apparent Babel of the variegated intonations lying behind the text.

The liberal theological project was paralleled by a shift in biblical studies. Just as theologians sought universality and certainty in the religious experiences to which the biblical writers bore witness, so also biblical scholars turned their attention to the history they thought lay behind text. They believed that they could sift through the biblical texts and peel off the mythical or theological accretions in an attempt to find the "facts"and then reconstruct "what really happened." Seeing themselves as neutral specialists, biblical scholars assumed that by dissecting the texts and combining the bits of data they discovered through this method, they could eventually piece together the true history of the ancient faith communities.

The Conservative Alternative

Eventually liberal scholars were joined in the critical task by recruits of a more conservative persuasion, who differed with their liberal colleagues only in degree, not in substance. These folks simply had a higher estimation of the

11. James A. Pike, "The Bible, God's Inspired Word," in *Spectrum of Protestant Beliefs*, ed. Robert Campbell (Milwaukee: Bruce Publishing Co., 1968), 34.

12. Harry Emerson Fosdick, *The Modern Use of the Bible* (New York: Macmillan Co., 1924), 97–130.

amount of the "real history" that was reflected in the biblical documents. Like the quest for the religious experiences that lay under the text, the attempts to reconstruct the underlying history treated the Bible as a problem rather than a solution. As a result, the voice of scripture was stifled as the Bible became the means to discover something more interesting than the text itself. In short, conservative biblical scholars often joined cause methodologically with their liberal colleagues, while differing radically with them over the results of that method. The situation in theology was somewhat parallel.

From its genesis in the nineteenth century and throughout its heyday in the twentieth, the liberal theological program was countered by a resurgent conservative theology that claimed as its pedigree the Reformation heritage of fidelity to scripture. Viewing themselves—and *not* their liberal opponents—as the true heirs not merely of the Reformation but also of the entire Christian tradition, conservative theologians emphasized their commitment to the Bible as the Word of God, against what they perceived to be the liberal attack on scripture. Hence, Charles Hodge's successors at Princeton, A. A. Hodge and B. B. Warfield, affirmed what they called "the great Catholic doctrine of Biblical Inspiration," namely, "that the Scriptures not only contain, but *are the Word of God*, and hence that all their elements and all their affirmations are absolutely errorless, and binding the faith and obedience of men."[13] In articulating this position, conservatives took pains to differentiate between what the Bible may "say" and what it actually "teaches." Thus, the Bible may report accurately the errant statements of a person (such as the friends of Job) without affirming that their assertions are in fact true.[14]

While claiming the inheritance of Protestantism, conservatives drew from the entire scholastic theological tradition, whose genesis actually predated the Reformation. As an extension of the scholastic legacy, conservatives viewed the Bible primarily (albeit not exclusively) as propositional revelation from God.[15] Foundational to scripture is divine revelation, which many conservatives—such as Carl F. H. Henry—asserted takes the form of "rational communication conveyed in intelligible ideas and meaningful words, that is, in conceptual-verbal form."[16] God, in turn, conservatives like Henry declared, is revealed "in the whole canon of Scripture which objectively communicates in propositional-verbal form the content and meaning of all God's revelation."[17]

The focus on propositional revelation led conservatives to view the Bible as above all the source for religious teachings. While these teachings also included

13. A. A. Hodge and B. B. Warfield, "Inspiration," *Presbyterian Review* (1881): 237.

14., Clark H. Pinnock, *Biblical Revelation—The Foundation of Christian Theology* (Chicago: Moody Press, 1971), 78.

15. For example, Gordon H. Clark, *Karl Barth's Theological Method* (Philadelphia: Presbyterian and Reformed Publishing Co., 1963), 150; Francis A. Schaeffer, *The God Who Is There* (Downers Grove, Ill.: InterVarsity Press, 1968), 92–93; Pinnock, *Biblical Revelation*, 66.

16. Carl F. H. Henry, *God, Revelation, and Authority*, 6 vols. (Waco, Tex.: Word Publishers, 1976–1983) 2:12; cf. 3:455.

17. Ibid., 2:87.

precepts for living, the central, foundational, and most significant dimension was that of doctrine: The Bible was fundamentally a doctrinal resource.[18] Hence, the great nineteenth-century, Princeton theologian, Charles Hodge, asserted,

> Revelation is the communication of truth by God to the understandings of men. It makes known doctrines. For example, it makes known that God is . . . that Christ is the Son of God; that he assumed our nature; that he died for our sins, etc. These are logical propositions.[19]

Conservatives, therefore, viewed the authoritative aspect of the Bible as its "stateable content,"[20] more specifically albeit not exclusively, the doctrines it teaches. And "believing the Bible" came to be linked most importantly with believing the doctrines that conservatives concluded the Bible itself teaches. Why this focus? Kelsey offers a clue. Speaking about Warfield, he writes,

> This fits with his view of the nature of saving faith. Saving faith necessarily includes belief that certain doctrines are true. Since it is important that the belief be utterly confident, the truths must be utterly trustworthy. That creates the need for an utterly trustworthy authority determining what those doctrines are. And scripture is, for the Protestant, that authority.[21]

Viewing the Bible as primarily a storehouse of theological facts,[22] conservative theologians set out to amass the true statements or factual propositions they believed were taught in the pages of scripture.[23] To this end, they crisscrossed the documents so as to bring together what they concluded the Bible "teaches" about any given topic.[24] And by bringing these biblical teachings together in a systematic whole, their goal became that of compiling the one, complete, timeless body of right doctrines, which they assumed constituted "all the counsel of God" (Acts 20:27, KJV).

Conservatives sincerely believed that in this manner they were returning the Bible to the very center of church life. What many apparently failed to see,

---

18. Richard J. Mouw, "The Bible in Twentieth-Century Protestantism: A Preliminary Taxonomy," in *The Bible in America: Essays in Cultural History*, ed. Nathan O. Hatch and Mark A. Noll (New York: Oxford University Press, 1982), 143.

19. Charles Hodge, "The Theology of the Intellect and That of Feelings," in *Essays and Reviews* (New York: Robert Carter & Bros., 1857), 609–610.

20. Kelsey, *Uses of Scripture,* 29.

21. Ibid., 21.

22. For example, Charles Hodge, *Systematic Theology,* 3 vols. (New York: Scribner, Armstrong, & Co., 1872), 1:18.

23. See, for example, Gordon R. Lewis and Bruce A. Demarest, *Integrative Theology,* 3 vols. (Grand Rapids: Zondervan, 1987–1994), 1:25-27.

24. Hence, Wayne Grudem, *Systematic Theology: An Introduction to Biblical Doctrine* (Grand Rapids: Zondervan, 1994), 21.

however, is how their efforts actually could engender the opposite result. In effect, the scholastic theological agenda meant that the ongoing task of reading the Bible as text was superseded by the publication of the skilled theologian's *magnum opus*. If the goal of theological inquiry was to extrapolate the system of propositions the divine Communicator had inscripturated in the pages of the text, it would seem that systematic theology could—and eventually would—make the Bible superfluous. Why should the sincere believer continue to read the Bible when biblical truth—correct doctrine—is more readily at hand in the latest systematic compilation offered by the skilled theologian? Why read, that is, for any reason except to determine for oneself that the theologian's conclusions are indeed biblical truth—that this theologian had captured the one, true biblical system of doctrine?

Hence, like the liberal project that conservatives struggled so untiringly against, the conservative's focus on the construction of the one true set of doctrines (together with the corresponding set of ethical principles or rules) replaced treating the Bible as text with the quest for the revelation that supposedly lies behind the texts of scripture. In this way, theologians exchanged the desire to give voice to the text itself for the attempt to read *through* the texts to the doctrinal system the texts concealed. Despite the well-meaning, lofty intentions of conservative thinkers to honor the Bible as scripture, their approach in effect contributed to the silencing of the text in the church.

Biblical Authority: Scripture as the "Norming Norm" of Theology

Our quick overview of the theological background to the current silence of the Bible in the church suggests that regaining the Bible's voice requires a rediscovery of the Bible as text. Yet as Wesley Kort argues, reading any text (let alone the biblical text) as scripture is not always a "pleasant" experience:

> As long as we do not read our scriptures as texts or texts as scriptures our locations and worlds can remain incontestable, taken for granted, or naturalized. But when we engage in such reading, we recognize that our locations are partial and our worlds are built on uncertainties. Understandably, we avoid such disconfirmations of adequacy and stability, and such avoidance is characteristic of our culture—in its religious as well as in its nonreligious segments, I would add.[25]

Despite our human inclinations to the contrary, however, the Bible must be read as text—first of all, and above all, in the church. In this process, theology

25. Wesley A. Kort, *Take, Read: Scripture, Textuality, and Cultural Practice* (University Park, Penn.: Pennsylvania State University Press, 1996), 14.

plays a key role. Theology ought to assist—not hinder—the community of Christ in reading canonical scripture as text. But for theology to contribute to the retrieval of the biblical voice, its practitioners must gain a renewed understanding of the role of scripture in theology. This takes us back to the issue of authority and, by extension, to the ancient confession of the Bible as the norming norm for theology.

The Bible, the Spirit, and Authority

A central disagreement dividing the Reformers and the church of the Counter-Reformation was the question as to what ought to function as the ultimate authority in theology. Yet the issue had already charted a two-hundred-year history by the time it came to a head in the sixteenth century. From the patristic era through the Middle Ages, theologians acknowledged the primacy of scripture, while simultaneously granting a certain importance to tradition. Not only did theologians sense no contradiction between these two authorities, but they also could not envision a possible conflict between the conclusions of biblical exegesis and the pronouncements of the church's teaching office. The renewed focus on the literal meaning of the texts beginning in the fourteenth century, however, led certain late medieval thinkers to assert that the exegesis of scripture carries primacy over the teaching authority of the papal office.[26]

As Protestants we side quite naturally with the intent of Luther's elevation of *sola scriptura* against the position that solidified at the Council of Trent. Nevertheless, we readily acknowledge that tradition plays an important (albeit subservient) role in theology. More specifically, as will be developed in the next chapter, the theological tradition of the church provides signposts for theological construction. And as we will see more clearly later in this chapter, the Christian tradition in general occasions the context for our reading the Bible.

The Protestant Principle of Authority

The point of departure for our affirmation of scripture as the norming norm lies in what evangelical theologian Bernard Ramm denoted "the Protestant principle of authority." Ramm writes, "The proper principle of authority within the Christian church must be . . . the Holy Spirit speaking in the Scriptures, which are the product of the Spirit's revelatory and inspiring action."[27] In some sense the Protestant principle belongs to the common heritage of all Christian traditions, yet this specific formulation captures especially well the sensitivities of the Reformation. More specifically, the principle received its definitive articulation in one of the most influential statements of the Reformed theological trajectory, the Westminster Confession of Faith:

---

26. Wolfhart Pannenberg, "The Crisis of the Scripture Principle," in *Basic Questions in Theology*, trans. George H. Kehm, 2 vols. (Philadelphia: Fortress Press, 1970), 1:4–5.

27. Bernard Ramm, *The Pattern of Religious Authority* (Grand Rapids: Wm. B. Eerdmans Publishing Co., 1959), 28.

> The Supreme Judge, by which all controversies of religion
> are to be determined, and all decrees of counsels, opinions of
> ancient writers, doctrines of men, and private spirits, are to
> be examined, and in whose sentence we are to rest, can be no
> other than the Holy Spirit speaking in the Scripture.[28]

Reflective of the Reformation concern to bind Word and Spirit together, the Westminister statement clearly links the Bible with the Holy Spirit. Bringing scripture and Spirit together provides the foundation for understanding in what sense the Bible is the norming norm in theology and, in turn, stands as the essential prerequisite for reading the Bible as text.

The declaration that the Spirit speaking in or through scripture is our final authority means that Christian belief and practice cannot be determined merely by appeal to either the exegesis of scripture carried out apart from the life of the believer and the believing community or to any supposedly private (or corporate) "word from the Spirit" that stands in contradiction to biblical exegesis. Instead, the reading of the text—and under this rubric we would place all our exegetical efforts—is for the purpose of listening to the voice of Spirit who seeks to speak through scripture to the church in the present.

The Protestant principle means the Bible is authoritative in that it is the vehicle through which the Spirit speaks. Taking the idea a step further, the authority of the Bible is in the end the authority of the Spirit whose instrumentality it is. As Christians, we acknowledge the Bible as scripture in that the sovereign Spirit has bound authoritative, divine speaking to this text. We believe that the Spirit has chosen, now chooses, and will continue to choose to speak with authority through the biblical texts.

The connection between the Spirit's enlivening of the text and our acknowledgment of biblical authority may actually be the point of the verses to which theologians routinely appeal as the *locus classicus* for the traditional doctrine of inspiration (2 Tim. 3:16–17).[29] Through the rare use of *theopneustos*, which may intend an allusion to God's breathing into the nostrils of Adam making him spring to life, Paul declared that "God breathes into the Scripture" thereby making it useful.[30] As the evangelical Greek scholar Edward Goodrick concludes, the text focuses on the surpassing value of the Spirit-energized scriptures and not on some purported "pristine character of the autographs."[31] The church, in short, came to confess the authority of scripture because the early believers experienced the power and truth of the Spirit of God through these

---

28. The Westminster Confession of Faith, 1.10, in *The Creeds of the Churches*, ed. John H. Leith, 3rd ed. (Atlanta: John Knox Press, 1982), 196.

29. Edward W. Goodrick, "Let's Put 2 Timothy 3:16 Back into the Bible," *Journal of the Evangelical Theological Society* 25/4 (December 1982): 479–87.

30. The Greek term *theopneustos* ("inspiration") occurs only here in the New Testament. Many expositors find the clue to its meaning in its etymology (*theos* [God] + *pneuma* [breath or spirit]), which yields the idea "God-breathed" or "expired by God." But the declaration itself does not spell out clearly what this means for the activity of the Spirit in scripture.

31. Goodrick, "Let's Put 2 Timothy 3:16 Back into the Bible," 486–87.

writings. They knew these documents were "animated with the Spirit of Christ."[32] Following the lead of the church of all ages, we too look to the biblical texts to hear the Spirit's voice.

Authority and Illumination

The affirmation of the Spirit speaking through scripture as our final authority that came to be codified in the Westminster Confession boasts a long and impressive pedigree in theology. Although in declaring the biblical canon closed in 397 C.E. the church in effect asserted that the Spirit's work in inspiration had ceased,[33] this did not mark the end of the Spirit's activity in connection with scripture. On the contrary, the Spirit speaks to succeeding generations of Christians through the text. Traditionally, this ongoing divine work has been known as "illumination."

Theologians routinely find the background for the idea of illumination in several biblical verses. An oblique reference to the idea may lie in Elihu's comment to Job: "But truly it is the spirit in a mortal, the breath of the Almighty, that makes for understanding" (Job 32:8, NRSV). However, several references in the New Testament seem to present the idea of illumination more clearly. Both John (1 John 5:7,11) and Paul (1 Cor. 2:6–16; 2 Cor. 3:14–17) emphasize the crucial importance of divine illumination if humans are to perceive spiritual truth. According to Paul, our depraved condition lies behind this necessity: Because our hearts are darkened, we no longer acknowledge the truth about God (Rom. 1:18–23), and consequently, we are dependent on divine illumination. John reports that in Jesus' farewell discourse he described more plainly in what form this provision would come: The Holy Spirit would guide the disciples into truth (John 14:26).

On the basis of texts such as these, Christians have always anticipated that the Spirit would guide *them* as well. Among the English Puritans, this expectation led to the idea of "further light." John Robinson's parting words to the Pilgrims as they set out from Holland for the New World provide a lucid example. On this occasion, the Puritan pastor purportedly admonished his flock to look for the further light that the Spirit of God would yet pour forth from the scriptures.[34] The Puritan doctrine of further light has been cast in the form of literary theory recently by the Canadian literary critic Northrop Frye. Frye notes that to an extent unparalleled in any other literature the biblical texts seem to invite the

32. Thomas A. Hoffman, "Inspiration, Normativeness, Canonicity, and the Unique Sacred Character of the Bible," *Catholic Biblical Quarterly* 44 (July 1982):457.

33. J. R. McRay, "Bible, Canon of," in the *Evangelical Dictionary of Theology*, ed. Walter A. Elwell (Grand Rapids: Baker, 1984), 141.

34. This remark has been preserved by Edward Winslow, who was present at Robinson's farewell speech. Winslow was among the original pilgrims on the Mayflower and later became governor of Plymouth. In his report, Winslow declares that Robinson "was very confident that the Lord had more truth and light yet to break forth out of his holy word." See Alexander Young, *Chronicles of the Pilgrim Fathers of the Colony of Plymouth, from 1602 to 1625*, (Boston: Charles C. Little and James Brown, 1841), 87, 396–97.

readers to bring their own experiences into a conversation with them, resulting in an ongoing interpretation of each in the light of the other.[35] For this reason, Frye suggests that readers properly approach the text with an attitude of expectation, anticipating that there is always more to be received from the Bible.[36]

In keeping with the example of Puritans like Robinson and critics like Frye, we would conclude that the Bible is the final authority in the church (and hence the norming norm in theology) precisely as the Spirit pours forth further light through the text. Through scripture, the Spirit continually instructs us as Christ's community in the midst of our life together as we face the challenges of living in the contemporary world.

Illumination and Subjectivism

At first glance, this proposal might appear to be beset with one potentially debilitating danger. Would not the close connection we are suggesting between biblical authority and the phenomenon of illumination lead inevitably to subjectivism? Does this link between Spirit and Word make the authority of the Bible dependent on our hearing the voice of the Spirit in its pages?

Of course, we should not minimize this danger. Several recent theologies of Word and Spirit have come close to subjectivism. Thinkers influenced by Karl Barth and neoorthodox Word of God theologies routinely differentiate between the Bible and the transcendent Word in a manner that seems to reduce biblical authority to our subjective reception of the divine address that confronts us through the human words of the Bible. The work of evangelical theologian Donald Bloesch stands as a lucid example. Drawing from a typical Barthian focus on revelation, Bloesch declares in no uncertain terms, "The Bible is not in and of itself the revelation of God but the divinely appointed means and channel of this revelation."[37] Consequently, Bloesch categorically denies that the Bible in itself is our authority:

> [T]he ultimate, final authority is not Scripture but the living God himself as we find him in Jesus Christ. Jesus Christ and the message about him constitute the material norm for our faith just as the Bible is the formal norm. The Bible is authoritative because it points beyond itself to the absolute authority, the living and transcendent Word of God.[38]

Echoing Barth, Bloesch then adds, "Revelation is God speaking and the human being responding through the power of God's Spirit. . . . Revelation is the

---

35. Northrop Frye, *The Great Code: The Bible and Literature* (New York: Harcourt Brace Jovanovich, 1982), 225.

36. Ibid., 220.

37. Donald G. Bloesch, *Holy Scripture: Revelation, Inspiration & Interpretation* (Downers Grove, Ill.: InterVarsity Press, 1994), 57.

38. Donald G. Bloesch, *Essentials of Evangelical Theology*, 2 vols. (San Francisco: HarperCollins, 1978), 1:62–63.

conjunction of divine revealing action and human response."[39] This perspective suggests that the presence of revelation is integrally tied to its human reception. As a consequence, Bloesch's view can easily be read (or misread) as involving a subjectivist understanding of the presence of the divine Word through the Bible.

A theology of Word and Spirit need not lapse into subjectivism, however. What leads to subjectivism is the articulation of such a theology in the context of a basically individualistic understanding of the event of revelation. In other words, the problem of subjectivism arises only when we mistakenly place the individual ahead of the community.

The declaration that our final authority is the Spirit speaking through scripture does not vitiate against acknowledging that the Bible remains scripture apart from our personal hearing of the Spirit's voice through it. On the contrary, the Bible's status as scripture is not dependent on whether or not we *individually* acknowledge the Spirit's voice speaking through scripture. Rather, the Bible remains objectively scripture because it is the book of the church. From its inception, the community of Christ—following the lead of the ancient Jewish community (e.g., Neh. 8:1–8)—has been a people who gather around the text to hear the Spirit's voice speaking through it. And throughout the ages this community has testified that the sovereign Spirit has spoken—and continues to speak—through the pages of the Bible.

We, in turn, acknowledge individually that the Bible is scripture because we participate in this listening and confessing people. And it is this corporate confession of the Bible as scripture that forms the context for our hearing the Spirit's voice in its pages as well. Our participation in the Spirit-illumined congregation facilitates our personal experience of the Spirit's illuminating work. The early twentieth-century Baptist theologian E. Y. Mullins got the epistemological order right when he declared,

> [S]alvation is not conditioned upon our belief in, or acceptance of a book. The knowledge of God of which we now speak is not derived from merely reading the pages of the Bible, or from the most rigidly scientific interpretation of its teachings. God's revelation of himself to us comes through his direct action upon our spirits. He comes to us in redeeming grace. There is a spiritual transaction within us. We are regenerated by his power, and lifted to a new moral and spiritual level. It is then that we acquire a new appreciation of the Bible.[40]

We would quickly add, however, that this divine regenerative work comes through the biblical *message.*

---

39. Ibid., 50.
40. Edgar Young Mullins, *The Christian Religion in Its Doctrinal Expression* (Philadelphia: Roger Williams Press, 1917), 41.

The Biblical Message

With the Westminster Confession, we acknowledge that the final authority in the church is the Spirit speaking through the scriptures. This confession directs us inevitably to ask about theology's "norming norm": In what sense is the Bible the forming source for our theological construction? The search for an answer to our question leads to the "biblical message" as the norming norm in theology. As we noted earlier, it is not the Bible as a book that is authoritative, but the Bible as the instrumentality of the Spirit; the biblical message spoken by the Spirit through the text is theology's norming norm. But what is the connection between this "message" and the text itself?

The Message behind the Text

Many modern theologians connect the biblical message, which is our ultimate theological norm, to a divine revelation they see as lying somehow "behind" the text. We noted earlier that liberal thinkers look for the "abiding experiences" whereas conservatives attempt to uncover the doctrinal teaching contained in the Bible. In this endeavor, they have been joined by proponents of the Word of God theologies, who view the Bible as the human witness to the transcendent Word.

The perspective that brings these seemingly diverse approaches together is the assumption that the Bible discloses an underlying divine revelation that constitutes the authoritative biblical message. Hence Anders Nygren asserts, "*Revelation* is the activity of God, his active and effective intervention in human life. It reaches its height in God's action in Christ. The *Bible* is the *message* about this action."[41] It is "a message about an action which God has effected for us."[42]

While some theologians view this revelation in personal-dynamic categories (i.e., through the Bible, God addresses the human individual), others see the locus of revelation, and hence the biblical message, in the sacred history to which the biblical documents point. In their estimation, history comprises the revelation standing behind the text. Bloesch, to cite one example, asserts, "From my perspective, the ultimate norm is the gospel of God based on the mighty acts of God." He then adds, "Revelation took place in a particular history in the past, the sacred history that constitutes the content of the Bible. It is this sacred history that can be described as the objective locus of revelation. . . . The Bible is the original witness to the mighty acts of God."[43] Bloesch's words echo the

---

41. Anders Nygren, *The Significance of the Bible for the Church*, trans. Carl C. Rasmussen (Philadelphia: Fortress Press, 1963), 7.

42. Ibid., 36.

43. Donald G. Bloesch, *A Theology of Word and Spirit* (Downers Grove, Ill.: InterVarsity Press, 1992), 187. For an example of an emphasis on the gospel as the reality standing behind the text, see Ted Peters, *God—the World's Future: Systematic Theology for a Postmodern Era* (Minneapolis: Fortress Press, 1992), 51–52, 57–59, 62–63. Even some conservatives speak of revelation as ultimately a saving encounter with God, of which the Bible is the medium. Hence, Francis I. Andersen, "We speak . . . in the words . . . which the Holy Ghost Teacheth," *Westminster Theological Journal* 22 (May 1960):118–19.

position of Canadian theologian Douglas John Hall, who speaks of "original revelation" as a sequence of foundational events.[44]

Other theologians offer a proposal that is not quite so specifically focused. Rather than looking solely to the specific history recounted in the texts, they bring into view the more general idea of the intention of the authors of the biblical writings. The authoritative revelation located behind the text is the message that the authors sought to communicate. Much of modern exegesis concentrates on the task of determining authorial intent as the vehicle that can connect us to the biblical message.

The genesis of the modern exegetical endeavor lies in the romanticism of Friedrich Schleiermacher.[45] Having observed that biblical texts are not systematic theological treatises but rather that each arose as a creative mind responded to particular circumstances, Schleiermacher argued that an interpreter must set a text in its context within the life of the author to get behind the printed words to the mind that wrote them. To this end, Schleiermacher differentiated between two aspects of interpretation:[46] the grammatical understanding, which looks for meaning in the words and phrases of the work itself, and the psychological understanding, which seeks to go behind the words to the mind of the author as expressed by the written text. Hence, Scheiermacher's method assumes (1) that to understand a work requires that we reconstruct it by retracing the process by which it came to be,[47] and (2) that the original creative process arose primarily from the author's personal outlook and life, which transpired within a wider social environment. What makes the exegetical project possible, in Schleiermacher's system, is the assumption that both author and interpreter are manifestations of universal life; as a result, not only can interpreters gain an understanding of the world of the author, but in a sense they can transform themselves into the author.[48]

These various attempts to engage the revelation behind the text provide a crucial reminder to us as we seek to understand how the biblical message is the norming norm of theology. Specifically, this approach stands as a warning against positing a simple, one-to-one correspondence between the revelation of

44. Douglas J. Hall, *Thinking the Faith: Christian Theology in a North American Context* (Minneapolis: Augsburg, 1989), 258.

45. See F. D. E. Schleiermacher, *Hermeneutics: The Handwritten Manuscripts*, ed. Heinz Kimmerle, trans. James Duke and Jack Forstman, American Academy of Religion Texts and Translation Series, no. 1 (Atlanta: Scholars Press, 1977).

46. Dilthey characterizes Schleiermacher's distinction in this manner: "Grammatical interpretation proceeds from link to link to the highest combinations in the whole of the work. The psychological interpretation starts with penetrating the inner creative process and proceeds to the outer and inner form of the work and from there to a further grasp of the unity of all his works in the mentality and development of their author." Wilhelm Dilthey, "Development of Hermeneutics," *Dilthey: Selected Writings*, ed. H. P. Rickman (Cambridge: Cambridge University Press, 1976), 259.

47. H. A. Hodges, *The Philosophy of Wilhelm Dilthey*, reprint ed. (1952; Westport, Conn.: Greenwood Press, 1974), 13.

48. For this characterization of Schleiermacher's position, see Hans-Georg Gadamer, *Truth and Method*, trans. Garrett Barden and John Cumming (New York: Crossroad, 1984), 166–67.

God and the Bible, that is, between the Word of God and the words of scripture.[49] Biblical scholars such as Paul Rainbow[50] and John Reumann[51] are in basic agreement that the New Testament writers rarely use the phrase "the word of God" to refer to the Hebrew scriptures but largely reserved the term for messages actually spoken by God to, or through, prophets.[52] Such messages center above all on the person and work of Jesus (e.g., Acts 6:7; 12:24; 19:20; 1 Pet. 1:23, 25). Elsewhere, this Word is viewed as an active agent before whom "no creature is hidden" (Heb. 4:12–13). We might conclude that ultimately "the word of God" is both Christologically and pneumatologically focused. In this sense, it is the Holy Spirit announcing the good news about Jesus Christ, which word the church speaks in the Spirit's power and by the Spirit's authority, and which is thereby connected to Christ himself.

At the same time, however, modern discourse about a biblical message that supposedly lies behind the texts brings us up short. Because no exegetical method can facilitate us in grasping the biblical message in its entirety, speaking of theology's norming norm as the "biblical message" is somewhat of a misnomer. As Colin Gunton observed, "*The* biblical message, in the sense of a finally adequate or even provisionally complete account of biblical teaching, is a chimera."[53] Equally unsatisfying, we quickly add, would be the more limited expression "*a* biblical message." This designation gives the impression that we simply choose from among the many messages we supposedly find disclosed through the various documents of the Bible. While no theological system can ever hope to encompass it in its entirety, the biblical message as a whole remains the norming norm that both provides the shaping influence for and stands in judgment over all our theological expressions.

Discourse about a biblical message lying behind the biblical documents involves an even more consequential difficulty, however. It too readily allows us to drive a wedge between the text and the message that supposedly stands behind it and to which the text gives us access. Of course, it is true that in an important sense the biblical message as the "word of God"—and hence revelation—precedes the Bible and can therefore be differentiated from the text. It is likewise the case that revelation carries logical priority, for the Bible presupposes

49. The tendency to make such an equation has been criticized by William J. Abraham, *The Divine Inspiration of Holy Scripture* (Oxford: Oxford University Press, 1981). For a historical precedence of this separation, see Donald G. Bloesch, *The Future of Evangelical Christianity: A Call for Unity Amid Diversity* (Garden City, N.Y.: Doubleday, 1983), 118.

50. Paul Rainbow, "On Hearing the Word of God," unpublished convocation address, North American Baptist Seminary, 1990.

51. John Reumann, "The New Testament Concept of the Word: Forms of the Word," *Consensus: A Canadian Lutheran Journal of Theology* 4/3 (July 1978):15–24; idem, "The New Testament Concept of the Word: Function of the Word," *Consensus: A Canadian Lutheran Journal of Theology* 5/1 (January 1979):15.

52. For a parallel perspective on the Old Testament use of the term to refer to prophetic utterance, see John Goldingay, *Models for Scripture* (Grand Rapids: Wm. B. Eerdmans Publishing Co., 1994), 204–8.

53. Colin Gunton, "Using and Being Used: Scripture and Systematic Theology," *Theology Today* 47/3 (October 1990): 254.

the reality of revelation.[54] Yet we ought not to posit too great a disjunction between the two.

Viewed historically, the relationship between revelation and text is actually somewhat fluid. Revelation arose not only prior to but also together with the process of canonical scripture. In part, God's revelatory work came in and through the formation of scripture, as under the guiding hand of the Spirit the community of faith sought to understand the ongoing work of God in the world in the light of God's earlier activity as described in the oral and written traditions of the community. The faith community sought as well to determine what God's covenant with their forebears meant for them as they sought to be God's covenant partners in the present. The canonical texts reflect this ongoing conversation within the ancient Hebrew community and the early church.

This, in turn, becomes the model of theologizing for us to follow. Treading the path blazed by the biblical communities of faith, we seek to discover and to understand the work of God in our day in the light of God's earlier working as set forth in the canonical texts. And in keeping with our forebears in the faith, we wrestle with what it means for us to be God's covenant partners on the basis of what covenant partnership meant to the biblical communities as indicated in the texts.

Yet one crucial difference separates their deliberations from ours. They engaged in the theological task with only certain texts (or oral traditions) in hand; we wrestle with these issues with the *complete* canonical text lying open before us. Since the end of the first century and especially since the Council of Carthage, the biblical text as a completed canon has taken center stage in the process of the community of Christ listening to the voice of the Spirit. Of course, this does not mean that our faith rests in the Bible itself. Biblical faith has always been centered in Jesus.[55] Nevertheless, as John Goldingay asserts, "Christian faith has to be biblical if it is to follow biblical faith in its centering on Jesus."[56] And as we will argue subsequently, we become "centered on Jesus" as we listen to the Spirit speaking through scripture.

The Biblical Message and the Scriptural Text

The biblical message is the norming norm for theology. In saying this we must be careful not to posit a nebulous, ethereal "something" standing behind the text to which we have at best only limited access. Rather, the biblical message is in some important sense bound to the canonical text itself. But how?

One significant recent proposal, "textual-sense interpretation," focuses on the "sense" of the text. Rather than looking for the meaning of the biblical text

---

54. James Barr, *The Scope and Authority of the Bible* (Philadelphia: Westminster Press, 1980),16; Dewey M. Beegle, *Scripture, Tradition and Infallibility* (Grand Rapids: Wm. B. Eerdmans Publishing Co., 1973), 307–308.

55. Barr is correct in noting, "In a certain sense the men of the Bible had no Bible." Nevertheless, once the canonical documents were collected and acknowledged, Christianity became a book-centered faith. See Barr, *Scope and Authority of the Bible*, 116.

56. Goldingay, *Models of Scripture*, 111.

as lying behind the text, textual-sense interpreters seek to discover the meaning of the biblical texts themselves. Hence, Hans Frei argues that the point of a biblical narrative does not lie in some event in ancient history that supposedly stands behind the text but in the meaning of the narrative itself.[57] In offering this insight, textual-sense interpretation marks an important antidote to modernist views of the Bible.

Yet if textual-sense interpreters assert that meaning is bound up entirely with intratextuality, their program provides neither a complete nor a completely satisfying answer to our quest for an understanding of the normativeness of the Bible as scripture. We affirm with the church throughout its history that God has acted and spoken; the biblical texts bear witness to God's acting and speaking to the communities of faith in the biblical era. But God acts and speaks today too, and the Bible is the Spirit's chosen vehicle for speaking authoritatively to us. Still the question remains: What does it mean to declare that the Spirit speaks through scripture? A final helpful suggestion emerges if we ask what it might mean to take the phrase literally. What would it mean to say that through the text the Spirit speaks—the Spirit actually addresses us?[58] This question leads us to contemporary speech-act theory as pioneered by J. L. Austin.[59]

Austin distinguished among three components in a total speech act: the locutionary act, the illocutionary act, and the perlocutionary act. These correspond roughly with how a sentence is enunciated (the locutionary act), what the speaker intended to do by this enunciation (the illocutionary act), and what the speaker achieved by the act of enunciating (the perlocutionary act).[60] For example, a person may ask another to open the door by simply enunciating the sentence, "Please open the door." The enunciation is the locutionary act through which the speaker performed the illocutionary act of requesting that the other person do the physical deed of opening the door.[61] Obviously, when we acknowledge that the Spirit speaks through the Bible, we are referring to an illocutionary, and not a locutionary, act.

How does the Spirit engage in the illocutionary act of addressing us through scripture? Nicholas Wolterstorff offers an intriguing explanation: The Bible constitutes "double agency discourse" or "double discourse."[62] That is, the Spirit speaks by way of the speaking of the biblical authors. Wolterstorff notes that the

---

57. Frei, *Eclipse of Biblical Narrative*, 280–81.

58. For an extended development of this idea, see Nicholas Wolterstorff, *Divine Discourse: Philosophical Reflections on the Claim that God Speaks* (Cambridge: Cambridge University Press, 1995).

59. See, especially, J. L. Austin, *How to Do Things with Words*, ed. J. O. Urmson and Marian Sbisa, 2nd ed. (Cambridge, Mass.: Harvard University Press, 1975).

60. For a helpful summary of speech act theory, see Kevin J. Vanhoozer, "The Semantics of Biblical Literature: Truth and Scripture's Diverse Literary Forms," in *Hermeneutics, Authority, and Canon*, ed. D. A. Carson and John D. Woodbridge (Grand Rapids: Zondervan, 1986), 85–92.

61. For this example, see Nicholas Wolterstorff, "The Importance of Hermeneutics for a Christian Worldview," in *Disciplining Hermeneutics: Interpretation in Christian Perspective*, ed. Roger Lundin (Grand Rapids: Wm. B. Eerdmans Publishing Co., 1997), 30.

62. Wolterstorff, *Divine Discourse*, 38–42, 52.

Spirit's speaking occurs in two basic ways.[63] Sometimes the Spirit speaks through deputized speech. Hence, the prophets often proclaimed the divinely given word as God enlisted them to bring a message to the community. In addition to containing such "deputized discourse," however, the Bible entails "appropriated discourse." The Spirit speaks by appropriating the discourse of the biblical author.

Although Wolterstorff is on the right track, at one crucial point his proposal comes up short. Perhaps against his own intentions, he also appears at times to fall prey to the modern tendency to elevate some other reality above the Bible as text. In calling for authorial-discourse interpretation, Wolterstorff appears to remain—at least at times—too closely focused on the author who produced the text, rather than on the text as itself being canon.

The Appropriated Text

If the final authority in the church is the Holy Spirit speaking through scripture, then theology's norming norm is the message the Spirit declares through the text. The Spirit does not address this message to us by means of a double discourse that centers on what the biblical author said (not merely *intended* to say) by authoring the text, as Wolterstorff suggests.[64] Rather—to push Wolterstorff's own terminology further—the Spirit speaks by "appropriating" the biblical text itself.

Because the Spirit speaks to us through scripture—through the text itself—the ongoing task of the community of Christ is to ask continually, What is the Spirit saying to the church? (Rev. 2:11, etc.). We inquire at every juncture, What illocutionary act is the Spirit performing in our midst on the basis of the reading of this scripture text? What is the Spirit saying to us in appropriating this text? In short, we inquire, What is the biblical message?

The Spirit's illocutionary act of appropriation does not come independently of what classical interpretation called "the original meaning of the text." Consequently, we must draw from careful exegesis to seek to understand this "original meaning," that is, to determine "what the author said" (to cite Wolterstorff's designation). At the same time, the Spirit's address is not bound up simply and totally with the text's supposed internal meaning. Indeed, as certain contemporary proponents of "textual intentionality" (e.g., Paul Ricoeur) remind us, although an author creates a literary text, once it has been written, it takes on a life of its own. The author's intention has been "distanced" from the meanings of the work, although the ways in which the text is structured shape the meanings the reader discerns in the text. In a sense, the text has its own intention, which has its genesis in the author's intention but is not exhausted by it.

Consequently, we must never conclude that exegesis alone can exhaust the Spirit's speaking to us through the text. Although the Spirit's illocutionary act

---

63. Ibid., 42–54, 186; Wolterstorff, "Importance of Hermeneutics," 45.
64. Wolterstorff, *Divine Discourse*, 188–89, 197–99.

is to appropriate the text in its internal meaning (i.e., to appropriate what the author said), the Spirit appropriates the text with the goal of communicating to us in *our* situation, which, while perhaps paralleling in certain respects that of the ancient community, is nevertheless unique.

Further, in appropriating the biblical text, the Spirit speaks, but the Spirit's speaking does not come through the text in isolation. Rather, we read the text cognizant that we are the contemporary embodiment of a centuries-long interpretive tradition within the Christian community (and hence we must take seriously the theological tradition of the church). And we read realizing that we are embedded in a specific historical-cultural context (and hence we must pay attention to our culture). In this process of listening to the Spirit speaking through the appropriated text, theology assists the community of faith both in discerning what the Spirit is saying and in fostering an appropriate obedient response to the Spirit's voice.

Biblical Creativity: Scripture as the Instrumentality of "World" Formation

The Spirit speaks to us today through the appropriated biblical text. Through scripture the Spirit acts. But what does the Spirit do? Of course, the basic answer is that the Spirit addresses us. This address can take several forms, in keeping with the manifold diversity of writings that constitute the Bible.[65] The Pauline statement to Timothy suggests that through scripture, the Spirit teaches, reproves, corrects, and instructs (2 Tim. 3:16). Also, through the text the Spirit offers divine promises and calls us to respond to the grace available through Christ. The Spirit even informs us as to how we might voice our thoughts, feelings, and emotions to God, as for example in certain of the Psalms.

In these and other ways, the Spirit speaks through the text; that is, the Spirit appropriates the text and thereby performs the illocutionary act of addressing us in these various ways. We must, however, probe deeper. The affirmation that the Spirit appropriates the text leads us to inquire about the *goal* of the Spirit's speaking. That is, what *perlocutionary* act does the Spirit seek to accomplish thereby? In response, we declare that *the Spirit creates "world."*

World and Word

Sociologist Peter Berger has pointed out that the world we inhabit as humans is not simply given, not merely prefabricated for us. Rather, we are world-builders. We live in a world of our own creation, a social-cultural world. This constructed world attains for us the character of objectivity, in the sense both

---

65. For a helpful delineation of the Bible as comprising four basic types of materials, see Goldingay, *Models for Scripture.*

of seeming to be external to our personal consciousness and of being experienced with others.[66] According to Berger, world construction entails above all the imposition of a meaningful order (a "nomos") on our variegated experiences. The ordering of experience involves language and "knowledge," the latter of which Berger understands not as objective statements about the universe as it actually is, but the "common order of interpretation" that a society imposes on experience.[67] The "universe" we inhabit, then, "is a socially constituted reality, which an individual member of society learns to take for granted as 'objective' knowledge about the world."[68]

Berger's main point, however, moves from society to religion. He notes that "[t]hroughout human history religion has played a decisive part in the construction and maintenance of universes."[69] More specifically, Berger defines religion sociologically as "the human enterprise by which a sacred cosmos is established."[70] According to Berger, the chief role of religion is that of legitimating the socially constructed world that participants in any society inhabit. Religion does this by locating a society and its institutions within a sacred and cosmic frame of reference, by bestowing on participants in a society a sense of being connected to ultimate reality, and by giving cosmic status to the nomoi (or common orders of interpretation) of that society.[71]

Sociologists like Berger point out that religion fulfills its role in part by devising a set of beliefs that together constitute the specifically religious *Weltanshauung*. Wesley Kort elaborates that certain specific types of beliefs are essential for "an adequate, workable world to appear," namely, beliefs about temporality, other people, borders, and finally norms and values. These types of beliefs, he asserts, are closely connected to languages and texts. In fact, in his estimation, they "can be textually identified because they and their relations to one another are borne by language." And this leads to the importance of "scriptures." Such texts, Kort adds, function by articulating "the beliefs that go into the construction of a world."[72] For this reason, as Paul Ricoeur noted, the meaning of a text always points beyond itself—it is "not behind the text, but in front of it"—for it projects a way of being in the world, a mode of existence, a pattern of life, and it "points towards a possible world."[73]

66. Peter L. Berger, *The Sacred Canopy: Elements of a Sociological Theory of Religion* (Garden City, N.Y.: Doubleday, 1969), 3–13.
67. Berger, *Sacred Canopy*, 20.
68. Peter L. Berger and Thomas Luckmann, "Sociology of Religion and Sociology of Knowledge," *Sociology and Social Research* 47 (1963): 421.
69. Ibid., 422
70. Berger, *Sacred Canopy*, 25.
71. Ibid., 32–36.
72. Kort, *Take, Read*, 10–14.
73. Paul Ricoeur, *Interpretation Theory: Discourse and the Surplus of Meaning* (Fort Worth, Tex.: Texas Christian University Press, 1976), 87; See also *Hermeneutics and the Human Sciences: Essays on Language, Action, and Interpretation*, ed. and trans. John B. Thompson (Cambridge: Cambridge University Press, 1981), 176–81.

As we noted at the beginning of this chapter, Christians are a "people of the book." The Bible stands at the center of our faith in that we read the biblical texts as scripture. Stated in another manner, we look to the Bible for the focus of the construction of our world. As John Goldingay declares, quoting Walter Brueggeman, "The biblical text 'has generative power to summon and evoke new life' . . . it 'anticipates and summons realities that live beyond the conventions of our day-to-day, take-for-granted world.' It calls a new world into being." Hence, there is in the text a "depth dimension," a capacity to speak beyond the context in which it was originally composed.[74]

The point we have continually made in this chapter, however, is that this world construction does not lie in the text itself, even though it is closely bound to the text. Rather, it is ultimately the Spirit's work. The Spirit speaks through the Bible. In so doing—in appropriating these texts as the instrumentality of this speaking—the Spirit performs the perlocutionary act of creating *world*. And the world the Spirit creates is not simply the world surrounding the ancient text itself. It is the eschatological world God intends for creation as disclosed in the text.

The Spirit's world-creating act does not arise out of nowhere, however. Rather, it emerges directly out of the Spirit's own particular role within God's creative activity.

Foundational to what became the pneumatology of the biblical faith communities is the linguistic—and consequently theological—connection between "spirit" and "breath," which the ancients, in turn, observed was linked phenomenologically to "life." The biblical peoples came to see "Spirit" as the divine power creating (Gen. 1:2; 2:7) and sustaining life (Ps. 104:29–30; Isa. 32:15; cf. Job 27:3; 34:14–15), so that wherever the Spirit is present life flourishes, whereas wherever the Spirit is absent life ceases. More significantly, the biblical writings link the Spirit with eschatological, new life. As the one who raised Jesus from the dead, the Spirit will give life to our mortal bodies (Rom. 8:11). In the meantime, the Spirit is already at work effecting our transformation (Rom. 8:10; 2 Cor. 3:18). As the author of life, the Spirit is the Creator Spirit, the divine power at work fashioning the universe, and in this sense, the Spirit is the author of the world.

The Spirit's world-creating work occurs through the Word and in accordance with the Word. As the Spirit speaks to us through scripture, the Spirit forms our world. What the Spirit thereby fashions is a "centered" world—a world that finds its cohesion in the Word. This leads us to Christology—more specifically to the role of the Word in the divine creative activity. The Genesis creation narratives depict God's act of creating "in the beginning" as occurring by means of speaking: God speaks and it is so (e.g., Gen. 1:3, 6, 9, 14, 20, 24, 26). The New Testament writers are more explicit. John and Paul, for example, declare that God created through the Word, whom they identify as the incarnate Jesus Christ (John 1:3, 10; Col. 1:16).

74. Goldingay, *Models of Scripture*, 256.

Just as God created the world "in the beginning" through the act of speaking the Word, so also God creates a world in the present by the Spirit speaking through scripture. And what the Spirit now constructs is a world centered in Jesus, who is the one through whom all things find their connectedness (Col. 1:17). Through appropriating the Word written—that is, by means of the biblical text—the Spirit creates a world centered on Jesus Christ, who is the Word disclosed.[75] But how does the Spirit perform this act? And what kind of world does the Spirit create?

The World the Spirit Forms

The Spirit performs the perlocutionary act of creating a world through the illocutionary act of speaking, that is, of appropriating the biblical text as the instrumentality of the divine speaking. This dynamic is closely connected to the literary nature of the Bible. As Edgar McKnight explains,

> A major role of literature in general is to enable readers (and readership) to create a world or worlds for themselves, cognitively, affectively, behaviorally—in all the ways that individuals and groups are related to their world. At implicit and explicit levels, readers create their own worlds in the process of reading. World and self do not exist in isolation, however, and the reader is transformed in the process. Biblical texts share in this role in a particular way; they provide resources for the creation of a comprehensive universe, which has space for the human and for the divine and which sees the human in the light of the divine and the divine in the light of the human.[76]

As Christians, we quickly add that we are not the primary agents in the creation of the world God intends. Rather, the constructing of a world through the biblical text is ultimately the act of the Spirit. The world that the Spirit creates is nothing less than a new creation centered in Jesus Christ (2 Cor. 5:17). And this world consists of a new community comprised of renewed persons.

The Spirit-formed Community of Persons

Above all, the world the Spirit creates through scripture is a communal world, that is, a community of the Word. Although the gospel comes to us personally, God's purposes for creation find their fulfillment not in the formation of an

---

75. This marks a reformulation of Barth's christologically informed bibliology. See Karl Barth, *Church Dogmatics*, 2nd ed., trans. G. W. Bromiley (Edinburgh: T. & T. Clark, 1975), I/1:88–124. See also G. C. Berkouwer, *Holy Scripture* (Grand Rapids: Wm. B. Eerdmans Publishing Co., 1975), 166.

76. Edgar V. McKnight, *Postmodern Use of the Bible: The Emergence of Reader-Oriented Criticism* (Nashville: Abingdon Press, 1988), 261–62.

aggregate of "saved" individuals but in a community of reconciled people. Consequently, the Spirit's task is to bring into being a new community—a fellowship of persons who gather around the name of Jesus the Christ, who is the Word. In this task, the Bible plays a crucial role, for the Spirit creates this new community by speaking through scripture, that is, by appropriating the biblical text.

The Roman Catholic theologian Francis Fiorenza characterizes the crucial place of scripture in the formation of the Christian community by what he calls the Bible's "constitutional" role. Fiorenza argues that as the product of the foundational stage in the history of the faith community—first in Israel and then in the church—the biblical writings set forth what constituted its communal identity at the beginning. Because they embody this foundational identity, these texts hold primary status at all stages in the life of the church. They function as "the constitution of an ongoing community,"[77] in that these texts provide the foundation (or what John Howard Yoder calls "the ground floor"[78]) for Christian communal identity throughout history.

Fiorenza's description provides a helpful image of the role of the Bible in the church and suggests why Christians acknowledge the Bible as authoritative scripture. Yet the question remains: Exactly how does scripture fulfill its role in the Spirit's work of creating a new communal world? How does the text carry out an ongoing, communal, identity-forming function? The search for an answer leads us to the concept of "paradigmatic events,"[79] together with the parallel idea of "interpretive framework."

A paradigmatic event may be defined as a historical occurrence that captures the imagination of a community in such a manner as to shape or form the community's way of conceiving the totality of reality and its understanding of its ongoing experience of reality. Because of the event's wide-ranging influence, the community preserves its memory, while both reinterpreting the event in the light of the subsequent situations in which the community finds itself and discovering in it the source of a renewed hope for the future. Hence, paradigmatic events connect the community and its participants with the past and the future. Through their appropriation of these events, succeeding generations understand themselves in relationship to the experiences of the past history of the community and in anticipation of a future that will bring about the actualization of the community's ideals.

By functioning in this manner, paradigmatic events are not merely occurrences in history. Rather than time-bound happenings, they have the potential to create a meaningful present. What sociologist Thomas F. O'Dea says about myths indicates the creative power of paradigmatic narratives:

77. Francis Schüssler Fiorenza, "The Crisis of Scriptural Authority: Interpretation and Reception," *Interpretation* 44 (October 1990): 363.

78. John Howard Yoder, "The Use of the Bible in Theology," in *The Use of the Bible in Theology/Evangelical Options*, ed. Robert K. Johnston (Atlanta: John Knox Press, 1985), 103.

79. See, for example, Richard J. Coleman, *Issues of Theological Conflict* (Grand Rapids: Wm. B. Eerdmans Publishing Co., 1980), 109–10.

> Mythic time is always present, and myth re-creates and re-presents what it portrays; it actualizes what it tells. Standing outside of time, making present what it presents, myth tells the event itself, not a mere description of it. It makes past and future immediately present.[80]

A paradigmatic narrative, therefore, goes beyond being a simple recounting of events in a dimly remembered past or expectations for a faintly anticipated future. Rather, such a narrative fuses past and future with the present in a manner that calls forth a new world in the here and now. The community that inhabits this world takes its identity from, and becomes the contemporary embodiment of, the paradigmatic narrative itself.

The Bible narrates the primary paradigmatic events that shape the identity of the Christian community, for as a people of the book, Christians comprise a fellowship of persons who gather around the story of Jesus Christ. As such, the Bible is the instrumentality of the Spirit. By orienting our communal and personal present on the basis of the past and in accordance with the vision of the future disclosed in the texts, the Spirit appropriates the biblical narrative to create in and among us a new world. And as we inhabit that world, we become the contemporary embodiment of the paradigmatic biblical narrative.

A central aspect of the Spirit's appropriating the biblical narrative is to connect us with the past. Read as our community scripture, the Bible narrates the primal events that originally constituted the biblical community. Perhaps no salvation-historical event was as important to the ancient Hebrew community as the exodus, which carries paradigmatic importance in both the Old and the New Testaments. The early church, however, was convinced that this event prefigured an even greater "exodus," namely, the divine salvation that came through Christ. Hence, for Christians, the life, passion, and resurrection of Jesus, together with the subsequent sending of the Holy Spirit—read in the context of the Old Testament story—comprise the central paradigmatic narrative of scripture. The Spirit appropriates this narrative in creating a new community in the present—the fellowship of disciples who take their identity from the narrative of Jesus. By looking to the biblical story as constituting our own identity, we become the contemporary embodiment of Jesus' narrative, and hence we are indeed "the body of Christ."

This goal of the Spirit in appropriating the text is not reached with the mere recounting of the biblical story. Instead, as the narrative is retold (or reread), the Spirit transports the contemporary hearers (or readers) into the text. Or, stated in the opposite manner, the Spirit recreates the past as narrated by the text within the present life of the community, both individually and corporately. As Goldingay rightly notes, "The telling of the biblical story is not a mere recounting of events from the past but a reenacting of a drama that involves people in the present."[81]

---

80. Thomas F. O'Dea, *The Sociology of Religion* (Englewood Cliffs, N.J.: Prentice-Hall, 1966), 43.
81. Goldingay, *Models of Scripture*, 256.

The Bible not only recounts paradigmatic stories of "long ago" but also declares God's intention for the world. In scripture we find a vision of a future, new creation in which humans live in harmony with each other, with God, and with all creation (e.g., Rev. 21:1–22:5). In addition to connecting us with our narrative past, therefore, the Spirit constructs our communal identity by linking us to this glorious future. The Spirit speaks to us through the text—appropriates the biblical vision of the divinely intended new creation—so that we might view our situation in the light of God's future and as a result open ourselves and our present to the power of that future, which in fact is already at work in us and among us (e.g., Rom, 8:9–30).

By narrating our foundational past and disclosing our glorious future, the Bible provides a paradigm of life as the believing community and as participants in that fellowship. That is, scripture mediates a specifically Christian "interpretative framework." A person's interpretive framework is that set of categories, beliefs, and values—whether consciously formulated or merely unconsciously presumed—which forms one's perception of reality and life. Hence, our interpretive framework facilitates our experiences and forms the outlook by means of which we make sense out of life.

Through the appropriated biblical text, the Spirit forms in us a communal interpretive framework that creates a new world. The Spirit leads us to view ourselves and all reality in light of an unabashedly Christian and specifically biblical interpretive framework so that we might thereby understand and respond to the challenges of life in the present as the contemporary embodiment of a faith community that spans the ages.[82] At times, this occurs as we simply read our situation through the lenses of the paradigmatic narratives of Scripture. At other times, we look to the more general beliefs, concepts, and values we find disclosed through the texts. In either case, by leading us to view life in the present through the lenses of a biblically based interpretive framework, the Spirit creates in the present a foretaste of the future, eschatological world and constitutes us as the eschatological people who serve as a sign pointing to the eschatological community.[83]

Theology assists the people of God in this process. The paradigmatic narratives of the Bible are meant to be read in the light of the whole of scripture, and our understanding of the biblical interpretative framework is to arise out of a reading of the whole. Theology seeks to enhance our ability as a community to read the Bible so as to understand its overarching narrative and to bring to the fore the interpretive framework by means of which the Spirit creates our communal world.

The Spirit-formed Self-in-Community

David Kelsey notes that through the text, the Spirit seeks "to nurture and reform the self-identity both of the community and of the individual persons

---

82. For a somewhat similar idea, see Barr, *Scope and Authority of the Bible*, 126–27.
83. Kelsey, *Uses of Scripture*, 89.

who comprise it."[84] As Kelsey's statement indicates, the world the Spirit creates is simultaneously communal and personal. That is, the Spirit creates a new community composed of persons who enjoy a new identity.

We noted in chapter 2 that certain contemporary thinkers have rejected the individualist epistemologies that predominated in the modern era in favor of a more communal understanding. They argue that the knowing process is connected to a cognitive framework—a web of belief—mediated to the individual by one's community of reference.[85] More significant for our discussion here, however, is the attendant awareness of the crucial role of community in personal identity formation.

We do not create our own identities; rather, our sense of self is socially produced.[86] Identity develops through the telling of a personal narrative in connection with which one's life makes sense,[87] a narrative that is always embedded in a transcendent story, that is, in the stories of the communities in which we participate.[88] This narrative forms the foundation for the interpretative framework, including the beliefs, concepts, and values, one's acceptance of which constitutes participation in the community and, in turn, a sense of personal identity as a member of the social group.

In this process of identity formation, religion plays a crucial role. Hence, Thomas O'Dea declares,

> Individuals, by their acceptance of the values involved in religion and the beliefs about human nature and destiny associated with them, develop important aspects of their own self-understanding and self-definition. Also, by their participation in religious ritual and worship, they act out significant elements of their own identity. In these ways, religion affects individuals' understanding of *who they are* and *what they are.*[89]

As Kingsley Davis noted in 1948, a religious community facilitates identity formation by connecting the individual with something transcendent: "[R]eligion gives the individual a sense of identity with the distant past and the limitless future. It expands his ego by making his spirit significant for the universe and the universe significant for him."[90]

---

84. Ibid., 214.

85. This opinion was recently articulated by George A. Lindbeck, "Confession and Community: How My Mind Has Changed," *Christian Century* 107/16 (May 9, 1990): 495.

86. See, for example, George Herbert Mead, *Mind, Self and Society: From the Standpoint of a Social Behaviorist*, ed. Charles W. Morris (1934; Chicago: University of Chicago Press, 1963), 144–64.

87. Robert N. Bellah et al., *Habits of the Heart: Individualism and Commitment in American Life* (Berkeley, Calif.: University of California Press, 1985), 81.

88. See, for example, Alasdair MacIntyre, *After Virtue*, 2nd ed. (Notre Dame, Ind.: University of Notre Dame Press, 1984), 221.

89. O'Dea, *Sociology of Religion*, 15.

90. Kingsley Davis, *Human Society* (New York: Macmillan Co., 1948), 531, 533.

Christians acknowledge the central place of the Spirit in this identity-creating process. The Spirit is the one who authors a new identity in us. And this work occurs through the Spirit's appropriation of the biblical text with its narrative of the past and its vision of the future. The biblical story of God at work in the world that begins at creation, continues through the ages, and climaxes in the future is the Spirit's instrumentality in bringing people to reinterpret their own life narratives in accordance with the paradigmatic narrative and the interpretive framework disclosed in the text. Hence, the Spirit appropriates the "old, old story of Jesus and his love" as the divinely chosen instrumentality in calling people into the family of God and in leading them to view all of life from the perspective of that story. As this occurs, they gain a new identity, an identity they receive as the Spirit's gift. Theology seeks to assist the Christian community in understanding the paradigmatic narrative and the Christian interpretive framework by means of which the Spirit creates in us a new identity through the appropriated text.

Biblical Literacy: The Bible as Theological Text

Our acknowledgment of the Bible as the final authority in the church and hence as the norming norm in theology has led to the conclusion that the Spirit performs the perlocutionary act of fashioning "world" through the illocutionary act of speaking through scripture, that is, through appropriating the biblical text. This world-constructing act occurs as the Spirit creates a community of persons who live out in the present the paradigmatic narrative of the Bible, that is, who view all of life through the interpretive framework the text discloses.

We must now take this discussion a step further. The Bible's pneumatical world-creative dimension implies that in the faith community the Bible functions as "theological text"—as "the Christian classic," to cite David Tracy's descriptor,[91] that is to be read theologically. Our task in this final section is to offer a summary exploration of the Bible as theological text and thereby bring into closer focus the reciprocal relationship between scripture and the theological enterprise. Before doing so, however, we must remind ourselves of one crucial presupposition: The reading of the biblical text must always take precedence over our theological constructions.

The Primacy of Text over Construction

In chapter 1 we set forth the premise that theological reflection is second-order discourse. In the present chapter, theology's second-order character came into view in our observation that theology serves the world-formative act the Spirit accomplishes through the appropriated text. This principle has far-reaching

91. David Tracy, *The Analogical Imagination* (New York: Crossroad, 1981), 249.

implications for our understanding of the connection between the biblical text and our theological constructions. Above all, it implies that, contrary to what some theologians might lead us to believe, the central purpose of the Bible is not to provide raw materials for erecting a systematic theological edifice. Rather, we engage in the theological enterprise conscious that we are servants of the Spirit and ministers within the community of those who seek to discern the Spirit's voice through the appropriated text. Although we believe his sights are too narrowly focused on the narrative dimension of scripture, Stanley Hauerwas is surely correct in reminding us that "[d]octrines . . . are not the upshot of the stories; they are not the meaning or heart of the stories. Rather they are tools . . . meant to help us tell the story better."[92] Theology, in other words, is not the attempt to codify the "meaning of the text" in a series of systematically arranged assertions, so that once this mission is accomplished we can then disregard, or even discard, the text. Rather, our theological construction ought always to lead us back to the Bible. Its goal is to place us in a position to be even more receptive to hear the voice of the Spirit, who appropriates the biblical text to refashion our world after the eschatological purposes of God.

To this end, the principle that the text takes primacy over construction provides the basic parameter for understanding the interface between exegesis and theological reflection. If our working presupposition is that theology serves the reading of the text (rather than that the text exists primarily for the sake of theology), then we can no longer follow slavishly what some take to be the traditional outlook, namely, that the logical flow of Christian thought consistently and necessarily moves *from* biblical studies *to* systematic theology. According to this view, biblical scholars deliver to theologians the authentic biblical teachings in their unsystematic multiplicity, and theologians, in turn, bring together these raw materials into a systematic statement of what purports to be *the* doctrinal system of the Bible.

This approach is helpful insofar as it provides a needed reminder of the importance of solid biblical scholarship in the theological enterprise. Indeed, theological construction ought never to proceed apart from a genuine wrestling with and a sound exegesis of the biblical texts. Exegesis, in other words, is a nonnegotiable participant in the theological enterprise. In an important way, theology *lives* from solid exegesis.

At the same time, however, the unidirectional pattern that moves from biblical studies to theology suffers from several debilitating difficulties. Not the least of these is its naivete about the purported objectivity of exegesis, a naivete that is indicative of the Enlightenment or modernist hermeneutical assumptions from which it operates. But as biblical scholar Robert Fowler notes, the presupposition of exegetical objectivity has come under severe attack. There is today, he reports,

---

92. Stanley Hauerwas, *The Peaceable Kingdom: A Primer in Christian Ethics* (Notre Dame, Ind.: University of Notre Dame Press, 1983), 26.

an increasing recognition that reading and interpretation is always interested, never disinterested; always significantly subjective, never completely objective; always committed and therefore always political, never uncommitted and apolitical; always historically-bound, never ahistorical. The modernist dream of disinterested, objective, distance, abstract truth is fading rapidly.[93]

George Aichele states this even more forcefully, perhaps to the point of overstatement:

Biblical scholars have been slow to awaken from the dream in which positivist science occupies a space apart from interests and values, to awaken to the realization that our representations of and discourse about what the text meant and how it means are inseparable from what we *want* it to mean, from how we *will* it to mean.[94]

Rather than following a strict unidirectional model, a truly helpful theological engagement involves a dialogue between the text and theological construction. As the comments of Fowler and Aichele indicate, this dialogical approach is necessitated by the nonobjectivity of all biblical exegesis. We simply cannot bracket our commitments, values, and worldviews in an attempt to approach the text as uninvolved, neutral observers.

Even more importantly, however, a dialogical engagement arises out of the purpose of Bible reading itself. We read knowing that the Spirit speaks through scripture, appropriating the text so as to create our communal world through it. While the world the Spirit fashions is specific to our situation and hence is not merely a transplanting of the world of the text into the present, the Spirit-constructed world we are to inhabit is nevertheless shaped by the world disclosed in the text. Our world is to be the contemporary embodiment of the paradigmatic narrative of scripture constructed through the interpretive framework that emerges from the Bible as a whole. For this reason, our goal must always be to read scripture theologically, and hence holistically, so that the world with which we are confronted through our reading is the eschatological world that arises from the vision of the whole of scripture.

The philosophical basis for dialogical engagement was articulated in the nineteenth century by the German thinker Wilhelm Dilthey. Dilthey argued that the goal of the hermeneutical enterprise is to understand the social and cultural meaning systems that underlie those past expressions of human experience that remain available for study in the present, especially as disclosed through writings.[95] Dilthey noted, however, that this task is complicated at its inception

93. Robert M. Fowler, "Post-modern Biblical Criticism," *Eastern Great Lakes & Midwest Bible Society Proceedings* 8 (September, 1989): 22.

94. George Aichele, et al., *The Postmodern Bible* (New Haven, Conn.: Yale University Press, 1995), 14.

95. Wilhelm Dilthey, "Construction of the Historical World," *Dilthey: Selected Writings*, 228.

by what he called the "hermeneutical circle": We can comprehend a complex whole only by appeal to its parts, but the parts acquire their meaning only within the whole.[96] Dilthey admitted that the circle is theoretically unresolvable. Nevertheless, he believed that, in practice, we could disentangle complex situations through an inductive, to-and-fro movement by means of which we make, and then revise, provisional conclusions. From the parts we obtain a preliminary idea of the sense of the whole. We then use this sense of the whole to determine more precisely the significance of the parts, which in turn serves to test and correct our idea of the whole.

Theological construction serves, in part, the task of bringing the community to hear the Spirit's voice through the text in that it facilitates our reading biblical texts with a view toward understanding the meaning system that characterized the early faith communities. This goal involves the kind of dialogical to-and-fro process Dilthey envisioned. The only way we can come to understand the faith of the biblical community is through the reading of individual texts. Hence, an exegesis of texts forms the basis of our theological construction.

Yet the bringing together of what we surmise to be the Christian worldview or interpretive framework on the basis of our exegesis of the various texts does not bring the theological enterprise to its culmination. Rather, the purpose of our theological constructions is to return us to the texts, acknowledging that the final authority in the church is not our theologizing about the texts but the Spirit speaking through them. Thus, we read the texts aware that our constructions are always partial, incomplete, and subject to revision. At the same time, however, we read convinced that the Spirit who speaks through scripture speaks with one voice and hence that through the Spirit's agency the multilingual texts become the one voice of the Spirit. Theological construction serves the Spirit's work as it assists us in discerning this pneumatic singularity in the midst of the diversity of the texts.

Theology, therefore, participates in the process of discerning the Spirit's voice through the texts by contributing to the hermeneutical process of reading scripture. A central aspect of theology's contribution is connected to the exegesis of the text on the basis of a hermeneutical key. Francis Watson suggests that theology supplies this key, insofar as theological themes "guide and shape the form and content of exegesis . . . while themselves being clarified and corrected by the progress of exegesis in accordance with the inescapable working of the hermeneutical circle."[97] However, if the goal of reading is to hear the Spirit speak, then the hermeneutical center to scripture does not lie so much in theology in general as in the biblical message as a whole, that is, in the overarch-

---

96. Idem, "The Development of Hermeneutics," in *Dilthey: Selected Writings*, 259. See also Robert C. Solomon, *Continental Philosophy since 1750: The Rise and Fall of the Self* (Oxford: Oxford University Press, 1988), 106–7.

97. Francis Watson, *Text, Church and World: Biblical Interpretation in Theological Perspective* (Edinburgh: T. & T. Clark, 1994), 241.

ing goal and purposes of God to create an eschatological world as indicated by scripture in its entirety. Theology provides a provisional guide in our attempt to hear this pneumatic singularity in scripture. It does so insofar as our theological construction seeks to provide a composite reading of the texts offered by the attempt to take a "global" view of the Bible from this side of the canonization process.

In the following two chapters, we will set forth two additional dimensions of this process. We will note that theology serves the discernment process in that theological construction also takes seriously the interpretive tradition of the church throughout the ages, together with the historical-cultural context in which the contemporary church listens to the Spirit speaking through scripture.

Theological Hermeneutics: Reading the Texts Theologically

Through the act of appropriating the biblical text, the Spirit creates the community that seeks to live the paradigmatic narrative of the Bible, which focuses on the story of Jesus. To this end, we read the various texts in the light of the whole of the biblical message, listening for the Spirit's voice guiding us as we seek to be the Spirit-constructed community of faith in the contemporary context. Theology serves this hermeneutical process in that it assists us in seeing the texts as the theological documents they are, that is, in reading them as scripture. But what does it mean to read the Bible theologically? We respond to this question by making explicit certain themes that have been implicit throughout the chapter.

Reading for the Spirit

What we have said thus far leads immediately to the conclusion that reading the texts theologically means reading with the intent of hearing the Spirit's voice. The beginning point for the theological reading is the presupposition that the Bible is the vehicle through which the Spirit speaks to us.

While claiming a theological tradition that dates to the early church, this understanding has been the central focus of the pietist movement connected historically with thinkers such as Philipp Jakob Spener (1635–1705) and August Hermann Francke (1663–1727). As the pietists asserted, through scripture the Spirit lays hold of the life of the reader and calls that life into divine service.[98] Hence, one crucial goal of Bible reading is spiritual formation. To this end, the pietists—following the patristic theologians—sought to bring to the reading of scripture both diligence in hermeneutical engagement with the text and patience in listening for God's voice speaking through it.[99] Donald Bloesch

---

98. John Weborg, "Pietism: Theology in Service of Living Toward God," in *The Variety of American Evangelicalism*, ed. Donald W. Dayton and Robert K. Johnston (Downers Grove, Ill.: InterVarsity Press, 1991), 176.

99. Michael Hardin, "The Authority of Scripture: A Pietist Perspective," *Covenant Quarterly* 49/1 (February 1991): 9.

reflects the pietist tradition when he declares that the reader must come to the text with "an open heart and a searching mind," because the spiritual meaning is only accessible to those who "are in experiential contact with the realities to which the text witnesses."[100]

As the pietist emphasis suggests, approaching the text with the desire to hear the Spirit's voice requires that we differentiate between exegesis and hermeneutics (or what Bloesch calls the "historical" and the "pneumatic" meanings of the text[101]), and that we acknowledge that exegesis is incomplete until it culminates in hermeneutics. Carl Braaten asserts that the goal of theological hermeneutics is to insure that "every new and serious interpretation is a creative synthesis of the results of historical research and the life situation of the present interpreter."[102] Another way of putting it is to declare that reading theologically entails listening to what the Spirit is saying through the text (exegesis) to us in our context (hermeneutics).

Consequently, the theological reading of the text always moves from, and returns to, the contemporary situation in which the faith community is living, even though this "hermeneutical circle" involves the use of exegetical methods. We read the text so that the Spirit might nurture us in the ongoing process of living as the contemporary embodiment of the paradigmatic narrative of scripture. Reading scripture theologically, then, entails reading the Bible as a whole, confident that the Spirit appropriates the text to create the eschatological world according to God's intentions as indicated in the Bible. Theology serves this hermeneutic purpose.

Reading As "Other"

Reading the text so as to hear the voice of the Spirit leads to a second dimension of what it means to read theologically. We approach the text conscious that we come to it as "other" to "other."

Fernando Segovia summarizes what it means to view both the text and the reader as "other": "Rather than positing any type of direct or immediate entrance into the text, the hermeneutic of otherness and engagement argues for the distantiation from the text as a working desideratum, emphasizing thereby the historical and cultural remoteness of the text." In the same way, Segovia adds, this approach views the reader as a socially and culturally conditioned "other" both to the text itself and to other readers. Consequently, a strict objectivity arising from the presumption of universality must give way to "a self-conscious exposition and analysis of the reader's strategy for reading, the theoretical foundations behind this strategy, and the social location underlying such a strategy."[103]

---

100. Bloesch, *Holy Scripture*, 190.
101. Ibid.
102. Carl E. Braaten, "Prolegomena to Christian Dogmatics," in *Christian Dogmatics*, ed. Carl E. Braaten and Robert W. Jenson, 2 vols. (Philadelphia: Fortress Press, 1984), 22.
103. Fernando F. Segovia, "The Text as Other: Towards a Hispanic American Hermeneutic," in *Text and Experience: Towards a Cultural Exegesis of the Bible*, ed. Daniel Smith-Christopher (Sheffield: Sheffield Academic Press, 1995), 294, 295.

As Segovia's explanation indicates, the theological reading requires that we acknowledge the integrity of the text within its own world, even though that world might appear strange to us. It means as well that we acknowledge the distance that stands between our world and the world of the text. Acknowledging this twofold distance leads to the realization that the goal of our theological reading is not to alter the text to fit our world. Indeed, attempting to do so merely undermines the integrity of the text. Neither should our intent be to alter ourselves to fit into the world of the text. Of course, the world of the text carries a certain primacy over our world. Thus, there is a sense in which the text "absorbs" the world of the reader, as George Lindbeck and others have suggested.[104] Yet this "absorption" does not transform the world of the reader—viewed as a pre-given, existing reality—into an earlier historical reality—the world the "biblical people" inhabited, to which we now have access through the text. Nor ought we to assume that our reading is intended to lead to the emergence of a third world, one that differs from both the world of the text and the reader's world but is the fusion of the two into a *tertium quid*.

Reading the text as "other" to "other" entails maintaining the integrity of the text while acknowledging that it is embedded in what to the contemporary reader is a strange and in some sense foreign world. At the same time, the contemporary reader expects that through this reading the Spirit will fashion a new world in the reader's present. And this new world that the Spirit calls the reader to inhabit is none other than the eschatological world of God's design. In short, to read the text theologically—as "other" to "other"—is to invite the Spirit to engage in the divine work in the lives of the readers through the text, which is the Spirit's instrumentality.

Reading the Patterns

We have noted earlier that we approach the Bible through a hermeneutical circle that reads the individual texts in light of the whole of scripture, while understanding that our perspective about the whole is informed by our reading of the individual texts. This suggests that we read the Bible theologically as we read with the intent of seeing the patterns of convergence in scripture.

Unfortunately, theological construction that seeks to take the biblical texts seriously routinely degenerates into mere proof-texting. Appealing to individual texts in reaching theological conclusions is, of course, crucial. The proof-texting approach errs, however, in that it merely picks verses from here and there in a willy-nilly, simplistic manner and in the process treats the Bible as a "flat" book rather than as theological scripture. Reading the Bible theologically provides an antidote to this mistaken use of scripture.

---

104. Lindbeck declares, "It is the text, so to speak, which absorbs the world, rather than the world the text." George A. Lindbeck, *The Nature of Doctrine: Religion and Theology in a Postliberal Age* (Philadelphia: Westminster Press, 1984), 118.

The theological reading views Scripture not as a storehouse of facts waiting to be systematized but as a testimony to the ongoing work of God with humankind, a work that climaxes with the Spirit calling into being the fellowship of Christ's disciples as the eschatological community. Consequently, we read the texts theologically as we seek in scripture the converging patterns present throughout the documents. The theological reading involves looking for "the ways in which different parts come together to make a whole,"[105] to cite Charles Scalise's appropriate description. Above all, we read the texts in the light of their convergence in the pattern that centers on God's work in Jesus Christ and the subsequent sending of the Spirit, that pattern that Christians believe lies at the heart of the Bible as a whole.

Obviously, the task of recognizing the patterns requires that we come to the texts with an assumption we mentioned earlier, namely, that canonical scripture is not merely a collection of distinctive writings representing a polyphony of voices; the Bible is more than God's *opera omnia*.[106] Rather, in keeping with the premise that motivated the church in bringing these specific books together into the one canon, we view the various books as comprising a whole. As such the Bible becomes a single voice. We must quickly add, however, that the singularity of voice does not ultimately rest with the inherent singularity of voice the texts themselves supposedly display. Nor is it dependent on any supposed singularity of the church's decision as to which books are canonical (for in fact the church has never been in complete, noncontroverted agreement on this point). Rather, the singularity of voice we claim for scripture is ultimately the singularity of the Spirit who speaks through the texts.

At the same time, we do acknowledge a certain "innate" singularity forming the various texts into one canonical scripture. Reading the Bible theologically means approaching the texts as embodying a unity of basic purpose. This unity of purpose brings the Old and New Testaments together as comprising one canon.

Reading the Bible as one canon forms the basis of reading the texts of the ancient Hebrews as Christian scripture, and it suggests what constitutes the interpretive center for reading both Testaments together. The unitary purpose of the Bible as a whole leads to the realization that the material realities given in the Hebrew scriptures are not merely shadows of spiritual realities more fully and accurately described in the New Testament. Rather, they are also promises of a spiritual reality given first to ancient Israel and later to Christians.[107] Reading the Bible in this theological manner provides what David Dawson terms a "triadic," in contrast to a "bipolar," perspective. This approach places "several readers of the text into relation with the same promising deity, and

---

105. Charles J. Scalise, *From Scripture to Theology: A Canonical Journey into Hermeneutics* (Downers Grove, Ill.: InterVarsity Press, 1996), 86–87.

106. Wolterstorff, "Importance of Hermeneutics," 45.

107. For a somewhat similar approach, see Luther's hermeneutic of the Old Testament as described in James Samuel Preus, *From Shadow to Promise: Old Testament Interpretation from Augustine to the Young Luther* (Cambridge, Mass.: Harvard University Press, 1969), 209.

therefore into relation with one another." More specifically, it claims "that the same promise of redemption by Christ is made in the events of Exodus and Baptism." This puts "Israelites and Christians into a metonymic relation to each other: they are related not because they share something metaphorically (or essentially)—which would make it easy for the Christian reader to set aside the Israelite reader's meaning as redundant—but because both readers stand in relation to the same promising God."[108]

As this approach to Christian scripture in two Testaments indicates, theology assists the reading of the Bible. It alerts the reader to read within the context of the unitive patterns that bring the texts into a canonical whole.

Reading within Community

We have noted repeatedly in this chapter that the Spirit appropriates the biblical text so as to fashion a community that lives the paradigmatic biblical narrative in the contemporary context. The goal of our reading the text, therefore, is to hear the Spirit's voice forming us into that community. This understanding leads to the conclusion that reading the text theologically entails reading "within community."

Reading within community occurs as we approach the text conscious that we are participants in the one faith community that spans the ages. This consciousness involves recognizing the theological heritage within which we stand as contemporary readers of the text. Because we come to the text as participants in a trajectory of faith—because we come as those who seek to understand the whole of scripture as the instrumentality of the Spirit's speaking to us—we do well to keep in view what the church through the ages has considered this biblical "whole" to be. An awareness of the theological heritage of the church can assist us in this process. Consciousness of our participation in the one church of Jesus Christ also involves acknowledging the Christian interpretive tradition in which our reading occurs, a tradition that, like the church in which it transpires, spans the ages. Like others before us, we desire to read the Bible Christianly. This process is advanced as we take seriously the attempts of our forebears to engage in the hermeneutical task that now occupies us, namely, that of listening to the Spirit speaking through the biblical texts.

Reading within community occurs as well as we approach the text conscious that we are participants in the contemporary church. This consciousness entails the desire to take seriously the attempts of other Christians to understand what the Spirit is saying to the faith community. Such attempts are both local and global. Hence, we do well to consider the manifold voices of faith communities in various settings around the world as they seek to discern how the Spirit is guiding them through scripture in the task of being Christ's disciples in their local context. We do well also to consider what the Spirit is saying to us as a global community regarding what it means to be the one church in the world today.

108. David Dawson, *Literary Theory* (Minneapolis: Fortress Press, 1995), 29.

Being conscious that we are participants in the church today means above all, however, reading the text within the local congregational setting. We come to scripture aware that we are participants in a concrete, visible fellowship of disciples in covenant with one another. In the end, our goal is to hear what the Spirit is saying to this particular congregation and to these particular believers who share together the mandate of being a fellowship of believers in this specific setting. Obviously this involves engaging in the hermeneutical task within the gathered community. In the words of Mennonite thinker Walter Klaassen, "[t]he text can be properly understood only when disciples are gathered together to discover what the Word has to say to their needs and concerns."[109] But sensitivity to reading within community extends to our individual interpretive efforts as well, as our private readings of the text are seasoned with the awareness that, even as the church scattered, each of us remains a participant in a particular gathered community.

It is in our participation in the gathered community that we are most clearly a "people of the book." And it is here that the Spirit's voice speaking through scripture can be most clearly discerned.

---

109. Walter Klaassen, "Anabaptist Hermeneutics: Presuppositions, Principles and Practice," in Willard M. Swartley, ed., *Essays on Biblical Interpretation: Anabaptist-Mennonite Perspective* (Elkhart, Ind.: Institute of Mennonite Studies, 1984), 10. For this idea, Klaassen cites John Howard Yoder, "Hermeneutics of the Anabaptists" *Mennonite Quarterly Review* 41 (October 1967): 301.

Chapter Four

Tradition: Theology's Hermeneutical Trajectory

What we have heard and known, what our fathers have told us. We will not hide them from their children; we will tell the next generation the praiseworthy deeds of the LORD, his power, and the wonders he has done. He decreed statutes for Jacob and established the law in Israel, which he commanded our forefathers to teach their children, so the next generation would know them, even the children yet to be born, and they in turn would tell their children. Then they would put their trust in God and would not forget his deeds but would keep his commands.
—Psalm 78:3–7

and what you have heard from me through many witnesses entrust to faithful people who will be able to teach others as well.
—2 Timothy 2:2 (NRSV)

The uncritical use of tradition *may leave the unwanted implication that Christian teaching is essentially an archaic or dogmatic traditionalism that is determined simply by rigid formulas and in-group prejudices. Rather "tradition," as Jews and Christians live it, is a vital social reality that receives and transmits the history of revelation. Tradition wants to be danced, sung, feasted upon, and celebrated. Tradition is shared in a social process through seasonal celebrations and the recollection of mighty events.*
—Thomas Oden[1]

1. Thomas C. Oden, *Systematic Theology: The Living God* (San Francisco: Harper & Row, 1987), 338.

Christianity is a historical phenomenon. Its teachings, practices, and ethos have been transmitted and preserved from generation to generation since its emergence in the first century as a movement distinct from Judaism. Throughout its history and in its contemporary manifestation, Christianity is to a significant degree the product of the historical circumstances and forces that have shaped it. It is, in short, a tradition. This is not to deny the centrality of scripture for Christian faith and practice. As we discussed in chapter 3, to be a Christian is to participate in a community whose corporate identity is shaped by the texts of canonical scripture. Hence, Christians are rightly viewed as a "book people." Nevertheless, Christianity is also a tradition; its beliefs and practices are rooted in its historical contexts as well as in its corporate reflection on scripture.

In chapter 3, we suggested that to read the biblical text theologically means to read with a conscious awareness of our participation in the historical faith community. This entails a recognition of the theological heritage that has shaped the corporate reflection of the people of God as they have read the text of scripture. We come to the texts as participants in the story of faith who seek to understand the whole of scripture as the instrumentality of the Spirit's speaking to us. Yet we realize that the Spirit has been speaking to the church through scripture over the course of history. Therefore, we do well to take account of the reception of the Spirit's voice mediated to us and passed on by the faith community through the ages.

The acknowledgment that the Spirit has been speaking to the church throughout its history naturally leads to the question, How ought the fruits of this heritage to bear on the process of theological reflection? The central concern of this chapter is to respond to this question. Our intent is to look at the role of Christian tradition in the task of contemporary theological construction. Introducing the idea of tradition as a source for theology raises a number of distinct but related issues. In the following pages, we will consider these issues by examining three crucial questions: What is the relationship between scripture and tradition? What is the nature of the Christian tradition and how can we account for the considerable diversity that characterizes the history of Christianity? How does the multifaceted and diverse tradition function in the task of contemporary theological construction? As we address these questions, however, we must note the context in which the contemporary discussion occurs. Just as the modern era has witnessed a loss of the Bible in the church, so also modernity has brought the demise of tradition.

The Rise and Demise of Tradition in Theology

Until recently, discussions of tradition—if they occurred at all—routinely took place within the context of the debates between Roman Catholics and Protestants over the question of the status of church tradition vis-à-vis scripture. The answers generally given to this question reflect the foundationalist commitments of participants on both sides of the historic confessional divide within the Western church. Moreover, both sides generally operate with a modern, static view of the nature of tradition. The postmodern situation provides the occasion to move beyond this impasse. However, making such a move requires that we come to understand how the concept of tradition developed in the church, how it hardened into static categories, and how this hardening led to the demise of tradition, at least among Protestants but in a certain sense among Catholics as well.

Scripture and Tradition before the Reformation

The genesis of the debate between Catholics and Protestants about the relationship between scripture and tradition is rooted in historical developments that took place well before the sixteenth century.[2] The discussion of this issue in the later medieval period focused particularly on the question of the authority of *extrascriptural* tradition. Prior to Basil in the East and Augustine in the West, however, the concept of an extrascriptural tradition functioning authoritatively in the life of the church would have been viewed as highly problematic.[3]

The Patristic Church

In the patristic era, scripture and tradition were not seen as mutually exclusive but as coinherent.[4] Kerygma—or scripture—and tradition completely coincide in the thinking of the early church. The church proclaims the gospel that is contained in written form in the canonical documents and is preserved and handed down in living form through the tradition of the church. The whole of the kerygma is found in both scripture and tradition. Viewed from this perspective, tradition is not an addition to the message contained in scripture but is the living, socially embodied expression of that message.

The conception of the coinherence of scripture and tradition came as the result of the assumption that both issue from the common source of divine revelation. This understanding constitutes an explicit repudiation of an extrascriptural tradition on a par with scripture as authoritative for the church. Writing in the latter half of the second century, Irenaeus set forth the most complete refutation of the appeal to traditions beyond scripure in his work *Against Heresies*.[5] He identified appeals to revelatory truth apart from scripture as a form of heretical Gnostic practice and maintained that only the "tradition which is derived

---

2. For a brief history of the discussion concerning scripture and tradition as it informed the Reformation, see George H. Tavard, *Holy Writ or Holy Church: The Crisis of the Protestant Reformation* (New York: Harper & Brothers, 1959), 3–79.

3. For a helpful summary of scripture and tradition in the early church, see J. N. D. Kelly, *Early Christian Doctrines*, 5th rev. ed. (London: Adam & Charles Black, 1977), 29–51.

4. Tavard, *Holy Writ or Holy Church*, 22.

5. St. Irenaeus, *Adversus Haereses*, ed. W. W. Harvey (Cambridge, 1857); also see St. Irenaeus, *Against the Heresies: Book 1* trans. by Dominic C. Unger. Further revised by John J. Dillon (New York: Paulist Press, 1992).

from the apostles" contained in scripture and preserved in the church was to serve as authoritative for the faith and practice of the Christian community.[6] In the midst of the fourth-century Arian controversy, Athanasius likewise insisted on the sufficiency of scripture for the determination of truth in the church.[7]

Beginning with Basil the Great, a transition in how the understanding of tradition is to be formulated occurs. In his treatise *De Spiritu Sancto*, Basil states that some aspects of the Christian faith and practice are to be found not in scripture but in the tradition of the church.[8] Historian Heiko Oberman pinpoints the significance of this work for the Catholic understanding of tradition: "We find here for the first time explicitly the idea that the Christian owes equal respect and obedience to written and unwritten ecclesiastical traditions, whether contained in canonical writings or in a secret oral tradition handed down by the Apostles through their successors."[9]

Oberman also highlights the importance of Augustine in the establishment of this new conception of tradition. On the one hand, Augustine reflects the coinherence of scripture and tradition characteristic of the early church, in that he repeatedly asserts the ultimate authority of scripture yet not in such a way as to oppose the authority of the church. On the other hand, Augustine also reflects the view evidenced in Basil. In Oberman's words, "In contrast to Irenaeus' condemnation of extrascriptural tradition, in Augustine we find mention of an *authoritative* extrascriptural oral tradition." According to Augustine, the church "moves" the faithful to "discover the authority of scripture" and scripture in turn "refers the faithful back to the authority of the church with regard to a series of issues with which the Apostles did not deal in writing." Oberman notes that Augustine appeals to this extrascriptural principle in his discussion of the baptism of heretics and then indicates the role that this theological move would play in subsequent history: "Abelard in the same manner would later treat Mariology, Bonaventura the *filioque* clause, and Thomas the form of the sacrament of confirmation."[10]

The Medieval Debate

In the fourteenth century, Basil's statement on the legitimacy of extrascriptural tradition and the two aspects of Augustine's thought gave rise to two competing conceptions as to the authority of scripture and tradition. Oberman labels these two understandings "Tradition I" and "Tradition II."[11] Tradition I repre-

---

6. Jaroslav Pelikan, *The Emergence of the Catholic Tradition (100–600)* (Chicago: University of Chicago Press, 1971), 115.

7. Athanasius, *Contra Gentes* (Oxford: Clarendon Press, 1971), 3.

8. St. Basil the Great, *De Spiritu Sancto* in *Patrologia Graeca*, ed. J. P. Migne (Paris: Migne, 1857–1912), 32:188. St. Basil the Great, *On the Holy Spirit* (Crestwood, N.Y.: St. Vladimir's Seminary Press, 1980), 98–99.

9. Heiko Oberman, *The Harvest of Medieval Theology: Gabriel Biel and Late Medieval Nominalism*, rev. ed. (Grand Rapids: Wm. B. Eerdmans Publishing Co., 1967), 369.

10. Ibid., 370–71.

11. Ibid., 371.

sents the single-source understanding in which the emphasis is on the suffi-ciency of scripture as the exclusive and final authority in the church. Oberman explains, "The horizontal concept of Tradition is by no means denied here, but rather understood as the mode of reception of the *fides* or *veritas* contained in Scripture." With the rejection of any appeals to extrascriptural tradition, eccle-siastical tradition is not to be understood as "self-supporting" but rather "depends on its relation to the faith handed down by God in Holy Scripture."[12] Tradition II maintains a two-source conception of authority in which both the written *and* the unwritten, oral components of the apostolic message, as approved by the church, are deemed to be equally authoritative. Here the emphasis shifts away from the interpreters, or doctors, of scripture and toward the bishops who determine the content of the authentic tradition. The church hierarchy is viewed as having its "own" oral tradition that is, to cite Oberman's characterization, "to a certain undefined extent independent, not of the Apostles, but of what is recorded in the canonical books. Ecclesiastical tradi-tions, including canon law, are invested with the same degree of authority as that of Holy Scripture."[13]

Prior to the fourteenth century, these two conceptions were held together without any conscious effort to distinguish between them or to integrate them. Nevertheless, a significant difference already existed between the theologians and the canon lawyers, a difference that was finally brought into relief during the fourteenth century. Throughout the early Middle Ages, canonists regularly refer to Basil's statement. In fact, the leading canon lawyer of the day, Ivo of Chartres, cites it in arguing for an equal standing for scripture and extrascrip-tural oral tradition.[14] Ivo's assertion, along with the Basilean passage on which it was based, is in turn included by Gratian of Bologna in his *Decretum*. From this highly influential source, the passage and its interpretation was widely dis-seminated into the standard textbooks of theologians as well as canon lawyers.[15]

From the perspective of the canon lawyers these developments were suffi-cient to establish the two-source theory with respect to canon law. Therefore, throughout the medieval period canon law stands on the foundations of scripture and tradition, the latter of which is understood as approved, extrascriptural oral tradition handed down from the apostles and preserved in the church.

The medieval theologians, in contrast, did not adhere to this understanding. Because they conceived of theology as the science of scripture, they elevated scripture itself as the final authority for matters of faith, as indicated in the use of the term *sacra pagina* to denote theology. This is the case despite the increas-ing tendency of the medieval theologians to comment on previous interpreta-tions in such a way as to appear to give them authority. Although their works

12. Ibid., 372.
13. Ibid., 373.
14. Ivo of Chartres, *Patrologia Latina*, ed. J.P. Migne (Paris: Migne, 1844–1890), 161:283.
15. Oberman, *The Harvest of Medieval Theology*, 369.

reflect acceptance of a close connection between scripture and its interpretation, the scholastic thinkers respected the distinction between text and gloss. They viewed the prior interpretive tradition as a vital and important component of theology without losing sight of the primacy of scripture in the assessment of various interpretations. These thinkers were convinced that final authority in questions of interpretation resided in the text of canonical scripture.[16]

In the fourteenth century, the prominence of canon lawyers resulted in a growing acceptance of the Basilean two-source theory in the church. Oberman points out that in the context of its historical circumstances, namely, the Great Schism and the final phase of the struggle between pope and emperor, canon lawyers were in high demand and perhaps even surpassed theologians in status at the papal *curia* and the royal courts. In his estimation, it is not surprising "that the canon-law tradition started to feed into the major theological stream in such a way that the Basilean passage became a genuinely theological argument, and the foundation of the position which we have called Tradition II."[17] The development and hardening of the position described by Tradition II in the later medieval period can be seen as a response to the increasing acceptance of the two-source theory that had its roots in Basil.

In the struggle between the curialists and the conciliarists to reform the church that began in the aftermath of the Western schism, members of both groups supported the legitimacy of authoritative extrascriptural tradition. The two differed merely over the location of highest authority, pope or council, in determining and defining the extrascriptural tradition. With this development, in the later Middle Ages, Tradition II increasingly came to be seen by the church as the more acceptable position. Reformers such as Bradwardine, Wycliffe and Hus, who supported Tradition I, were viewed as dangerous radicals by the church hierarchy because they challenged the authority of the pope and the received church tradition.

The Elevation of Scripture over Tradition in the Reformation

By the sixteenth century the debate in the church regarding scripture and tradition had undergone further development.[18] Three main schools of thought can be identified. The first, corresponding to Tradition I, maintained that all truth necessary for salvation could be found either explicitly or implicitly in scripture. Tradition was required for the task of correctly interpreting scripture, particularly those elements regarding salvation that were deemed to be merely implicit in the text. This is often referred to as the "classical" view. The second position, which corresponds to Tradition II, asserts that Christian revelation is

16. For an outstanding study on biblical interpretation and the use of scripture in the medieval period, see Beryl Smalley, *The Study of the Bible in the Middle Ages*, 2nd ed. (Oxford: Oxford University Press, 1952).

17. Oberman, *The Harvest of Medieval Theology*, 372.

18. For an overview of the discussion on scripture and tradition in the sixteenth century see Yves Congar, *Tradition and Traditions* (New York: Macmillan & Co., 1967).

only partly contained in the canonical text, with another part lodged in the oral traditions of the apostles passed down through their disciples. Finally, a third outlook, which came to prominence among curial canonists and theologians in the late Middle Ages, taught that the Holy Spirit abides constantly with the Catholic Church and gives new inspiration or illumination to the Church. In this view the teaching of popes and councils is binding on the faithful, even where such teaching is unsupported by scripture or the oral traditions of the apostles.[19]

Sola Scriptura

In response to the increasing emphasis on extrascriptural tradition and papal authority, the northern European humanists of the fifteenth and sixteenth centuries advocated a reformist agenda characterized by the slogan *ad fontes*, "back to the sources." This program gave clear priority to the teaching of scripture as the source for Christian faith and was highly critical of the elevation of tradition in the practices of the medieval church.[20] The emphases of the humanists on the sufficiency of scripture and the related rejection of the distorting influence of the medieval tradition were adopted by the early Reformers, such as Luther and Zwingli, and provided the basis for their appeal to the principle of *sola scriptura*,[21] that is, the claim that scripture alone was normative for the faith and life of the church.

The elevation of *sola scriptura* effectively set the agenda for what became Protestant antitraditionalism, at least as it characterized the Protestant attitude toward the theological developments in the first 1500 years of church history.[22] Predictably, the implications of *sola scriptura* were often applied against those who were committed to the principle by other reformists who believed that one doctrine or another had been too greatly affected by tradition. Thus, Luther was so critiqued by Zwingli on the sacraments, Zwingli by the Zurich Anabaptists on the question of infant baptism, and more extremely, Calvin by Servetus on the doctrine of the Trinity.

The Reformers, at least those of the magisterial reformation, did not intend to sever themselves entirely from the Christian past. Calvin's writings in particular contain numerous references to the Church fathers, and he clearly attempts to align the program of the Reformation with Augustine.[23] The significance of

---

19. These three positions and their proponents are described in greater detail by Tavard, *Holy Writ or Holy Church*, 47–66.

20. Ibid., 67–79.

21. For an account of the influence of humanism on the Reformation, see Alister McGrath, *The Intellectual Origins of the European Reformation* (Oxford: Basil Blackwell Publisher, 1987), 32–68.

22. Jaroslav Pelikan, *The Vindication of Tradition* (New Haven, Conn.: Yale University Press, 1984), 11.

23. On Calvin's use of the early church and medieval traditions, see Anthony N. S. Lane, "Calvin's Use of the Fathers and Medievals," *Calvin Theological Journal* 16 (November 1981): 149–205.

Calvin in this regard is noted by Pelikan, who states that the Geneva Reformer became the one figure who, "more than any other, enabled the leaders of the Reformation to claim that they were not throwing over the Christian past after all."[24] Yet in spite of attempts by some of the Reformers to maintain a place, albeit a limited one, for the tradition of the Church, the *trajectory* of Protestantism coupled with its ongoing polemic against the Catholic Church inevitably served to diminish, if not eclipse, the significance of tradition for Protestant theology.

The Council of Trent

The separation of scripture and tradition occasioned by the Protestant insistence, *contra* the Catholic Church, on scripture as the *sole* source for theology was intensified by the developments at the Council of Trent.[25] In addition to the formulating and clarifying of official Catholic doctrine, the Council was also clearly concerned with the refutation of Protestantism. Thus, while the Council engaged in lengthy deliberations about the precise nature of the relationship between scripture and tradition, the participants were in fundamental agreement that the Protestant position was inadequate.[26]

The Catholic theologians at Trent almost unanimously agreed that the canonical scriptures were not in themselves sufficient as a source of doctrine. Further, the Roman Catholic divines were united in claiming that even if scripture contained all truth, it could not be sufficiently understood without reliance on the tradition enshrined in the works of the fathers and in ecclesiastical decisions.[27] The draft text of the Council, adopted by majority vote, seemed to favor the position that not all of divine revelation was contained in scripture. However, according to Catholic theologian Avery Dulles, the final text left open the possibility that all revelation was contained in scripture alone, but also the possibility that all revelation was found in tradition.[28] In any case, Trent certainly affirmed the value of both scripture and tradition as means of the transmission of revelation. The Council appropriated the phrase from Basil's *De Spiritu Sancto* that spoke of scripture and apostolic tradition as having equal value for piety.[29] Although the precise meaning of the Basilean expression has been debated, it certainly implies that tradition is to be received as being in some sense equal with scripture.[30] On the strength of this historical precedent,

24. Pelikan, *The Vindication of Tradition*, 19.

25. For a brief commentary on the doctrinal position of Trent on tradition see Joseph Ratzinger, "On the Interpretation of the Tridentine Decree on Tradition" in Karl Rahner and Joseph Ratzinger, *Revelation and Tradition* (New York: Herder & Herder, 1966), 50–78.

26. For a discussion of the Council's deliberations on scripture and tradition, see Tavard, *Holy Writ or Holy Church*, 195–209.

27. Avery Dulles, *The Craft of Theology: From Symbol to System* (New York: Crossroad, 1992), 88.

28. Ibid., 89.

29. Basil the Great, *De Spiritu Sancto*, 27:66.

30. Congar, *Tradition and Traditions*, 163.

the Tridentine decree asserted that the Catholic Church "accepts and venerates" apostolic tradition with the same sense of "loyalty and reverence" with which it "accepts and venerates" all the books of both the Old and New Testaments.[31]

In short, although Trent did not formally speak of scripture and tradition as two sources of revelation, it at least seemed to suggest such a construction. And it certainly held that the authority of tradition was not in any way less than that of scripture, insofar as both came from God and therefore both carried divine authority.[32] Thus, the decrees of the Council clearly struck at the Protestant conception of *sola scriptura*, connected as it was to a disdain for church tradition.

According to George Tavard, Catholic opposition to *sola scriptura* became so strong in the wake of Trent that despite the Council's careful attempt to set forth a doctrine of scripture and tradition that did not move in the direction of suggesting two separate sources of revelation, the classical or traditional conception nearly vanished from the highly polemical theology of the Counter-Reformation. Tavard goes so far as to note, "A study of this new period would show that the main post-Tridentine theologians misinterpreted the formula of the Council."[33] Theologians such as Perez de Ayala and Melchior Cano propagated the concept of two sources of revelation or faith and influenced polemicists such as Cardinal Bellarmine to read the mistaken interpretation into the Tridentine decree. Tavard maintains that for the most part later Catholic theology followed the formulations of Cano and Bellarmine and asserted that scripture and tradition constitute two sources of revelation.[34] In addition, in response to the Protestant denial of the authority and infallibility of the Catholic hierarchy, Catholic polemical theologians placed great emphasis on this doctrine as an extension of the ongoing authority of the Church's tradition.[35]

In the centuries since Trent, Catholic theologians have continued to explore the principle of the primacy of the Church and the role of the ecclesiastical magisterium. In the nineteenth century, John Henry Newman argued that scripture never exists by itself alone, but only in the context of the Church, and hence cannot be properly interpreted without the ongoing commentary of the Church. According to Avery Dulles, this interpretation "can express itself in irreversible doctrinal decisions, such as creeds and conciliar definitions," and it develops through "a harmonious interaction between the ecclesiastical magisterium and the sense of the faith inherent in the Church as a whole."[36] The Jesuits of the Roman school worked closely with the Church in promoting the dogmas of Vatican I, affirming papal primacy and infallibility. In keeping with this conception of the authority of the Holy See, the Jesuit theologian J. B. Franzelin

31. H. Denzinger and A. Schonmetzer, eds., *Enchiridion Symbolorum*, 33rd ed. (Freiburg: Herder, 1965), 1501.

32. Dulles, *The Craft of Theology*, 89.

33. Tavard, *Holy Writ or Holy Church*, 244.

34. Ibid., 245.

35. James P. Mackey, *Tradition and Change in the Church* (Dayton, Ohio: Pflaum Press, 1968), 138–39.

36. Dulles, *The Craft of Theology*, 91.

emphasized the role of the magisterium for the purpose of developing the explicit content of the Christian faith as well as safeguarding it from corruption.[37] Catholic thinkers distinguished between "active tradition" and "passive tradition" in which the magisterium is viewed as the bearer of the "active tradition." Dulles suggests that in this conception the role of the magisterium was not "simply to authenticate what was believed by the faithful as a body, but to clarify and explicate the contents of faith. The 'passive tradition' borne by the faithful as a body was simply a reflection of what had been taught by the magisterium."[38]

The Protestant Reaction

The post-Tridentine Catholic position on tradition that arose in due course as a response to *sola scriptura* occasioned, in turn, the hardening of the Protestant attitude toward tradition. The Reformers maintained that theology must be subject only to the direct authority of God who has spoken through the Bible and not to any merely human authority, such as the creeds and traditions of the church. They averred that their teachings were based solely on scripture apart from any other source.[39] Moreover, they developed hermeneutical principles, such as the perspicuity of scripture and the idea that scripture interprets scripture, aimed at minimizing the need for human interpretation.[40]

In accordance with these principles, Protestant thinkers rejected the Catholic claim to an infallible ecclesiastical magisterium, arguing instead that the only infallible interpretive authority for scripture is scripture itself. In this way, Protestant theologians believed that they had secured the sole authority of God in the church and that they could access divine commands and instructions in a relatively unmediated fashion through the Bible, without recourse to human means and traditions that are subject to error.[41] It would clearly be an overstatement to suggest that this antipathy toward tradition characterizes all Protestant denominations and churches equally. Nevertheless, it certainly describes the general trajectory of the movement as set forth in its confessional statements, a trajectory that has influenced Protestant theology to the present.

The Loss of Tradition in Protestant Theology

On the basis of loyalty to scripture, the Reformation mounted a serious theological challenge to tradition. The Reformers argued that theology must be subject solely to the direct authority of the Bible, which alone is the written Word of God. To be under the authority of the Bible was to be under the authority

---

37. James Mackey, *The Modern Theology of Tradition* (New York: Herder & Herder, 1963), chapter 1.

38. Dulles, *The Craft of Theology*, 91.

39. Pelikan, *Vindication of Tradition*, 11–12.

40. For a brief discussion of hermeneutics in the Reformed confessions see Jan Rohls, *Reformed Confessions: Theology from Zurich to Barmen*, trans. by John Hoffmeyer (Louisville, Ky.: Westminster John Knox Press, 1998), 38–41.

41. Rohls, *Reformed Confessions*, 42–43.

of God. To add human traditions to this authority was to compromise the lord-ship of Christ over his church. Although this conception minimized the impor-tance of tradition and even brought it under suspicion, some Reformers, such as Calvin, still valued the ancient tradition of the early church and did not com-pletely diminish the significance of the Christian past. Yet even Calvin warned with respect to tradition that the "safety of that man hangs by a thread whose defense turns wholly on this—that he has constantly adhered to the religion handed down to him from his forefathers."[42]

Since the sixteenth century, Protestants have generally looked on tradition with considerable suspicion. The constant polemic against the Catholic posi-tion became, and continues to be in some contexts, a staple of Protestant theo-logical exposition. In many respects, the denial of tradition as an authoritative source for theological construction, contra the Catholic position, has even con-stituted the Protestant raison d'etre. This negative attitude toward tradition born in the Reformation came to maturation in three contexts.

1. *The devaluation of tradition in Protestant orthodoxy.* As the sixteenth cen-tury gave way to the seventeenth, the churches of the magisterial Reformation sought to codify the theological insights of the early Reformers through the use of a scholastic approach to theology reminiscent of medieval Catholic theol-ogy.[43] In each of the Protestant ecclesiastical contexts, theologians carefully con-structed systems of theology that sought to be comprehensive accounts of doctrine faithful to the distinctive concerns of the Lutheran and Reformed churches.

A common theme in the development of both Lutheran and Reformed dog-matics in Protestant scholasticism is, in keeping with the theology of the Reformers, a heavy emphasis on scripture alone as the cognitive foundation for the theology.[44] In scholastic theological treatises, the doctrine of scripture is rou-tinely treated first among the theological *loci* for the purpose of establishing scripture as the sole source and foundation on which the theological enterprise is based. In the task of establishing scripture as the *sole* source for theology and diminishing the role of tradition, theologians formulated several important concepts. Protestant scholastics declared that the authority of scripture was self-authenticating and thus valid apart from the faith of the church.[45] Further, they asserted that scripture was sufficient, that is, that nothing was needed in addi-tion to the teaching of scripture, for instruction in Christian life and faith.[46] In addition, they conceived of scripture as perspicuous, thereby eliminating the

---

42. John Calvin, "Reply to Sadolet" in J. K. S. Reid, *Calvin: Theological Treatises* (Philadelphia: Westminster Press, 1954), 221–56.

43. Alister McGrath notes the irony of this development in *The Intellectual Origins of the European Reformation* (Oxford: Basil Blackwell Publisher, 1987), 191–196.

44. For a detailed account of these developments in the Reformed theological community, see Richard A. Muller, *Post-Reformation Reformed Dogmatics, Volume 2: Holy Scripture: The Cognitive Foundation of Theology* (Grand Rapids: Baker, 1993).

45. Ibid., 270–302.

46. Ibid., 327–40.

need for an authoritative magisterium.[47] Closely related to this concept is the hermeneutical assertion that the only authoritative interpreter of scripture is scripture itself, that is to say, "Scripture interprets Scripture."[48] These formulations effectively served to eliminate the role of tradition in theology, or at least to render it completely subservient to scripture.

2. *The elimination of tradition in Anabaptist theology.* The Anabaptists churches also sought to deny the role of tradition by means of an emphasis on scripture alone as the standard for theology.[49] However, in Anabaptist circles this emphasis took on a shape quite different from that developed by the Lutheran and Reformed theologians. In contrast to the scholastics who composed numerous systems of theology, along with confessions and catechisms, in order to reinforce their doctrinal teachings as based on the Bible, the Anabaptists for the most part avoided producing such documents. Their reticence arose out of a concern that such efforts would eventually result in the establishment of new, but nevertheless human, authoritative traditions. The Anabaptists, therefore, sought to preserve the sole authority of scripture by refraining from drafting any humanly devised authoritative works that might take on, at least de facto, a status that could only be properly ascribed to the Bible.

Typical of the Anabaptist viewpoint was the attitude evidenced by Menno Simons. Menno maintained that, despite their intentions, the Reformers were too dependent on human traditions in the development of their theology.[50] Accordingly, Menno decried scholasticism in both its Catholic and Protestant manifestations.[51] Since the sixteenth century, Mennonite scholars have generally been content to engage in the discipline of biblical theology, and Mennonite churches have produced no creeds beyond the more ad hoc statements of faith that typify Believers' Church groups in general. This form of antitraditional "traditionalism" has, in turn, seeped into much of North American Protestant evangelicalism.

3. *The undercutting of tradition in the Enlightenment.* The most severe attack on the concept of tradition, however, came from neither the Protestant scholastics nor the Anabaptists. Rather, it was launched in the Enlightenment. The appeal to reason that characterized the Age of Reason provided a powerful acid that effectively dissolved the role of tradition in theology.

In the Enlightenment the reliance on received authorities, whether the Bible or the church, as a source for knowledge came to be viewed with scorn. In fact, such reliance was even thought to be intellectually irresponsible. The responsible

47. Ibid., 340–57.
48. John H. Leith, ed., *Creeds of the Churches: A Reader in Christian Doctrine from the Bible to the Present,* 3rd ed. (Atlanta: John Knox Press, 1982), 196.
49. On the Anabaptist conception of *sola scriptura,* see William R. Estep, *The Anabaptist Story: An Introduction to Sixteenth-Century Anabaptism,* 3rd ed. (Grand Rapids: Wm. B. Eerdmans Publishing Co., 1996), 190–196.
50. Timothy George, *Theology of the Reformers* (Nashville: Broadman Press, 1988), 274–6.
51. Ibid., 276.

thinker, in contrast, was the *individual* who did not accept matters as true simply on the basis of pronouncements by so-called authorities. Instead, such persons would think for themselves and carefully scrutinize all knowledge claims, refusing to accept long-held convictions of society and demanding that all assertions of truth be supported with rational evidence of an objective and unbiased nature.[52] Beliefs that could not be supported on the basis of such rational investigation were to be jettisoned as irrational or superstitious. In this context, thinkers and patterns of thought that embodied the intellectual traditions of the past were viewed with special suspicion. In short, the Enlightenment set forth as the best approach to knowing, whether the field be theology or any other area of inquiry, cutting oneself loose from the influence of tradition in order to pursue knowledge in an objective, dispassionate manner, unencumbered by the authorities of the past.[53]

The Demise of Tradition in Modern Theology

The factors that emerged in the aftermath of the Reformation converged in the modern era to spell the demise of tradition not only in Protestant theology but eventually in certain Roman Catholic circles as well. The elimination of tradition from the theological radar screen has been pronounced in both liberal and conservative Protestantism since the nineteenth century.

The Overthrowing of Tradition in Protestant Liberalism

The mind-set of suspicion toward tradition, the emphasis on objectivity, and the priority of the individual in the task of knowing were the basic characteristics of the liberal theological program spawned in the wake of the Enlightenment. Hence, one of the chief concerns of liberal theology is to render an account of Christian faith that is intelligible, credible, and convincing to the honest, objective inquirer.[54] In line with this concern, liberals came to view formulations of the past as a hindrance to the task of theology, in that such formulations were based on conceptions of reality that had been superseded by those of the modern world. What is needed, according to the liberal perspective, is a reformulation or revision of Christian doctrine consonant with modern sensibilities, not a retrieval of the particular doctrines of the ancient Christian past.[55]

In one sense, liberal theology is a logical trajectory of Protestantism. Luther, Zwingli, and, especially, Calvin critically appropriated and revised the traditions

---

52. For a discussion and critique of objectivity, see Michael Polanyi, *Personal Knowledge: Towards a Post-Critical Philosophy* (Chicago: University of Chicago Press, 1958), 3–17.

53. Trevor Hart, *Faith Thinking: The Dynamics of Christian Theology* (Downers Grove, Ill.: InterVarsity Press, 1995), 168.

54. H. P. van Dusen, *The Vindication of Liberal Theology* (New York: Charles Scribner's Sons, 1963), 27.

55. Bernard M. Reardon, ed., *Liberal Protestantism* (Stanford, Calif.: Stanford University Press, 1968), 73–78.

of the ancient Church in their reformist theological programs. For Protestants, therefore, the call to scrutinize critically received traditions and confessions was not a new idea.

Although liberalism can claim a certain continuity with the aims and concerns of the Protestant Reformation at least on the formal level, we dare not overlook the significant difference between the two. The Reformers were concerned that the Christian tradition had been deformed by the medieval Church, and, as the antidote, they appealed to one of the central premises of the tradition—the primacy of scripture—as the corrective. They claimed that their reform program as developed on the basis of scripture alone was rooted in a proper understanding of the tradition itself.

With the liberal movement, in contrast, the problem shifted—in the words of Brian Gerrish—"from the inside to the outside: it is not so much that the tradition itself has been corrupted by the infidelity of the church as that the church's tradition in the modern world has become insecure."[56] The issue for liberalism, then, is not scripture and tradition but the legitimacy of the classical Christian tradition itself, including its commitment to scripture, as viewed from the perspective of modernity. Further, unlike the program of the sixteenth-century Protestants, which emphasized *sola scriptura,* the characteristic expression of liberal Protestantism is "the recognition that Scripture can no longer serve alone as the exclusive critical norm for the language which the believing community is to hand on."[57]

The liberal stance almost inevitably leads to the denigration of the entire tradition prior to the Reformation as well as that of the Reformation itself in terms of its material concerns, inasmuch as both are committed, in one way or another, to the centrality of scripture. Gerrish asserts that liberal Protestantism is at once both "less and more radical than the classical, Reformation model: less radical because there is a stronger consciousness of continuing what is right in the tradition (rather than correcting what is wrong); more radical because the tradition is brought to the test of norms from outside the entire Christian heritage."[58] Although Gerrish is partially correct, liberalism can only be thought less radical in its stance toward the formal, revisionist character of the Reformation, which liberalism maintains, but not in terms of the material commitments of the Reformation contained in its creeds and confessions, which liberals largely reject. This perspective is evident in Edward Farley and Peter Hodgson, who, in their assessment of the Reformation hallmark, conclude that the negative impact of *sola scriptura* was to turn Christianity into a book religion—a logical extension of the scripture principle not unlike the logical extension of institutional authority in the dogma of infallibility. The positive insight behind the assertion of *sola*

---

56. B. A. Gerrish, *Tradition and the Modern World: Reformed Theology in the Nineteenth Century* (Chicago: University of Chicago Press, 1978), 7.
    57. Ibid.
    58. Ibid.

scriptura (as well as *sola fide, sola gratia,* and ultimately *solus Christus*) was the critical questioning of all authorities.[59]

The standard liberal approach urges the cultivation of a hermeneutic of suspicion with regard to the classical Christian tradition and for all intents and purposes mutes the voice of that tradition in theology. Where an appeal to tradition is made, it tends to claim the heritage of the revisionist character of the Protestant Reformation. Scripture is collapsed into the Christian tradition, which is then subject to the critique of modernity. Hence, the modern world "absorbs" the classical Christian tradition, including the biblical text—to use Lindbeck's characterization—demanding its conformity to modernist conceptions of rationality and thus effectively silencing the distinctive material concerns of the tradition in the name of making it credible to modern sensibilities.[60] This liberal theological paradigm is characterized by its commitment to reason as an independent authority set over against the Christian tradition. The assumption that follows from this commitment is that the most responsible use of the Christian theological tradition is "initially to rebel against its authority, to test its worth, and only to afford it respect when one can establish the truth of its offerings on other independent grounds, and thereby commend its truth to those who do not belong to the tradition."[61]

In keeping with this paradigm, when liberal Protestants have discussed the Christian tradition, the focal point has been not on the authority of that tradition but on the question of the origins of the confessional tradition of orthodoxy. As Richard Lints notes, having cut themselves loose from the authority of the Bible and the church, "they sought to explain the development of doctrine in the history of the church in naturalistic terms, focusing on political, social and economic factors."[62] This interest in the historical development of doctrine, coupled with the concern of biblical scholarship to get behind the text in order to reconstruct the true history of the ancient faith communities, led to the conclusion that the church in its many expressions had corrupted the true meaning of the gospel.[63]

Examples of this perspective abound in nineteenth- and twentieth-century liberal writings. Hence, Friedrich Schleiermacher maintained that the teaching

59. Edward Farley and Peter C. Hodgson, "Scripture and Tradition" in Peter C. Hodgson and Robert H. King, *Christian Theology: An Introduction to Its Traditions and Tasks,* 2nd ed. (Philadelphia: Fortress Press, 1985), 72.

60. George Lindbeck, *The Nature of Doctrine: Religion and Theology in a Postliberal Age* (Philadelphia: Westminster Press, 1984), 118.

61. Hart, *Faith Thinking,* 168.

62. Richard Lints, *The Fabric of Theology: A Prologomenon to Evangelical Theology* (Grand Rapids: Wm. B. Eerdmans Publishing Co., 1993), 88.

63. On the development of the discipline of historical theology, see Owen Chadwick, *From Bossuet to Newman: The Idea of Doctrinal Development* (London: Cambridge University Press, 1957); and Jaroslav Pelikan, *Historical Theology: Continuity and Change in Christian Doctrine* (New York: Corpus Publishers, 1971). On the development of biblical scholarship and its relationship to theology, see Roy A. Harrisville and Walter Sundberg, *The Bible in Modern Culture: Theology and Historical-Critical Method from Spinoza to Käsemann* (Grand Rapids: Wm. B. Eerdmans Publishing Co., 1992).

of Christ had been undermined by Greek and Roman influences. Similarly, Adolf Harnack attempted to demonstrate that the original teaching of Jesus had been distorted due to the overlay added by the later "orthodoxy" of the church. Likewise, on finding that some of the epistles had elements of doctrine that were similar to later orthodoxy, F. C. Bauer asserted that this similarity shows that the tradition of the church had distorted the simple message of Jesus and concluded that the New Testament provides more information about the faith of the early Christian community than it does about the real Jesus of history. This conclusion triggered the scholarly search for those recorded words of Jesus that supposedly truly belonged to him and were thus free from the corruption of the church and its tradition.[64]

In the estimation of many liberals, the tradition of the church merely codifies and defines the prejudices of the past, as those in power attempt to impose their will on the church. They argue that the history of the church tells us more about who was influential and who wielded power than it does about who properly interpreted the texts that were studied. In this paradigm, the results of the struggle to define various doctrines are viewed as the products of an essentially political procedure that was controlled by those in power, who were able to determine effectively the shape of orthodoxy to suit their own ends. This view has been most prominently defended by Walter Bauer, who argued that doctrinal pluralism was the norm in the early church and was only later suppressed by the rise of orthodoxy.[65] In keeping with nineteenth-century liberalism, Bauer claimed not only that there were numerous and significant doctrinal differences between the pure teaching of Jesus and that of the early church but also that doctrinal diversity was at the center of the early tradition.[66]

The widespread acceptance of Bauer's thesis has effectively silenced the voice of the classical Christian tradition in contemporary liberal theology.[67] In their dismissal of the Christian tradition as a corruption of the true teachings of Jesus and genuine Christianity, liberal theologians seek to free themselves from the constraints of that tradition in order to open up the possibility of new formulations and interpretations of the faith that they believe are more in keeping with contemporary cultural assumptions.

---

64. The "Jesus Seminar" provides an example of the contemporary manifestation of this search for the historical Jesus who is distinct from the Jesus of faith and tradition. On the work of the Jesus Seminar see Robert W. Funk, ed., *The Five Gospels: The Search for the Authentic Words of Jesus* (New York: Macmillan Publishing Co., 1993); and Robert W. Funk, ed., *The Acts of Jesus: The Search for the Authentic Deeds of Jesus* (San Francisco: HarperSanFrancisco, 1998).

65. Walter Bauer, *Orthodoxy and Heresy in Earliest Christianity*, ed. Robert A. Kraft and Gerhard Krodel (Philadelphia: Fortress Press, 1971).

66. For a contemporary defense of Bauer's position, see Helmut Koester, "Gnomai Diaphorai: The Origin and Nature of Diversification in the History of Early Christianity" in James M. Robinson and Helmut Koester, eds., *Trajectories through Early Christianity* (Philadelphia: Fortress Press, 1971), 114–57.

67. On the continuing influence of Bauer's work, see Daniel J. Harrington, "The Reception of Walter Bauer's *Orthodoxy and Heresy in Earliest Christianity* during the Last Decade," *Harvard Theological Review* 73, nos. 1–2 (1980): 289–98.

The Ignoring of Tradition in Evangelical Protestantism

While the influence of the classical Christian tradition in contemporary theology has been largely negated in liberalism, the situation is somewhat different, although not altogether more positive, in the conservative wing of Protestantism.[68] This is especially the case among evangelicals, who have often been characterized by a disdain for tradition,[69] despite their claims to hold to the faith of the ancient church.

Richard Lints notes three fundamental characteristics of contemporary evangelicalism that work against the appreciation and appropriation of tradition: the emphasis on inductive methods of Bible study, the pervasive parachurch or transdenominational orientation of the movement, and its "ahistorical devotional piety."[70] In many evangelical contexts, the emphasis in Bible study is often primarily on the question of the meaning of the text for the individual reader. Although such an approach may well stimulate a greater interest in individual Bible study, it also encourages reading according to subjective interests. In such circumstances the Bible can be enslaved by the whims of individual readers whose only interest is in the "meaning" of the text for their particular situation. Lints points out that if this is the primary concern in the examination of the text, the church will have to contend with as many different interpretations of the biblical text as there are interpreters. He writes,

> In banishing all mediators between the Bible and ourselves, we have let the Scriptures be ensnared in a web of subjectivism. Having rejected the aid of the community of interpreters throughout the history of Christendom, we have not succeeded in returning to the primitive gospel; we have simply managed to plunge ourselves back to the biases of our own individual situations.[71]

The parachurch orientation of evangelicalism is related to the fact that the movement has no cohesive tradition or ecclesiology of its own. The evangelical community is a patchwork of communities bound together in part by shared theological, social, and cultural concerns. The basis for the unity of the evangelical

---

68. Increasingly, the two-party Protestant paradigm is being called into question with the emergence of theological approaches that do not fit well into either the liberal or the conservative type. These various positions or movements have been described by terms such as neoorthodox, postcritical, postliberal, and postconservative. Nevertheless, the liberal-conservative typology has come to characterize much of the historiography of Protestantism and still serves as a useful way of broadly distinguishing between major segments of the Protestant tradition. For a helpful discussion of the basic distinctions between these types, see Nancey Murphy, *Beyond Liberalism and Fundamentalism: How Modern and Postmodern Philosophy Set the Theological Agenda* (Valley Forge, Penn.: Trinity Press, 1996).

69. David Wells, *No Place For Truth; or, Whatever Happened to Evangelical Theology?* (Grand Rapids: Wm. B. Eerdmans Publishing Co., 1993).

70. Lints, *The Fabric of Theology*, 92.

71. Ibid., 93.

movement has typically been thought to rest on a narrow core of theological distinctives around which a diversity of theologies is represented.[72] The best-known set of essential doctrines are the so-called "five fundamentals" set forth in 1910 by the Presbyterian General Assembly and adopted by the fundamentalist coalition, which formed the precursor of the contemporary neoevangelical movement.[73] The resultant tendency among evangelicals has been, in the name of unity, to relegate to insignificance the differences among the particular theologies and church traditions represented in the coalition. As Lints explains, it "is sometimes claimed that theology divides communities and that appeals to theological distinctives perpetuate this divisiveness. In the powerful desire for unity that drives the evangelical vision, theological distinctives are viewed as roadblocks."[74]

This tendency has given evangelicalism its transdenominational character, so that an "evangelical Presbyterian often feels closer to an evangelical Methodist than to a liberal Presbyterian." According to Lints, "The effect of this is that evangelical Presbyterians and Methodists typically locate their identity less in the Presbyterian or Methodist heritage than in the nebulous theological heritage of evangelicalism."[75]

To a significant extent this transdenominational orientation effectively severs evangelicalism from the richness of the many theological traditions that are part of the movement. The result is a truncated theology that emphasizes certain "essentials" while virtually ignoring other elements of traditional Christian faith. Above all, the almost mandatory neglect of ecclesiology, characteristic of the movement, effectively eliminates tradition from playing any major role in evangelical theology. As Lints comments, "Where there is no 'church,' there will be little 'tradition' to nurture the group."[76] Of course, the irony of the evangelical situation is the similarity it bears to the modern ecumenical movement that it has so vehemently opposed.

The final factor that Lints cites as inhibiting the reception of tradition in the evangelical movement is the "ahistorical character of its devotional piety." He writes that the classics of evangelical devotional literature go back no further than the 1950s and suggests that evangelicals have removed themselves from the works of Christian writers from the nearly two thousand years of prior Christian history. Evangelicals "have convinced themselves that every important thing has happened in the present century and every important book (excepting the Bible, of course) has been written in their own lifetime."[77] Lints

72. An alternative approach to evangelical identity is set forth in Stanley J. Grenz, *Revisioning Evangelical Theology: A Fresh Agenda for the 21st Century* (Downers Grove, Ill.: InterVarsity Press, 1993), 21–35.

73. For a discussion of the five fundamentals, see Stewart Grant Cole, *The History of Fundamentalism* (New York: R. R. Smith, 1931); on the use of these doctrines in the fundamentalist coalition, see George Marsden, *Fundamentalism and American Culture: The Shaping of Twentieth-Century Evangelicalism 1870–1925* (New York: Oxford University Press, 1980).

74. Lints, *The Fabric of Theology*, 94.

75. Ibid.

76. Ibid.

77. Ibid., 96.

acknowledges that it is certainly true that the twentieth century is substantially different from the preceding centuries due to the rise of modern technologies that have altered contemporary life in significant ways. In addition, the secularism and pluralism of our culture have decisively altered our outlook on the world and transformed the ways we think and live. However, Lints suggests that these dramatic changes ought not to invalidate the wisdom of the past but should provide all the more reason to seek out the counsel of those who lived in contexts that were not shaped by these extraordinary pressures.[78] The history of the evangelical movement as a largely twentieth-century coalition, however, works against the appropriation of the more distant past and leaves evangelicalism less able to critique the biases of its own perspective.[79]

There are signs of change brewing in the wings. Moreover, the evangelicalism previously described does not encompass all that properly goes by the designation conservative Protestantism. This anomaly is connected to the events that gave birth to evangelicalism in the modern era.

Conservatives entered the twentieth century largely focused on the struggle with theological liberalism.[80] For many, this battle centered on the defense of certain central doctrines, considered to comprise the "fundamentals" of the faith. Richard Lints comments perceptively that the net result of this broad coalition was the loss of a theological framework:

> Theological truth was separated from the fabric in which it inhered. Truth still mattered to evangelicals, but no longer as an expression of the full organic unity of the revelation of God in Scripture. It became a political platform, the assemblage of a disparate collection of dogmas that had been gathered with the intent of avoiding offense to any of the diverse theological traditions represented in the evangelical coalition. The theological task degenerated into the faithful repetition of core dogmas rather than a harvesting of the rich fields of Scripture with the help of the community of interpreters of the past.[81]

Eventually, cracks emerged in the turn-of-the-twentieth-century coalition, cracks that were often rooted in the differing ecclesiastical and theological convictions that coexisted in the context of the fundamentalist crusade against the perceived influence of liberalism.[82] In the aftermath of the fundamentalist-liberal controversy, a nonconfessionally oriented trajectory emerged out of

---

78. Ibid.

79. On the origins and history of American Evangelicalism, see Marsden, *Fundamentalism and American Culture;* and George Marsden, *Reforming Fundamentalism: Fuller Seminary and the New Evangelicalism* (Grand Rapids: Wm. B. Eerdmans Publishing Co., 1987).

80. See Douglas W. Frank, *Less Than Conquerors: How Evangelicals Entered the Twentieth Century* (Grand Rapids: Wm. B. Eerdmans Publishing Co., 1986).

81. Lints, *The Fabric of Theology*, 42–3.

82. Marsden, *Fundamentalism and American Culture*, 176–95.

fundamentalism that became the neoevangelicalism of the post-World War II period. In addition, however, the breakup of the older coalition launched a confessional trajectory consisting of those ecclesiastical bodies that sought to return to their roots in the creeds of the magisterial Reformation, whether Lutheran, Reformed, or Anglican. Thus, while the larger segment of contemporary evangelicalism has until recently evidenced little place for tradition, another segment of conservative evangelical Protestantism has continually maintained a very strong, confessional approach to tradition as a vital component of theology. It is this wing of the movement that explains why evangelicals are "so often accused by the larger theological community of having a Roman Catholic view of tradition" and why it is "a common perception of modern theologians that the evangelical movement relies on its confessions as infallible interpreters of the Scriptures."[83]

Finding their theological bearings in the authority of the confessions and catechisms of their various traditions, these groups have often been critical of the disregard for the traditions of confessional Protestantism they see in evangelicalism. Yet such groups often give evidence to a static, rather than living, view of tradition. And as a consequence the theology that often emerges in such circles routinely becomes little more than a confessional variety of the foundationalism that typifies modern theology in general.

Scripture and Its Hermeneutical Trajectory: The Place of Tradition in Theology

As we discussed in chapter 3, Protestants are especially aware of the central role of scripture in their lives. This commitment to the centrality of the Bible for faith and practice is captured in the sixteenth-century Reformation formula, *sola scriptura*, and stands as a corrective, from the Protestant perspective, to the Catholic elevation since the Council of Trent of tradition as an authority equal with scripture. Yet, while acknowledging the significance of *sola scriptura* as establishing the principle that canonical scripture is the *norma normans non normata* (the norm with no norm over it), it is also true that in another sense *scriptura* is never *sola*. Scripture does not stand alone as the sole source in the task of theological construction or as the sole basis on which the Christian faith has developed historically. Rather, scripture functions in an ongoing and dynamic relationship with the Christian tradition, as well as with the cultural milieu from which particular readings of the text emerge.

Scripture must be interpreted, and this activity is always shaped by the theological and cultural context within which interpreters participate. It is simply not possible to step back from the influence of tradition in the act of interpretation or in the ascription of meaning. Interpretive communities that deny the reality of this situation and seek an interpretation unencumbered by the

83. Lints, *The Fabric of Theology*, 91.

"distorting" influence of fallible "human" traditions are in fact enslaved by interpretive patterns that are allowed to function uncritically precisely because they are unacknowledged. Such a mind-set is labeled by Richard Lints as "anti-traditional traditionalism" in which the disdain for tradition becomes an ironic form of tradition.[84] Trevor Hart adds that the notion of a "pure" reading of the text "must be shown up for the self-deception that it is."[85]

The task of this section is to set forth an understanding of the "tradition" component in the theological task. More specifically, we argue that tradition provides the hermeneutical trajectory though which theological construction that is truly Christian emerges.

The Renewed Conversation about Tradition

Our first order of business in the process of clarifying in what sense tradition serves as theology's hermeneutical trajectory is to pursue the question of the relationship between the tradition of the Christian church and the canonical scriptures. And the place to begin this discussion is with the recent renewal of conversations between Roman Catholics and Protestants about the nature of tradition. Avery Dulles reports that developments among Catholics took shape at two significant meetings, Vatican II and the Montreal Conference on Faith and Order, both held in the 1960s.

The watershed in the renewed ecumenical discussion between Catholics and Protestants was clearly the Second Vatican Council. Vatican II echoes Trent in affirming that both scripture and tradition are to be "accepted and honored" with equal "devotion and reverence"[86] and affirms that the word of God exists in the twofold form of scripture and tradition.[87] Commenting on the relationship between scripture and tradition set forth by Vatican II, Catholic theologian Avery Dulles says that the Council describes tradition primarily in terms of its function, namely, that of preserving and handing on the word of God. He explains that this does not imply that tradition is not itself the word of God, or that it is merely derivative and secondary to the word of God in scripture. Rather, the process of traditioning began before the composition of the inspired books and continues without interruption through the ages.[88] He explains, "Thus tradition has a certain priority, in view of which *Dei Verbum* found it advisable to treat tradition before turning to Scripture."[89] Dulles summarizes the thrust of Vatican II by noting that scripture is understood as formally insufficient and that tradition is deemed necessary in order to gain "a sufficient grasp of the word of God, even though it be assumed that all revelation is somehow contained in Scripture. It is not from scripture alone that the Church draws its

---

84. Ibid.
85. Hart, *Faith Thinking*, 167.
86. Dulles, *The Craft of Theology*, 97.
87. Ibid.
88. Ibid., 96.
89. Ibid., 96–7.

certainty about everything that has been revealed. Tradition is the means by which the full canon of the sacred books becomes known, and by which the meaning of the biblical text is more profoundly understood and more deeply penetrated."[90]

In Dulles's estimation, Vatican II broke with the traditional two-source theory of revelation, while still acknowledging tradition as a conduit of revelation. The Montreal Conference on Faith and Order, in turn, acknowledged the indispensability of tradition as providing a proper context for the interpretation of scripture.[91] In so doing, Catholic scholars have contended against the older Catholic position that scripture and tradition are not in fact two separate "reservoirs," each containing a certain portion of divinely revealed truth. Nevertheless, they continue to maintain, contrary to the traditional Protestant understanding of *sola scriptura*, that Christians read the Bible in the context of the church, and in the understanding of the use made of it by the church. Thus, the Bible does not function alone.[92] In light of these developments Dulles concludes that "while they do not totally overcome all the historic disputes between Catholics and Protestants, [they] go a long way toward reconciliation. As a result, it is no longer safe to assume that either Protestants or Catholics adhere to the classical orthodoxies of their own churches, as expressed in past centuries."[93]

Although it is certainly true that these developments represent a move in the right direction, significant and fundamental differences still remain.[94] In the traditional discussion between the Catholics and the Protestants the question is, Which has priority, scripture or the tradition of the church? This fundamental difference still animates contemporary dialogues between Catholics and Protestants. We suggest that posing the question in this matter is ultimately unhelpful in that it rests on a foundationalist understanding of the derivation of knowledge as discussed in the second chapter. Consequently, a shift to a nonfoundationalist conception can assist in moving the discussion beyond this impasse.

A Nonfoundational Conception of Scripture and Tradition

In chapter 3 we suggested that the authority of scripture does not ultimately rest with any quality that inheres in the text itself but with the work of the Spirit who speaks in and through the text. Scripture is authoritative because it is the

---

90. Ibid., 97.
91. Avery Dulles, "Scripture: Recent Protestant and Catholic Views," in *The Authoritative Word*, ed. Donald McKim (Grand Rapids: Wm. B. Eerdmans Publishing Co., 1983), 250.
92. Ibid., 260.
93. Ibid., 250.
94. For an example of the strong Catholic emphasis on the magisterial teaching office of the Church, see Aidan Nichols, *The Shape of Catholic Theology* (Edinburgh: T. & T. Clark, 1991), 248–60. On the Protestant side the lack of engagement with tradition continues in both the mainline and evangelical contexts.

vehicle through which the Spirit speaks. That is to say, the authority of the Bible is ultimately the authority of the Spirit whose instrumentality it is. Similarly, it is the work of the Spirit that accounts for the formation of the Christian community, the church. It is the Spirit who calls the community into existence and empowers it to accomplish his purposes, not least in the production and authorization of the biblical texts. These observations point in the direction of a helpful understanding of tradition.

The Faith Community and the Development of Scripture

Crucial in this context is an impulse from Dulles's observation about the genesis of "traditioning." This observation stands as a reminder that the community precedes the production of the scriptural texts and is responsible for their content and for the identification of particular texts for inclusion in an authoritative canon to which it has chosen to make itself accountable. Apart from the Christian community, the texts would not have taken their particular and distinctive shape. Apart from the authority of the Christian community, there would be no canon of authorized texts. In short, apart from the Christian community the Christian Bible would not exist.

The Bible, then, is the product of the community of faith that produced it. The compilation of scripture occurred within the context of the community, and the biblical documents represent the self-understanding of the community in which they were developed. In light of these phenomena, Paul Achtemeier comments that the "major significance of the Bible is not that it is a book, but rather that it reflects the life of the community of Israel and the primitive church, as those communities sought to come to terms with the central reality that God was present with them in ways that regularly outran their ability to understand or cope."[95]

Thus, the Bible represents the understanding of those members of the faith community who formed the enduring trajectory of that community. The scriptures witness to the claim that they are the final written deposit of a trajectory—a traditioning—that incorporates a number of varied elements in their composition, including oral tradition and other source documents. Within the community of faith these writings were recognized as authoritative materials that were interpreted and reapplied to various contemporary situations. Through the work of the Spirit these materials were collected and brought together throughout the course of the community's life in response to their corporate concerns. However, these concerns were subject to the sense of responsibility, induced by the guidance of the Spirit, to preserve for the sake of the community's continuity the witness to the events that shaped it, as well as the interpretation of those events and their particular applications to the life of the community.

---

95. Paul J. Achtemeier, *The Inspiration of Scripture* (Philadelphia: Westminster Press, 1980), 92.

That same faith community has corporately confessed the Spirit-inspired character of the canonical texts as a distinctive collection of documents to which it makes itself accountable.[96] Awareness of the role of the community in the production of the writings of scripture, that is, to the process of traditioning present already within the biblical era, leads to a broader concept of inspiration. While inspiration includes the composition of particular writings produced by individuals, it also incorporates the work of the triune God in the midst of the Hebrew and early Christian communities, leading these people to participate in the process of bringing scripture into being. By extension, the direction of the Spirit permeated the entire process that climaxed in the coming together of the canon as the book of the Christian community. Thus, although the church precedes scripture chronologically and is responsible for its formation, it has nevertheless, by it own corporate affirmation in the establishment of the canon, made itself accountable to scripture as the norming norm for its life, faith, and practice. In this sense, the text produces the community.

The Act of the Spirit

What unifies this relationship between scripture and communal tradition of the church is the work of the Spirit. It is the Spirit who stands behind both the development and formation of the community as well as the production of the biblical documents and the coming together of the Bible into a single canon as that community's authoritative texts. The community found these texts to be the vehicle through which they were addressed by the Spirit of God. The illuminating work of the Spirit brought forth these writings from the context of the community in accordance with the witness of that community. This work of illumination has not ceased with the closing of the canon. Rather, it continues as the Spirit attunes the contemporary community of faith to understand scripture and apply it afresh to its own context in accordance with the intentions of the Spirit.

The contemporary process of illumination parallels that experienced by the ancient faith communities insofar as the Bible contains materials that represent the appropriation by the community of the writings and oral traditions of their heritage, some of which are rejected as being contrary to the established trajectory of the community. Hence, the scriptures contain sharp critique and condemnation of some of the attitudes and actions of the ancient faith communities. At the same time, however, there is also a significant difference between the experience of the ancient faith communities and our relationship to scripture. The people of Israel and the early Christian communities engaged in the interpretive task *within* the process of the formation of the canon. Subsequent to the closure of the canon, the Christian community receives the illumination of the Spirit speaking through canonical scripture. Thus, in terms

96. Gabriel Fackre, *The Christian Story: A Narrative Interpretation of Basic Christian Doctrine*, 3rd ed. (Grand Rapids: Wm. B. Eerdmans Publishing Co., 1996), 19.

of the basic character of the relationship between scripture and the tradition of the church, canonical scripture is on the one hand constitutive of the church, providing the primary narratives around which the life and faith of the Christian community is shaped and formed, and on the other hand is itself derived from that community and its authority. In the divine economy scripture and tradition are in this manner inseparably bound together through the work of the Spirit.

For this reason, to suggest that the Protestant slogan *sola scriptura* implies an authority apart from the tradition of the church—its creeds, teachings, and liturgy—is to transform the formula into an oxymoron.[97] Separating scripture and church in such a manner was certainly not the intention of the Reformers. Indeed, historian Heiko Oberman contends that the issue of the Reformation was not scripture *or* tradition but rather the struggle between two differing concepts of tradition.[98] Commenting on the role of the community in the process that led to the production and identification of scripture, Achtemeier notes, "If it is true, therefore, that the church, by its production of Scripture, created materials which stood over it in judgment and admonition, it is also true that Scripture would not have existed save for the community and its faith out of which Scripture grew. That means that church and Scripture are joint effects of the working out of the event of Christ."[99] And this "working out" is carried on under the guidance and illumination of the Spirit.

In this conception, the authority of both scripture and tradition is ultimately an authority derived from the work of the Spirit.[100] Each is part of an organic unity, so that even though scripture and tradition are distinguishable, they are fundamentally inseparable. In other words, neither scripture nor tradition is inherently authoritative in the foundationalist sense of providing self-evident, noninferential, incorrigible grounds for constructing theological assertions. The authority of each—tradition as well as scripture—is contingent on the work of the Spirit, and both scripture and tradition are fundamental components within an interrelated web of beliefs that constitutes the Christian faith. To misconstrue the shape of this relationship by setting scripture over against tradition or by elevating tradition above scripture is to fail to comprehend properly the work of the Spirit. Moreover, to do so is, in the final analysis, a distortion of the authority of the triune God in the church.

A nonfoundational understanding of scripture and tradition locates ultimate authority only in the action of the triune God. If we must speak of a "foundation" of the Christian faith at all, then, we must speak of neither scripture nor tradition in and of themselves, but only of the triune God who is disclosed in

97. Robert Jenson, *Systematic Theology: Volume 1, The Triune God* (New York: Oxford University Press, 1997), 28.

98. Heiko A. Oberman, "Quo Vadis Petre? The History of Tradition from Irenaeus to Humani Generis," *Scottish Journal of Theology* 16 (September 1963): 225–55.

99. Achtemeier, *The Inspiration of Scripture*, 116.

100. For a treatment of scripture in the context of the work of the Holy Spirit, see Stanley J. Grenz, *Theology for the Community of God* (Grand Rapids: Wm. B. Eerdmans, 2000), 494–527.

polyphonic fashion through scripture, the church, and even the world,[101] albeit always normatively through scripture.

The same illuminating work of the Spirit that served to guide the community in the process of the composition, compilation, and canonization of scripture continues to lead and direct that community by speaking through the texts of scripture. In this way the action of the Spirit enables the Christian community to fulfill its task of living as the people of God in the various historical and cultural locations in which it is situated. This broader conception of the Spirit's illumination in the production of scripture and the ongoing life of the community leads not only to a more adequate understanding of the process by which scripture came into being but also to a greater appreciation for the theological significance of the tradition of the Christian community. We have suggested that the Christian tradition provides an important reference point and numerous resources for the contemporary community in its struggle to understand the meaning of scripture and engage in the task of theology in the context of the complex issues that characterize the present age. This assertion raises the following question: How does the Christian tradition provide these resources? Or put another way, How does the Christian tradition function in the task of theological construction?

The Nature of the Christian Tradition

Our response to this question begins with the nature of tradition itself. According to Alaisdair MacIntyre, a tradition begins with some contingent historical starting point, most often a text or a set of related texts, and develops from this starting point as a historically extended, socially embodied argument as to how best to interpret and apply the formative text(s).[102] From this conception of tradition in general, we can conceive of the Christian tradition as the history of the interpretation and application of canonical scripture by the Christian community, the church, as it listens to the voice of the Spirit speaking through the text. *The Christian tradition is comprised of the historical attempts by the Christian community to explicate and translate faithfully the first-order language, symbols, and practices of the Christian faith, arising from the interaction among community, text, and culture, into the various social and cultural contexts in which that community has been situated.*

In this understanding tradition is viewed not as static but rather as a living, dynamic concept in which development and growth occur. A tradition grows as it confronts new challenges and as it faces new situations and difficulties over the course of time and in various contexts. The Christian tradition is thus char-

---

101. On the development of the notion of God as the foundation for theology in the thought of Karl Barth, see William Stacy Johnson, *The Mystery of God: Karl Barth and the Postmodern Foundations of Theology* (Louisville, Ky.: Westminster John Knox Press, 1997).

102. Alasdair MacIntyre, *Whose Justice? Which Rationality?* (Notre Dame, Ind.: University of Notre Dame Press, 1988); and idem, *Three Rival Versions of Moral Enquiry: Encyclopaedia, Genealogy, and Tradition* (Notre Dame, Ind.: University of Notre Dame Press, 1990).

acterized by both continuity and change as the faith community, under the guidance of the Spirit, grapples with the interaction between scripture and the particular challenges of changing situations.

As we today examine this past heritage, we gain wisdom and insight from the results of the Spirit-guided reflection of the community on scripture. Gabriel Fackre rightly notes that the gift of the Christian community "comes to us in creed and council, catechism and confession, dialogue and proclamation. It meets us in the ancient lore of the Church and the present learnings of the Christian community. This common life and its wisdom, brought to us by the constant activity of the Holy Spirit, is a fundamental resource in our engagement with the biblical source."[103]

Insofar as the tradition of the Christian church is the product of the ongoing reflection of the Christian community on the biblical message, it is in many respects an extension of the authority of scripture. Thus, theologian Tom Oden suggests that the history of theology may be viewed in large measure as the history of biblical exegesis.[104] In addition to mediating the kerygma, the narrative of God's redemptive action toward human beings, scripture also provides a record of some of the basic Christian teachings and practices that developed in the earliest church. The canonical documents witness to these teachings and the concern of the early church that these basic teachings be communicated from one generation of Christian believers to the next. The narratives of God's redemptive activity and these basic teachings and practices of the early Christian community constitute what scripture calls "the faith which was once for all delivered to the saints"(Jude 3, KJV). This sense of passing on the teachings of the community from generation to generation is the most basic expression of the operation of tradition. Speaking of this body of early Christian beliefs, Robert Webber notes that its content "is basic to and even prior to theological formulation."[105] The contemporary believing community stands in the tradition of the ancient community who maintained and passed on this basic body of beliefs on which the church reflects theologically.

Although this commitment to pass on "the faith once delivered to the saints" is an important component of the Christian tradition, it can also be misconstrued and as a consequence used as the basis for oversimplifying a complex phenomenon. The assumption that tradition comprises an unchanged body of Christian doctrines articulated by the ancient church for all time, while in one sense true, can also be indicative of an understanding that fails to comprehend properly the dynamic character of tradition, viewing it instead in static terms. The dynamism of tradition, however, emerges out of its very nature within the life of the faith community.

---

103. Fackre, *The Christian Story*, 18.

104. Thomas C. Oden, *Systematic Theology: The Living God* (San Francisco: Harper & Row, 1987), xiii.

105. Robert Webber, *Common Roots: A Call to Evangelical Maturity* (Grand Rapids: Zondervan, 1979), 139.

From its inception, the Christian community has been concerned with the task of proclaiming its message to the ends of the earth in order that all humankind might know and experience the love of the Creator. In keeping with this concern the church has undertaken the mission of establishing communities of believers throughout the world. As a consequence, the Christian church as been located in a wide variety of social, historical, and cultural contexts, and it has faced the numerous challenges presented by these various situations. These challenges have called on the Christian community to exercise wisdom and creative judgment in addressing questions in a manner that best promotes its mission to announce the gospel and establish communities of Christ's disciples. A canonical example of this activity is the story of the Jerusalem Council (Acts 15), in which the church had to address the cultural issues raised by the conversion of Gentiles and their coexistence in the community of the new covenant with ethnic Jews who were concerned to preserve their social distinctiveness. Viewed from this perspective, tradition is comprised by the ongoing deposit of "wisdom" emerging from this dynamic movement of the community under the Spirit's guidance.

The multicultural character of the Christian community alerts us to an additional insight about tradition. All expressions of the faith are contextualized. This includes not only the confessions, creeds, and theological constructions of the church but also the content of the biblical documents themselves. All texts of the Christian faith were formulated within the social, cultural, linguistic, and philosophical frameworks of the times in which they were produced. This fact does not detract from the authority of scripture as the inspired and canonically constitutive standard of the Christian community. It merely alerts us to the incarnational character of the Bible and the challenges of contextualizing its message into new, varied, and changing settings. This observation calls likewise for a nuanced understanding of the tradition of the church as a source for theology.

Tradition as Theological (Re)Source

With these considerations in view, we are now in a position to suggest how tradition takes its rightful place in theological construction. To summarize what follows, the tradition of the Christian church serves as a source or a resource for theology, not as a final arbiter of theological issues or concerns but a hermeneutical context or trajectory for the Christian theological enterprise. Tradition provides this context as the constructive theologian examines the history of Christian worship, the history of Christian theology, and past theological formulations for the sake of articulating the belief-mosaic in the contemporary context.

The History of Worship

One of the most significant components of the Christian tradition is the history of worship and liturgy. The content and form of Christian worship throughout the history of the church provides an understanding of the context in which theologians have worked and insight into the primary commitments of the church. Recently, a renewed emphasis on the role of faith for theology has reminded us that theologians have not worked in isolation from the church to produce systems of theology untouched by the concerns of the community. Theologians are part of the community that prays and worships, and this context informs the nature and shape of their theological reflection.

The phrase *lex orandi, lex credendi*—the way you pray determines what you believe—addresses the intimate connection between the life of prayer and the content of faith. This phrase points to the interaction between theology and worship. What Christians believe shapes the content and approach of their worship, and their worship reflects what they believe. This connection alerts us to the importance of liturgical history as insight into the first-order commitments of the Christian community that have shaped its theological reflection.

Contemporary theology has recently developed a renewed interest in the relationship between worship and theology. Of particular significance is the work of Geoffrey Wainwright, whose systematic theology is written from the perspective of the liturgical forms of the church.[106] He examines the connection between liturgy and theology and draws attention to the ways in which the earliest Christian communities incorporated theological motifs into worship. He points out that the liturgy of the church is not simply or purely emotive in character, but includes intellectual elements as well, and that the connection between the two is entirely natural. Thus, Wainwright suggests that doing theology from a liturgical perspective serves to ground theology in the life and faith of the historical and ecumenical Christian community by pointing to the beliefs and concerns that have been expressed and emphasized in the forms and practices of Christian worship.

The History of Theology

Another aspect of the tradition of the Christian church that is particularly beneficial to the task of theology is the complex and multifaceted story of theological history that describes the responses of the Christian community to past challenges. Throughout its history the church has continually sought to proclaim and affirm the gospel in the context of the specific cultural situations in which it has been situated. The story of theological history is the narrative of the attempts by the Christian community to explicate the gospel message within these shifting historical circumstances.[107]

This theological history is important for contemporary theology for a number of reasons. Previous theological models and constructions are helpful for theology in that they provide the present community with a record of some of

---

106. Geoffrey Wainwright, *Doxology: The Praise of God in Worship, Doctrine, and Life* (New York: Oxford University Press, 1980).

107. For an excellent recent account of the narrative of theological history, see Roger Olson, *The Story of Christian Theology: Twenty Centuries of Tradition & Reform* (Downers Grove, Ill.: InterVarsity Press, 1999).

the failures of past efforts over the course of time. Ideas have consequences. But the long-term consequences of ideas are seldom fully discernable. The history of theology provides the opportunity to observe the long-term consequences of various theological formulations and approaches to theology in a number of different contexts.

Some of these formulations and approaches have clearly failed to sustain the community throughout its history. For example, overly accommodationist approaches to the relationship between theology and culture have had devastating long-term consequences for the church. Perhaps the most telling example of such accommodation has been the close linking of Christian faith with the goals and aspirations of particular nationalities or political ideologies at the cost of faithfulness to the gospel and the integrity of the community.[108]

The history of theology also brings us into contact with another type of failure, namely, that which has traditionally been labeled *heresy*. Awareness of those thinkers whose ideas about theology and Christian faith have been rejected by the Christian community remain instructive for contemporary theology. As Roger Olson points out, it is "almost impossible to appreciate the meaning of orthodoxy without understanding the heresies that forced its development."[109] The Christian community did not simply receive orthodox belief and pass it on in a static fashion. Rather, the community has struggled to determine the content and application of orthodoxy in ways that are faithful to the canonical narratives. This process grew through the challenges presented by those whose teachings were eventually deemed heretical. To cite one especially important example, understanding the development of orthodox conceptions of the Trinity requires that we grasp those views that both prompted and shaped the formation of the early conceptions of this doctrine.

Another significance of the history of heresy is the realization that, paraphrasing Luther, God sometimes strikes significant blows with a crooked stick. In other words, those who have held views that have been declared heretical by the church have often been of great importance in the development of theology. Perhaps the most striking example of this is found in the life and work of the early Alexandrian theologian Origen. One of the leading thinkers of his day, Origen may be considered the first systematic or constructive theologian in the history of the church. While many of his ideas were declared unorthodox and heretical after his death, his contribution to the development of early Christian thought and his intellectual achievement places him among the most significant theologians in the history of the church. His speculative theology provided the impetus for much of the theological reflection of the early Christian community and his essential vision of the Christian faith has remained highly influential throughout the history of the church.

---

108. For a fascinating study of this phenomenon as it manifested itself in Nazi Germany, see Robert P. Ericksen, *Theologians Under Hitler: Gerhard Kittel, Paul Althaus and Emanuel Hirsch* (New Haven: Yale University Press, 1985).

109. Olson, *The Story of Christian Theology,* 21.

More importantly, however, the history of theology suggests directions that might hold promise for the contemporary attempts of the community to fulfill its calling. Especially important in this respect are those formulations and symbols that have come to be regarded as "classic" theological statements.

"Classic" Theological Formulations and Symbols

Emerging from the history of worship and the history of theology is another particularly important aspect of tradition that informs contemporary theological construction: the preservation of classical theological formulations, symbols, and communal practices that have survived the test of time and thereby have remained an integral part of the community's life in its various cultural locations. For example, the near universal acceptance by the worldwide Christian community of ecumenical statements such as the Apostles' Creed and the Nicene Creed serves to make these "classic" symbols of the faith a vital resource for theology. Gabriel Fackre highlights this aspect of tradition viewed as an ecumenical consensus inherited from the past:

> Found in both official documents and formal statements of the undivided Church, such as the Apostles' and Nicene Creeds, the doctrines of the Person of Christ and the trinity, the patterns of affirmation implicit in the worship and working of faith of the church universal, tradition is a weighty resource in Christian theology.[110]

These "classic" statements and symbols of the historical community stand as milestones in the thought and life of the church universal and therefore have a special ongoing significance for the work of theology.[111]

The role of classic theological formulations is made clearer as we recall the broader historical implications of Christian confessions of faith for our own confession and our own theological statements. Throughout the history of the church, Christian believers from successive generations and various social, cultural locations have confessed and witnessed to faith in the God revealed in Christ. In this act they have participated in the faith of the one church and have been coconfessors with all who have acknowledged the one faith throughout the ages. So also, in confessing the one faith of the church in the present we become the contemporary embodiment of the legacy of faith that spans the ages and encompasses all the host of faithful believers. Rather than standing alone in this act, we confess our faith in unison with, and in solidarity with, the whole company of the church universal. Hence, although our expression of faith is to be contemporary, in keeping with our task of speaking the biblical message to the age in which we live, it must also place us in continuity with the faith of the

---

110. Fackre, *The Christian Story*, 18.
111. For a compilation of such "milestones" in the history of the church in its various expressions see Leith, *Creeds of the Churches*.

one people of God, including both our forebears who have made this confession in ages past and our successors who will do so in the future. When we engage in the second-order task of theology, therefore, we do so conscious that we stand in the context of a community of faith that extends through the centuries and that has engaged in this task before us. Because we are members of this continuous historical community, the theological tradition of the church must be a crucial component in the construction of our contemporary theological statements, so that we might maintain our theological or confessional unity with the one church of Jesus Christ.

As we have noted already, statements that have stood the test of time and have received broad affirmation among Christians of many generations and in many contexts comprise a type of "ecumenical theology." This "ecumenical theology" has come to expression as well in the great corpus of theological literature written over the centuries. The library of theological literature can be read with great benefit in the contemporary context, for it provides a considerable resource for the task of theology that, with few exceptions, has been largely untapped by Protestant theologians.[112]

Having asserted the essential significance of these past symbols of the faith, we must now voice an important reminder. These past creeds, confessions, and theological formulations are not binding in and of themselves. They are helpful as they provide insight into the faith of the church in the past and as they make us aware of the presuppositions of our own context. In addition, they stand as monuments to the community's reception and proclamation of the voice of the Spirit. Despite their great stature, such resources do not take the place of canonical scripture as the community's constitutive authority. Moreover, they must always and continually be tested by the norm of canonical scripture.

In addition, in our reading of the great theological literature we must keep in mind the culturally situated nature of all such statements and hence understand them within their particular historical and cultural contexts. For this reason, it is the *intent* of the creeds, confessions, and formulations, and not the specific construction and order of their wording, that is significant for contemporary theology.

An "Open" Confessional Tradition

The reminder stated previously stands as a challenge to those Christian confessional bodies and denominations who ascribe full authority to past confessional statements and demand complete subscription to these as criteria for participation in their fellowship. Such groups run the risk of transforming their creeds, even if unofficially or unintentionally, into de facto substitutes for scripture. In

---

112. A fine example of engaging the resources in this body of historical-theological literature to address contemporary theological issues is Ellen Charry, *By the Renewing of Your Minds: The Pastoral Function of Christian Doctrine* (New York: Oxford University Press, 1997).

the interest of securing an absolute authority in the church beyond the scriptures themselves, this approach can actually hinder such a community from hearing the voice of the Spirit speaking in new ways through the biblical text.

One especially significant confessional community is the Reformed tradition. Reformed denominations tend to be strongly confessional, often adopting a statement such as the Westminster Confession as a doctrinal standard and in some cases demanding a strict subscription to it for ordination into the ministry of the denomination. Unfortunately, some Reformed church bodies readily fall into the ironic position of evidencing methodological commitments similar to the medieval Catholic position rejected by their Reformation forebears and thus departing from one of the central concerns of the early Reformed communities, namely, the principle that the truly Reformed church must always be reforming itself in accordance with the teaching of scripture. As Jan Rohls points out in contrasting the Reformed and Lutheran traditions, in Lutheranism "the process of confessional development came to a conclusion with the Formula of Concord (1577) and the Book of Concord (1580). On the Reformed side there is nothing that corresponds to this conclusion."[113]

Jack Stotts provides a distinction that is helpful in this context, namely, the differentiation between "open" and "closed" confessional traditions. He writes,

> A closed tradition holds a particular statement of beliefs to be adequate for all times and places. An open tradition anticipates that what has been confessed in a formally adopted confession takes its place in a confessional lineup, preceded by statements from the past and expectant of more to come as times and circumstances change.[114]

Stotts then adds that an "open" confessional tradition understands its obligation to develop and adopt new confessions in accordance with shifting circumstances. Although such confessions are "extraordinarily important" for the integrity, identity, and faithfulness of the church, "they are also acknowledged to be relative to particular times and places." In addition, he adds that the "occasional" nature of confessions is a reminder "that statements of faith are always subordinate in authority to scripture."[115]

This concept of an "open" confessional tradition brings into relief the major function of tradition in the task of theology. In contrast to the demand for a strict subscription to a particular symbol or confession characteristic of a "closed" confessional tradition, the truly Reformed tradition is by its very nature "open." And this "openness," in turn, preserves the dynamic nature of tradition.

---

113. Rohls, *Reformed Confessions*, 9.
114. Jack L. Stotts, "Introduction: Confessing after Barmen" in Rohls, *Reformed Confessions*, xi.
115. Ibid.

Tradition's Eschatological Orientation

The tradition of the Christian community provides the context in which to hear the Spirit's voice speaking through the canonical texts of scripture in continuity with the church universal. We can conceive of this context as establishing and providing a Spirit-directed hermeneutical trajectory for theological reflection. This hermeneutical trajectory is not institutionalized, as Roman Catholic theologians have argued, but must be discerned through participation in the fellowship of the Christian community and its practices of worship, prayer, Bible reading, and service, as well as through study and reflection on the symbols and literature of the tradition.[116] That is to say, the task of Christian theology begins with commitment to and participation in the tradition of the church.[117] To participate in the fellowship of the Christian community is to participate in this hermeneutical trajectory and to embrace the joint responsibilities of maintaining continuity with the community of the past and addressing the context in which the community is situated. Many thinkers are now aware that we can only read and interpret scripture properly in light of hermeneutical history and the way in which the church uses the Bible. Clark Pinnock, to cite one example, points out that in this way tradition becomes "a defense in the church against individualism in interpretation."[118]

To understand the tradition of the church as providing a hermeneutical trajectory is to acknowledge the importance of tradition without elevating it to a position of final authority because of the ongoing life of the church as it moves toward its eschatological consummation. Throughout the course of the ebb and flow of the history of the church the Spirit is at work completing the divine program and bringing the people of God as a community into a fuller comprehension of the implications of the gospel. This activity of the Spirit will reach consummation only in the eschatological future. Until then the church must grapple with the meaning and implications of the biblical message for its context as it listens patiently and expectantly for the voice of the Spirit speaking afresh through scripture yet still continuous with the Spirit-guided trajectory of Christian tradition.

The unfolding of this trajectory has been characterized by the dialectic of continuity and change. In his overview of the history of theology, Roger Olson tells the story of the conversations and conflicts between "traditionalists," who were particularly concerned with maintaining the continuity of the faith, and "reformers," whose concern was primarily focused on correcting past formulations and addressing their particular context.[119] In the back and forth of these

---

116. On the importance of participating in the practices of the Christian community as crucial for engagement in the task of theology, see the works of James Wm. McClendon, particularly *Systematic Theology: Ethics* (Nashville: Abingdon Press, 1986).

117. Hart, *Faith Thinking*, 192–194.

118. Clark H. Pinnock, *The Scripture Principle* (San Francisco: Harper & Row, 1984), 217.

119. This dialectical tension is highlighted in the subtitle of Olson's work, *The Story of*

conversations in the midst of the life and ministry of the Christian community, its tradition has taken shape. The comment of Gabriel Fackre regarding the state of affairs in the church is helpful:

> The circle of tradition is not closed, for the Spirit's ecclesial Work is not done. Traditional doctrine develops as Christ and the Gospel are viewed in ever fresh perspective. Old formulations are corrected, and what is passed on is enriched. The open-endedness, however, does not overthrow the ancient landmarks. As tradition is a gift of the Spirit, its trajectory moves in the right direction, although it has not arrived at its destination.[120]

In short, at the heart of tradition and the role of tradition in theology is the eschatological directedness of the Spirit's work in guiding the community of faith into the purposes and intentions of God that form a divinely given *telos* ultimately realized only at the consummation.

Tradition and Performance

One final aspect of the function of the hermeneutical trajectory in the task of theology remains to be noted. This dimension emerges through the metaphor of performance.[121] Tradition provides an interpretive context for the task of living out or "performing" the deepest intentions of an established, historical community. The ultimate purpose of theology is not simply to establish "right belief" but to assist the Christian community in its vocation to *live* as the people of God in the particular social-historical context in which they are situated. The goal of theology is to facilitate and enable authentic "performance" of the Christian faith by the community in its various cultural locations. Tradition provides an essential component in this process.

Like a Mozart symphony that has only one score but many possible interpretations, the text of scripture has been subject to numerous interpretations over the centuries. While the score of the symphony is authoritative, it demands performance in order to realize the intention for which it was produced, and performance requires interpretation. However, not all interpretations of Mozart have equal integrity in the history of the performance of his works; some are too radical or idiosyncratic. Determinations as to the

---

Theology: Twenty Centuries of Tradition & Reform. Olson has also used this distinction between traditionalists and reformers to characterize current tensions in contemporary evangelical theology. Roger Olson, "The Future of Evangelical Theology," *Christianity Today* 42 (February 9, 1998): 40–48.

120. Fackre, *The Christian Story*, 18–9.

121. For the development of the metaphor of performance with respect to scripture, see Frances Young, *The Art of Performance: Towards a Theology of Holy Scripture* (London: Darton, Longman & Todd, 1990).

legitimacy or illegitimacy of particular interpretations and performances emerge in the context of tradition.

Frances Young offers a helpful perspective on the performative metaphor. She writes, "For classic performance, tradition is indispensable. A creative artist will certainly bring something inspired to the job, but an entirely novel performance would not be a rendering of the classic work. Traditions about appropriate speed and dynamics are passed from master (or mistress) to pupil, from one generation to another, and a radical performance will be deliberate reaction against those traditions if it violates them."[122] The tradition of the Christian community functions in much the same manner. It establishes a context for authentic interpretation and performance of the biblical message and its implications, which allows for creativity in addressing new situations while providing a basis for identifying interpretation that is not consonant with the historic position of the community.

N. T. Wright suggests a model of biblical authority that moves along similar lines.[123] He uses the analogy of a five-act Shakespeare play in which the first four acts are extant but the fifth has been lost. In this model the performance of the fifth act would be facilitated not by the writing of a script that "would freeze the play into one form" but by the recruitment of "highly trained, sensitive, and experienced Shakespearean actors" who would immerse themselves in the first four acts and then be told "*to work out a fifth act for themselves.*"[124] The first four acts would serve as the "authority" for the play, but not in the sense of demanding that the actors "should repeat the earlier parts of the play over and over again." Instead, the authority of these extant acts "would consist in the fact of an as yet unfinished drama, which contained its own impetus, its own forward movement, which demanded to be concluded in the proper manner but which required of the actors a responsible entering into the story as it stood, in order to first understand how the threads could appropriately be drawn together, and then to put that understanding into effect by speaking and acting with both *innovation* and *consistency*.[125]" Wright then suggests that this model closely corresponds to the pattern of the biblical narratives.

Such a model brings the role of Christian tradition in the task of theology into sharp relief. A key component of Wright's model, although not one he emphasizes, is the role of tradition. His actors were not only immersed in the first acts of the play, the textual authority, but also in the Shakespearean interpretive *tradition*, which also functions in an authoritative fashion, albeit a secondary one, in the performance of the final act. The Christian tradition provides a historically extended, socially embodied context in which to interpret, apply, and live out the communally formative narratives contained in the canonical texts.

122. Ibid., 45.
123. N. T. Wright, "How Can the Bible be Authoritative," *Vox Evangelica* 21 (1991): 7–32.
124. Ibid., 18.
125. Ibid., 19.

In this manner, the biblical narratives function as the norming norm for Christian faith and life. Nevertheless, the tradition of the community provides a crucial and indispensable hermeneutical context and trajectory in the construction of faithfully Christian theology. But this performance always occurs in a particular historical-cultural context. Therefore, in the next chapter we turn our attention to this dimension of the theological enterprise.

Chapter Five

Culture: Theology's Embedding Context

All the world's a stage,
And all the men and women merely players.
They have their exits and their entrances,
And one man in his time plays many parts.
> —William Shakespeare, *As You Like It*

The nations will walk by its light, and the kings of the earth will
bring their glory into it. . . . People will bring into it the glory and
the honor of the nations.
> —Revelation 21:24, 26 (NRSV)

According to Phyllis A. Tickle, contributing editor in religion to *Publishers Weekly,* "more theology is conveyed in, and retained from, one hour of popular television than from all the sermons that are also delivered on any given weekend in America's synagogues, churches, and mosques."[1] Tickle's observation captures a significant trend in contemporary life. Pop culture in general—and the entertainment industry in particular—has emerged as a potent shaper of the fundamental convictions of North American society, rivaling, if not surpassing, the church itself. Cognizant of this, certain voices today are suggesting that theology ought to engage with pop culture.

The current call to engagement with pop culture is one contemporary embodiment of a long-standing, crucial issue in theological method: What is the role—if any—of culture in theology?

Christian theologians have always been interested in the cultural context in

---

1. Phyllis A. Tickle, *God-Talk in America* (New York: Crossroad, 1997), 126.

which they lived. For the early centuries of church history, this context was largely shaped by the Greek philosophical tradition. As the gospel spread into the Roman Empire, Christian evangelists—beginning with Paul—sought to convey the Christian story to a Hellenistic world. Later, the second-century apologists expressed sympathy for philosophy, arguing that Christianity is the true philosophy.[2] Early in the third century, Clement of Alexandria even went so far as to suggest that Greek philosophy served as a "schoolmaster" bringing the Greeks to Christ.[3] Not all theologians, however, have agreed that culture has a role to play in theology. The rhetorical question "What does Athens have to do with Jerusalem?" has been trumpeted since Tertullian's day[4] by those who find no place for philosophy, and hence for culture, in theological construction.

Chapters 3 and 4 explored the relationship of theology to scripture and to heritage. We determined first that theology's norming norm lies in the Spirit speaking through the biblical text. Then we suggested that the heritage of the church marks the hermeneutical trajectory through which we hear the Spirit's voice in the Word. This chapter explores the third in the triad of sources that together constitute the perichoretic dance that informs and forms our theology. In this chapter, we seek to clarify the relationship of theology to culture, aware that the suggestion that theological construction ought to take culture seriously has been, and remains, controversial. Our purpose is to weigh into this debate as it impinges on the development of theological method. Setting forth our understanding of the place of culture in theology, however, will inevitably lead us to raise several fundamental questions as to the nature of theology itself.

What Is Culture?

En route to our goal, we must get clear in our minds what we mean by culture. Therefore, we begin our discussion with the idea of culture itself: What is culture? And how does culture function? These questions bring us directly into contemporary discussions in cultural anthropology.

The Rise of Cultural Anthropology

The word *culture* is derived from the Latin *cultivare* ("to till the soil"). This etymological connection to the practice of "cultivation" led to the original meaning of *culture*, namely, "the care and tending of crops or animals,"[5] especially as this

---

2. For a helpful summary, see Roger E. Olson, *The Story of Christian Theology: Twenty Centuries of Tradition and Reform* (Downers Grove, Ill.: InterVarsity, 1999), 54–67.

3. Clement of Alexandria, *The Stromata*, I.5.

4. Tertullian, *The Prescription Against Heretics*, ch. 7. It might be an overstatement to say that Tertullian espoused a radical rejection of classical philosophy and culture *per se*. What he objected to were the heresies that often resulted from the syncretism of pagan philosophy and Christian theology. See Justo L. González, *The Story of Christianity* (San Francisco: HarperSanFrancisco, 1984), 1:53–54.

5. For this background, see Michael Warren, *Seeing Through the Media: A Religious View of Communications and Cultural Analysis* (Philadelphia: Trinity Press International, 1997), 41.

activity is aimed at improving or perfecting its object. The idea of a specifically *human* culture, indicative of our use of the term, was likely a metaphorical extension of this "tending" process to the human person. Perhaps humans could also be "cultivated." As a result of this extension in meaning, *culture* came to be connected with the "development" or "refinement" of the human person.

For the ancient philosophers, the cultivation of the human person involved above all the mind, and it occurred through teaching.[6] The breakdown of the feudal system in Europe and the rise of the middle class led to a renewed emphasis on the idea of the cultured person, especially in intellectual circles in France, Germany, and Britain. The process was now understood, however, to be in keeping with the idea captured in the German term *Bildung*. The cultured person (*der gebildete Mench*) was one who had been educated to possess both intellectual capabilities and aesthetic sensibilities. Culture, in turn, was connected to the process of educating and refining the individual as well as denoting the artistic and intellectual products (such as art and literature) deemed to be the means to becoming, or to be expressions of, the "refined" person.

The resulting preference for what we might call "high culture" formed a marked contrast to the practices, customs, and even the language of the "uneducated" lower classes. Understood in this manner, culture was often used somewhat interchangeably with *civilization*, especially by Enlightenment thinkers in France. The civilizing task involved overcoming the chaotic diversity characteristic of the life of the "common people," which, the proponents of "civilization" concluded, marks a stage on the way toward the cultured society. In short, as Kathryn Tanner explains, "civilization or culture was a self-conscious construction of human beings, a self-directed form of education, something made rather than found, the product of reason rather than blind habit."[7]

While the idea of "high culture" still lives on in certain quarters, in the 1920s it was replaced by a far-reaching shift in the meaning of the term *culture*, especially in intellectual circles in the United States in the 1920s. Rather than denoting the ideal—the goal of an education process—*culture* came to refer to an already given dimension of human social life. Culture now consisted of the customs and rituals of a particular social group.

According to some historians, the genesis of this shift lay in the work of the British human scientist, Sir Edward Burnett Tylor. Tylor understood culture not so much as the refinement of the human person but as the high cultural achievements sustained through social institutions. Hence, he declares,

---

6. Hence, Cicero writes, "Moreover, to continue the same comparison, just as a field, however good the ground, cannot be productive without cultivation, so the soul cannot be productive without teaching. So true is it that the one without the other is ineffective. Now the cultivation of the soul is philosophy; this pulls out vices by the roots and makes souls fit for the receptions of seed, and commits the soul and as we may say, sows in it seeds a kind to bear the richest fruit when fully grown." Cicero, *Tusculan Disputations*, 2.5.13 in *Cicero in Twenty-eight Volumes*, trans. J. E. King, rev. ed. (Cambridge, Mass.: Harvard University Press, 1971), 18:159.

7. Kathryn Tanner, *Theories of Culture: A New Agenda for Theology* (Minneapolis: Augsburg 1997), 7.

"Culture or Civilization, taken in its wide ethnographic sense, is that complex whole which includes knowledge, belief, art, morals, law, custom, and any other capabilities and habits acquired by man as a member of society."[8]

Perhaps more significant in inaugurating the shift in meaning, however, were thinkers such as Franz Boas,[9] who introduced into the English discussion the German idea of *Kultur*, understood as the highest achievements of a particular society. Under this rubric, the customs and cultural forms of a particular people came to be viewed as a self-contained whole comprising the culture of that social group. As a result, *culture* could now be used in the plural.[10] There are many human societies; consequently, there are likewise a variety of human cultures.

This new social understanding of culture lay at the heart of the fledgling field of cultural anthropology that emerged after the 1920s. Seen from the anthropological perspective, culture—in the words of one writer—"refers to the whole way of life of a people." No longer limited to intellectual and artistic activity, culture was now viewed as extending to "behavior patterns, customs, beliefs, rituals, and the whole material apparatus of life, from tools to textiles, totems to sacred texts," to cite Martha Bayles's helpful description.[11] This broad anthropological understanding is evident in the typical cultural-anthropological description offered in 1948 by Melvin Herskovitz:

> [C]ulture is essentially a construct that describes the total body of belief, behaviors, knowledge, sanctions, values and goals that mark the way of life of a people. . . . In the final analysis it comprises the things that people have, the things they do, and what they think.[12]

Armed with this concept, modern anthropologists explored the specific pattern of behaviors that distinguishes any given society from all others.[13]

One goal of their work was to overcome the ethnocentrism often connected with the process of *Bildung*. The Enlightenment outlook tended to assume that one's own culture, together with its norms and values, comprises the standard by which the practices of all other societies are to be judged. In the place of such ethnocentrism, cultural anthropologists advocated "cultural relativism." This approach seeks to evaluate ideas, actions, and objects according to the norms

8. Edward Burnett Tylor, *Primitive Culture* (London: J. Murray, 1871), 1.

9. For this assessment, see Tanner, *Theories of Culture*, 19.

10. See George Stocking, *Race, Culture and Evolution* (Chicago: University of Chicago Press, 1982), 203. Writing as a historian of anthropology, Stocking describes here the shift in usage from "culture" to "cultures," a shift that he suggests was begun by Frank Boas.

11. Martha Bayles, "Immunity Not Surgery: Why It Is Better to Exert Cultural Authority than to Impose Censorship," in *Toward the Renewal of Civilization: Political Order and Culture*, ed. T. William Boxx and Gary M. Quinlivan (Grand Rapids: Wm. B. Eerdmans Publishing Co., 1998), 152–53.

12. Melvin Herskovitz, *Man and His Works* (New York: Alfred A. Knopf, 1948), 625.

13. See, for example, John W. Bennett and Melvin M. Tumin, *Social Life* (New York: Alfred A. Knopf, 1948), 208–9.

and values of the culture in which they are found, rather than on the basis of the observer's cultural norms and values.[14]

An episode of *Star Trek: The Next Generation* that aired several years ago provides an illuminating illustration of the anthropological idea of cultural relativism. An accident had robbed the Klingon member of the Enterprise crew, Lt. Worf, of the use of his legs. In Klingon society this tragedy meant that Worf was as good as dead and that aided by his next of kin he must take his life. Because the only other Klingon on the ship is his son, Alexander, who is too young to be involved, Worf has asked the ship's first officer and his best friend, Will Riker, to fill this role in the death ritual. Riker, however, is loath to cooperate in what in his society is a reprehensible act of suicide. Desiring advice as to how to respond to the request, Riker has gone to his commanding officer, the ship's captain, Jean-Luc Picard. In the ensuing conversation, the good captain attempts to help his second-in-command view the situation from Worf's perspective within the context of the Klingon community, with its unique set of beliefs, mores, and rituals. Picard points out that what appears immoral to Riker, being embedded in one particular moral community, is perfectly acceptable to the Klingon Worf.

The practice and principles of cultural anthropology have enjoyed wide influence. Even Christian anthropologists have drawn heavily from the cultural-anthropological model. This is evident, for example, in Stephen Grunlan and Marvin Mayers, who describe culture as including learned and shared attitudes, values, and ways of behaving, together with the material artifacts created by the members of a cultural group.[15] Similarly, Paul Hiebert defines culture as "the integrated system of learned patterns of behavior, ideas, and products characteristic of a society."[16] As this terse definition indicates, Hiebert—following cultural anthropology in general—places great emphasis on the unified character of culture. He explains, "Culture is an 'integrated system,' not a random assortment of quaint customs. Ideas, behavioral patterns, and material products are related to one another in cultural traits, and these are linked to each other in broader patterns called 'cultural configurations.'"[17]

Rethinking Culture

Modern cultural anthropology reigned nearly unchallenged for half a century. Yet in the 1980s and 1990s it came increasingly under attack. Once launched, the critique became so thoroughgoing that it brought some thinkers to the verge of discarding the term *culture* as hopelessly inadequate. Rather than eliminating the concept entirely, however, in the end the criticisms led to a

14. See, for example, William Graham Sumner, *Folkways* (Boston: Ginn and Company Publishers, 1906), 13, 58–59.

15. Stephen A. Grunlan and Marvin K. Mayers, *Cultural Anthropology: A Christian Perspective*, 2nd ed. (Grand Rapids: Zondervan, 1988), 39.

16. Paul G. Hiebert, *Cultural Anthropology*, 2nd ed. (Grand Rapids: Baker, 1983), 25.

17. Ibid., 30.

"chastened," postmodern understanding of culture that takes seriously the historical contingency of human personal and social life. Hence, most anthropologists agree with James Clifford's grudging acknowledgment: "Culture is a deeply compromised idea I cannot yet do without."[18]

At the heart of the newer understanding is a rejection of the "integrated" focus found in modernist definitions of culture such as that of Hiebert cited above. This critique includes a rethinking of how culture functions as an ordering principle, that is, how culture orders a society. Postmodern anthropologists have discarded the older assumption that culture is a given reality, a preexisting social-ordering force that is transmitted externally to members of a cultural group who in turn passively internalize it. This view errs in that it isolates culture from the ongoing social processes that produce and continually alter it, as well as from the human agents who are active in such processes.[19] The newer voices agree that culture is not a "thing";[20] it is not an entity standing above or beyond human products and learned mental structures.

The older understanding likewise focused on the idea of culture as what integrates the various institutional expressions of social life and binds the individual to society. This focus on the integrative role of culture is now suspect. According to Anthony P. Cohen, it has become one of the casualties of the demise of the "modernistic grand theories and the advent of 'the interpretive turn' in its various guises." These developments have spawned a tendency to treat culture "as that which *agg*regates people and processes, rather than *int*egrates them." In Cohen's estimation, the distinction between aggregating and integrating is important, because it elevates difference, rather than similarity, among people.[21] Thus, like their modern predecessors, postmodern anthropologists consider cultures as wholes; but rather than being monolithic, these wholes are internally fissured.[22]

The elevation of difference that typifies postmodern thinking has triggered a heightened awareness of the role of persons in culture formation. Rather than being sui generis and exercising a determining power over people, culture is the outcome and product of social interaction. Consequently, people are active creators, rather than passive receivers, of culture.[23]

This awareness leads, in turn, to a conflict model of society and culture. While continuing to acknowledge that culture functions as an agent of consensus building, postmodern anthropologists speak about an ongoing struggle to determine the meaning of public symbols and thereby to build a consensus.

18. James Clifford, *The Predicament of Culture: Twentieth Century Ethnography, Literature, and Art* (Cambridge, Mass.: Harvard University Press, 1988), 10.

19. Tanner, *Theories of Culture*, 50.

20. Roy G. D'Andrade, *The Development of Cognitive Anthropology* (Cambridge: Cambridge University Press,1995), 250.

21. Anthony P. Cohen, *Self Consciousness: An Alternative Anthropology of Identity* (London: Routledge & Kegan Paul, 1994), 118–19.

22. Tanner, *Theories of Culture*, 56.

23. Cohen, *Self Consciousness*, 118–19.

Within any society, they point out, human actors struggle over cultural elements so as to imbue them with preferred meanings and to appropriate them to support certain forms of social organization.[24] Consequently, as Alain Touraine points out, what binds people together is not so much a general framework of social relations, a clearly understood body of beliefs and values, or a dominant ideology as much as "a set of resources and models that social actors seek to manage, to control, and which they appropriate or whose transformation into social organization they negotiate among themselves."[25]

Of greatest importance to our discussion is the postmodern movement away from the focus on common human behaviors as comprising the essence of culture in favor of a greater concern for the connection between culture and meaning. Contemporary "cognitive anthropologists" no longer see culture as simply the customs, artifacts, and oral traditions of a people. Nor is it primarily the specific modes of behavior in which persons participate and thereby are integrated into a society. Rather it now denotes—to cite Cohen's description—"the framework of meaning, of concepts and ideas, within which different aspects of a person's life can be related to each other without imposing arbitrary categorical boundaries between them."[26] In other words, culture consists of "shared knowledge." It includes what people need to know so as to behave as functioning members of their society—to act the way they do, to make the things they make, and to interpret their experience in the distinctive way they do. In the words of Naomi Quinn and Dorothy Holland, culture involves the "presupposed, taken-for-granted models of the world that are widely shared (although not necessarily to the exclusion of other, alternative models) by the members of a society and that play an enormous role in their understanding of that world and their behavior in it."[27]

Anthropologists routinely look to Clifford Geertz (albeit not uncritically) for providing the impetus in this direction. Geertz described culture using the metaphorical language of the "web." Cultures comprise the "webs of significance" that people spin and in which they are then suspended.[28] As he expressed in his well-known, terse definition,

> [culture] denotes an historically transmitted pattern of meanings embodied in symbols, a system of inherited conceptions expressed in symbolic forms by means of which [people] communicate, perpetuate, and develop their knowledge about and attitudes toward life.[29]

24. Tanner, *Theories of Culture*, 56.

25. Alain Touraine, *Return of the Actor*, trans. Myrna Godzich (Minneapolis: University of Minnesota Press, 1988), 8, 26–27, 54–55.

26. Cohen, *Self Consciousness*, 96.

27. Naomi Quinn and Dorothy Holland, "Culture and Cognition," in *Cultural Models in Language and Thought*, ed. Dorothy Holland and Naomi Quinn (Cambridge: Cambridge University Press, 1987), 4.

28. Clifford Geertz, *The Interpretation of Cultures* (New York: Basic Books, 1973), 5.

29. Ibid., 89.

In Cohen's estimation, Geertz was thereby responsible for "shifting the anthropological view of culture from its supposedly objective manifestations in social structures, towards its subjective realisation by members who compose those structures." As a result, Geertz "was seminal in leading anthropologists to regard culture as more a matter of thinking than of doing."[30]

Connected to the shift to understanding culture as meaning has been a renewed interest in the role of the person in determinating and internalizing cultural meanings. Postmodern anthropologists are aware that even though a symbol or metaphor may be shared by the participants in a social group, its meaning is subject to private interpretation. Hence, the meaning of a public metaphor may actually differ from person to person,[31] for what a word, an object, or an event means to a particular individual depends on what one is experiencing at the moment as well as on the interpretive framework one brings to the moment, which in turn is a result of one's past experiences.

Postmodern anthropologists quickly add, however, that an awareness of the personal nature of meaning does not deny its public dimension.[32] Given that people share similar life experiences, a word, object, or event will typically evoke in them a similar interpretation. The frequently occurring or widely shared aspects of any such interpretation is its "cultural meaning." It is a *cultural* meaning, in that the object or event would evoke a different interpretation in people with different characteristic life experiences.[33] Hence, Claudia Strauss and Naomi Quinn define a cultural meaning as "the shared cognitive-emotional state that results when the mental structures of a group of people respond to typical objects and events in their world."[34]

The focus on the personal determination of cultural meaning has led to a more interactive understanding of the self. The self is social and cultural, acted on rather than autonomous. Yet, rather than being merely a passive creation of society and culture, the self is an active, proactive, and creative agent. As Cohen explains, "Constituted by society and made competent by culture, individuals make their worlds through their acts of perception and interpretation. The external world is filtered and, in the process, remade, by the self. It is in this sense that the self is the centre and the premise of the individual's world."[35]

The interplay of self and society, communal meaning and personal internalization, has led to the realization that culture is two sided: simultaneously public and private, "out there" and "in here, part of the social milieu and lodged in people's minds."[36] Culture resides in a set of meaningful forms and symbols that

30. Cohen, *Self Consciousness*, 135.

31. Ibid., 142.

32. For an example of a discussion of this relationship in the case of religious beliefs, see Melford E. Spiro, *Culture and Human Nature: Theoretical Papers of Melford E. Spiro*, ed. Benjamin Kilborne and L. L. Langness (Chicago: University of Chicago Press, 1987),161–84.

33. Claudia Strauss and Naomi Quinn, *A Cognitive Theory of Cultural Meaning* (Cambridge: Cambridge University Press, 1997), 6.

34. Ibid., 15.

35. Cohen, *Self Consciousness*, 115.

36. Strauss and Quinn, *Cognitive Theory*, 256.

from the point of view of any particular individual are largely given.[37] Yet these forms are only meaningful because human minds have the ability to interpret them.[38]

As a result of this realization, contemporary thinkers look at the interplay of cultural artifacts and the internalizing individual in the formation of meaning. In contrast to the earlier assumption that meaning lies in signs or in the relations among them, anthropologists now suggest that meanings are bestowed by the users of signs. Hence, meanings reside in people and not in things or in some nebulous space between people and things,[39] an emphasis that gives rise to the individual side of the culture equation. At the same time, individuals do not discover or make up cultural meanings on their own. Even the mental structures by which they interpret the world are developed through explicit teaching and implicit observation of others. Consequently, cultural meanings are both psychological states and social constructions.[40]

Ulf Hannerz represents the more complex understanding of culture that typifies contemporary thinking. He indicates that culture involves the interrelations of three dimensions: first, the shared way that people within a social unity think—that is, the host of mental entities and processes, concepts, and values—in short, the *meanings*—they share; second, the meaningful *external forms* a people share—that is, the vehicles through which these meanings are made public and hence accessible to the senses; and third, the *manner* in which cultural meanings and their external forms are spread over a population and its social relationships.[41] Terming his approach "interactionist," Hannerz argues that through their contacts with one another, people shape social structures. Societies and cultures, in turn, emerge and cohere "as results of the accumulation and aggregations of these activities."[42]

The Function of Culture

Our survey of the discussion in cultural anthropology leads to the conclusion that the primary focus of concern among contemporary thinkers lies in the making of cultural meaning as connected to world construction and identity formation. Hence, postmodern anthropologists view *culture* as a shorthand way of talking about the shared dimension of meaning making. But how does "culture" function in this process? And what types of cultural items contribute to the construction of meaning, world, and identity?

37. Geertz, *Interpretation of Cultures*, 45.
38. Ulf Hannerz, *Cultural Complexity: Studies in the Social Organization of Meaning* (New York: Columbia University Press,1992), 3–4.
39. Strauss and Quinn, *Cognitive Theory*, 253.
40. Ibid., 16.
41. Hannerz, *Cultural Complexity*, 7.
42. Ibid., 15.

Culture and Meaning

To pursue this question, we must remind ourselves of the socially constructed character of the world we inhabit and our personal identity within that world. We noted in chapter 3 the thesis of social constructionists such as Peter Berger that rather than inhabiting a prefabricated, given world, we live in a social-cultural world of our own creation.[43] At the heart of the process whereby we construct our world is the imposition of some semblance of a meaningful order on our variegated experiences. For the interpretive framework we employ in this task, we are dependent on the society in which we participate.[44] In this manner, society mediates to us the cultural tools necessary for constructing our world. Similar to Berger's model, Paul Hiebert declares,

> [C]ulture is made up of systems of shared concepts by which people carve up their worlds, of beliefs by which they organize these concepts into rational schemes, and of values by which they set their goals and judge their actions. Viewed in this way, culture is the model that provides the people in a society with a description and an explanation of reality.[45]

Berger's work continues to provide the foundation for contemporary thinking about culture.[46] Yet in keeping with postmodern sensitivities, contemporary anthropologists are less inclined to speak about grand, overarching cultural forms. Instead, they highlight the smaller and seemingly simpler cultural units, together with the connections among them. These "cultural schemas"[47] or "cultural models" are what bring persons together into social groups. Naomi Quinn and Dorothy Holland offer this summary: "The prototypical scenarios unfolded in the simplified worlds of cultural models, the nestedness of these presupposed models one within another, and the applicability of certain of these models to multiple domains all go far to explain how individuals can learn culture and communicate it to others, so that many come to share the same understandings."[48]

By means of these shared cultural schemas persons construct and internalize cultural meanings. Viewed from this perspective, people may be said to share a culture to the extent that they have similar experiences (i.e., experiences that follow the same general patterns as those of other members of the society)[49]

---

43. Peter L. Berger, *The Sacred Canopy: Elements of a Sociological Theory of Religion* (Garden City, N.Y.: Doubleday, 1969), 3–13.

44. Ibid., 20. See also Peter L. Berger and Thomas Luckmann, "Sociology of Religion and Sociology of Knowledge," *Sociology and Social Research* 47 (1963):417–27.

45. Hiebert, *Cultural Anthropology*, 28–29.

46. See, for example, David Morgan, *Visual Piety: A History and Theory of Popular Images* (Berkeley, Calif.: University of California Press, 1998), 7.

47. Strauss and Quinn, *Cognitive Theory*, 6–7.

48. Quinn and Holland, "Culture and Cognition," 35.

49. Strauss and Quinn, *Cognitive Theory*, 48.

mediated by shared humanly created products and learned practices, which lead them to develop a set of similar meaning-creating cultural schemas. The schemas provide the tools for ongoing identity formation, in that they comprise the framework for reconstructing memories of past events, for imparting meaning to ongoing experience, and for devising expectations for the future.[50]

Taken together, the cultural schemas constitute the world a person inhabits. They form what Pierre Bourdieu calls the "*habitus*," that is, the "*matrix of perceptions, appreciations, and actions*"[51]—"the range of conscious and unconscious codes, protocols, principles and presuppositions"[52]—that people enact as they fulfill their roles in their socially constructed world. Building from Bourdieu's concept, David Morgan offers this description of the "habitus": "We might say that a world or habitus consists of all the roles, scripts, stages, and past performances that form the common fund of a society and are instantiated or remembered in the choices an individual makes when interacting with others."[53] This habitus informs, modifies, and determines what a person does. And it generates the strategies that enable a person to cope with unforeseen and ever-changing situations.[54] Or as Quinn and Holland declare using the language of cultural models, "Cultural models frame our understanding of how the world works, including our inferences about what other animate beings are up to, and, importantly, our decisions about what we ourselves will do."[55]

Although this constructed world gives the semblance of being a given, universal, and objective reality, it is actually—to use Morgan's picture—"an unstable edifice that generations constantly labor to build, raze, rebuild, and redesign." He then adds,

> To use a literary metaphor, a world is a story that is told and retold in order to fortify its spell of enchantment. And there is never just one story, never just one world. Worlds collide with one another as well as contain within themselves the contradictions and disjunctures that must be mediated or concealed for the sake of a world's endurance.[56]

While maintaining the focus on the social construction of a meaning-filled world, contemporary thinkers home in on the construction of meaning as the task of the person within the social context. This suggests that the focal point of culture is not beyond, but rather within, the individual. The various aspects of

---

50. Ibid., 49.

51. Pierre Bourdieu, *Outline of a Theory of Practice*, trans. Richard Nice (Cambridge: Cambridge University Press, 1977), 82–83.

52. Morgan, *Visual Piety*, 7.

53. Ibid., 205.

54. Bourdieu, *Outline of a Theory of Practice*, 82–83, 72.

55. Quinn and Holland, "Culture and Cognition," 22.

56. Morgan, *Visual Piety*, 9.

culture assist a person in putting into practice the routines that constitute one's symbolic world. This process is not dictated by some ontologically superior, transcendent domain—the "mind" of culture, as it were. Rather the process arises from the storehouse of behaviors a person has observed, the stories one has heard, the images one has seen, and the material objects one possesses. As Morgan succinctly states, "The habitus is not situated above the clouds but in the memory, in the body of each social actor."[57]

Likewise the goal of the meaning-making task is the formation of personal identity within the context of the social group, that is, the socially constructed self. But this task, like that of the construction of culture itself, is never complete and is thus an ongoing process. Again we cite Morgan, who offers a lucid statement of the point:

> When we think of all the duties a person routinely per-
> forms, we realize that the self must be a dense, lifelong
> weave of roles, internalized templates, scripts awaiting
> completion and performance. We are each relatively
> unique deposits of enactments, of countless reinforcing
> strata. Invested in the historical forms that generate it, the
> self draws in its every act and decision from the habitus.
> . . . As each self's evolved uniqueness in turn interacts with
> others and with the institutions of society, new roles are
> created. We each enact roles that we create, rewrite, inherit,
> or have thrust upon us. The self, then, is not a loose con-
> figuration of roles but a vast repertoire cohering around a
> tightly knit core, itself a historical formation but one whose
> origin occurred so early in life that it is unavailable to
> memory and, in its earlier phases, hardly distinguishable
> from the biology of pleasure and pain that make up the
> infant's life.[58]

Purveyors of Cultural Meaning

According to Hannerz, culture involves the meanings people share, the external forms that embody those meanings, and the manner in which meanings are filtered throughout a society. Through cultural meanings, persons construct the world they share with others as well as their own identity within that world. But what are the central contributors to and carriers of cultural meaning? For the answer, anthropologists look to a variety of types of cultural items, including language, material objects, images, and rituals. What brings these seemingly disparate items together is their role as symbols, that is, their function as both builders and conveyers of meanings that lie beyond themselves.

57. Ibid., *Visual Piety*, 205.
58. Ibid., 204–5.

Symbols and the Symbolic World

Geertz's "classic" definition of culture—"an historically transmitted pattern of meanings embodied in symbols, a system of inherited conceptions expressed in symbolic forms"[59]—reminds us of the central importance of symbols to culture. The world we inhabit is a symbolic world. We construct our world and communicate our understanding of ourselves and the world through a variety of symbols that together form elaborate systems. In fact, the primary purpose of humanly devised symbolic systems is to convey meanings and thereby facilitate the world-constructing task. Hence, the value of symbols lies in their connection to meaning, which in turn resides in the mind rather than in the symbols themselves. As Paul Hiebert explains, "[Symbols] link physical things with mental concepts, and these concepts can be distinguished from the form and immediate context of the symbols and can be combined in new contexts to create new ideas. . . . Symbols thus become labels for abstract concepts."[60]

Despite our tendency to confuse symbols with their meanings, there is no necessary connection between a symbol and what it symbolizes; the assigning of meanings to symbols is arbitrary. At the same time, symbols are generally a public, rather than merely a private, matter. It is this public aspect of symbols that leads to their importance as purveyors of cultural meaning. And the public dimension of symbols, in turn, fosters participation in social groups. Again we cite Hiebert's conclusion:

> The fact that symbol systems can be held in common with other people makes cultures possible. Ideas and knowledge can be passed from one generation to the next, accumulating and changing as people have and create new experiences and reinterpret old ones. Thus, people learn the symbol systems of their particular culture.[61]

Foundational to the working of symbols is their representative character: A symbol represents something else. But through this representing function, a symbol participates in the power and meaning of what it stands for.[62] Further, a symbol becomes a means to opening up a level of meaning for which nonsymbolic communication is inadequate.[63] According to Paul Tillich, symbols are able to disclose the deepest dimension of human existence. He writes,

---

59. Geertz, *Interpretation of Cultures*, 89. Similarly, Raymond Williams declares that culture functions as a "signifying system through which a social order is communicated, reproduced, experienced and explored." Raymond Williams, *The Sociology of Culture* (New York: Schocken Books, 1982), 13.
60. Hiebert, *Cultural Anthropology*, 115.
61. Ibid., 118–19.
62. Paul Tillich, *Theology of Culture*, ed. Robert C. Kimball (New York: Oxford, 1959), 54.
63. Ibid., 56.

We can call this the depth dimension of reality itself, the dimension of reality which is the ground of every other dimension and every other depth, and which therefore, is not one level beside the others but is the fundamental level, the level below all other levels, the level of being itself, or the ultimate power of being.[64]

Language

Symbols come in various shapes and sizes. Yet perhaps the most widely employed—even paradigmatic—symbolic systems are linguistic. Indeed, language ranks as the central cultural form involved in the world-constructing and meaning-creating task.[65]

Language provides the conceptual tools through which we construct the world we inhabit. As Paul Hiebert asserts, "We cannot perceive nature or think or communicate about it without language, but language, to a great extent, also molds what we see and how we see it."[66] In addition, linguistic concepts serve as the vehicles through which we communicate and thereby share meaning with others. In the words of Peter Berger and Thomas Luckmann, "Language objectivates the shared experiences and makes them available to all within the linguistic community, thus becoming both the basis and the instrument of the collective stock of knowledge."[67]

Rather than speaking the language of grand, unified linguistic worlds, contemporary cognitive anthropologists focus on the function of words in "framing" a simplified world in which prototypical events unfold. To cite one widely used example, in a world in which men marry at a certain age and marriages last for life, *bachelor* denotes a man who stays unmarried beyond the usual age and thereby has become eminently marriageable.[68] Multiplying this example and applying it to the various dimensions of life leads to the importance of language in the process of making and transferring cultural meaning.

Things

As central as language is in the world-creation process, it is not the only purveyor of meaning. Thinkers today are exploring the role of other vehicles that have taken on increased importance in our contemporary consumer society. One such means to the production of meaning is what we might call "things."[69]

---

64. Ibid., 59.

65. Quinn and Holland, "Culture and Cognition," 9.

66. Hiebert, *Cultural Anthropology*, 119.

67. Peter L. Berger and Thomas Luckmann, *The Social Construction of Reality: A Treatise in the Sociology of Knowledge* (New York: Anchor Books, 1967), 68.

68. See Charles J. Fillmore, "An Alternative to Checklist Theories of Meaning," in *Proceedings of the First Annual Meeting of the Berkeley Linguistics Society*, ed. Cathy Cogen et al. (Berkeley, Calif.: Berkeley Linguistics Society, 1975), 128. See also Quinn and Holland, "Culture and Cognition," 23.

69. Examples of such studies include Grant McCracken, *Culture and Consumption: New*

Things are significant aspects of the world we inhabit. In fact, we might say that we construct a world populated by things, and the kinds of things that populate it carry a powerful influence on the character of the world we construct. Material objects also play a crucial role in the formation and maintenance of selfhood in contemporary social life. According to Mihaly Csikszentmihalyi, things counter the process through which the self fades into unfocused, chaotic activity. To this end, material objects invest the human self with a degree of objectivity, for they assert and maintain a person's identity in the face of an omnipresent flux of sensation and mental activity. For example, material objects display power and social status. They secure the continuity of the self over time by acting as focal points in the present, perpetuating traces from the past and encapsulating expectations for the future. And things provide material evidence of one's position in the web of social relations.[70]

The automobile is one obvious example. Not only has it been a potent shaper of contemporary society through its function as the dominant form of transportation, the automobile has become a symbol representing deeper dimensions of personal identity and our socially constructed world.

More recently, this world has become not only populated by but also constructed by the "screen" — by the movie, television, and computer screens.[71] For many people, what—and only what—is seen on the screen, especially the television screen, is deemed truly important.[72] The symbolic power of the screen also functions at a somewhat less obvious level. In the world of the screen the contrast between the subjective self and the objective world is blurred. The screen is not merely an external object we look at. Rather than being either "out there" (merely on the screen) or in us,[73] what "happens" on the screen seems to occur in some "space" (cyberspace) between the two. The screen brings us into its world, just as it enters into ours. Further, the screen creates a world in which truth and fiction are easily blurred. And it fosters an outlook that views the self as a collector of experiences, as a repository of the transitory, fleeting images produced and fostered by the diversity of contemporary media forms.

Approaches to the Symbolic Character of Consumer Goods and Activities (Bloomington, Ind.: University of Indiana Press, 1990); Daniel Miller, *Material Culture and Mass Consumption* (Oxford: Basil Blackwell Publisher, 1987); Steven Lubar and W. David Kingery, eds. *History from Things: Essays on Material Culture,* (Washington, D.C.: Smithsonian Institution Press, 1993).

70. Mihaly Csikszentmihalyi, "Why We Need Things," in Lubar and Kingery, *History from Things,* 22–23. See also Mihaly Csikszentmihalyi and Eugene Rochberg-Halton, *The Meaning of Things: Domestic Symbols and the Self* (New York: Cambridge University Press, 1981), esp. 90–120.

71. For a fuller treatment, see Stanley J. Grenz, *A Primer on Postmodernism* (Grand Rapids: Wm. B. Eerdmans Publishing Co., 1996), 31–36.

72. Arthur Kroker and David Cook, *The Postmodern Scene: Excremental Culture and Hyper-Aesthetics* (New York: St. Martin's Press, 1986), 268.

73. Jean Baudrillard, "The Ecstasy of Communication," in *The Anti-Aesthetic,* ed. Hal Foster (Port Townsend, Wash.: Bay Press, 1983), 126–34.

Images

Also crucial in the making of meaning are "images." In fact, Western society has become what Michael Warren calls an "image culture."[74] Warren differentiates between two broad types of images, iconic (or representational) and metaphoric-perceptual.

Iconic images are pictures that we actually see with our eyes. They depict some person, place, object, event, or narrative. Such images are significant because of their power to invoke mimesis, that is, their ability to move the viewer to imitate the behavior the image represents. En route to this end, iconic images tend to create assumptions about the world and determine the ways we relate to others. In Warren's words, "What we see tends to construct a way of seeing and can, even further, become institutionalized in patterns of interaction between persons."[75]

Not only do we look *at* images; more important, we look *through* images. The images through which we see are what Warren calls "metaphoric images."[76] As humans, we understand and name the world we inhabit by means of images. These images provide the lens through which we see, in that they form our underlying "sense of things." Thereby they bring a fundamental pattern to our experience and provide coherence to our world. Charles Davis goes so far as to assert that metaphoric images "are the constitutive elements of the world of human meaning."[77] Such images are culturally specific, for they are operative within a particular social order.

While providing a composite vision of life, images also participate in the collision of worlds that characterizes culture. Images often serve either to mend or to conceal places of disjuncture and contradiction. They may buttress one of the colliding worlds, safeguard the boundaries of the more familiar world, or mend the tears that occur when the fabric of a world wears thin. According to Morgan, images accomplish this task by "tirelessly repeating what we have always known, as if the ritual act of repetition might transfigure a belief into a condition of nature."[78]

Ritual

Morgan's comment leads us to what Roy Rappaport considers "*the* basic social act,"[79] ritual.[80] Ritual carries this foundational importance, he argues, because societies rest on shared understandings of reality that are constituted ritually,

74. Warren, *Seeing Through the Media*, 122.
75. Ibid., 132.
76. Ibid., 152, 154.
77. Charles Davis, "Religion and the Sense of the Sacred," *Proceedings of the Catholic Theological Society of America* 31 (1976): 90.
78. Morgan, *Visual Piety*, 9–10.
79. Roy Rappaport, *Ecology, Meaning, and Religion* (Richmond, Calif.: North Atlantic Books, 1979), 174, 197.
80. For a discussion of the role of rituals, see Tom F. Driver, *The Magic of Ritual: Our Need for Liberating Rites that Transform Our Lives and Our Communities* (San Francisco: HarperSanFrancisco, 1991).

that is through shared performance, long before they come to be privately or inwardly believed.[81] In addition, ritual brings together what language, by its very nature, divides. According to Rappaport, whereas the distinctions of language "cut the world into bits—into categories, classes, oppositions, and contrasts"—ritual unites or reunites "the psychic, social, natural, and cosmic orders which language and the exigencies of life pull apart."[82]

As a dimension of culture, rituals provide a foundation for society, in that they create and maintain order.[83] This function of rituals arises from their ability to represent a structured world by marking times and spaces, and by symbolizing realities. Hence, the performance of a ritual does not merely remind the performers of an underlying order; it actually establishes that order.[84] For this reason, rituals can be "factive," to cite Rappaport's characterization; they can cause things to happen. Such rituals establish the propriety and obligatory character of particular acts. But the role of ritual goes even deeper. Ritual performance, Rappaport writes,

> is not always performative in a simple way, merely bringing into being conventional states of affairs through conventional actions. It is, rather *meta*-performative and *meta*-factive, for it *establishes*, that is, it stipulates and accepts, the conventions in respect to which conventional states of affairs are defined and realized.[85]

One crucial aspect of the means by which ritual establishes social order is through what Driver calls the "confessional mode" of ritual.[86] Through their participation in ritual, people accept the social order denoted by the ritual. Because participation in ritual marks a public acceptance of a public order, ritual forms a powerful basis for the public order it maintains.[87] But even more significant is the fact that ritual is able to link temporal order with an ultimate, absolute transcendent order, of which the temporal order is merely a contingent part.[88] Consequently, as Rappaport concludes regarding ritual,

> We are confronted, finally, with a remarkable spectacle. The unfalsifiable supported by the undeniable yields the unquestionable, which transforms the dubious, the arbitrary, and the conventional into the correct, the necessary, and the natural. This structure is, I would suggest, the foundation upon which the human way of life stands, and it is realized in ritual.[89]

81. For example, Rappaport, *Ecology, Meaning, and Religion*, 193–94.
82. Ibid., 206.
83. Huizinga, for example, links this role of ritual with its character as "play." Johan Huizinga, *Homo Ludens: A Study of the Play-Element in Culture* (London: Paladin, 1970), 22–23.
84. Rappaport, *Ecology, Meaning, and Religion*, 197.
85. Ibid., 194.
86. Driver, *The Magic of Ritual*, 148.
87. Rappaport, *Ecology, Meaning, and Religion*, 194.
88. Ibid., 214.
89. Ibid., 217.

The Cultural "Stage"

Our discussion of the contemporary conversation in cultural anthropology yields the conclusion that we inhabit socially constructed worlds to which our personal identities are intricately bound. The construction of these worlds, as well as the formation of personal identity, is an ongoing, dynamic, and fluid process, in which the forming and reforming of shared cultural meanings play a crucial role. Culture includes the symbols—the language, material objects, images, and rituals—that provide the shared meanings by means of which we understand ourselves, pinpoint our deepest aspirations and longings, and construct the worlds we inhabit. And through the symbols of our culture we express and communicate these central aspects of life to each other, while struggling together to determine the meaning of the very symbols we employ in this process.

Drawing from the famous line of Shakespeare, then, we might say that all the world's a stage, albeit a stage of our own construction. By participating in the making of meaning, we contribute to the creation of the context in which we act out our socially designed roles and gain our sense of identity. Yet rather than being fixed and stable, this socially constructed stage is in constant flux—sometimes imperceptible to us, sometimes obvious to all, but changing nonetheless. Over the course of our life narratives, our sense of personal identity (and hence the parts we play) shifts along with the changes in our constructed world.

Theology and Culture

To be human means to be embedded in culture. Some aspects of culture appear to come to us as a preexistent given, for we sense that we are products of a cultural tradition that predates us and forms us. At the same time, we interpret for ourselves and internalize the cultural meanings that we share with other participants in the ongoing conversation about meaning that marks the shifting context we call "our" culture. But what does all this have to do with theology? To this question we now turn our attention. Our answer begins as we add one additional aspect to the discussion of culture that has occupied us thus far in this chapter.

Culture and Religion

In our sketch of developments in cultural anthropology, we left out one important dimension of the contemporary understanding of culture—one that we hinted at, however, when we mentioned that ritual links the temporal order with the transcendent. This additional dimension is the connection between culture and religion. Indeed, a variety of thinkers find a close, even integral, relationship between the two. But what is this connection?

Aspects of the Connection

One way of understanding the connection between religion and culture emerges when one looks at religious artifacts as a dimension of a broader phenomenon called *culture*. In this view, religious forms provide one vehicle for the expression of the deeper sensitivities endemic to a particular people, sensitivities that manifest themselves in a variety of forms, which are therefore deemed "cultural." Hence, Bernard Meland declares, "[R]eligious expression is, itself, a cultural occurrence, not only in the sense of partaking of a cultural coloring but in the deeper sense of giving voice to human hungers, anxieties, and appreciations which, in turn, exemplify and articulate the cultural psyche."[90]

At the same time, the connection could conceivably move in the opposite direction. We might see cultural artifacts as giving expression to the underlying religious ethos of a particular society. T. S. Eliot reflects this understanding: "We may . . . ask whether what we call the culture, and what we call the religion, of a people are not different aspects of the same thing: the culture being, essentially, the incarnation (so to speak) of the religion of a people."[91] According to Paul Tillich, "religion is the substance of culture, culture is the form of religion." Consequently, the one "who can read the style of a culture can discover its ultimate concern, its religious substance."[92]

While not rejecting either of these approaches, the understanding propounded in cultural anthropology tends to develop a sociological connection between culture and religion, the foundation for which lies in the social construction theories of Peter Berger. As we noted earlier, Berger theorizes that we construct our world as we draw from a culturally mediated interpretive framework—a "common order of interpretation" we share within a society—so as to impose a meaningful order on the multiplicity of experiences we encounter.[93] Berger does not focus his attention on society, however, but moves to religion. "Throughout human history," he and Thomas Luckmann write, "religion has played a decisive part in the construction and maintenance of universes," that is, in the socially constructed worlds humans inhabit.[94] Religion's role is to legitimate the world endemic to any particular society by locating it and its institutions within a sacred, cosmic frame of reference, by bestowing on its members a sense of being connected to ultimate reality, and by giving cosmic status to its interpretative framework.[95] In short, religion is "the human enterprise by which a sacred cosmos is established."[96] And insofar as cultural expressions speak about what a society believes to be ultimate, they are religious.

In this way, Berger draws a connection between religion and the process of legitimating a society and its institutions. More recently, other thinkers have pushed his seminal idea into the realm of personal identity formation. They speak about the role of religion in legitimating—that is, in safeguarding—the

90. Bernard Eugene Meland, *Faith and Culture* (Carbondale, Ill.: Southern Illinois University Press, 1953), 82.

91. T. S. Eliot, *Notes Towards the Definition of Culture* (London: Faber & Faber, 1948), 28.

92. Tillich, *Theology of Culture*, 42–43.

93. Berger, *Sacred Canopy*, 20.

94. Berger and Luckmann, "Sociology of Religion and Sociology of Knowledge," 422.

95. Berger, *Sacred Canopy*, 32–36.

96. Ibid., 25.

identity of the self within the socially constructed world. Hence, David Morgan asserts, "It is the function of religious images in visual piety to secure the world or sense of reality in which the self finds its existence."[97]

Christianity and Cultural Artifacts

There was a time in Western society when what we often call "culture" was closely connected to the Christian church. Especially in the Middle Ages, artistic productions—whether in music or in the fine arts—focused almost exclusively on religious themes and served the worship life of the church. Even the linguistic world that inhabitants of medieval Europe populated was largely oriented around church teachings. However, beginning in the Renaissance and advancing in the Enlightenment art came to be increasingly disengaged from its former ecclesiastical setting, opening the way for the secularization of artistic work in particular and cultural expression in general that typifies modern society.

One intriguing aspect of the postmodern situation is what we might refer to as the "respiritualization" of cultural expression. In a manner unprecedented in the late modern era, contemporary North Americans appear to be open to the spiritual,[98] even though participation in traditional organized religion has nosedived.[99] Tom Beaudoin explains the sensitivities behind this development among members of his generation: "Xers take symbols, values, and rituals from various religious traditions and combine them into their personal 'spirituality.' They see this spirituality as being far removed from 'religion,' which they frequently equate with a religious institution."[100]

Many of Beaudoin's generation transfer the religious quest from institutionalized ecclesiastical forms to pop-cultural expression. Their "lived theology" is not expressed in the sacred practices of traditional religions, especially Christianity, but in and through popular culture.[101] In a sense, pop culture as we know it today is the invention of the baby boomer generation. Boomers not only elevated pop-culture icons, from Elvis Presley to the Beatles, into international heroes but also transformed them into objects of veneration. The popcultural realm boomers inaugurated has for subsequent generations become a

---

97. Morgan, *Visual Piety*, 205.

98. See, for example, John Naisbitt and Patricia Aburdene, *Megatrends 2000: Ten New Directions for the 1990s* (New York: Avon Books, 1990), 295–96.

99. According to a recent poll, eight out of ten adult Canadians say they believe in God, 82 percent consider themselves to be "somewhat" or "very spiritual," and about half report that their lives have become more spiritual in the last several years (Sharon Doyle Driedger, "On a Higher Plane," *Maclean's* 108/52 [Dec. 25, 1995–Jan. 1, 1996]: 23). Nevertheless, less than 25 percent attend church regularly. Similarly, although 80 percent of the students in David Batstone's religion classes at the University of San Francisco claim that they are "not religious," the same percentage think of themselves as "spiritual" (Martin Wroe, "American Pie in the Sky," *Third Way* 18/7 [September 1995]:13).

100. Tom Beaudoin, *Virtual Faith: The Irreverent Spiritual Quest of Generation X* (San Francisco: Jossey-Bass, 1998), 25.

101. Ibid., 18.

given, a central dimension of life in which they are steeped nearly from the cradle. As Beaudoin says, "[W]e are nurtured by the amniotic fluid of popular culture with the media as a primary source of meaning. . . . We express our religious interests, dreams, fears, hopes, and desires through popular culture."[102] In addition, Beaudoin notes that the shared set of cultural referents that shape the meaning systems and values of his generation consists largely of certain pop-culture "events."[103]

The findings of Beaudoin and others reaffirm the presence of a integral connection between culture and religion. Many of the cultural symbols by means of which we construct our world and form our identity are fundamentally religious or take on a religious character. This observation raises crucial questions for theological method. What are the implications of the connection between culture and religion for theology? Is there—or ought there to be—a corresponding connection between theology and culture? And to what extent should Christian theologians take culture seriously in their constructive work?

A Culture-Sensitive Theology?

As we noted earlier, the question of the relationship between culture and theology has been with us since the first century. However, beginning in the late nineteenth century with the advent of the liberal-theological project, it took on a new sense of urgency, a situation that has continued unabated into the present.

The Liberal-Conservative Context

Following in the footsteps of Schleiermacher, liberals were committed to the task of reconstructing Christian belief in the light of modern knowledge. They believed that theology dared not ignore the new scientific and philosophical understandings that had arisen in Western society. The survival of Christianity, they believed, depended on its ability to adapt to the new thinking.[104] Liberal theology, therefore, was characterized, in the words of Claude Welch, by a "maximum acknowledgment of the claims of modern thought."[105] In keeping with this concern, liberal thinkers sought to give place to culture in their theological reflections—so much so that it is now fashionable to fault them for linking theology too closely to the culture of the day.[106] Concerned about the risks

102. Ibid., xiv.
103. Ibid., 22.
104. In the words of one student of liberalism, adherents of the movement "would have agreed on the necessity of giving renewed strength and currency to Protestant Christianity by adapting it to the spiritual wants of the modern man, even if much that the past had accepted without demur would have to be discarded." Bernard M. G. Reardon, *Liberal Protestantism* (Stanford, Calif.: Stanford University Press, 1968), 10.
105. Claude Welch, *Protestant Thought in the Nineteenth Century, Volume I, 1799–1870* (New Haven and London: Yale University Press, 1972), 142.
106. See, for example, Gordon R. Lewis and Bruce A. Demarest, *Integrative Theology*, 3 vols. (Grand Rapids: Zondervan, 1987–1994), 1:89.

entailed in what they saw as blatant cultural accommodation, many conservatives argued that theology involves the discovery of transcultural truth[107] and consequently that theologians need give little, if any, thought to culture.[108]

While the dangers involved in accommodating the faith to culture are real, the quest to construct a culture-free theology is misguided. We simply cannot escape from our particular context into some transcultural intellectual vantage point. On the contrary, all theology is by its very nature as a human enterprise influenced by its cultural context. In fact, when we look back to the supposedly grand, culture-free, timeless theological systems of past eras, we can see how culturally conditioned they actually were.

The quest for a culture-free theology is also theologically and biblically unwarranted. Rather than coming to us in transcultural form, divine truth is always embedded in culture. As Lesslie Newbigin points out, this is the case with the gospel itself: "We must start with the basic fact that there is no such thing as a pure gospel if by that is meant something which is not embodied in a culture. . . . Every interpretation of the gospel is embodied in some cultural form."[109] Justo González confirms this assessment. "The knowledge of Christ never comes to us apart from culture, or devoid of cultural baggage," he writes. González then explains,

> From its very inception, the gospel was proclaimed within a culture. Jesus came to his contemporaries within the circumstances of the Jewish culture of his time and place. It was as Jews—more concretely, as Galilean Jews—that his first disciples received him. Ever since, in the passage to the various forms of Hellenistic culture, in the conversion of the Germanic peoples, and in every other missionary enterprise and conversion experience, people have met Christ mediated through cultures—both theirs and the culture of those who communicated the gospel to them.[110]

As González's statement suggests, the culture-specific nature of divine truth arises directly out of the doctrine of the incarnation, with its reminder that the

107. Hence, Lewis and Demarest alert the reader of their systematic theology that "the study of each basic Christian doctrine begins with a problem of permanent, transcultural significance." Lewis and Demarest, *Integrative Theology*, 1:9. At the same time, Lewis and Demarest favor contextualization in some sense of the term. They assert that in addition to being faithful to revealed truth, theology must also be "clear and significant for the present generation of Christians and the unreached people we serve." *Integrative Theology*, 1:38.

108. Following in the footsteps of the nineteenth-century conservative theologian Charles Hodge, Wayne Grudem does not include a section on culture in his systematic theology. Nor does the term appear in the index to the volume. See Wayne Grudem, *Systematic Theology: An Introduction to Biblical Doctrine* (Grand Rapids: Zondervan, 1994).

109. Lesslie Newbigin, *The Gospel in a Pluralist Society* (Grand Rapids: Wm. B. Eerdmans Publishing Co., 1989), 144.

110. Justo L. González, *Out of Every Tribe and Nation: Christian Theology at the Ethnic Roundtable* (Nashville: Abingdon Press, 1992), 30.

Word became flesh in a specific cultural context (John 1:14). As the incarnate one, Jesus ministered to culturally embedded people in first-century Palestine in a culturally sensitive manner. Indicative of this, he approached the Samaritan woman (John 4:1–24) in a manner quite different from his response to Nicodemus (John 3:1–21). Similarly, Paul readily drew from Greek cultural artifacts, including the works of pagan poets, in his conversation with the Athenian philosophers (Acts 17:28). John Goldingay notes, "Paul is *the* great discursive theologian in scripture, but his systematic, analytic thinking characteristically takes the form of contextual theological reflection."[111] These examples suggest that our calling is likewise to serve the present generation by speaking within and to the cultural context in which God has placed us. Hence, González rightly criticizes theological descriptions that retreat from culture in "arrogant abstinence" for "failing to take seriously the Christian insistence on the particular incarnation in human history and culture of the creating and consummating God."[112]

Considerations such as these have led a chorus of voices to call for cultural relevance. But theologians display a variety of understandings as to what this actually means. According to Geoffrey Wainwright, to cite one example, relevance is largely a Christological affirmation: Jesus is "culturally relative." This involves the recognition that as a particular historical event, the incarnation occurred "in the cultural form appropriate to that time and place," and consequently that "the particular man Jesus is—criteriologically—related to all culture and history."[113] More significant—and controversial—than Wainwright's proposal have been two suggestions as to what the desire for cultural relevance means for theological method: the programs of correlation and contexualization.

The Method of Correlation

One theologian who sought to negotiate a position between the seemingly opposite extremes of liberalism and conservatism (while rejecting the Roman Catholic approach as well) was Paul Tillich. Tillich argued that the "supernaturalistic" method of conservatives, whether of the fundamentalist or the neoorthodox variety, is inadequate in that it ignores the questions and concerns (the "situation") of humans who are to receive the message. By assuming that the Word of God itself creates the possibility for its acceptance,[114] this approach fails to realize that humans cannot receive answers to questions they have never asked.[115] Tillich found the liberal "naturalistic" or "humanistic" method, which

111. John Goldingay, *Models for Scripture* (Grand Rapids: Wm. B. Eerdmans Publishing Co., 1994), 365.

112. David Dawson, *Literary Theory* (Minneapolis: Fortress Press, 1995), 16–17.

113. Geoffrey Wainwright, *Doxology: The Praise of God in Worship, Doctrine and Life* (New York: Oxford University Press, 1980), 360.

114. Paul Tillich, *Systematic Theology*, 3 vols. (Chicago: University of Chicago Press, 1951) 1:64–65.

115. Ibid., 1:65.

attempts to derive theological answers from the natural human state, equally suspect. It overlooks the estrangement of human existence and the fact that revelation (which contains the answers) is something spoken *to* humans, not *by* them to themselves.[116]

In their stead, Tillich proposed his well-known method of correlation, which, in his words, "explains the contents of the Christian faith through existential questions and theological answers in mutual interdependence."[117] Because the questions are raised by philosophy through careful examination of human existence, the theologian must first function as a philosopher. Then in a second step, the theologian draws on the symbols of divine revelation to formulate answers to the questions implied in human existence, which philosophy can discover but not answer. The theologian's task is to interpret the answers of revelation so that they remain faithful to the original Christian message while being relevant to the questions asked by secular men and women.

Recently several theologians have offered variants on the general theme of correlation. One important example is Gordon Kaufmann, who understands theology through its connection to the universal human question of meaning posed within the context of the mysteriousness of life. Theology provides the Christian response to the quest for a pattern of fundamental categories (a worldview) that can orient, guide, and order human life so as to promote "human flourishing and fulfillment," that is, "human wholeness, well-being, or salvation."[118] In a somewhat similar manner, David Tracy seeks to correlate the specific symbols and categories of Christianity to what he sees as universal human realities.[119]

During his own lifetime, Tillich's method of correlation received mixed reviews. Critics chided him for giving autonomous philosophy too much independence from and authority over revelation. More specifically, they wondered how such a discipline, disrupted by the tensions inherent in finite reason, can be trusted to formulate the right questions in the right manner. Critics worried that the substance and form of the questions set forth by a philosophy that had not been fully "converted" by the Christian faith would lead to a distortion or obscuring of the Christian "answers."[120]

More recently the whole correlationist approach has come under fire for its inability to take seriously the emphasis of contemporary cultural anthropology on the specificity and plurality of cultures. Rather than searching for the characteristics of some universal culture-in-general, anthropologists are interested in particular cultures. This development in anthropology would seem to disallow

116. Ibid., 1:65.

117. Ibid., 1:60.

118. Gordon Kaufman, *In Face of Mystery* (Cambridge, Mass.: Harvard University Press, 1993), 41–42, 47.

119. David Tracy, *The Analogical Imagination: Christian Theology and the Culture of Pluralism* (New York: Crossroad, 1981), 405.

120. George F. Thomas, "The Method and Structure of Tillich's Theology" in Charles W. Kegley, ed., *The Theology of Paul Tillich* (New York: Pilgrim Press, 1982), 137–38

the attempt to engage in a method of correlation that formulates human universals as the context into which theological constructions are subsequently fitted. Instead, contemporary cultural anthropology encourages theologians to focus on the particular and to see theology as a part of a concrete, specific, communally shaped way of life.[121]

This appraisal suggests that the chief difficulty with any method of correlation is its inherent foundationalism. The correlating enterprise assumes some discoverable universal human reality—some structure of human existence or some essential human characteristic—on which the theological edifice can be constructed. As we have already noted, the foundationalist project has become highly suspect. Consequently, we must be wary of all attempts to correlate Christian faith with supposed human universals.

Contextualization

Another attempt to craft a theological method leading to a culturally relevant theology in the wake of liberal-conservative debate has its genesis not in theology itself but in missiology, more particularly in the missiological question of "gospel and culture." In response to the changing global situation of the church and developments in the missionary movement, missiologists have called for the inculturation or, more preferably, the contextualization[122] of the gospel. A reoccurring theme among missiologists is the importance of engaging in the inculturation process with a view toward culture, rather than from the perspective of assuming the gospel (that is, with a particular understanding of the gospel) as a transcultural given.

Robert Schreiter provides a typical example.[123] He rejects the model that pictures the process as the gospel encountering culture. According to this model, the gospel seeks to "purify" the culture by affirming what is good and true in it, while challenging and correcting what it deems to be evil or sinful. This approach assumes that although the gospel can become inculturated in any culture, it in fact transcends every culture.

While not denying "the transcending character of the gospel or the power of faith to criticize and transform culture,"[124] Schreiter nevertheless questions whether the model of the gospel encountering culture can really bring about inculturation. He avers that lying behind such an approach is a misunderstanding as to how intercultural communication takes place. In Schreiter's words, "It assumes that a message communicated by someone from one culture will be received and understood by someone in another culture precisely in the

121. For this critique and proposal, see Tanner, *Theories of Culture*, 66–67.
122. For the preference of this term, see Stephen B. Bevans, *Models of Contextual Theology* (Maryknoll, N.Y.: Orbis Books, 1992), 22.
123. See, for example, Robert Schreiter, "Inculturation of Faith or Identification with Culture?" in *Christianity and Cultures: A Mutual Enrichment*, ed. Norbert Greinacher and Norbert Mette (London: SCM Press, 1994).
124. Ibid., 16.

way that its sender intended."[125] Schreiter, in contrast, is convinced that "the gospel never enters a culture in pure form" but "is always already inculturated— embedded in the culture of the evangelizer," so that the "already inculturated faith" will naturally "emphasize some features of the message and necessarily de-emphasize others."[126]

Instead of this questionable approach, Schreiter advocates looking to the dynamics of culture as the starting point. Genuine inculturation, he believes, requires that one

> begin with the culture to be evangelized, and imagine a more dialectical approach to the relation between gospel and culture in which the presentation of the gospel is gradually disengaged from its previous cultural embeddedness and is allowed to take on new forms consonant with the new cultural setting.[127]

More influential in evangelical circles has been Fuller Seminary missiologist Charles Kraft, who devised a contextualizing missions strategy that elevated meaning above form. He begins with the anthropological principle that meanings can be conveyed to humans only through cultural forms or symbols. Humans, in turn, develop and perpetuate cultural forms within a cultural system, because these forms serve as conveyers of meaning from and to those who use them. According to Kraft, the forms are essentially neutral, in contrast to the "non-neutral, subjective use that human beings make of their cultural patterns."[128] This distinction provides Kraft with the basis for contextualization, in that it allows him to conclude that Christian meanings can be communicated through human cultural forms. Hence, he asserts that "relative cultural forms" are able to serve as the vehicles for expressing "absolute supracultural meanings," for the divine message, "while appropriately expressed in terms of those forms, transcends both the forms themselves and the meanings previously attached to those forms."[129]

The missiologists' call for contextualization suggests a parallel model for theological construction. Consequently, contextualization as a theological method has won a hearing across the theological spectrum.[130] Evangelical theologians have been especially interested in this approach,[131] welcoming it as a way of overcoming the ahistorical nature of conservative theologies that, by focusing on the transcultural nature of doctrinal construction, fail to take seriously the social context

---

125. Ibid.
126. Ibid.
127. Ibid.
128. Charles H. Kraft, *Christianity in Culture: A Study in Dynamic Biblical Theologizing in Cross-Cultural Perspective* (Maryknoll, N.Y.: Orbis Books, 1979), 391.
129. Ibid., 99.
130. For a helpful summary of the major approaches to contextualization prevalent today, see Bevans, *Models of Contextual Theology*.
131. See, for example, John Jefferson Davis, *Foundations of Evangelical Theology* (Grand Rapids: Baker, 1984), 60–72.

of the theological task and the historicity of all theological reflection. Evangelical proponents of contextualization fault their conservative forebears' approach for its tendency to promote a repetition of traditional formulations of biblical doctrine, rather than attempting to offer appropriate recontextualizations of the doctrines in response to changing cultural and historical conditions.[132]

While being critical of the lack of contextualization in conservative theology, evangelicals nevertheless generally maintain their forebears' focus on doctrine. Hence, Millard Erickson defines theology as "that discipline which strives to give a coherent statement of the doctrines of the Christian faith, based primarily upon the Scriptures, placed in the context of culture in general, worded in a contemporary idiom, and related to issues of life.[133]

While seeking to avoid the cultural accommodation that in the eyes of critics beset the older theologies of correlation, "mainline" theologians, in contrast, have tended to pursue the contextualization of theology through the pattern of correlation articulated so well by Tillich, a pattern that has its roots in liberalism. Douglas John Hall provides a typical example. On the one hand, he advocates a theological method that, reminiscent of Tillich, begins squarely with the contemporary cultural context:

> [C]ontextuality in theology means that the *form* of faith's self-understanding is always determined by the historical configuration in which the community of belief finds itself. It is this world which initiated the questions, the concerns, the frustrations and alternatives, the possibilities and impossibilities by which the *content* of the faith must be shaped and reshaped, and finally confessed.[134]

On the other hand, Hall cautions against acquiescing to dominant cultural values. Appealing to the example of the biblical prophets, he calls for a theology that is "inherently suspicious of dominant values and trends," is characterized by "neither a priori approval nor a priori disapproval of society," and seeks engagement or dialogue with society.[135]

With this caution, Hall is echoing a fear acknowledged earlier by David Kelsey: "In being conditioned by the limits culture sets on what is seriously imaginable, theological proposals may turn out to be merely restatements of what is already imagined in the culture apart from Christianity's central reality."[136] The potential toward radical cultural accommodation remains one of the chief criticisms voiced by critics of the program of contextualization.

132. Ibid., 67.
133. Millard J. Erickson, *Christian Theology,* 3 vols. (Grand Rapids: Baker, 1983), 1:21.
134. Douglas John Hall, *Thinking the Faith: Christian Theology in a North American Context* (Minneapolis: Fortress Press, 1991), 84.
135. Ibid., 114–15.
136. David H. Kelsey, *The Uses of Scripture in Recent Theology* (Philadelphia: Fortress Press, 1975), 173.

Of equal importance is another criticism Hall voices. He fears that taking seriously the contextual dimension will lead theology to become narrowly focused on its own social setting. In an insightful statement, he explains what this unwholesome process might look like:

> Wishing to be witnesses to the Eternal within its own time and place, the disciple community may find itself the captive of currents and ever-changing trends within its host society. Because it seeks to respond concretely to these currents and trends, it may lose sight of long-range questions to which its greater tradition tried to speak. A tendency to permit the issues of the historical moment to determine its witness may emerge. Then the theological community ceases to recognize, not only that these issues may be transient, but that matters of greater magnitude may be hidden by the surface concerns with which it has busied itself. Perhaps it will even go so far as to let its context, rather glibly conceptualized, become the touchstone for any kind of theological 'relevance,' so that it retains out of the long tradition only what seems pertinent to the moment, and disposes of the rest as being *passe*.[137]

Hall worries that this process will result in theology having "nothing of its own to bring to the analysis of its host society or the resolution of that society's ills," becoming "little more than a religious variation on existing opinions and mores." He is also concerned that the construction of local theologies could fragment the church into "theological provinces which are no longer capable of communicating with one another meaningfully, being so thoroughly identified with the problematic of their separate cultures." If this were to occur, the church would forfeit its ecumenical character and its potential for "worldwide witness" at the very time in the history of the planet when "both analysis and cure must be *global*."[138]

Warnings such as these are important. Yet they do not pinpoint the most significant potential difficulty with contextualization as a theological method. Similar to correlation, with which it shares certain common features, contextualization generally functions in a foundationalist manner. Yet the foundationalist character it evidences moves in a direction opposite from what the method of correlation displays. Rather than acknowledging the particularity of every human culture, correlationists are prone to universalize the culture pole and fit theological construction into it. Contextualizers, in contrast, can all too readily overlook the particularity of every understanding of the Christian message. Despite their heroic attempts to the contrary (and some notable exceptions[139]),

---

137. Hall, *Thinking the Faith*, 111–12.
138. Ibid., 112.
139. These exceptions include those who engage in what Bevans calls "the synthetic model." See Bevans, *Models of Contextual Theology*, 81–96.

contextualizers are tempted to assume too readily a Christian universal, which in turn functions as the foundation for the construction of the theological superstructure, even though its architects articulate this superstructure in the language of the culture to whom they are seeking to speak. This is especially evident in Kraft's model, based as it is on a distinction between the transcultural gospel and its expression through neutral cultural forms. Yet even as cautious a missiologist as Schreiter moves in this direction, in that his model likewise seems to assume the existence of some pure, Platonic gospel with a "transcending character."

Despite the debilitating difficulty they share from their foundationalist roots, taken together correlation and contextualization point the way forward. Held in tandem, the two models suggest that our theological method must employ an interactive[140] process that is both correlative and contextual. Theology emerges through an ongoing conversation involving both "gospel" and "culture."

While drawing in this manner from both methods, in one vital way the process of theologizing we are envisioning stands apart from both. Unlike either correlation or contextualization, this model presupposes neither gospel nor culture—much less both gospel and culture—as preexisting, given realities that subsequently enter into conversation. Rather, in the interactive process both gospel (that is, our *understanding* of the gospel) and culture (that is, our *portrayal* of the meaning structure, shared sense of personal identity, and socially constructed world in which we see ourselves living and ministering) are dynamic realities that inform and are informed by the conversation itself. Hence, we are advocating a specifically nonfoundationalist, interactionalist theological method.

The Interaction between Theology and Culture

Apart from a few noteworthy exceptions, a near consensus has emerged among theologians today that says theology must take culture seriously. Colin Gunton states the point starkly but succinctly: "[W]e must acknowledge the fact that all theologies belong in a particular context, and so are, to a degree, limited by the constraints of that context. To that extent, the context is one of the authorities to which the theologian must listen."[141] But what form should this "listening" take? We concluded the previous section by calling for an interactional model that brings "gospel" and "culture" together in critical and mutually informing conversation. Now we want to fill in a few of the details regarding what such a conversation involves.

---

140. For this descriptor we are indebted to William Dyrness, *Learning about Theology from the Third World* (Grand Rapids: Zondervan, 1989), 29.

141. Colin Gunton, "Using and Being Used: Scripture and Systematic Theology," *Theology Today* 47/3 (October 1990): 253.

Addressing the Context

One purpose of theological reflection is to facilitate the community of Christ in addressing contemporary people. If people inhabit a "socially constructed reality," as sociologists such as Berger and Luckmann suggest,[142] culture must become a crucial tool in this aspect of theological work. Discerning what characterizes the socially constructed worlds people around us inhabit places us in a better position to address the generation God calls us to serve. Doing so, however, necessitates that we conceptualize and articulate Christian beliefs— the gospel—in a manner that contemporary people can understand. That is, we must express the gospel through the "language" of the culture—through the cognitive tools, concepts, images, symbols, and thought forms—by means of which people today discover meaning, construct the world they inhabit, and form personal identity. This aspect of our missiological calling is advanced as well, as we come to understand how Christian faith addresses the problems, longings, and ethos of contemporary people, knowing that the social context in which we live presses on us certain specific issues that at their core are theological.

Viewed from this perspective, the task of theology includes "understanding the times" to assist the community of Christ in living as a gospel people in the wider contemporary social context and proclaiming the gospel message in that context. To this end, the theological enterprise does well to draw from "cultural artifacts," for they offer a window into the psyche of people with whom we desire to engage the gospel. This dimension of the use of culture in theology involves three interrelated steps, which are logically separable but in practice occur almost simultaneously.

The first, "hearing," entails being observant of the various venues that provide a cultural voice, that give expression to the ethos of our day, or that embody the often unexpressed inner longings and structure of meaning indicative of people in our society. Examples of these venues include literature, music, film, television programming, art, even newspapers and magazines, as well as expressions of our institutional life.

In the process of "hearing," however, we must bear in mind that our exegesis of cultural phenomena will not be an "objective" hearing. Rather than viewing culture as neutral observers, we will engage with our context as participants in the faith community. We will bring the categories of our own meaning structures and beliefs to the conversation we seek to have with culture. In short, just as there is no culture-free reading of the biblical text and no culture-free construction of Christian theology, so also there can be no "theology-free" reading of culture and cultural artifacts. What we hear will come filtered through our particular Christian-theological hearing aid.

"Hearing" is closely connected to "scrutinizing." This act involves the process of bringing to the surface the particular assumptions, beliefs, or meaning

142. Berger and Luckmann, *Social Construction of Reality*, 189.

structure lying behind,[143] motivating, or being expressed in cultural phenomena. The goal of our "scrutinizing" activity is to gain a window into what people actually think, sense, and believe about themselves and the world they inhabit, as well as to determine what cultural meanings are exercising a molding influence on people today.

To this end, we engage cultural artifacts in conversation by asking the specific questions that our particular theological stance raises. Hence, we will seek to understand the conceptions of God, ourselves, and the world that are bound up with the cultural items under scrutiny. We raise such questions as, How does this cultural item disclose what people today believe about themselves, the world, and transcendent meaning? And in the scrutinizing process, we seek to determine why the particular cultural item "resonates" with people today.

"Hearing" and "scrutinizing" remain incomplete without "responding." This includes, of course, offering a theologically informed appraisal of the beliefs and meaning structures expressed in cultural phenomena. Hence, we seek to determine the extent to which the cultural meanings and underlying belief assumptions square with Christian outlooks. "Responding" also involves ascertaining the extent to which the cultural artifact offers a bridge for engaging the Christian faith with those who find in the item an expression of their own sensitivities—that is, asking in what sense (if any) the item serves as a point of contact with the gospel or even an expression of gospel sensitivities.

Culture and the Spirit

"Responding" cannot end here, however. If rather than seeing "gospel" and "culture" as preexisting realities, we realize that both our understanding of the gospel and the meaning structures through which people in our society make sense of their lives are dynamic, the conversation between them ought to be mutually enriching. Not only does the theological interplay between gospel and culture serve to optimize our ability to address our context; it also ought to enrich our theological construction. For this reason, we must consider the extent to which our cultural context in general and any particular cultural expression in particular ought to lead us to reconsider our understanding of the Christian faith. Indeed, whether occurring directly or, more likely, indirectly, culture can be a means through which we gain theological insight. In short, reading our culture can assist us in reading the biblical text to hear more clearly the voice of the Spirit. But on what basis and in what sense can we speak of culture as the voice of the Spirit?

In chapter 3 we developed an understanding of the Spirit's speaking through scripture. We noted that the Spirit, who always speaks in accordance with the Word, speaks most clearly through the word and, since the completion of the

143. For a similar suggestion, albeit following a more Tillichian approach, see Bernard E. Meland, *Fallible Forms and Symbols: Discourses of Method in a Theology of Culture* (Philadelphia: Fortress Press, 1976), 123.

canon, more particularly through the inscripturated word. Yet the Spirit's speaking through scripture is always a contextual speaking; it always comes to its hearers within a specific historical-cultural context. Of course, throughout church history the Spirit's ongoing provision of guidance has always come, and now continues to come, as the community of Christ as a specific people in a specific setting hears the Spirit's voice speaking in the particularity of its historical-cultural context. But the same principle was operative even during the biblical era. In fact, the canon itself was the product of the faith communities that heard the Spirit speaking within their changing contexts, often speaking through literary materials that they had gathered and preserved, but leading to the composition of additional texts.

The specificity of the Spirit's speaking means that the conversation with culture and cultural context is crucial to the hermeneutical task. We seek to listen through scripture to the voice of the Spirit, who speaks to us in the particularity of the historical-cultural context in which we live. Hence, Douglas John Hall rightly argues that because theology must be in touch with life in the here and now, the questions and concerns it brings to the scriptures are not necessarily identical with those of the exegetes. Instead, he says, "[w]hat theology needs from its ongoing discourse with the biblical text is determined in large measure by its worldly context," so that it might "address its world from the perspective of faith in the God of Abraham, Isaac, and Jacob, the God whom Jesus addressed as 'Abba.'"[144]

This hermeneutical process occurs in part as contemporary "knowledge"— the discoveries and insights of the various disciplines of human learning— informs our theological construction. For example, theories about addictions and addictive behavior can provide insight into the biblical teaching about sin. Likewise, current discoveries about the process of human identity formation assist us in becoming aware of the many dimensions entailed in the new identity the Spirit seeks to create in us through our union with Christ. Our theological reflections can draw from the so-called "secular" sciences, because ultimately no discipline is in fact purely secular. More important, because God is the ground of truth, as Wolfhart Pannenberg so consistently argues, all truth ultimately comes together in God. Theology therefore draws from all human knowledge, for in so doing it demonstrates the unity of truth in God.[145]

Christian thinkers have always drawn images from the surrounding world as well as insights from the "latest scientific findings" to facilitate them in understanding and articulating Christian truth. A classic example is the profound effect that sociopolitical changes—such as the rise of feudal society and later the advent of nation-states—had on the development of atonement theories. Perhaps a more mundane area is that of church music, which has a long history of drawing from popular culture. Hence, typical of compositions of that era,

144. Hall, *Thinking the Faith*, 263.
145. Wolfhart Pannenberg, *Systematic Theology*, trans. Geoffrey Bromiley, 3 vols. (Grand Rapids: Wm. B. Eerdmans Publishing Co., 1990), 1:59–60.

the lyrics of the nineteenth-century gospel song, "Let the Lower Lights Be Burning," draw from the perils of ocean travel to state a Christian truth. Because the piece avoids completely the "language of Zion," it could easily be sung at a gathering of the local Maritime Rescue Society. Yet within the Christian context for which it was written, it issues a powerful call to believers to remain faithful in the task of evangelism.

These considerations, however, have not yet brought us to the heart of the pneumatological basis for hearing the Spirit's voice in culture. Much of Western theology has focused on the church as the *sole* repository of all truth and the *only* location in which the Holy Spirit is operative. The biblical writers, however, display a much wider understanding of the Spirit's presence, a presence connected to the Spirit's role as life-giver. As we noted in chapter 3, the pneumatology of the biblical faith communities arose out of the connection of "spirit" with "breath" and consequently with "life." The ancient Hebrew writers speak of the Spirit as the divine power creating (Gen. 1:2; 2:7) and sustaining life (Ps. 104:29–30; Isa. 32:15; cf. Job 27:3; 34:14–15), and hence causing creaturely life to flourish.

Because the life-giving Creator Spirit is present wherever life flourishes, the Spirit's voice can conceivably resound through many media, including the media of human culture. Because Spirit-induced human flourishing evokes cultural expression, we can anticipate in such expressions traces of the Creator Spirit's presence. Consequently, we should listen intently for the voice of the Spirit, who is present in all life and therefore who "precedes" us into the world, bubbling to the surface through the artifacts and symbols humans construct.

A cautionary note is in order here, however. Whatever speaking that occurs through other media does not come as a speaking against the text. To pit the Spirit's voice in culture against the Spirit speaking through scripture would be to fall prey to the foundationalist trap. It would require that we elevate some dimension of contemporary thought or experience as a human universal that forms the criterion for determining what in the Bible is or is not acceptable. Darrell Jodock pinpoints the difficulty:

> The problem here is not that one's world view or experience influences one's reading of the text, because that is inescapable. The problem is instead that the text is made to conform to the world view or codified experience and thereby loses its integrity and its ability to challenge and confront our present priorities, including even our most noble aspirations.[146]

Hence, while being ready to acknowledge the Spirit's voice wherever it may be found, we still uphold the primacy of the text. Even though we cannot hear the Spirit speaking through the text except by listening within a particular

---

146. Darrell Jodock, "The Reciprocity Between Scripture and Theology: The Role of Scripture in Contemporary Theological Reflection," *Interpretation* 44/4 (October 1990): 377.

historical-cultural context, nevertheless hearing the Spirit in the text provides the only sure canon for hearing the Spirit in culture, because the Spirit's speaking everywhere and anywhere is always in concert with this primary speaking through the text. In fact, culture and text do not comprise two different moments of communication; rather, they are but one speaking. And consequently we engage not in two different "listenings," but one. We listen for the voice of the Spirit who speaks the Word through the word within the particularity of the hearers' context, and who thereby can speak in all things.

Theology and the Community of Christ as a Culture

There remains one additional aspect of the relationship of theology to culture yet to be developed—one that we hinted at earlier. We turn our attention finally to the connection between Christian theology and one particular culture—the Christian community.

The Church as a Culture

Doing so, however, raises immediately the question of whether, or in what sense, it is appropriate to use the language of culture to refer to the church. And our response to this question, in turn, is closely tied to a view of the church that sees it as a distinct social group. Although the fuller treatment of the church as "community" will need to wait until chapter 7, in this context we must offer some preliminary remarks about its social character.

While we dare not push the point too far, several considerations suggest that the church is a distinctive social group with its own particular culture. According to contemporary sociologists, a group consists of two or more people who are related to or oriented toward one another, who share "unit awareness" (i.e., the persons consider themselves a distinct entity), and between whom there is interaction or communication in the form of observable behavior, behavior that takes on significance in relation to symbolic objects that carry meaning within the social setting.[147] Measured according to this criterion, the church in both its universal and local expressions is a group.

Further, as a community or society, the church seeks to perpetuate itself institutionally as well as propagate a particular vision of meaning making and world construction. As Peter Berger notes, "The reality of the Christian world depends upon the presence of social structures within which this reality is taken for granted and within which successive generations are socialized in such a way that this world will be real *to them*."[148]

More important for our purposes, however, the "unit awareness" that participants in the church share is theological and ethical in scope. Hence, the church is made up of people who share, albeit in varying degrees, a particular

---

147. H. F. Taylor, *Balance in Small Groups* (New York: Van Nostrand Reinhold Co., 1970), 1–2
148. Berger, *Sacred Canopy*, 46.

set of values, beliefs, and loyalties, all of which arise out of a fundamental commitment to the God revealed in Christ. Consequently, the church forms a people committed—at least in principle—to order all their relationships according to these beliefs and values, and to do so in the light of a pattern they find embodied in the biblical narrative of God acting in, and being in relationship with, creation. Although they may disagree on the practicalities connected to the outworking of this pattern, Christians are nevertheless united by this shared concern.

As this particular group, the church forms a particular culture, for participants share a group of symbols that serve as both building blocks and conveyors of meaning. These symbols cover the range indicative of all cultures: a particular language, as well as specific images (e.g., the crucifixion and the empty tomb), material things and rituals (e.g., baptism and the Lord's Supper). While they share many symbols in common, participants are not necessarily in agreement about the meaning these symbols are to convey. On the contrary, meaning making is an ongoing task in the church, one that involves lively conversation, intense discussion, and often even heated debate among participants.

Finally, the church is a social group in that participants share a common sense of mission. The nature of this mission is likewise a topic of debate. Yet perhaps nearly all Christians would agree that their common mandate includes worship, edification, and outreach, although they may differ on the definition and outworking of the three. The concept of mission leads to one final point, one that tempers our understanding of the church as a particular society. Christians are not called to be a group that exists over against the rest of humankind. In fact, they are not called to be anything but truly human. Consequently, in engaging in the cultural task of meaning making, throughout its history the church has readily appropriated elements from the social contexts—the cultures—in which it has found itself. In short, Christians are co-participants with people around them in an ongoing conversation about what it means to be human. What makes this particular group unique—that is, what makes it uniquely "Christian"—is the participants' desire to engage in this process from a particular vantage point, namely, that of viewing all things in connection to the God of the Bible who they believe is revealed supremely in Jesus Christ. This above all marks the connection between the Christian communal culture and the theological enterprise.

Theology as a Cultural Practice

Karl Barth begins his monumental *Church Dogmatics* by declaring, "[T]heology is a function of the Church."[149] Insofar as the church is a social group, we might alter Barth's statement to read, "Theology, as a function of the church, is linked to Christian cultural practice." The developments in cultural anthropology out-

---

149. Karl Barth, *Church Dogmatics*, I/1, trans. G. W. Bromiley (Edinburgh: T. & T. Clark, 1975), 3.

lined in this chapter warn us against understanding *theology* in this context as primarily constituting the "high culture" of the church.[150] Rather, theology is linked to the meaning-making activity of the people who comprise the community of Christ. Hence, theology is related to the various Christian symbols and activities in their function as purveyors—as building blocks and conveyors—of what we might call "Christian cultural meaning."

To this end, theology engages with church practices or, more specifically, with that dimension of church practices that transforms them from mere disjointed physical acts into socially meaningful patterns. In fact, at their core all Christian activities are theological. All such practices are linked to, informed by, or expressions of some underlying theological belief or core value. Theology makes explicit the connection all Christian practices have to their underlying meaning and to the particular Christian symbols or carriers of meaning to which they are related.

Hence, reflection on the practices of the community belongs to what we might call the "critical task" of theology. Hans Frei aptly describes this aspect of the theological enterprise as "the Christian community's second-order appraisal of its own language and actions under a norm or norms internal to the community."[151] Such critical reflection on the practices of the community includes the attempt to bring to light the meaning structures that inform them. It involves as well, however, evaluating individual practices by how well they reflect sound Christian teaching.[152] Of course, in this process theologians will be influenced by their own conclusions about the meanings that ought to motivate and come to expression in Christian practices in general and the specific practice under scrutiny in particular.

There is another, more intimate manner in which theology is connected to Christian culture. Not only do theologians reflect on the practices of the community, they also seek to express Christian communal beliefs and values as well as the meaning of Christian symbols in a more direct manner. That is, the theological enterprise entails not only a critical but also a constructive task. In its constructive dimension, theology is directly a cultural practice of the church. As Tanner states succinctly, "[T]heology . . . is a material social practice that specializes in meaning production."[153] Connected as it is with this particular social group, such theological construction has as its goal the setting forth of a particular understanding of the particular "web of significance," "matrix of meaning," or "mosaic of beliefs" that lies at the heart of the community of Christ.

In understanding theology's constructive task as a cultural practice we must avoid a foundationalist approach that starts with some complete whole as a given reality which theologians in turn simply explicate or on which they erect

---

150. Tanner, *Theories of Culture*, 70.

151. Hans W. Frei, *Types of Modern Theology*, ed. George Hunsinger and William C. Placher (New Haven: Yale University Press, 1992), 2.

152. Ronald Thiemann, *Revelation and Theology: The Gospel as Narrated Promise* (Notre Dame, Ind.: University of Notre Dame Press, 1985), 75.

153. Tanner, *Theories of Culture*, 72.

the theological knowledge edifice. Rather, the constructive task of theology emerges out of the process of give and take, as participants in the community converse over their shared cultural meanings as connected to the symbols they hold in common as Christians. And as we noted in chapter 3, theological construction, in turn, serves the church's ongoing, ever-necessary calling to listen to the one voice of the Spirit speaking through text within the interpretive community embedded in its cultural context.

If theology is both the reflection of church practices and the articulation of the church's mosaic of beliefs for the sake of hearing the Spirit's voice, then ultimately all theology is "local." That is, it is the reflection and articulation of a particular group in a particular moment of their ongoing existence in the world. But the specificity of theology leads inevitably to the question, "What—if anything—do these local theologies have in common?" to which we answer, "A similar pattern, shape, or 'style.'"[154] And what characterizes this particularly Christian theological style? What makes a local theology *Christian*? What unites these local theologies together within the one designation "Christian theology"? Our methodological proposal offers this answer: All truly Christian local theologies are trinitarian in content, communitarian in focus, and eschatological in orientation. The explication of this assertion will occupy us in Part 3 of this volume.

---

154. According to Kroeber, culture provides "a far more natural and fit medium" for "style" to grow in than does "life." Alfred L. Kroeber, *Style and Civilizations* (Ithaca, N.Y.: Cornell University Press, 1957), 76.

PART THREE
THEOLOGY'S FOCAL MOTIFS

Chapter Six

The Trinity:
Theology's Structural Motif

It is part of the pathos of western theology that it has often believed that while trinitarian theology might well be of edificatory value to those who already believe, for the outsider it is an unfortunate barrier to belief, which must therefore be facilitated by some non-trinitarian apologetic, some essentially monotheistic 'natural theology.' My belief is the reverse: that because the theology of the Trinity has so much to teach about the nature of our world and life within it, it is or could be the centre of Christianity's appeal to the unbeliever, as the good news of a God who enters into free relations of creation and redemption with his world. In the light of the theology of the Trinity, everything looks different.

—Colin Gunton[1]

Go therefore and make disciples of all the nations, baptizing them in the name of the Father and of the Son and of the Holy Spirit.
—Matthew 28:19 (KJV)

By its very definition, theology—the teaching about God—has as its central interest the divine reality, together with God's actions in creation. The chief inquiry for any theology, therefore, is the question of the identity of God. The Christian answer to the question "Who is God?" ultimately leads to the

---

1. Colin Gunton, *The Promise of Trinitarian Theology*, 2nd ed. (Edinburgh: T. & T. Clark, 1997), 7.

doctrine of the Trinity. The one God, Christians assert, is triune—Father, Son, and Spirit, to cite the traditional designations for the trinitarian persons—and consequently the confession of the triune God is the sine qua non of the Christian faith. In keeping with this fundamental Christian confession, both the Apostles' Creed and the Nicene Creed, the ancient and ecumenical symbols of the church, are ordered around and divided into three articles that correspond to the three persons of the triune God: the Father and creation; the Son and reconciliation; the Spirit and salvation as well as consummation. For much of the history of the church this creedal pattern gave rise to a trinitarian structure in the construction and exposition of theology.

This observation leads us to the first of three focal motifs that provide unity and coherence for the various local, contextual expressions of theology and thus constitute them as authentically *Christian* theology. Because Christian theology is committed to finding its basis in the being and actions of the God of the Bible, it should be ordered and structured in such a way as to reflect the primacy of the fundamental Christian confession about the nature of this God. Because the structuring motif of the Christian confession of God is trinitarian, a truly Christian theology is likewise necessarily trinitarian. In a truly trinitarian theology, the structuring influence of God's triunity goes well beyond the exposition of theology proper, extending to all aspects of the delineation of the Christian belief-mosaic.

This present chapter focuses on the Trinity as the content, or structural motif, of theology and thus on the trinitarian character of Christian theology. Our goal is to make a case for the centrality of the Trinity in the explication of theology and, in the process, to describe what we mean by a theology that is trinitarian in structure. We do so, however, conscious of the continuing skepticism regarding the doctrine of the Trinity and its usefulness for theology that typifies much of contemporary theology, a skepticism that raises the question of whether the doctrine of the Trinity is truly significant for Christian theology as a whole.

The Case for a Trinitarian Theology

Throughout much of church history, theologians, following the pattern of ancient creed, have structured theology in a trinitarian manner. Although various interpretations of the Trinity abounded in the early and medieval church, the doctrine was universally considered central to the task of theology.[2] The rise of the Enlightenment, however, altered the situation, resulting in the marginalization of the doctrine of the Trinity, which came to be regarded as little more than an abstract and indefensible example of the excesses of speculative theology. The twentieth century witnessed a renaissance of trinitarian theology that

2. For a survey of the various views on offer, see Edmund Fortman, *The Triune God: A Historical Study of the Doctrine of the Trinity* (Philadelphia: Westminster Press, 1972).

has spawned a wealth of studies of and proposals for a renewed understanding of the doctrine.[3] Despite this renewed interest, however, the question of its proper role in theology remains the subject of considerable debate.

On one side of this debate are those theologians who continue to give little place to the doctrine of the Trinity. Cyril Richardson, for example, views it as an artificial intellectual construction that is racked with "inherent confusions,"[4] and John Hick dismisses the doctrine as the product of an outmoded understanding of the world that must be left behind."[5] Other critics avoid trinitarian speculation because they are convinced that God's eternal triune nature is fundamentally mysterious and therefore lies beyond the capacity of finite humans to grasp. On this basis, Friedrich Schleiermacher, who devoted a scant fifteen pages to the doctrine of the Trinity in the conclusion to his 750-page magnum opus, surmised that delving into this mystery would go against the very nature of theology.[6] Another group of naysayers are convinced that the Trinity is of little practical significance. Immanuel Kant, to cite one extreme example, declared that the doctrine leads to "absolutely nothing worthwhile" for practical, everyday life.[7] This suspicion is given voice by Dorothy Sayers in her characterization of the average churchgoer's view of the Trinity: "The Father incomprehensible, the Son incomprehensible, and the whole thing incomprehensible. Something put in by theologians to make it more difficult—nothing to do with daily life or ethics."[8]

Colin Gunton summarizes well this aspect of the contemporary theological climate: "Overall, there is a suspicion that the whole thing is a bore, a matter of mathematical conundrums and illogical attempts to square the circle."[9] Many view the doctrine as at best a theological terminus. They might admit that it remains a necessary support for the Christian consciousness, for Christian worship, or for Christian orthodoxy. But they are convinced that giving it a place in the theological enterprise—beyond merely clarifying how the doctrine is to be articulated—is to invite worthless, even detrimental, speculation.

Standing on the other side of the debate are those who suggest that because theology is particularly interested in God as well as God's actions in creation, the reality of God as triune lies at the heart of any truly *theological* exposition. These theologians are convinced that rather than being mere speculation, unpacking the eternal trinitarian relations is endemic to the theological task and

---

3. Catherine Mowry LaCugna, "Philosophers and Theologians on the Trinity," *Modern Theology* 2/3 (April 1986): 169–81. LaCugna notes this renaissance of trinitarian thought in conjunction with the citation of a number of recently published major works on the doctrine of the Trinity.

4. Cyril Richardson, *The Doctrine of the Trinity* (New York: Abingdon Press, 1958), 148–9.

5. John Hick, *God Has Many Names* (Philadelphia: Westminster Press, 1982), 124.

6. Friedrich Schleiermacher, *The Christian Faith*, ed. H. R. Mackintosh and J. S. Stewart (Edinburgh: T. & T. Clark, 1928), 748.

7. Cited in Jürgen Moltmann, *The Trinity and the Kingdom of God*, trans. Margaret Kohl (London: SCM Press, 1981), 6.

8. Dorothy Sayers, *Creed or Chaos* (New York: Harcourt, Brace & Co., 1949), 22.

9. Gunton, *Promise of Trinitarian Theology*, 2–3.

is warranted by the now-famous dictum known as Rahner's rule: "The 'economic' Trinity is the 'immanent' Trinity and the 'immanent' Trinity is the 'economic' Trinity."[10] The trailblazer in the revival of trinitarianism was clearly Karl Barth. Barth returned the focus of theology to God as triune by recognizing that present in the economy of salvation is none other than God as God is within the eternal divine reality.[11] Since Barth's pioneering work, a host of theologians have taken up the trinitarian theme. In fact, David Cunningham recently commented that studies on the Trinity have become so prevalent that "the phenomenon begins to look not so much like a renaissance as a bandwagon."[12]

We are convinced that the theologians who comprise this second group are correct. The Christian understanding of God as triune offers a fruitful starting point for theological and ethical reflection. In fact, we would go further, claiming that the Trinity provides the structuring motif for Christian theology. Building from the sources for theology set forth in the previous chapters, we argue that theology must be trinitarian because this structure reflects the biblical narrative, dominates the Christian tradition, and resonates with the cultural moment. Unpacking this thesis implicitly indicates in part what it means to pursue a theology that is truly trinitarian.

Trinitarian Theology and the Biblical Narrative

The word "trinity" is not found in the Bible, nor is the theological concept developed or fully delineated in scripture. The absence of any explicit reference to God as triune in the Bible led Swiss theologian Emil Brunner to conclude, "The ecclesiastical doctrine of the Trinity, established by the dogma of the ancient Church, is not a Biblical *kerygma*, therefore it is not the *kerygma* of the Church, but it is a theological doctrine which defends the central faith of the Bible and the Church."[13] In this terse statement Brunner calls our attention to the fact that the doctrine of the Trinity as we know it was not formulated in scripture itself, but by the church during the patristic era. Nevertheless, by the fourth century the Christian community had come to the conclusion that understanding God as triune was a nonnegotiable aspect of the gospel, because it capsulized the Christian conception of God.

Brunner is surely correct in this judgment. At the same time, the doctrine of the Trinity that unfolded in the patristic era is a natural—and perhaps even necessary—outworking of the faith of the New Testament community. Above all, it is based on the concrete witness of the biblical narrative. It emerges as the

10. Karl Rahner, *The Trinity* (New York: Herder & Herder, 1970), 22.
11. John Thompson, *Modern Trinitarian Perspectives* (New York: Oxford University Press, 1994), 3.
12. David S. Cunningham, *These Three Are One: The Practice of Trinitarian Theology* (Malden, Mass.: Blackwell Publishers, 1998), 19.
13. Emil Brunner, *The Christian Doctrine of God*, trans. Olive Wyon (Philadelphia: Westminster Press, 1950), 206.

fundamental theological conclusion arising from and embodying that narrative. In fact, the trinitarian conception of God is so closely tied to the biblical narrative that it serves as a shorthand way of speaking not only about the God of the narrative but about the narrative itself as the act of the God of the Bible.

The Trinity and the New Testament Community

The doctrine of the Trinity is often portrayed as a highly abstract teaching that emerged from the philosophical concerns and speculations of third- and fourth-century theologians, rather than from the content of the biblical witness. The fact is, however, that the doctrine arose as a response to the concrete historical situation encountered by the early Christian community. The early Christians faced a grave theological problem, namely, how to reconcile their inherited commitment to the confession of the one God with the lordship of Jesus Christ and the experience of the Spirit. Far from a philosophical abstraction, therefore, the doctrine of the Trinity was the culmination of an attempt on the part of the church to address the central theological question regarding the content of the Christian faith, a question that arose out of the experience of the earliest followers of Jesus.

The early Christians, following their Jewish heritage, vigorously maintained the belief in one God together with the attendant rejection of the polytheistic practices of other nations. This commitment was rooted in their claim that the Christian faith was a continuation of what God had initiated in the covenant with Abraham. The Hebrew community that had been shaped by the promises contained in the Abrahamic covenant asserted unequivocally that there is only one God and that this God alone was to be the object of their loyalty and worship (e.g. Deut. 6: 4). The early Christians viewed themselves as the continuation of the one people of the one God, and consequently they steadfastly continued in the Old Testament tradition of monotheism. The followers of Jesus asserted that the God they worshiped is none other than the God of the patriarchs, the one and only true God. This commitment to one God of the Hebrew community provided the Christian community an indispensable framework in which to reflect on its experience of the living God in the person of Jesus Christ.

Although the early Christians continued the Jewish practice of worshiping only one God, they also believed that this God had been revealed preeminently in the person of Jesus of Nazareth. They confessed that this Jesus is the head of the church and the Lord of all creation. This confession resulted in a second core belief. In addition to the commitment to one God, the early church asserted the deity and lordship of Jesus (John 1:1; John 20:28; Rom. 9:5; Titus 2:3). At the same time, the followers of Jesus made a clear distinction, following the pattern of Jesus himself, between Jesus as the Son of God and the God of Israel, the Creator of the world, whom he addressed as "Father." In short, the Church asserted that while Jesus is divine, he is nevertheless distinct from the Father.

In addition to the belief in one God and the confession of Jesus as Lord, the early Christian community also experienced the living God present among them through Another, who is neither Jesus nor his heavenly Father. This Other is the Holy Spirit, through whose ministry the early Christian believers enjoyed an intimate fellowship with the living God and therefore whom they equated with the presence of God among and within them. The community believed that through the presence of the Spirit, Christians individually and corporately comprise the true temple of God (Rom. 8:9; 1 Cor. 3:16; 2 Cor. 3).

This assertion is particularly striking in light of the significance of the Temple in first-century Judaism. As the focal point of all aspects of Jewish national life, the Temple was regarded as the place where God lived and ruled.[14] Thus, the connection between the presence of the Spirit in the life of the Christian community as constituting that community as the temple of God intimately linked the Spirit with God. In addition, the early Christians also closely connected the Holy Spirit to the risen Lord (2 Cor. 3:17; Phil. 1:19), while also making a clear and definite distinction between the Spirit and both the Father and the Son. This distinction among the trinitarian members is evident in the trinitarian formulations found in the documents of the New Testament canon (e.g. 2 Cor. 13:14).

The early Christians were faced with the task of integrating into a coherent, composite understanding these three commitments borne out of their experience of God. More particularly, they were faced with the challenge of maintaining both the unity and the differentiated plurality of God. They did not want to posit three Gods, yet the three differentiated experiences of God were far too concrete to be seen as simply different "modes" of the one God. As a result, trinitarian theology is rooted in the practical, concrete concern to provide a Christian account of God that is in accord with the experience and witness of the community. Of course, subsequent attempts to provide such an account drew from the philosophical terminology and thought forms of the Greek culture in which the patristic church was embedded. Yet this does not mean that the doctrine itself is merely the product of philosophical speculation. As David Cunningham points out, when Christian theologians engaged in the attempt to make sense of the God of the Bible, "they (quite naturally and appropriately) turned to the philosophical categories that were available to them. But this fact should not be allowed to eclipse the concrete reality of the particular narratives that gave rise to trinitarian thought."[15]

The Trinity and the Eternal "History" of God

The biblical narratives speak of three historical encounters with God: with the one God of Israel, with Jesus the incarnate Son, and with the Spirit as the

---

14. On the significance of the Temple, see N. T. Wright, *The New Testament and the People of God* (Minneapolis: Fortress Press, 1992), 224–226.
15. Cunningham, *These Three Are One*, 22.

manifestation of the ongoing presence and guidance of God in the community and in the world. While the constitutive narratives of the Christian tradition bear witness to the engagement of God with the world, they also point beyond this encounter to the eternal divine life. In addition to acting in the history of the world, the biblical materials view God as having a "history." In this history, creation is not the beginning point but an event in the continuing story of God's life, which stretches from the eternal past into the eternal future. Catherine LaCugna notes that although the acts of God in history were the original subject matter of the doctrine of the Trinity, theologians have come to understand that "God's relations to us in history are taken to be what is characteristic of the very being of God."[16] In other words, God has an internal "history" (the inner divine life) as well as an external history (God's actions and engagement with the world). The narratives of scripture invite theologians to take account of both the internal and external aspects of God's life and to think through the details and the implications of this history.

The Return of the Narrative

The significance of God's internal and external history was taken for granted throughout much of the history of theology, and numerous systems of speculative theology were produced, based in no small part on this distinction arising out of the biblical narrative.[17] In the aftermath of the Enlightenment, however, the biblical narratives began to suffer neglect due to incredulity toward the truth of the narratives displayed in the Age of Reason and the corresponding rise of biblical criticism.[18] The effect of this suspicion toward the biblical narratives was a shift away from the accounts of scripture as providing the basis for Christian belief, a shift that led in turn to the rejection of Christian doctrines such as the Trinity as being the product of abstract philosophical speculation.

In the twentieth century, however, proponents of trinitarian theology sought once again to link the doctrine of the Trinity with the biblical narratives. Karl Barth's *Church Dogmatics* stands out as a monumental attempt to reassert the centrality of the Trinity for the task of theology by grounding the doctrine in the narratives of God's relationship with Israel and the church. For Barth, trinitarian theology is the story of God and God's action in the world, which finds its ultimate center in Christ.[19]

Like Barth, Robert Jenson is committed to showing that the doctrine is grounded in the concrete narratives of the Christian faith that witness to the life, death, and resurrection of Christ and therefore that the Trinity is not the

---

16. LaCugna, "Philosophers and Theologians on the Trinity," 173.

17. Cunningham, *These Three Are One*, 22.

18. On the history of this development, see Hans Frei, *The Eclipse of Biblical Narrative: A Study in Eighteenth and Nineteenth Century Hermeneutics* (New Haven, Conn.: Yale University Press, 1974).

19. David Ford, *Barth and God's Story* (Frankfurt: Perter Lang, 1985).

product of mere abstract philosophical speculation.[20] To this end, he seeks to free the doctrine of God in particular and Christian theology in general from its excessive dependence on the categories of Hellenistic philosophy, such as divine timelessness, simplicity, and impassability. Although agreeing that the communities of ancient Israel and the church experienced God as eternal, Jenson argues that they did not understand this eternity as timelessness but as faithfulness through time. The God of the biblical narratives does not transcend time by being immune from it but by maintaining faithful continuity through time, a continuity that Jenson describes as "personal." The eternity of the Christian God, he therefore concludes, is intrinsically a matter of relationship with God's creatures.[21] By working from the biblical texts in this manner rather than drawing from Greek philosophical categories, Jenson seeks to ensure that trinitarian theology remains firmly grounded in the narrative of the experience of Israel and the church with the God of the Bible.

Perhaps the most widely hailed attempts to link trinitarian theology with the biblical narratives are those of Jürgen Moltmann and Wolfhart Pannenberg. Although they differ from each other at a number of important points, both seek to liberate the doctrine of the Trinity from abstract speculation about a distant being and to connect the triune God with the historical process. To this end, both thinkers have followed Barth in linking the doctrine of the Trinity with the doctrine of revelation, albeit by asserting that God, as the one who is active in history, is revealed in history. Their emphasis on revelation, whether in a Barthian manner or after the fashion of the theologians of hope, has served to reconnect the doctrine of God in general and the understanding of the Trinity in particular with the biblical story.

Some scholars find in the separation of the doctrine of God from the biblical narratives the genesis of modern atheism, which emerged in the wake of Enlightenment theology, with its propensity to develop generic conceptions of God believed to be demonstrable by reason.[22] In the estimation of these observers, the rationalist approach of the Enlightenment led to the belief that the existence of God could be "proved" rationally, an assumption that, when it was subsequently undermined, led to the undermining of the conception of God as well.[23] This historical appraisal implies that modern atheism emerged in part as the result of the neglect of the biblical narratives in theology, as theologians discarded the biblical witness to the active presence of God in the world in favor of speculation about a generic, completely transcendent deity.

The renewed emphasis on the narratives of the Christian faith as the narratives of God's history has reinvigorated trinitarian theology by asserting that its

---

20. Robert W. Jenson, *The Triune Identity: God According to the Gospel* (Philadelphia: Fortress Press, 1982).

21. Ted Peters, *GOD as Trinity: Relationality and Temporality in Divine Life* (Louisville, Ky.: Westminster John Knox Press, 1993), 129.

22. The most detailed account of this development is Michael J. Buckley, S. J., *At the Origins of Modern Atheism* (New Haven: Yale University Press, 1987).

23. Cunningham, *These Three Are One*, 24.

claims are not grounded in abstract philosophical speculation but in the intellectual challenges about God and God's relationship to creation raised by these narratives. Moreover, as David Cunningham notes, the biblical narrative is properly read and interpreted "not according to the supposedly context-independent assumptions of rationalism, but in the context of Christian participation in concrete practices of worship, education, and discipleship."[24]

To summarize: The doctrine of the Trinity is not the product of philosophically speculative theology gone awry but the outworking of communal Christian reflection on the concrete narratives of scripture, which call for coherent explanation. For this reason, the centrality of the Trinity in giving shape to theology is likewise demanded by these narratives, which witness to the revelation of God in Christ. The biblical narratives lead to the conclusion that the affirmation of God as the triune one lies at the very heart of the Christian faith and comprises its distinctive conception of God. Therefore, insofar as the theological enterprise is embedded methodologically in the biblical narratives, a truly Christian theology must be trinitarian in structure, and in this way theology becomes the study of the God of the Bible, who is the triune one.

Trinitarian Theology and the Theological Heritage of the Church

A truly Christian theology must be trinitarian because the biblical narrative, which speaks about the history of God, focuses on the triune God. Not only does the Trinity as theology's structural motif emerge out of the biblical narrative, however; it also arises from the theological heritage of the church. The doctrine of the Trinity has stood at the heart of theology throughout church history, providing impetus to the theological task and giving shape to the theological deposit that has continually arisen from that enterprise. In fact, we might suggest that in one sense the history of theology is the history of the genesis and development of the doctrine of the Trinity, the engagement with the trinitarian conception of God, and the quest to set forth a theology that is truly trinitarian.

The Emergence of Trinitarian Theology

We noted previously that the early Christians faced the challenge of coming to grips with the theological situation spawned by their confession of the lordship of Jesus, their experience of the Holy Spirit, and their commitment to the one God of the Old Testament. The preoccupation with the unity of God thrust on the second-century church by their struggle with paganism and Gnosticism initially left the theologians of the day with little interest in exploring the eternal relations of the trinitarian persons or in devising a conceptual and linguistic apparatus capable of expressing these relations.[25] The situation soon changed,

---

24. Ibid., 25.
25. J. N. D. Kelly, *Early Christian Doctrines*, rev. ed. (San Francisco: Harper & Row, 1978), 109.

however, as the church became embroiled in theological controversy that would eventually insure that all subsequent theology would be cast in a trinitarian die.

The first crucial, specifically theological question to which the church devoted its attention centered on the relationship between Jesus of Nazareth and God. Because by the latter half of the second century Hellenism loomed as the chief audience to which Christian thought needed to be directed,[26] the early Christian apologists busied themselves with the task of finding common ground between the Christian message and the Greek philosophical tradition.[27] For this reason, the attempt to articulate the relationship between Jesus and God took on a decidedly Greek philosophical flavor. And this led to, as well as framed, the emerging theological controversy about the person of Christ.

The particular formulation of Christology that eventually climaxed in the formal development of the doctrine of the Trinity arose in the context of the Arian controversy. In his desire to protect the absolute uniqueness and transcendence of God, Arius, who agreed with Origen that the Father begets or generates the Son, argued that, rather than an eternal movement within the divine life, this begetting occurred at a temporal point. The Father made the Son, he asserted, and this meant that the Son is a creature who must have had a beginning.[28] In concluding that there was a time when the Son was not, Arius in effect made the trinitarian distinctions external to God and claimed that in the divine, eternal nature God is one, not three.[29] The church, however, disagreed with Arius, unequivocally affirming the full deity of Christ at the Council of Nicea in 325. The creed issued by the Council asserted that the Son is "begotten of the Father as only begotten, that is, from the essence of the Father, God from God, Light from Light, true God from true God, begotten not created, of the same essence as the Father."[30]

At Nicea, the church set the Christological basis for a trinitarian theology. A second theological debate occurring in the aftermath of Nicea provided the corresponding pneumatological basis. The dispute about the Holy Spirit likewise had its roots in Arius's teaching about the Son, for his followers, including Macedonius, the bishop of Constantinople[31] for whom the controversy is often named, asserted that not only was the Son the first creature of the Father, the Holy Spirit was the first creature of the Son.[32] The church father Athanasius countered this claim by showing that the full deity of the Spirit, like that of the

26. Jaroslav Pelikan, *The Emergence of the Catholic Tradition (100–600)* (Chicago: University of Chicago Press, 1971), 27.

27. For a discussion of the early Christian apologists, see Robert M. Grant, *Greek Apologists of the Second Century* (Philadelphia: Westminster Press, 1988).

28. "The Letter of Arius to Eusebius," in *Documents of the Christian Church*, ed. Henry Bettenson, 2nd ed. (London: Oxford University Press, 1963), 39.

29. Tillich, *A History of Christian Thought* (New York: Harper & Row, 1968), 61–79.

30. See "The Creed of Nicaea," in *Creeds of the Churches: A Reader in Christian Doctrine from the Bible to the Present*, ed. John Leith, 3rd ed. (Atlanta: John Knox Press, 1982), 30–31.

31. Kelly, *Early Christian Doctrines*, 259.

32. Ibid., 256.

Son, was a necessary component of Christian faith,[33] especially the Christian teaching about salvation. He asserted that if the Spirit who enters the hearts and lives of the faithful is not fully divine, believers do not enjoy true community with God. The Council of Constantinople (381 C.E.) agreed with Athanasius,[34] articulating the orthodox position in a statement, popularly known as the Nicene Creed, that speaks of the Holy Spirit as "worshiped and glorified together with the Father and the Son."[35]

The decisions of the ecumenical councils at Nicea and Constantinople provided the framework for the future development of trinitarian theology. Yet, although the Councils affirmed the full deity of the Son and the Spirit along with the Father, the creeds that articulated the results of the conciliar deliberations did not address the question of how the three comprise one God or what the implications of this doctrine were for the Christian message. The task of providing a formulation of the relationship among Father, Son, and Spirit fell to the Cappadocian fathers: Basil the Great, Gregory of Nyssa, and Gregory of Nazianzus.[36] In developing their conception of the triune God, the Cappadocians appropriated two Greek terms, *ousia* and *hypostasis*, theorizing that God is one *ousia* ("essence") but three *hypostaseis* ("independent realities") who share the one essence. The Cappadocian formulation of the Trinity provided the church with a fixed reference point, but it did not bring the discussions of the doctrine to an end. On the contrary, it opened the door for an ensuing debate about the exact way of construing the threeness and oneness of God, a debate that eventually led to a theological parting of ways between the Eastern and Western churches.

The theologians of the East sought to draw out the implications of the distinction posited by the Cappodicians between the words *ousia* and *hypostasis*. Gunton notes that by the time of the Cappadocians, the Greek term *hypostasis* had come to be used in distinction from the term *ousia* in order to refer to the concrete particularity of Father, Son, and Spirit.[37] In this rendering the three are not to be viewed simply as individuals but rather as persons whose reality can only be understood in terms of their relations to each other. By the virtue of these relations they together constitute the being or *ousia* of the one God. The persons are therefore not relations, but concrete particulars who are in relation to one another.[38] Gunton notes that this conceptual development not only provided a way to understand the threeness of the Christian God without loss to the divine unity but also established a new relational ontology: For God to be means that God is in communion. This theological conclusion arose out the linguistic connection between the terms *hypostasis* and *ousia*, which, although being conceptually distinct, are inseparable in thought because of their mutual

33. Tillich, *A History of Christian Thought*, 73–4.
34. Leith, *Creeds of the Churches*, 32.
35. See the "Constantinopolitan Creed" in *Creeds of the Churches*, 33.
36. Kelly, *Early Christian Doctrines*, 258.
37. Gunton, *The Promise of Trinitarian Theology*, 39.
38. Ibid.

involvement with one another.[39] The Eastern understanding was also characterized by the tendency to focus on the three individual members of the Trinity
rather than on the divine unity.[40] Although not denying that Father, Son, and
Spirit possess the one divine essence, the Eastern thinkers tended to highlight
the specific operations of the Father, the Son, and the Spirit in the divine acts
of creation, reconciliation, and consummation.

The linguistic differences between Latin and Greek as well as the differing
cultural and theological temperaments of East and West[41] led the Western
theologians to travel a somewhat different pathway. Their use of Latin meant
that Western theologians were not fully cognizant of the nuances of the linguistic formulations emerging from the East. Instead, they drew on the work of
Tertullian, whose formula *tres personae, una substantia* became a staple of the
Latin conception. Tertullian's formula served to complicate the discussion with
Eastern thinkers, however, in that the term *substantia* was the usual Latin translation of *hypostasis*, not *ousia*. The linguistic difficulties were compounded by
the continuing influence of Athanasius, who had understood *ousia* and *hypostasis* as synonyms.[42] Use of the formula *tres personae, una substantia* led Western
theologians to emphasize the one divine essence or substance rather than the
plurality or threeness of divine persons characteristic of the East.

The classic statement of the Western understanding of the Trinity came in
Augustine's influential work *De Trinitate*. Augustine appeals to the nature of
human beings who, because they are created in the image of God, display "ves-
tiges" of the Trinity, an approach that leads him to look for analogies of the
Trinity in the nature of the human person.[43] In his estimation, the key to understanding the Trinity is found in the concept of love. According to Augustine,
the human mind knows love in itself and as a consequence knows God, for God
is love. This leads to a knowledge of the Trinity in that love implies a Trinity:
"he that loves, and that which is loved, and love."[44] Actually, Augustine offered
a long series of analogies based on humans as the *imago dei*, the most central of
which is the triad of *being, knowing,* and *willing.*[45] Augustine's psychological
analogy of the Trinity, with its focus on the oneness of God, in contrast to the
Eastern emphasis on the divine threeness, and with its starting point in the
divine essence, rather than in the saving act of God in Christ, set the stage for

39. Ibid.

40. For a discussion of the development of the Trinity in Eastern thought, see Jaroslav
Pelikan, *The Spirit of Eastern Christendom (600–1700)* (Chicago: University of Chicago Press,
1974).

41. For a discussion of these differences, see Kelly, *Early Christian Doctrines*, 3–28.

42. Fortman, *The Triune God,* 72–83.

43. Cyril C. Richardson, "The Enigma of the Trinity" in *A Companion to the Study of St.
Augustine,* ed. Roy Battenhouse (Oxford: Oxford University Press, 1955), 248–255.

44. Augustine, *On the Trinity,* 8.10.14, trans. Arthur West Haddon, vol. 3, first series of The
Nicene and Post-Nicene Fathers (hereafter NPNF), reprint ed. (Grand Rapids: Wm. B. Eerdmans
Publishing Co., 1980), 124.

45. Augustine, *Confessions* 13.11.12, trans. Henry Chadwick (Oxford: Oxford University
Press, 1992), 279–280.

the trinitarian theologizing prominent in the West.[46] In the case of both East and West, however, the conception of God as triune, though definitely not the only topic of discussion, clearly framed the dominant theological agenda and structured the theologizing of the great minds of the day.

The Trinity in Medieval Theology

The linguistic and cultural differences between the Eastern and Western churches contributed to the Great Schism that came in the wake of the *filioque* controversy.[47] Yet the ecclesiastical breech did not terminate discussions of the doctrine or move the Trinity from the center of Christian theology, especially in the West. Throughout the medieval period the doctrine of the Trinity continued to receive considerable attention from both scholastic and mystical theologians who viewed God's triune nature as a central concern for Christian faith. This period is characterized by an emphasis on metaphysical speculation as well as by attempts to systematize and explicate trinitarian doctrine.

During the twelfth century a number of significant works on the Trinity served to codify and standardize the insights of the early Fathers and thereby provided a basis in tradition for the speculations of the following century. Leading thinkers such as Anselm of Canterbury and Peter Abelard developed a dialectical approach to theology that attempted to demonstrate the coherence between revealed and rational truth. But perhaps the most significant twelfth-century contribution to trinitarian theology was that of Richard of St. Victor, whose treatise *De Trinitate* stands as one of the most learned expositions of the Trinity in the Middle Ages.

In keeping with the classical understanding of theology as faith seeking understanding, Richard attempted to provide a rational demonstration of the Trinity and to discover "necessary reasons" for God's unity and triunity[48] that could be coupled with faith and experience.[49] Hence, he declared, "While God's unity and Trinity are beyond independent proof by reason, human reason can offer lines of reasoning that support and explicate what faith declares."[50] Of particular interest is Richard's discussion of the necessary plurality of persons in the Godhead.[51] To develop this point, he turns to the concept of divine goodness and observes that supreme goodness must involve love.[52] Richard argues that because self-love cannot be true charity, supreme love requires another, equal to the lover, who is the recipient of that love.[53] In addition, because supreme love

46. Fortman, *The Triune God*, 141.

47. Jaroslav Pelikan, *The Melody of Theology: A Philosophical Dictionary* (Cambridge: Harvard University Press, 1988), 90.

48. Fortman, *The Triune God*, 193.

49. Ewert Cousins, "A Theology of Interpersonal Relations," *Thought* 45 (1970): 59.

50. Grover A. Zinn, ed. *Richard of St. Victor* (New York: Paulist Press, 1979), 46.

51. For an English translation of book 3 of Richard's *De Trinitate*, see Zinn, *Richard of St. Victor*, 373–397.

52. Ibid., 375–6.

53. Ibid., 374–5.

is received as well as given, such love must be a shared love, one in which each person loves and is loved by the other.[54] Cognizant that the witness of Christian faith declares that the one God is three, and not merely two persons,[55] Richard claims that further analysis of supreme love demonstrates that indeed three persons are required.[56] He argues that for love to be supreme it must desire that the love it experiences through giving and receiving be one that is shared with another. Consequently, perfect love is not merely mutual love between two but is fully shared among three and only three.[57]

Richard's work is significant in that it provides a relationally based alternative to Augustine's psychological approach to the Trinity. As Gunton notes regarding Richard, "Unlike Augustine, the fountainhead of most Western theology of the Trinity, he looks not at the inner soul for his clues to the nature of God, but at persons in relation."[58] Moreover, Richard's conception of the interior life of God demands a fully personal Trinity. By extension, the relationality within the divine life captured in Richard's theological model carries implications for a theological understanding of humans as the *imago dei* as well, a point we will pick up later. As Zinn explains, "[T]he reflection of this life should lead to a renewed appreciation of charity as a love lived in community with others, involving interpersonal sharing of the deepest kind."[59] In short, whereas Augustine's conception of the individual soul as an image of the Trinity provided the basis for an interior approach to spirituality that emphasizes the ascent of the individual to union with God, Richard's approach suggests the possibility of spirituality based on interpersonal community.[60] Although it would be misleading to say that Richard developed a fully relational view of the person in his thought, he provided, as Gunton points out, "an approach to the doctrine of the Trinity that contains possibilities for the development of a relational view of the person."[61] Commenting on the significance of Richard's theological program, Fortman declares that henceforth "there will be two great trinitarian theories in the medieval theological world, the Augustinian that St. Thomas will systematize, and the theory of Richard of St. Victor, whose principal representative will be St. Bonaventure."[62]

The thirteenth century was the high point of medieval theology. During this century, the theologians of the Dominican and Franciscan orders produced what one historian calls "the greatest contribution to trinitarian systematization that the Western Church ever had seen or would see."[63] Clearly the most significant figure of this period is Thomas Aquinas. The comprehensive detail and

---

54. Ibid., 380.
55. Ibid., 384.
56. Ibid., 386–393.
57. Fortman, *The Triune God*, 194.
58. Gunton, *The Promise of Trinitarian Theology*, 89.
59. Zinn, *Richard of St. Victor*, 46.
60. Cousins, "A Theology of Interpersonal Relations," 59.
61. Gunton, *The Promise of Trinitarian Theology*, 91.
62. Fortman, *The Triune God*, 191.
63. Ibid., 233.

philosophical precision of his trinitarian theology has won for him the admiration of many who would affirm with Fortman that there can be "little doubt that Aquinas produced the finest metaphysical synthesis of trinitarian doctrine that had thus far appeared in West or East."[64] In sum, Aquinas provides an outstanding example of a comprehensive understanding of the Christian faith and the created order developed into a coherent whole through the doctrine of the triune God, "to which everything was made tributary and in the light of which all things were viewed," to cite McGiffert's characterization.[65]

The approach of the medieval scholastic theologians to the doctrine of the Trinity has recently come under scrutiny, largely because of its focus on the unity of God. As the leading theologian of the time, Aquinas in particular is the recipient of much of the criticism. Karl Rahner, for example, suggests that by turning first to the doctrine of the one God and only later developing an understanding of God as triune, Aquinas contributed to the decline of robust trinitarian theology in the life of the church.[66]

Critiques such as Rahner's often leave the impression that Aquinas was not genuinely interested in the doctrine of the Trinity and that his relative lack of concern was symptomatic of the decline of the doctrine over the course of the Middle Ages. This is, however, manifestly not the case. Medieval theology is marked by extensive trinitarian discourse motivated by a robust concern for a proper understanding of the nature of God as triune. To the criticism that Aquinas's method of beginning with the doctrine of the one God effectively marginalized the doctrine of the Trinity, Cunningham replies that the medieval doctor knew that it would not even have crossed the minds of his readers "to imagine God in anything *other* than trinitarian categories." Cunningham then adds, "Centuries later, audiences may no longer operate with this assumption; we need to take this into account, but it can hardly be blamed on Thomas."[67] Evident in the thought of the medieval theologians in general and Aquinas in particular is a deep commitment to the trinitarian faith and witness of the early church coupled with an earnest desire to provide a compelling account of that confession as an integral component of the faith of the Christian community.

The Decline of Trinitarian Theology

In many ways the medieval period was the high water mark of trinitarian discourse in the history of the church, at least until the twentieth century. As the cultural ethos of the medieval world gave way to the Renaissance and the emergence of the modern world, the theological concerns of the church shifted. The most significant development in the Western church was, of course, the

---

64. Ibid., 234.

65. Arthur C. McGiffert, *A History of Christian Thought*, vol. 2 (New York: Scribner's, 1933), 293.

66. Rahner, *The Trinity*, 16–7. For a similar critique, see Catherine Mowry LaCugna, *God for Us: The Trinity and the Christian Life* (San Francisco: HarperCollins, 1991), 145.

67. Cunningham, *These Three Are One*, 33.

Protestant Reformation with its focus on the nature of authority and the doctrine of individual salvation. The advent of the Reformation and the emergence of the modern world inaugurated a period of decreased theological interest in the Trinity and the waning of trinitarian discourse in the church.

The doctrine of the Trinity was not central in the theological debates of the Reformation. The magisterial Reformers essentially affirmed the trinitarian doctrine of the ancient creeds as expressing the teaching of scripture on the doctrine, while doing little to advance trinitarian theology itself. Although the Reformers were committed to the confession of the Trinity, they had only a paltry interest in speculative reflection. This disinterest was due in part to their aversion to the speculative theology characteristic of scholasticism and their desire not to move beyond the testimony of the biblical writings.

The magisterial Reformers were content merely to affirm the classical Western position. Some leaders in the radical tradition of the Reformation, however, transformed the general reticence to engage in speculative matters into an actual rejection of the doctrine of the Trinity. A few went so far as to claim that the doctrine is an unbiblical human construction and therefore ought to be dropped from the Christian confession.

Perhaps the best known of the antitrinitarians is Faustus Socinus. Socinus accepted scripture as the supreme authority in matters of faith but insisted that it be interpreted in accordance with reason and not in the context of the traditional creeds. On this basis, he argued that God was one in both essence and person. In Socinius's estimation, if the divine essence is one in number, there cannot "be several divine persons in it, since a person is nothing else than an intelligent, indivisible essence."[68] Thus, although orthodox theology had always carefully distinguished between essence and person, Socinus equated the two and as a consequence asserted that God is a single person. The Socinian understanding later provided the theological basis for Unitarianism in England and America.

In the Enlightenment, the doctrine of the Trinity came under widespread attack as the benign neglect of earlier years turned into outright hostility. The thinkers of the Age of Reason eschewed revealed religion in favor of a religion based solely on reason. Because the basis for the traditional understanding of the Trinity lay in divine revelation and church tradition rather than in universal reason, the doctrine was cast aside as a relic of a superstitious and uninformed past. In challenging the concept of the Trinity, the Enlightenment thinkers called into question the possibility of structuring an entire theology around it.

The hegemony of Enlightenment thought came to an apex in the work of Immanuel Kant, who represented both the culmination and the destruction of the rationalist mind-set.[69] Kant opened the way for the modern theological

---

68. *Racovian Catechism*, qq. 21–23. Cited in Fortman, *The Triune God*, 244.
69. Jaroslav Pelikan, *From Luther to Kierkegaard* (St. Louis: Concordia Publishing House, 1950), 97.

situation through the rejection of both the classical orthodox and the purely rationalist understandings of theology. His abnegation of any special revelation as the source for religious truth or any church authority as the interpreter of theological truth undermined the classical understanding of the Trinity. And his claim that "scientific" knowledge must be limited to the realm of experience shaped by the rational structures of the mind meant that claims to knowledge of God through pure reason were impossible. Although Kant provided a telling critique of many of the claims of the Enlightenment, he also sealed off the possibility of any rational knowledge of God and thereby made traditional trinitarian discourse both impractical and superfluous.

In the wake of Kant's "Copernican revolutions" in philosophy, nineteenth-century theologians followed three basic trajectories, each of which continued to play a major role in the twentieth-century discussion. One approach, that of the conservatives who sought to maintain traditional, confessional orthodoxy, simply held fast to the classical position on the basis of scripture or tradition. Despite their commitment to the orthodox doctrine, however, conservatives gave little place to the Trinity or to a trinitarian structure in their constructive theological work. As a result, in conservative circles the doctrine of the Trinity increasingly came to be viewed as a mystery to be confessed on the basis of scripture and tradition, but not as a motif that can provide content and structure to the theological enterprise.

A second approach was pioneered by Schleiermacher, who denied that the doctrine of the Trinity is an essential component of Christian faith. As has been noted earlier, in his major theological work, *The Christian Faith*, he provides only a brief discussion of the Trinity, which comes as little more than an addendum to the whole. In this short discussion, Schleiermacher confesses that he is unable to provide an adequate construction of the doctrine,[70] largely because the Trinity is "not an immediate utterance concerning the Christian self-consciousness but only a combination of several such utterances."[71]

For Schleiermacher, therefore, trinitarian theology is the product of synthetic construction based on a variety of faith utterances that lead to the doctrine of the Trinity only after the fact. He works on the assumption that the primary Christian experience and therefore the primary Christian symbols are bound up with the concept of the one God, the God of monotheism. In this understanding, the threeness of God is not a part of the primary witness of Christian faith but merely the product of the attempt to pull together the various elements of early Christian experience. As Ted Peters points out, the assumption that trinitarian doctrine is "a synthesis of otherwise random convictions regarding a more fundamental monotheism renders the Trinity systematically superfluous."[72] In this way, Schleiermacher shifts the triunity of God to the

---

70. Schleiermacher, *The Christian Faith*, 751.
71. Ibid., 738.
72. Peters, *GOD as Trinity*, 85.

margins of Christian faith, effectively "relegating it to the status of a second-rank doctrine."[73]

Hegel stands at the genesis of the third nineteenth-century approach to the Trinity. According to Hegel, God is the Absolute Spirit, whose nature is to differentiate himself in order to determine himself. God accomplishes this task through a dialectical process that develops under three determinations, which correspond to the three members of the Trinity.[74] Despite its innovative way of understanding God as triune, at several points Hegel's speculative trinitarianism falls short of the classical conception. For example, his model suggests that the reality of God is fully manifest only in the third mode, the Spirit, thereby effectively denying the traditional doctrine, with its clear assertion that all three persons participate equally in deity. In addition, Hegel reduces the Christian theological conception of God as Trinity to a symbolic illustration of a philosophical truth accessible through human reason apart from Christian revelation or experience. In short, as Peters concludes, Hegel and his followers affirm a philosophical trinitarianism in which the Trinity "is the equivalent of a metaphysical truth that can be established more or less independently of the Christian revelation."[75]

In spite of shortcomings such as these, Hegel is important in that he broke with his Enlightenment philosophical predecessors and many of his contemporaries, who saw the concept of the Trinity as an embarrassing relic from the ancient Christian past. Going against the philosophical grain, he boldly reestablished the concept of the Trinity as a crucial component in both philosophy and theology. As a consequence, Hegel's reaffirmation of the importance of the trinitarian conception of God opened the way for the revival of trinitarian theology in the twentieth century. In this sense, his understanding of the Trinity marked the first stage in the contemporary recovery of the doctrine.

Conclusion: Trinitarian Theology as "Church Dogmatics"

We have argued that Christian theology must be trinitarian because the understanding of God as triune reflects the biblical narrative and because, apart from a hiatus generated by the Enlightenment, it has informed—and even shaped—the theological conversation throughout the history of the church. Modern theology did mark a momentary move away from this approach, one that led to the marginalization of the Trinity, as both liberal and conservative theologians pursued the agenda of the Enlightenment, even if in differing ways. Yet the twentieth century launched a renewal of trinitarian theology, characterized by a return to the classical supposition that the Trinity ought to be a central concern for Christian faith and life, and that the

---

73. Ibid., 83.
74. G. W. F. Hegel, *The Phenomenology of Mind*, trans. J. B. Ballie (New York: Harper & Row, 1967), 766–85.
75. Peters, *GOD as Trinity*, 83.

entire content and exposition of theology should be ordered around the trinitarian conception of God.

The renewed commitment to the centrality of the Trinity that typifies the contemporary theological environment is in keeping with the historical trajectory of the Christian community 's reflection on the content of theology. As has been mentioned repeatedly in this chapter, the particularly Christian answer to the question of God's identity is rooted in the doctrine of the Trinity. The one God is Father, Son, and Spirit. This confession reflects the Christian experience of God and stands as the chief hallmark of the Christian faith. The ecumenical symbols of the Christian tradition are ordered around this confession, and the history of Christian theological reflection has been decisively shaped by it. Consequently, any theology that would claim to be *Christian* theology must be trinitarian. That is, because the Christian community has, in a fundamental way, been committed to finding its basis in the being and action of the triune God, truly *Christian* theological reflection must continue in this tradition if it is to make any claim of continuity with the past. Faithful Christian theology should thus be ordered and structured in such a way as to reflect the primacy of this fundamental Christian confession.

This is not to say that there is no room for revisioning the exact content of the doctrine of the Trinity. This can and should be an important part of the faithful Christian theological agenda, which continually seeks a better understanding of the message of the gospel and its implications. What we are claiming is simply that any theology that would call itself Christian in any meaningful sense has an obligation not only to contemporary theological concerns but also to past reflections of the Christian community. As we maintained in chapter 4, the Christian tradition provides the hermeneutical trajectory for contemporary theology. Theology that is faithful to this hermeneutical trajectory must be trinitarian.

There remains yet a third reason that we must mention. A trinitarian theology reflects the understanding of theology that arises from the contemporary understanding of the nature of theology itself. Because this point emerges from the previous chapter, along with the argument of this chapter's previous sections, and because we will touch on the topic again in chapter 7, we need devote only a paragraph to the idea here.

In chapter 5 we asked whether or not theology is a cultural practice, that is, an act of the Christian community viewed as a culture. In that discussion, we concluded that in its constructive dimension, theology is directly a cultural practice of the church, insofar as theology is connected to the production of meaning. Viewed from this perspective, the goal of theological construction is exploring and articulating an understanding of the particular belief-mosaic of the Christian community. This goal is attained as participants in the community engage in an ongoing conversation about the meanings of the symbols they hold in common as Christians. Of the various topics about which Christians converse, none is more central to the faith than the conception of God, and as we have argued in this chapter, the understanding of God that lies at the heart of the faith is of God as triune. In this sense, we might speak of the Trinity as the central symbol of the Christian community. Theology, in turn, is the community's conversation about the meaning of this central symbol, and consequently, Christian theology is inherently trinitarian in content and structure. In short, as will be argued again in chapter 7, theology is "church dogmatics," and the "dogmatics" of the *Christian* church must by its very nature be trinitarian.

The Character of a Trinitarian Theology

The biblical witness, the theological heritage of the church, and contemporary understandings converge to indicate that a truly Christian theology must be trinitarian. In setting forth our case for a trinitarian theology we have implicitly indicated what characterizes a theology whose contents and structure are informed by the Christian conception of God as triune. What remains is to present our understanding in a more explicit manner. The place to begin this discussion is with the resurgence of trinitarian theology in the twentieth century.

The Renewal of Trinitarian Theology
and the Trinitarian Structure of Theology

As noted previously, the twentieth century witnessed a renewed interest in the doctrine of the Trinity and consequently in trinitarian theology. Although several theologians at the turn of the century were busily unfolding the implications of Hegelian trinitarianism, arguably the most significant thinker responsible for launching theology on a new path was Karl Barth.

Barth and Revelational Trinitarianism

A central aspect of Barth's agenda was clearly to reestablish the significance of the Trinity for theology. In his *Church Dogmatics* the doctrine functions both as a type of prolegomenon and as the structural motif for his presentation of Christian theology.

At the heart of Barth's program is his assertion that the revelation of God that provides the basis for theology is a trinitarian event in which the divine self-disclosure involves three moments: Revealer, Revelation, and Revealedness. He maintains that these correspond to Father, Son, and Spirit.[76] Departing from Schleiermacher's model of synthesis, Barth engages in analysis of the biblical witness that leads him to the conclusion that the doctrine of the Trinity is a logical necessity.[77]

Actually, for Barth it is the Christocentric focus of the biblical witness that necessitates a trinitarian revelational theology. He is convinced that the biblical

---

76. Karl Barth, *Church Dogmatics*, trans. G. W. Bromiley, 2nd ed. (Edinburgh: T. & T. Clark, 1975), 1/1:295.

77. Peters, *GOD as Trinity*, 87.

affirmation that God has reconciled the world to himself through the mission of Jesus Christ leads to a trinitarian conception of God. Moreover, the scriptural witness to the life and mission of Jesus and the New Testament confession that this Jesus is Lord entail the corresponding belief that God is triune. Hence, for Barth, the threefoldness indicated by the terms Father, Son, and Spirit is in the words of Claude Welch, "a threefoldness in the structure or pattern of the one act of God in Christ and therefore the structure of all divine activity and of the being of God."[78] In short, Barth is convinced that the doctrine of the Trinity is deeply embedded in the biblical witness and consequently is in fact, contra Schleiermacher, a primary Christian symbol.[79]

Barth's Christocentric, revelational trinitarianism emerges as well from his conviction that the Christian conception of God does not begin with a generic monotheism to which Christology is added at a later point. Instead, the Christian understanding of God begins with the Son through whom God is revealed as Father, and it is through the revelation of the Son that God is known as the triune one. Thus, for Barth the Christian understanding of God as triune is distinct from all other conceptions of the divine reality.

In Barth's estimation, then, the doctrine of the Trinity follows directly from the Christian confession that God has revealed himself to the world in Jesus Christ. Claude Welch praises Barth's Christocentric revelational approach, in that in it the Trinity is "an immediate consequence of the gospel" due to the fact that the revelation "on which everything depends" cannot be developed or stated except in a trinitarian fashion. Welch then adds, "The doctrine of the Trinity is of all-embracing importance because it is the objective expression, the crystallization of the gospel itself. It is not just one part of the doctrine of God, but is integral to every aspect of the doctrine of God and to every other doctrine as well."[80]

Barth's great accomplishment, therefore, was to argue conclusively that the Christian community's primary experience of revelation is trinitarian in nature and, as a consequence, that the doctrine of the Trinity is a logically necessary component of the early Christian experience and confession of Jesus Christ as Lord and as revealer of God. In so doing, Barth avoided "splitting up" elements of the Christian experience that had in fact been received by the early community as a whole. Welch summarizes the far-reaching theological implications of this innovation: "It not only prevents us from identifying God simply with a Creator-God of nature and natural theology, thus falling into a 'unitarianism of the Father,' but it also makes impossible a Christology that is not wholly theocentric or a pneumatology that is not genuinely Christocentric and theocentric."[81] These implications are evident in the *Church Dogmatics* itself, as the

---

78. Claude Welch, *In This Name: The Doctrine of the Trinity in Contemporary Theology* (New York: Charles Scribner's Sons, 1952), 234.
    79. Peters, *GOD as Trinity*, 87.
    80. Welch, *In This Name*, 238.
    81. Peters, *GOD as Trinity*, 88.

renewed emphasis on the threefold nature of God as a primary component of Christian faith provides structure for everything that follows.

We noted previously Hegel's importance in opening the way for a revival of trinitarian theology. Despite its shortcomings, Hegel's work leads to an important insight for theological method. Taking Hegel's impulse seriously, we conclude that insofar as the triune God is connected to the historical process (even if not in the manner Hegel himself proposed), the doctrine of the Trinity is not merely a subtheme of theology proper but is in fact the topic of the entire, systematic theological construction, which views all the theological loci as in some sense participants in the central topic of theology, namely, the triune God. Barth's renewal of the doctrine of the Trinity took this Hegelian implication a step further. In his estimation, all theology is the explication of the being and action of God in Christ. As a consequence of this Barthian insight, a truly trinitarian theology is one that is structured around the self-disclosure of the triune God as centered in Christ and given through scripture to the believing community. Building from Barth, we would add that a truly trinitarian theology is one in which all of the theological loci are informed by and, in turn, inform the explication of the Trinity that, following Hegel, stands at the heart of the constructive systematic-theological enterprise.

Trinitarian-structured Theology

Following the trail blazed by Barth, many theologians[82] have risen to the challenge of placing the doctrine of the Trinity back into the center of constructive theology. Often ranked with Hegel and Barth in setting the theological agenda is Karl Rahner. Rahner articulated the important thesis that the economic Trinity is the immanent Trinity and the immanent Trinity is the economic Trinity.[83] This thesis, known as Rahner's rule, marks out the new phase that trinitarian discourse has entered, as this basic principle has engendered a broad consensus of opinion among theologians of various traditions.[84]

Rahner's rule indicates that rather than God's relating to the world in the unity of the divine being, God's ongoing interaction with creation always comes as the work of one or another of the three divine persons. Because the Christian experience of God occurs through the economy of salvation, that is, through God's redemptive activity in history, knowledge of God is never simply knowledge of God in general but always knowledge of God in God's triune being. At the same time, Rahner argues that the experience of God that arises in the economy of salvation remains a genuine experience of the eternal God, for through the process of salvation the eternal God reveals his own true self to humans.

82. For helpful summaries of several recent contributions as well as an overview of the issues under consideration in the contemporary discussion, see John Thompson, *Modern Trinitarian Perspectives* (New York: Oxford University Press, 1994); and Peters, *GOD as Trinity*.

83. Rahner, *The Trinity*, 22.

84. Walter Kasper, *The God of Jesus Christ*, trans. Matthew J. O'Connell (London: SCM Press, 1983), 274.

Thus, Rahner declares that God is "actually internally just the way we experience the divine in relation to us, namely, as Father, Son, and Spirit."[85] Although theologians such as Moltmann and Jenson subsequently developed the idea that God finds his identity in the temporal events of the economy of salvation, Rahner himself did not move in this direction. He retains the classical belief that God's eternal being is independent of historical events. He views "Rahner's rule" as postulating that the way in which God relates to the world must be understood with reference to each of the three persons and not as emerging from a prior understanding of God as a unity.[86]

Hegel, through his connection of the Trinity and the unfolding historical process; Barth, through his insistence on the connection between the Trinity and revelation as the basis for all theological assertions; and Rahner, through his connection of the immanent Trinity and the economic Trinity as one identical reality, set the context for the discussion of trinitarian theology in the twentieth century.[87] Jüngel, Moltmann, Jenson, and Pannenberg in turn, attempted to develop a trinitarian theology within the context of the framework and insights provided by the three pioneers. All of these theologians are committed to a relational interpretation of the Trinity and to the methodological premise that the revelation of God as Trinity, along with the corresponding trinitarian theology, must be grounded solely in the historical person of Jesus and not based on alien philosophical categories and structures.[88] Their work launched a relatively new emphasis that bases the doctrine of the Trinity on relationality and as such represents, at least to some degree, an extension and development of ancient trinitarian thought.[89]

Of these, Pannenberg's proposal offers perhaps the most rigorous and highly developed statement of the doctrine and its interrelatedness to the whole of theology.[90] He asserts that rather than relegating the Trinity to the status of a footnote, we ought to place God's triune nature at the very heart of theology. In a manner reminiscent of Barth, Pannenberg asserts that all of systematic theology is in some sense the explication of this central doctrine. At the same time, Pannenberg is also critical of the theological tradition from Augustine to Barth. He claims that, by viewing the trinitarian members as the internal relations within the one God, theologians have made God into a fourth person above the three members of the Trinity. Rather than speaking of the one God who is above the three, Pannenberg argues

---

85. Peters, *GOD as Trinity*, 96–7.

86. Peters, *GOD as Trinity*, 97.

87. Faye E. Schott, "God is Love: The Contemporary Theological Movement of Interpreting the Trinity as God's Relational Being" (Th.D. dissertation, Lutheran School of Theology at Chicago, 1990), 62.

88. Schott, "God is Love," 9.

89. Catherine Mowry LaCugna, "Current Trends in Trinitarian Theology," *Religious Studies Review* 13/2 (April 1987): 141–47.

90. For a summary and discussion of Pannenberg's conception of the Trinity, see Stanley J. Grenz, *Reason for Hope: The Systematic Theology of Wolfhart Pannenberg* (New York: Oxford University Press, 1990), 46–54, 71–75.

that the one God is the three, and that there is no God other than the Father, Son, and Spirit.[91]

These insights from Rahner and Pannenberg are significant for a theological method that seeks to structure theology in a trinitarian manner. They provide assurance that the explication of the triune God in God's self-disclosure in and to creation is at the same time the explication of the triune God in the divine reality. This assertion takes us back to our earlier discussion of the history of God. At that point we noted that throughout much of church history theologians assumed that God's internal history corresponded to God's external history. This assumption, however, eventually led to a focus on God's internal history that elevated a speculative trinitarian theology separate from the concrete historical narratives of the Bible. This produced a "theology from above" that no longer had much interest in the "theology from below" to which it was necessarily linked and on which it depended. In the aftermath of the attendant loss of trinitarian theology, Rahner and Pannenberg have reunited God's internal and external histories and, in so doing, brought together once again theology "from above" and "from below."

Methodologically, this means that trinitarian-theological explication runs in two directions. On the one hand, it moves *from* the self-disclosure of God in and to creation, centered on the coming of Christ and the ongoing work of the Spirit, *to* the eternal life of the triune God. Viewed from this perspective, theology (proper) is dependent on Christology and pneumatology. On the other hand, theological construction moves as well *from* the eternal reality of the triune God, which is confessed by the ecumenical church of all ages, *to* an understanding of the trinitarian persons in the creative and redemptive work of the one God. In this sense, Christology and pneumatology can only be ventured in the light of theology (proper).

Trinitarian Theology and the *Imago Dei*

The methodological insights we drew from the architects of the renewal of trinitarian theology brought the doctrine of the Trinity into play within the loci of systematic theology. More specifically, we asserted that in a trinitarian theology the three central aspects—theology (proper), Christology, and pneumatology—are interrelated. One further aspect of a truly trinitarian theology remains to be mentioned, a dimension that links the divine and the human or the theological and the anthropological. This aspect is crucial if our systematic-theological articulation is to draw insight from the Christian understanding of God in a manner that can inform our human purpose as creatures of the triune God. The path to this goal leads through the traditional theological conviction that God's triune nature forms the transcendent grounding for human rela-

---

91. This theme is addressed repeatedly in Pannenberg's work. For example, see Wolfhart Pannenberg, "The Christian Vision of God: The New Discussion on the Trinitarian Doctrine," *Trinity Seminary Review* 13/2 (Fall 1991): 53–60.

tionships, which in turn is connected to the theological concept of humans as the *imago dei*. Because venturing in this direction leads us beyond what has been the methodological focus to date of the renewed interest in trinitarian theology, we must flesh out this aspect of the trinitarian structuring of theology in somewhat greater detail.

The Relationality of God

Perhaps the single most significant development in the contemporary renaissance of trinitarian theology has been the emphasis on relationality. The category of relationality enjoys a considerable degree of consensus among recent interpreters of trinitarian theology, who see it as providing an alternative to the metaphysics of substance that dominated theological reflection on the Trinity throughout much of church history. The traditional emphasis on an abstract property of substance, or a divine essence, standing under God has come under scrutiny in recent trinitarian studies. Theologians today routinely critique the concept as one that implies that God is an isolated, solitary individual.

The question of the nature of a substance was initially placed on the theological table by the early church father Tertullian through his famous formula *una substantia, tres personae*. Theologians, especially in the West, subsequently took up the challenge of devising an understanding of the nature of substance when used with reference to God. Hence, Augustine spoke of God as a substance that was eternal and unchangeable. Later Thomas Aquinas defined God as pure act, thereby excluding such ideas as *becoming* or *potency* as inapplicable to God, insofar as these would imply change in the immutable God in the act of becoming or in the transition from potency to act. The definitional link these theologians forged between substance and unchangeability meant that they viewed God as eternal and unchanging, in contrast to creation, which is temporal and in a constant state of change in its relation to God.

The substantialist conception carried within itself the distinction between absolute essence and relational attributes. According to this understanding, essence is absolute, and therefore it must remain unchanged in order to preserve its identity. If change occurs in the essence of an entity its identity is lost. Relationality, in turn, was deemed to belong to the dimension of attributes, not substance. Consequently, substantialist theologians suggested that God is absolute and immutable in his essential nature, whereas he maintains relationality to creation through the divine attributes. As Ted Peters notes regarding the classical position, "What could not be countenanced is the notion that the divine essence is contingent upon the relational dimensions of its being."[92] The result, however, has been the obscuring of God's internal relationality and of God's loving relationship to creation in much of the classical literature on the nature of God.

In recent years, the classical commitment to a substantialist conception of God's nature has been critiqued. At the heart of this critique is the apparent

92. Peters, *GOD as Trinity*, 31.

incompatibility of an eternal, essentially immutable God with the portrait in the biblical narratives of a God who has entered into loving relationship with creation. Although the debate continues regarding the degree to which the category of substance ought to be abandoned, theologians voice considerable agreement that the primary accent should be placed on the category of relationality.

Catherine LaCugna, to cite one example, asserts that *person* rather than *substance* is the primary ontological category, and notes that the ultimate source of reality is not a "by-itself" or an "in-itself" but a person, a "toward-another." She concludes that the triune God is "self-communicating" and exists from all eternity "in relation to another."[93] Likewise, Robert Jenson writes, "The original point of trinitarian dogma and analysis was that God's relations to us are internal to him, and it is in carrying out this insight that the 'relation' concept was introduced to define the distinction of identities."[94] In a similar manner, Elizabeth Johnson claims that the priority of relation in the triune God challenges and critiques the concentration of classical theism on "singleness" in God. Because the persons are "constituted by their relationships to each other, each is unintelligible except as connected with the others."[95] The assertion that each of the persons in the triune life is constituted only in relationship to the others leads Johnson to the conclusion that the "very principal of their being" is to be found in the category of relation.[96]

David Cunningham notes that the breadth of the current consensus about the priority of relationality in trinitarian discourse is evidenced by the fact that both Jenson and Johnson may be cited in support of it, even though the two thinkers "are not usually noted for being in close agreement with one another."[97] This theological consensus encompasses a variety of thinkers, including Jürgen Moltmann,[98] Wolfhart Pannenberg,[99] Leonardo Boff,[100] Ted Peters,[101] Colin Gunton,[102] and Alan Torrance,[103] although these theologians may differ from one another on the precise construction of relationality.

93. Catherine Mowry LaCugna, *God for Us: The Trinity and Christian Life* (San Francisco: HarperCollins, 1991), 14–15.

94. Robert W. Jenson, *The Triune Identity: God According to the Gospel* (Philadelphia: Fortress Press, 1982), 120.

95. Elizabeth A. Johnson, *She Who Is: The Mystery of God in Feminist Theological Discourse* (New York: Crossroad, 1992), 216.

96. Ibid.

97. Cunningham, *These Three Are One*, 26.

98. Moltmann, *The Trinity and the Kingdom of God*, 171–72.

99. Pannenberg, "The Christian Vision of God: The New Discussion on the Trinitarian Doctrine," 53–60.

100. Leonardo Boff, *Trinity and Society*, trans. Paul Burns (Maryknoll, N.Y.: Orbis Books, 1988), 134–48.

101. Peters, *GOD as Trinity*, 30–34.

102. Colin Gunton, *The One, the Three and the Many: God, Creation and the Culture of Modernity* (Cambridge: Cambridge University Press, 1993), 164.

103. Alan J. Torrance, *Persons in Communion: Trinitarian Description and Human Participation* (Edinburgh: T. & T. Clark, 1995).

At the heart of the contemporary consensus of the divine relationality is the apostolic witness that God is love (e.g., 1 John 4:8, 16). Developing the doctrine of the Trinity in accordance with the category of relationality indicates how this biblical assertion is to be understood. Throughout all eternity the divine life of the triune God is aptly characterized by the word *love*, which, when viewed in the light of relationality, signifies the reciprocal self-dedication of the trinitarian members to one another. Indeed, there is no God other than the Father, Son, and Spirit bound together in love throughout eternity. The term *love*, in turn, provides a profound conception of the reality of God as understood by the Christian tradition. Love expressed and received by the trinitarian persons among themselves provides a description of the inner life of God throughout eternity apart from any reference to creation. In addition to enjoying the support of the biblical witness, *love* is an especially fruitful term as an explication of the divine life because it is a relational concept. Love requires both subject and object. Because God is triune—that is, multiplicity within unity—the divine reality comprehends both love's subject and love's object. For this reason, when viewed theologically, the statement "God is love" refers primarily to the eternal, relational, intratrinitarian fellowship among Father, Son, and Holy Spirit, who together are the one God. In this way, God is love within the divine reality, and in this sense, through all eternity God is the social Trinity, the community of love.

Two significant factors have influenced the contemporary interest in relationality among theologians. One is the recovery and introduction into Western thought of certain impulses from the Eastern or Greek theological tradition. The primary focus of attention in this "turn to the East" has been the Cappadocian emphasis on *relation* over *substance*[104] as developed by Orthodox theologians such as Vladimir Lossky[105] and John Zizioulas.[106] In the process, thinkers from other traditions have critiqued and modified the particularly Orthodox perspective on the Cappadocian understanding of relationality, yet they have generally retained the basic impulse toward relationality in preference to substantiality that goes back to this element in the patristic legacy.[107] The other crucial influence in the contemporary focus on relationality is the reconceptualization of the nature of personhood and the self that has emerged recently in reaction to the radical individualism spawned by the Enlightenment, with its elevation of the individual viewed in isolation and as fundamentally detached from the world. This facet of the contemporary situation requires further exploration.[108]

104. Cunningham, *These Three Are One*, 26–7.

105. Vladimir Lossky, *The Mystical Theology of the Eastern Church*, trans. Fellowship of St. Alban and St. Sergius (Cambridge: James Clark & Co., 1957; reprint, Crestwood, N.Y.: St. Vladimir's Seminary Press, 1976).

106. John D. Zizioulas, *Being as Communion: Studies in Personhood and the Church* (Crestwood, N.Y.: St. Vladimir's Seminary Press, 1985).

107. For a recent and significant engagement with the thought of Zizioulas from a Protestant perspective, see Miroslav Volf, *After Our Likeness: The Church As the Image of the Trinity* (Grand Rapids: Wm. B. Eerdmans Publishing Co., 1998).

108. For a fuller exposition of the developments described here, see Stanley J. Grenz,

The Rise and Demise of the Self

Humans from the beginning to the present have sought to understand the nature of identity and personhood. Thinkers in every culture since ancient times have pondered the question of personal identity. For example, the Hebrew psalmist, while contemplating the vastness and majesty of the universe, asks in wonder and amazement, "[W]hat are human beings that you are mindful of them, mortals that you care for them?" (Ps. 8:4, NRSV). In recent years, however, this seemingly universal human quest to fathom the nature of personal identity has occurred in the context of the widespread cultural movement away from the outlook of modernity. The demise of the Enlightenment project has shifted the focus of the search for a sense of personhood. To understand this shift requires that we briefly consider the view of the self in modernity.

Whereas the psalmist placed humans within the context of creation, in the modern era the human person was pried loose from creation, now understood as "nature." And in contrast to the psalmist, who viewed human identity from a vantage point within the created order, the modern response to the question of human identity came in the form of the construction of the self. In the wake of the Enlightenment, for the determination of what it means to be a human many philosophers looked to reason, understood as the innately human ability to disengage from one's natural environment and social context and objectify the world. Disengagement from the objectified world formed the foundation for the modernist ideal—namely, individual autonomy—understood as the ability to choose one's own purposes from within oneself apart from the controlling influence of natural and social forces[109] and hence to create one's own identity or self. Society, in turn, was seen as a collection of autonomous, independent selves pursuing their personally chosen ends. In this manner, the modern self became self-created and self-sufficient, the highly centered "true inner person" persisting through time and standing above the vacillations and shifting relationships that characterize day-to-day living. The self was seen as the autonomous, individual subject, who enters into relationships (whether with other humans, with "nature," or even with God) as a preexisting "given."

Postmodern theorists have vigorously challenged this modern conception of the self, a process that has led to the demise of the modern self. Whatever else it may be, viewed from the perspective of anthropology the postmodern ethos is marked by the rejection of—or even more strongly stated, the deconstruction of—the modern self. Postmodern thinkers assert that rather than the disengaged, isolated observer who exists prior to society and thus forms the primary building block for the supposedly purely contractual social order, the human

---

"Belonging to God: The Quest for a Communal Spirituality in the Postmodern World," *Asbury Theological Journal* 54/2 (Fall 1999): 41–52.

109. Charles Taylor, *Human Agency and Language: Philosophical Papers*, vol. 1 (Cambridge: Cambridge University Press, 1985), 4.

self is in some sense constituted by social relationships. Postmodern thinkers routinely picture this engaged self as a position in a vast web, a nexus, a point of intersection. The postmodern self is a bundle of fluctuating relationships and momentary preferences. Of course, in a fast-changing world, this image leads to a highly unstable, impermanent self. As the French philosopher Jean-Francois Lyotard observed, "[E]ach exists in a fabric of relations that is now more complex and mobile than ever before."[110]

The postmodern condition, therefore, arises out of the loss of the stability and consistency that characterized the self of the modern ideal. The destruction of the modern self leaves as its residue only the radically decentered postmodern "self," whose fleeting "existence" is limited to whatever tastes, preferences, and relationships happen to be juxtaposed in the existential moment. The result of this is what Fredric Jameson refers to as "psychic fragmentation."[111] And this splintering of the self into multiple subjectivities gives birth to, in the terminology of Johann Roten, the "chaotic self,"[112] which "attempts to absorb 'alterity' in all its forms to overcome separation and isolation, only to find itself in the end in a state of spiritual chaos."[113]

The Christian response to the demise of the self brought on by the postmodern ethos brings us to the Christian teaching that humans are created in the image of God.

The Image of God

Christian theologians have traditionally constructed theological anthropology around the concept of the *imago dei*. Human identity (or the self) is bound up with the idea that human beings are created in the image of God and therefore are bearers of the divine image. In keeping with this conviction, theologians have offered various suggestions as to the nature or content of the *imago dei*.[114]

Perhaps the most long-standing interpretation of the *imago* sees it as a structure of the human person. In this understanding, the divine image consists of the properties that constitute human beings as human with special emphasis placed on the capacity for rationality coupled with our moral nature. This view is widespread in the writings of the church fathers and the medieval scholastic theologians. It was challenged to some extent in the Protestant Reformation, regained ascendancy in Protestant orthodox theology, and continues to be influential in those traditions influenced by the scholastic traditions. In spite of

110. Jean-Francois Lyotard, *The Postmodern Condition: A Report on Knowledge*, trans. Geoff Bennington and Brian Massumi (Minneapolis: University of Minnesota Press, 1984), 15.

111. Fredric Jameson, *Postmodernism, or the Cultural Logic of Late Capitalism* (Durham, N.C.: Duke University Press, 1995), 90.

112. Johann G. Roten, "The Marian Counterpoint of Postmodern Spirituality," in *Divine Representations: Postmodernism and Spirituality*, ed. Ann W. Astell (New York: Paulist Press, 1994), 113–14.

113. Roten, "The Marian Counterpoint of Postmodern Spirituality," 114.

114. For a fuller delineation of the *imago dei*, see Stanley J. Grenz, *Theology for the Community of God* (Grand Rapids: Wm. B. Eerdmans Publishing Co., 2000), 168–80.

its venerable pedigree, the substantialist view ultimately fails to do justice to the dynamic nature of the divine image.

Two concepts have served to move the discussion forward: relationality and destiny. The former finds its genesis in the Reformers, who tended to place primary focus on the special standing before God that characterizes human existence rather than on a formal structure supposedly found within the human person. According to the biblical narratives this relationship was tarnished by human sin but is restored through Christ. The relational view fostered by the Reformers found support in the twentieth century in the work of so-called neoorthodox theologians, such as Emil Brunner.[115]

The Reformers also opened the door to the other concept, namely, the idea that links the *imago dei* to our human destiny, although the groundwork for this idea lay in Irenaeus's fruitful christological proposal that Jesus is the "recapitulation" of the human story. In his discussion of Genesis 9:6, to cite one example from the Reformation, Luther declared that although humankind lost the image of God through sin, "it can be restored through the Word and the Holy Spirit."[116] This restoration, which begins now and reaches completion only on the Last Day, raises humans to a stature that is even higher than what was lost in the fall. The perfection of the divine image is the eternal life for which Adam was "fitted."[117] Hence, in this sense the *imago dei* is ultimately God's intention and goal for humankind.

The more formal development of the anthropological concept of destiny arose in the context of German romanticism, particularly in the work of Johann Gottfried Herder (1744–1803).[118] Working from the idea of "openness to the world," Herder's followers, including such eminent proponents as Wolfhart Pannenberg,[119] posit a link between the biblical concept of the image of God and our future human destiny. This link introduces a dynamic dimension into the concept of the divine image. The image of God is a destiny toward which human beings are moving and entails what they are en route to becoming. It is what resurrected humans will bear in the new creation and hence a future reality that is present now only as a foretaste or only in the form of our human potential. As Daniel Migliore states, "Being created in the image of God is not a state or condition but a movement with a goal: human beings are restless for a fulfillment of life not yet realized."[120]

This dynamic conception of the *imago dei* arising out of the relational model launches us on the road toward an understanding of the self that can speak

115. Emil Brunner, *The Christian Doctrine of Creation and Redemption*, trans. Olive Wyon (Philadelphia: Westminster Press, 1953), 55–56.

116. Martin Luther, *Lectures on Genesis*, in *Luther's Works*, ed. Jaroslav Pelikan, trans. George V. Schick, American Edition (St. Louis: Concordia Publishing House, 1958), 2:141.

117. Luther, *Lectures on Genesis*, 1:64–5.

118. See, for example, J. G. Herder, *Ideen zur Philosophie der Geschichte der Menschheit* (Berlin: G. Hempel, 1879), 9.5.

119. Wolfhart Pannenberg, *Systematic Theology*, trans. Geoffrey W. Bromiley, vol. 2 (Grand Rapids: Wm. B. Eerdmans Publishing Co., 1991), 218–31.

120. Daniel L. Migliore, *Faith Seeking Understanding: An Introduction to Christian Theology* (Grand Rapids: Wm. B. Eerdmans Publishing Co., 1991), 128.

within the postmodern context. At the heart of the divine image is human destiny as designed by God. Human beings are the image of God insofar as we have received, are now fulfilling, and one day will fully actualize the divine design for human existence, which is our destiny. But what is this design? This question takes us to the biblical texts.

The Genesis creation narratives suggest that the divinely given destiny of human beings begins with a special standing before God. As created in the divine image, human beings are the recipients of God's commands and thus have a special responsibility before God. Above all, however, Genesis 1 connects the human task with the concept of "dominion," which Genesis 2 elaborates further by suggesting that the special calling of humanity lies in our role in creation: "The LORD God took the man and put him in the Garden of Eden to work it and take care of it" (Gen. 2:15 NIV).

Rather than reading "dominion" against the background of the ideology of modern industrial society, however, we must place the concept within the context of the royal theology of the Old Testament.[121] The kings of the ancient Near East often left images of themselves in cities or territories where they could not be present in person. Such images served to represent their majesty and power.[122] Gerhard von Rad draws the parallel to humankind as the image of God:

> Just as powerful earthly kings, to indicate their claim to dominion erect an image of themselves in the provinces of their empire where they do not personally appear, so man is placed upon earth in God's image as God's sovereign emblem. He is really only God's representative, summoned to maintain and enforce God's claim to dominion over the earth.[123]

Thus, "image" and "likeness" carry the sense of "representation." God has entrusted to humans a special task with reference to creation, namely, that we serve as God's representatives. We are to reflect to creation the nature of God.

Viewing the *imago dei* as pertaining to our divinely given purpose to represent God suggests that all persons are "in the image of God" (e.g., Gen. 9:6), in that all share in the one human *telos*. Yet the New Testament writers apply the concept of the divine image particularly to Jesus Christ (2 Cor. 4:4, 6; Col.

---

121. See, for example, Phyllis A. Bird, "'Male and Female He Created Them': Gen. 1:27b in the Context of the Priestly Account of Creation," *Harvard Theological Review* 74 (April 1981): 137–44; H. Paul Santmire, "The Genesis Creation Narratives Revisited: Themes for a Global Age," *Interpretation* 45/4 (October 1991):374–75.

122. Gerhard von Rad, "*Eikon*," in the *Theological Dictionary of the New Testament*, ed. Gerhard Kittel, trans. Geoffrey W. Bromiley (Grand Rapids: Wm. B. Eerdmans Publishing Co., 1964), 2:392. See also Henri Blocher, *In the Beginning: The Opening Chapters of Genesis*, trans. David G. Preston (Downer's Grove, Ill.: InterVarsity Press, 1984), 81.

123. Gerhard von Rad, *Genesis*, trans. John H. Marks, in the Old Testament Library, ed. G. Ernest Wright (Philadelphia: Westminster Press, 1972), 58.

1:15), who is the clear representation of the character and glory of God. By extension, those who are united to Christ share in his role as the *imago dei*. All who are "in Christ" are being transformed into the image of Christ so that their lives may reflect his glory (2 Cor. 3:18). In fact, it is to conformity to Christ (as the likeness of God) that God has destined us (Rom. 8:29; 1 John 3:2). For this reason, Paul proclaims the hope that "just as we have borne the likeness of the earthly man, so shall we bear the likeness of the man from heaven" (1 Cor. 15:49). And this, he adds, will be accomplished through our participation in Christ's resurrection (1 Cor. 15:50–53). In short, the entire biblical panorama may be read as presenting the purpose of God as that of bringing into being a people who reflect the divine character and thus are the *imago dei*. At the eschaton, God will complete what was the divine intention from the beginning and has from the beginning been set before us as our human destiny. On that eschatological day we will reflect fully the divine image as God's representatives after the pattern of Christ.

The Trinity and the Social Image

While providing a necessary and helpful starting point, even the dynamic understanding of the *imago dei* as the eschatological destiny of human beings does not constitute the entire basis for recasting the self in response to the postmodern problematic. It too readily retains a potential indebtedness to the individualistic focus characteristic of the modern self.

Perhaps the most significant postmodern insight into identity formation is the observation that whatever the self may be, it is a social reality. That is to say, rather than arising sui generis, personal identity emerges *extra se*, as Luther, following Paul, observed. As a nexus, a bundle of relationships, the chaotic self that emerged from the deconstruction of the autonomous, self-positing, centered self of modernity looks to relationships for any semblance of identity.[124] Viewed from a Christian perspective, this "turn to relationships" is not misguided. On the contrary, it offers a perspective from which to view the *imago dei* and engage Christian anthropology with the postmodern condition. The contemporary acknowledgment of the relationality of personal identity suggests that the divine image is a shared, communal reality. It implies that the image of God is fully present only in relationships, that is, in "community."[125] And this aspect of the contemporary situation provides an occasion for us to return to the biblical texts with new insight into the strong communitarian strand already in the biblical concept of the *imago dei*.

The foundation for the understanding of the image of God as social lies in the creation narratives. As many thinkers since Karl Barth have noted, the first

---

124. See, for example, George Herbert Mead, *Mind, Self and Society*, ed. Charles W. Morris (Chicago: University of Chicago Press, 1934, 1974), 138–58.
125. For a development of the philosophical basis for the social understanding of personhood, see Alistair I. McFadyen, *The Call to Personhood: A Christian Theory of the Individual in Social Relationships* (Cambridge: Cambridge University Press, 1990).

creation story connects the *imago dei* with humans in relationship. What is indicated in Genesis 1:26–28 is even more explicit in the second creation narrative: God creates the first human pair in order that humans might enjoy fellowship with each other. Specifically, the creation of the woman is designed to deliver the man from his isolation. This primal community of male and female then becomes expansive, producing the offspring that arise from the sexual union of husband and wife and eventually giving rise to the development of societies. In the biblical narrative, what begins in the Garden of Eden finds its completion at the consummation of history, when God establishes the new creation, the realm in which humans enjoy perfect fellowship with each other, creation, and the Creator (e.g., Rev. 21:1–5; 22:1–5). The second creation narrative links God's creation of humans in the image of God, which includes the creation of a plurality of sexes, to a plurality found within the divine self-reference: "Let us make humankind in our image" (Gen. 1:26, NRSV). Although the verse is not explicitly trinitarian, the use of the plural pronouns does suggest that the narrator intends the reader to make a connection between human relationality and the Creator, whom through their relationality humans represent.

It is not surprising that ultimately the image of God should focus on relationality, fellowship, or "community." Indeed, as we have seen, God is inherently relational. As the doctrine of the Trinity asserts, throughout all eternity God is "community," namely, the fellowship of the three trinitarian persons who comprise the triune God. As the triune one, the fellowship of the trinitarian persons, God is love. God's goal for humankind, in turn, is that we represent God by reflecting the divine nature (love) and thereby be the *imago dei*, which is our divinely intended destiny. According to the New Testament, the focus of this image-bearing function is humans-in-relationship but, more specifically, the church as the foretaste of the new humanity. Hence, the divine design for Christ's community is that we be a people who, because we share in the Holy Spirit and thereby participate in the eternal love of God, represent God in the midst of the fallenness of the present through relationships that reflect God's own loving character. The creation of humankind in the divine image, therefore, can mean nothing less than that humans express the relational dynamic of the God whose representation we are called to be. Consequently, each human is related to the image of God ultimately only within the context of life in relationship. Only in community can we truly show what God is like, for God is the community of love, the eternal relational dynamic enjoyed by the three persons of the Trinity.

The doctrine of the Trinity indicates why the image of God is, and can only be, expressed in human relationships. The God we know is the triune one— Father, Son, and Spirit united together in perfect love. Because God is "community"—the fellowship of Father, Son, and Spirit—the creation of humankind in the divine image must be related to persons-in-relationship as well. God's own character can only be mirrored by humans who love after the manner of the perfect love present within the heart of the triune God. Only as

Christians who live in fellowship can we show forth what God is like. And as we reflect God's character—love—we also live in accordance with our own true nature and find our true identity.

This conception of God as a relational, trinitarian fellowship of love and the corresponding social reflection of the divine image by human beings in relationship leads us back to the question as to what characterizes a trinitarian theology. Theological construction that is truly trinitarian in content and structure brings the Christian confession of the triune God into its explication of the Christian belief-mosaic at every turn. As we noted earlier, this entails a thoroughly trinitarian approach to the three theologically oriented foci—theology (proper), Christology, and pneumatology. But it means as well that, by drawing from a relational understanding of the *imago dei* as derived from its transcendent theological grounding, the structuring principle of God as triune and therefore inherently relational informs the other foci as well. This method leads to a truly relational anthropology, a fully theological ecclesiology, and a completely trinitarian eschatology, as systematic theology from start to finish becomes, as Pannenberg notes, the explication of the Christian declaration that God is love.[126]

Relationality as characterizing the triune God and as marking our human calling as the *imago dei* suggests likewise the primacy of community in the construction of Christian theology. The deepest intentions of God in creation are fulfilled in the establishment of community, for indeed human beings have been created for fellowship and community with God, one another, and all of creation. This community will ultimately be established at the consummation of God's program for creation when the people of God, together with all creation, will be drawn into participation in the divine life. Given the social nature of God, a theology that is truly trinitarian will find coherence, or its integrative motif, in the concept of community, which is reflective of the nature of God and God's intention for creation. Thus, the trinitarian content of theology points to the concept of community as providing the integrative motif for theology and eventually to eschatology as its orienting motif. It is to these two focal motifs that we turn our attention in the remaining chapters of this volume.

126. Pannenberg, *Systematic Theology*, 1:448.

Chapter Seven

Community: Theology's Integrative Motif

They devoted themselves to the apostles' teaching and fellowship, to the breaking of bread and the prayers. . . . All who believed were together and had all things in common; they would sell their possessions and goods and distribute the proceeds to all, as any had need. Day by day, as they spent much time together in the temple, they broke bread at home and ate their food with glad and generous hearts, praising God and having the goodwill of all the people. And day by day the Lord added to their number those who were being saved.

—Acts 2:42–47 (NRSV)

We find ourselves not independently of other people and institutions but through them. We never get to the bottom of our selves on our own. We discover who we are face to face and side by side with others in work, love, and learning. All of our activity goes on in relationships, groups, associations, and communities ordered by institutional structures and interpreted by cultural patterns of meaning. . . . We are parts of a larger whole that we can neither forget nor imagine in our own image without paying a high price. If we are not to have a self that hangs in the void, slowly twisting in the wind, these are issues we cannot ignore.

—Robert Bellah et al.[1]

1. Robert N. Bellah et al., *Habits of the Heart: Individualism and Commitment in American Life* (New York: Harper & Row, 1986), 84.

According to Arthur Dyke, the assumption that humans are social creatures reigned from the time of Socrates until the seventeenth century.[2] Dyke's observation leads to the second motif that characterizes the pattern uniting the various local theologies, constituting them as expressions of *Christian* theology. In keeping with the realization that humans are social creatures—to which we quickly add, following the conclusions of chapter 6, that the triune God is in a primary way social—we maintain that a Christian theology that is truly trinitarian will also be completely communitarian. We maintain that theology, with its trinitarian structure, finds its integration through the concept of *community*. Community forms the theme that integrates the various strands of theological reflection into a single web or mosaic.

This chapter focuses on community as the integrative motif of theology and thus on the communitarian character of Christian theology. Our goal is to suggest why community lies at the heart of Christian theology and to indicate in what sense theology is by its very nature communitarian. To accomplish this task, we begin by exploring the concept of community itself. Then we turn our attention to the connection between community and Christian theology.

The Concept of Community

Our introduction of "culture" in chapter 5 as the embedding context for theological reflection plunked us in the middle of a discussion within contemporary anthropology. In a similar manner, the claim that Christian theology is communitarian parachutes us into an ongoing conversation among theorists in several fields, including sociology, philosophy, and political philosophy. Invoking the word *community* places us in the middle of an ongoing discussion between contemporary individualists and the "new communitarians." That is, it brings us into the so-called "liberal-communitarian" debate.[3]

The Two Traditions

It has become the vogue in recent years to speak of contemporary Western society as heir to two traditions—the individualist and the communal—each of which is the bearer of a distinctive set of values.[4] While present elsewhere, including Britain,[5] this tendency is especially pronounced in the United States. Perhaps to an unparalleled degree the American psyche has been stamped by

2. Arthur J. Dyke, *Rethinking Rights and Responsibilities: The Moral Bonds of Community* (Cleveland: Pilgrim Press, 1992), 12.

3. For this designation, see Michael J. Sandel, *Liberalism and the Limits of Justice*, 2nd ed. (Cambridge: Cambridge University Press, 1998), ix.

4. For example, Gerry C. Heard, *Basic Values and Ethical Decisions: An Examination of Individualism and Community in American Society* (Malabar, Fla.: Robert E. Krieger, 1990), 3.

5. See, for example, Raymond Plant, *Community and Ideology: An Essay in Applied Social Philosophy* (London: Routledge & Kegan Paul, 1974), 34.

both the individualist impulse and a keen awareness of the importance of communal relationships. The presence of these two streams is reflected in Robert Nisbet's telling appraisal of 1950s' America:

> On the one hand, we prize equalitarian democracy, moral neutrality, intellectual liberation, secular progress, rationalism, and all the liberating impersonalities of modern industrial and political society. On the other we continue to venerate tradition, secure social status, the corporate hierarchies of kinship, religion, and community, and close involvement in clear moral contexts.[6]

Therefore, to understand the current debate, as well as the importance of the renaissance in communitarian thought, we must look briefly at these two traditions.

The Dominance of Liberal Individualism

The first impulse, the individualist tradition, elevates the human person as the logical primus of all forms of social life and views the contract between individuals as the basis of all social interaction. This tradition promotes such values as personal freedom, self-improvement, privacy, achievement, independence, detachment, and self-interest.[7] Although the exercise of these values may bring a person into contact with others, the essential meaning of such values is not connected to interaction among persons but to the rights and needs of individuals separate from their relationships with others.[8] Thus, lying at the basis of this tradition is what Robert Bellah calls "ontological individualism," that is, "the belief that the truth of our condition is not in our society or in our relation to others, but in our isolated and inviolable selves."[9]

The individualist tradition is closely connected to liberalism as a political theory. The modern conception of the political order is based on social atomism together with the idea of the "social contract." According to this theory, autonomous selves come together to form the state, contracting with each other to give up a certain amount of their personal prerogatives to the whole for the sake of personal advantage. As a corollary, political liberalism—in the words of British theologian David Fergusson—"asserts the right of each person to free and equal treatment." Fergusson then explains: "Since modern societies comprise citizens with divergent notions of the good life, the state should adopt a

6. Robert A. Nisbet, *The Quest for Community: A Study in the Ethics of Order and Freedom* (New York: Oxford University Press, 1953), 212–13.

7. Heard, *Basic Values and Ethical Decisions*, 3.

8. Ibid.

9. Robert N. Bellah, "Community Properly Understood: A Defense of 'Democratic Communitarianism,'" in *The Essential Communitarian Reader*, ed. Amitai Etzioni (Lanham, Md.: Rowman & Littlefield, 1998), 17.

position of relative neutrality with respect to these. Its function is to maintain the equality and freedom of each citizen."[10]

As a term, *individualism* is of relatively recent origin. In fact, it may date only to the nineteenth century. It gained wide use through the writing of Alexis de Tocqueville,[11] who called it "a novel expression, to which a novel idea has given birth." Tocqueville offered a largely civic definition of individualism, speaking of it as "a mature and calm feeling, which disposes each member of the community to sever himself from the mass of his fellows and to draw apart with his family and his friends, so that after he has thus formed a little circle of his own, he willingly leaves society at large to itself." And the "novel idea" that gave it birth, Tocqueville added, was democracy.[12]

While Tocqueville may have brought the term into common use, the individualist tradition—especially as an understanding of the constitutive nature of the self—predates the French thinker's conclusions about the presence of the phenomenon in nineteenth-century America. For the impulse toward individualism, Raymond Plant,[13] following the lead of Robert Nisbet,[14] looks to those thinkers in the seventeenth and eighteenth centuries who sought to cope intellectually with the demise of the rigid status systems endemic to the older feudal society and with the rise of the modern world, characterized by a market economy, industrialization, specialization, and urbanization. In response to the changed situation, philosophers such as Thomas Hobbes (1588–1679), David Hume (1711–1776), and Jeremy Bentham (1748–1832), sought to provide an understanding of human nature that could justify the loss of the older communal social relationships. The emerging understanding looked to the contract between and consent of free persons, rather than to custom or tradition, as the basis for all human interactions. Social rules, economic structures, and even the forming of family are artificial, these thinkers argued; such matters are arrangements of convenience, derived from contracts between individuals who attain personal identity and self-consciousness without them. On this basis, Hobbes broke with the past by elevating rights, rather than responsibilities, as the foundational moral concept.[15]

In the United States, individualism took on two distinct forms. The first to emerge was "utilitarian individualism," the belief that—to cite the characterization of the Bellah group—"in a society where each vigorously pursued his own interest, the social good would automatically emerge."[16] This attitude was especially pronounced in the economic realm, where it fosters a laissez

10. David Fergusson, *Community, Liberalism and Christian Ethics* (Cambridge: Cambridge University Press, 1998), 139.

11. Bellah et al., *Habits of the Heart*, 37.

12. Alexis de Tocqueville, *Democracy in America*, trans. Henry Reeve, Francis Bowen, and Phillips Bradley, Vintage Books ed., vol. 2 (New York: Alfred A. Knopf, 1945), 104.

13. Plant, *Community and Ideology*, 30–32.

14. Robert A. Nisbet, *The Sociological Tradition* (New York: Basic Books, 1966), 48–51.

15. Dyke, *Rethinking Rights and Responsibilities*, 12.

16. Bellah et al., *Habits of the Heart*, 33.

faire capitalism that encourages all persons to pursue their own material interest.

In the mid-nineteenth century, utilitarian individualism bred a reaction spawned by American Romanticism. Yet rather than marking the rejection of individualism as a whole, Romantic thinkers such as Ralph Waldo Emerson (1803–1882) and Walt Whitman advocated merely replacing one form by another. Donald Gelpi labels their proposal "expressive individualism" and describes it as declaring that "at the heart of each person lies a unique core of intuition and feeling that demands creative expression and needs protection against the encroachments both of other individuals and of social institutions."[17]

In contrast to earlier understandings, the architects of the political theory associated with individualism did not view freedom as lying within association. Rather, freedom both entailed and demanded emancipation from such bonds.[18] Hence, in his essay *On Liberty*, the nineteenth-century, British utilitarian thinker John Stuart Mill extols the importance of individuality for a person's well-being in general and creative abilities in particular.[19] In this manner, what grew out of the emphasis in the Christian tradition on the ethical primacy of the person, became—to cite Robert Nisbet's characterization—"a rationalist psychology devoted to the ends of the release of man from the old and a sociology based upon the view that groups and institutions are at best mere reflections of the solid and ineffaceable fact of the individual."[20]

Individualism retains a powerful influence in contemporary American society. The assumption that the self is autonomous, self-determining, and "unencumbered"—that it exists independently of and outside any tradition or community—continues to color the manner in which many people view themselves and life itself. It is evident, for example, in the tendency to define ourselves fundamentally through reference to the choices we make, including the choice to join whatever "communities" we prefer.[21] According to Robert Bellah and his associates, writing in their seminal study *Habits of the Heart*, for most Americans the meaning of life is "to become one's own person, almost to give birth to oneself."[22] In keeping with this ideal, society encourages us to "cut free from the past, to define our own selves, to choose the groups with which we wish to identify,"[23] a goal that is especially depicted in "the upward mobility of the middle-class individual who must leave home and church in order to

17. Donald L. Gelpi, "Conversion: Beyond the Impasses of Individualism," in *Beyond Individualism: Toward a Retrieval of Moral Disclosure in America*, ed. Donald L. Gelpi (Notre Dame, Ind.: University of Notre Dame Press, 1989), 2. See also Bellah et al., *Habits of the Heart*, 33–35.

18. Nisbet, *The Quest for Community*, 228.

19. John Stuart Mill, *On Liberty*, ed. Curran V. Shields (1859; Indianapolis: Bobbs-Merrill Co., 1956), 67–90.

20. Nisbet, *Quest for Community*, 226.

21. See, for example, Bellah et al., *Habits of the Heart*, 65.

22. Ibid., 82.

23. Ibid., 154.

succeed in an impersonal world of rationality and competition."[24] This unencumbered, autonomous self, in turn, is viewed by many today as the foundational building block of the social orders, including the political order.

The Retrieval of Community

The communal tradition marks a strong contrast to individualism in its various forms, for it emphasizes the social nature of human existence. Its proponents are convinced that the self is formed by its relationships, roles, and attachments, that is, by a person's connection with other people as well as with institutions and traditions. Thus, the communal tradition holds to the primacy of the group, elevates the importance of relationships for personal existence, and suggests that interaction among people takes on meaning only within the social context in which it occurs. This tradition values relational qualities, including intimacy, benevolence, fellowship, belonging, dependence, social involvement, and the public good.[25] Further, advocates of the communal tradition believe that conceptions of what is right and proposals as to how society should be organized always presuppose some vision of the common good. Consequently, a society should promote civic ties and foster those institutions that form its citizens in accordance with the common good and through which its citizens can find fulfillment.[26]

The contemporary retrieval of the communal tradition is often traced to the work of several scholars,[27] including Alasdair MacIntyre,[28] Michael J. Sandel,[29] Charles Taylor,[30] and Michael Walzer,[31] who are often dubbed "the new communitarians." In the 1980s these thinkers launched a sustained critique of liberal political theory and the attendant orientation toward the language of "rights."

Underlying this critique was an attempt to tackle again the philosophical question of how the self is constituted. In this context the new communitarians attacked the individualistic atomism linked to political liberalism. Typical is Sandel's rejection of the individualistic notion of the "unencumbered self," a concept that in his opinion denies to the self "the possibility of membership in

24. Ibid., 152–53.

25. Heard, *Basic Values and Ethical Decisions*, 3.

26. Fergusson, *Community, Liberalism and Christian Ethics*, 139.

27. For this appraisal, see Amitai Etzioni, "Introduction: A Matter of Balance, Rights and Responsibilities," in *Essential Communitarian Reader*, ed. Etzioni, ix; Sandel, *Liberalism and the Limits of Justice*, ix.

28. Alasdair MacIntyre, *After Virtue: A Study in Moral Theory*, 2nd ed. (Notre Dame, Ind.: University of Notre Dame Press, 1984), first published in 1981; idem, *Whose Justice? Which Rationality?* (Notre Dame, Ind.: University of Notre Dame Press, 1988).

29. Sandel, *Liberalism and the Limits of Justice*. Note: this book was first published in 1982.

30. Charles Taylor, *Philosophical Papers, Vol. I: Human Agency and Language; Vol. II: Philosophy and the Human Sciences* (Cambridge: Cambridge University Press, 1985); idem, *Sources of the Self: The Making of Modern Identity* (Cambridge, Mass.: Harvard University Press, 1989).

31. Michael Walzer, *Spheres of Justice: A Defense of Pluralism and Equality* (New York: Basic Books, 1983).

any community bound by moral ties antecedent to choice." This individualistic self, he adds, "cannot belong to any community where the self *itself* could be at stake."[32]

Thus, the new communitarians see as the fundamental shortcoming of radical individualism its disregard for the social dimension of life and for the importance of that dimension in the shaping of the self. Imbued as we are by the focus on the unencumbered self, the new communitarians theorize, we do not see ourselves as discovering our personhood, our deepest beliefs, and our most cherished values—in short, our world—in and through the community in which we participate. Bellah et al. point out that the "language of radical individualism" blinds us to such truths, which they enumerate:

> We find ourselves not independently of other people and institutions but through them. We never get to the bottom of our selves on our own. We discover who we are face to face and side by side with others in work, love, and learning. All of our activity goes on in relationships, groups, associations, and communities ordered by institutional structures and interpreted by cultural patterns of meaning. . . . Finally, we are not simply ends in ourselves, either as individuals or as a society. We are parts of a larger whole that we can neither forget nor imagine in our own image without paying a high price.[33]

In contrast to radical individualism with its loss of the social self, the new communitarians emphasize the importance of the social unit for certain crucial aspects of human existence. Thus, the community is integral to epistemology. Communitarians argue that we can no longer hold to the modern epistemological paradigm that focuses on the self-reflective, autonomous subject, for the knowing process is dependent on a cognitive framework mediated to the individual by the community. This critique forms the basis for the replacement of the individualistic, foundationalist rationalism of modernism with an understanding of knowledge and belief that views them as socially and linguistically constituted, an epistemological shift that we sketched and appropriated in the first two parts of this work.

Further, contemporary communitarians argue that the community is crucial to the sustaining of character, virtue, and values, and provides the necessary basis for involvement in public discourse. For this reason, they add, the sense of community is integral to the well-being of the broader society. Communitarians argue that a society is not merely an aggregate of individuals. Instead, the grounding of society lies in the communities that transmit traditions from one generation to another. Bellah and associates explain:

---

32. Michael J. Sandel, "The Procedural Republic and the Unencumbered Self," in *Communitarianism and Individualism*, ed. Shlomo Avineri and Avner De-Shalit (New York: Oxford University Press, 1992), 19.

33. Bellah et al., *Habits of the Heart*, 84.

> In short, we have never been, and still are not, a collection of
> private individuals who, except for a conscious contract to
> create a minimal government, have nothing in common.
> Our lives make sense in a thousand ways, most of which we
> are unaware of, because of traditions that are centuries, if not
> millennia, old. It is these traditions that help us to know that
> it does make a difference who we are and how we treat one
> another.[34]

Roots of the New Communitarianism

Rather than being a completely new development, the sociopolitical communitarianism of the 1980s emerged as a recent embodiment of a critique of
Enlightenment liberalism that dates two hundred years earlier. *Community*
emerged as an ideal in social and political theory in late eighteenth- and early
nineteenth-century Germany. The fragmentation of social contacts among persons that came on the heels of industrialization and the advent of urban society, with its division of labor, triggered a "rediscovery of community" that in
Robert Nisbet's opinion is "unquestionably the most distinctive development in
nineteenth-century social thought."[35]

Especially prominent in this renaissance of communitarian thinking were the
German Romantic thinkers, such as Johann Gottfried Herder (1744–1803),
Johann Christoph Friedrich von Schiller (1759–1805), and G. W. F. Hegel
(1770–1831). For the paradigmatic *polis*, these philosophers harkened back to
the Greek city-states, especially Athens.[36] In their estimation, community
involves the whole person; interactions take place within a web of inclusive ties,
as people meet each other in the totality of their social roles rather than in a fragmented manner.[37] The rediscovery of community, therefore, emerged in part as
an attempt "to recapture some sense of the wholeness of human nature which
has been lost sight of in modern mass society,"[38] as Raymond Plant notes.

The largely Romantic ethos that stamped the "rediscovery of community" set
the tone for subsequent attempts to speak about the concept. Hence Sheldon
Wolin observes, "[T]he political and social thought of the nineteenth and twentieth centuries largely centered on the attempt to restate the value of community,
that is, of the need for human beings to dwell in more intimate relationships with
each other, to enjoy more affective ties, to experience some closer solidarity than
the nature of urbanized and industrialised society seemed willing to grant."[39]

---

34. Ibid., 282.
35. Nisbet, *Sociological Tradition*, 47.
36. Derek L. Phillips, *Looking Backward: A Critical Appraisal of Communitarian Thought*
(Princeton, N.J.: Princeton University Press, 1993), 5.
37. Plant, *Community and Ideology*, 16.
38. Ibid., 18.
39. Sheldon S. Wolin, *Politics and Vision: Continuity and Innovation in Western Political
Thought* (Boston, Mass.: Little, Brown & Co., 1960), 363–64.

Perhaps the most influential work for the retrieval of community as a socio-logical concept[40] was Ferdinand Toennies's *Gemeinshaft und Gesellschaft* (1887).[41] In this book, Toennies drew a distinction between two paradigmatic types of human social orders, the community (*Gemeinschaft*) and the society (*Gesellschaft*). Basically, *Gemeinschaft*, which for Toennies characterizes most traditional groups, designates any social order in which human relationships are intimate and such relationships encompass persons in the entirety of their being rather than in a seg-mented or limited aspect of their existence. *Gesellschaft*, in contrast, denotes a social order in which relationships are determined by contracts rather than cus-tom or tradition. In such a society, authority is based on ideas such as consent, volition, and contract, which leads to an individualistic account of the legal order.[42] Further, relationships are determined by specific, perhaps even formal, obligations. And transactions may occur between persons who remain otherwise quite anonymous.[43] These characteristics, obviously, typify modern nations.

Since the publication of Toennies's work, the distinction between *Gemeinshaft* and *Gesellschaft* has become common parlance among sociologists, especially those who see the "communal" as a major conceptual focus of sociol-ogy.[44] For example, Robert Nisbet and Robert Perrin use Toennies's vocabulary while offering only a passing reference to him as the one to whom they owe "primarily the sociological interest in these types of relationship."[45] Nisbet and Perrin then offer helpful explications of each social type. By *Gemeinschaft* they mean those social groupings that involve

> relationships encompassing human beings as full personali-ties rather than the single aspects or roles of human beings. These are relationships characterized by a high degree of cohesion, communality, and duration in time. . . . What is essential is the quality of strong cohesiveness of persons to one another and the quality of rooted, persisting collective identity.

Gesellschaft, in contrast, denotes the type of aggregate that

> engages the individual in only one of the aspects or parts of his or her total being, or, at most, only a few aspects. From

40. For an example, see Peter L. Berger and Brigitte Berger, *Sociology: A Biographical Approach* (New York: Basic Books, 1972), 304.

41. Ferdinand Toennies, *Community and Society* , trans. Charles P. Loomis (East Lansing, Mich.: Michigan State University Press, 1957).

42. Plant, *Community and Ideology*, 23–24.

43. For this interpretation, see Kaspar D. Naegele, "The Institutionalization of Action," in *Theories of Society: Foundation of Modern Sociological Theory*, 2 vols., ed. Talcott Parsons et al. (New York: Free Press, 1961), 1:184.

44. For a helpful summary of the development of the communal as a central sociological theme, see Nisbet, *Sociological Tradition*, 47–106.

45. Robert Nisbet and Robert G. Perrin, *The Social Bond*, 2nd ed. (New York: Alfred A. Knopf, 1977), 98.

the individual's point of view his relationship with others in *Gesellschaft* is more tenuous, loose, and less deeply rooted in his allegiances or commitments. *Gesellschaft* is commonly founded around a few specific interests or purposes, whether religious, economic, recreational, or political.[46]

These descriptions find parallels in[47] and seem to stand behind the contrast the Bellah group articulates between a true "community" and a "lifestyle enclave," with the latter being the end product of the shift toward *Gesellschaft* that accompanied the birth of modern society. In *Habits of the Heart*, Bellah et al. write, "Whereas a community attempts to be an inclusive whole, celebrating the interdependence of public and private life and of the different callings of all, lifestyle is fundamentally segmental and celebrates the narcissism of similarity." Emerging as "an outgrowth of the sectoral organization of American life" that resulted from industrialization and the emergence of a national market, lifestyle enclaves are both individually and socially segmental. "They involve only a segment of each individual," our authors explain, "for they concern only private life, especially leisure and consumption. And they . . . include only those with a common lifestyle."[48] Thus, in keeping with a strand of American thought that sees social life as merely an arrangement for the fulfilment of the needs of individuals, a lifestyle enclave is a group of persons who are united merely by shared interests and activities and who join together only to maximize individual good.[49] The distinction between these two types of social groups provides the background for the call voiced by Bellah et al. for a retrieval of the communal tradition in contemporary American life.

Toward a Synthesis

In certain respects, the communitarian critique of individualism has been devastating. Already in 1953, Robert Nisbet cut to the heart of the situation by noting that individualism is dependent on communalism insofar as the values individualists prize are in fact group characteristics. He writes,

> What we can now see with the advantage of hindsight is that, unconsciously, the founders of liberalism abstracted certain moral and psychological attributes from a *social organization* and considered these the timeless, natural, qualities of the *individual*, who was regarded as independent of the influences of any historically developed social organization. Those qualities that, in their entirety,

46. Nisbet and Perrin, *Social Bond*, 98–99.
47. Bellah notes, however, that "community" means more than merely the "small-scale, face-to-face groups" that many people associate with the German term *Gemeinschaft*. Bellah, "Community Properly Understood," 15.
48. Bellah et al., *Habits of the Heart*, 72.
49. Ibid., 134.

> composed the eighteenth-century liberal image of man were qualities actually inhering to a large extent in a set of institutions and groups, all of which were aspects of historical tradition.[50]

Elsewhere Nisbet provides the flip side to Mill's thesis, asserting that community is crucial to both personal freedom and personal achievement, in that "the perspectives and incentives of the free creative mind arise out of communities of purpose."[51] Considerations such as these have led even many proponents of sociopolitical liberalism to use the language of community—at least sparingly[52] or as an aspect of liberal political theory.[53]

Communitarianism, however, has also not been without its critics.[54] Opponents accuse its advocates of being sentimental or nostalgic, guilty of constructing a past golden age while forgetting the oppressive conditions under which people lived prior to the advent of liberalism.[55] Critics likewise worry that even in its contemporary form communitarianism harbors a latent oppressiveness.[56]

The ranks of its critics are not limited to proponents of political liberalism but include as well scholars often associated with the new communitarianism. Some thinkers, such as Charles Taylor, question the usefulness of the opposing labels, suggesting that the terms are too ill-defined to be of assistance.[57] Others eschew the label "communitarian,"[58] especially if by it is meant either "majoritarianism" (i.e., the view that "the values of the community or the will of the majority should always prevail") or "the idea that rights should rest on the values that predominate in any given community at any given time," to cite Sandel's characterizations.[59]

The concern to retain the gains of political liberalism and avoid the pitfalls of majoritarianism typifies even those who willingly carry the communitarian

50. Nisbet, *Quest for Community*, 225–26.

51. Ibid., 235.

52. For an example, see John Rawls, *A Theory of Justice* (Cambridge, Mass.: Harvard University Press, 1971), 520.

53. See, for example, Ronald Dworkin, "Liberal Community," in *Communitarianism and Individualism*, ed. Avineri and De-Shalit, 205–23.

54. For an early overview and critique, see Amy Gutmann, "Communitarian Critics of Liberalism," in *Communitarianism and Individualism*, ed. Avineri and De-Shalit, 120–36. For a more recent overview written from a critical posture, see Bruce Frohnen, *The New Communitarians and the Crisis of Modern Liberalism* (Lawrence, Kan.: University Press of Kansas, 1996).

55. For a thoroughgoing critique of the new communitarianism as being guilty of historical revisionism and nostalgia, see Philips, *Looking Backward*.

56. See, for example, Marilyn Friedman, "Feminism and Modern Friendship: Dislocating the Community,"in *Communitarianism and Individualism*, ed. Avineri and De-Shalit, 104–13.

57. Charles Taylor, "Cross-Purposes: The Liberal-Communitarian Debate," in *Liberalism and the Moral Life*, ed. Nancy L. Rosenblum (Cambridge, Mass.: Harvard University Press, 1989), 159–82.

58. Daniel Bell, *Communitarianism and Its Critics* (Oxford: Clarendon Press, 1993), 4. See also the review of this book by Alasdair MacIntyre, "The Spectre of Communitarianism," *Radical Philosophy* 70 (March/April 1995): 34–35.

59. Sandel, *Liberalism and the Limits of Justice*, ix–x.

label. Reflecting on the movement of which he has been a prominent part, Amitai Etzioni observes,

> The new communitarians made the question of balance between individual rights and social responsibilities, between autonomy and the common good, a major concern. We assumed from the beginning that the theory of a good society will need to deal simultaneously with both dangers; with a society whose communal foundations are crumbling and with one in which they have risen to the point that they block out individual freedoms.[60]

Consequently, most contemporary communitarians would readily acknowledge that genuine community emerges only through the promotion of independent judgment and honest self-expression, and through the refusal to minimize or ignore differences among individuals.

In recent years, the liberal-communitarian debate has given rise to a movement toward convergence[61] or even synthesis. Thus, many social theorists today would agree with Gerry Heard that "the concepts of individualism and community are interdependent. Each needs the presence of the other to be able to reach its highest level."[62] Similarly, Daniel A. Helminiak would strike a resounding chord with many today when he asserts that

> the human phenomenon is always and simultaneously and inextricably both social and individual . . . there is no human being apart from the social group in which he or she participates, and there is no group apart from the individual members who constitute that group.[63]

Seyla Benhabib typifies thinkers who see value in both positions. She borrows the communitarian thesis that traditions, communities, and practices shape our identities. At the same time, she advances the liberal concern for maintaining reflective distance, on the basis that it facilitates the ability to criticize, challenge, and question the content of these identities and the practices they prescribe.[64]

Despite a movement toward convergence, differences remain. Sandel offers a succinct characterization that both sets forth the key issue dividing the two positions and indicates the contribution of the communitarian proposal to

---

60. Etzioni, "Introduction," xi.

61. For a helpful summary, see Fergusson, *Community, Liberalism and Christian Ethics*, 149–55.

62. Heard, *Basic Values and Ethical Decisions*, 103.

63. Daniel A. Helminiak, "Human Solidarity and Collective Union in Christ," *Anglican Theological Review* 70/1 (January 1988): 37.

64. Seyla Benhabib, *Situating the Self: Gender, Community and Postmodernism in Contemporary Ethics* (New York: Routledge & Kegan Paul, 1992), 74.

social and political thought, a contribution that carries overtones for theological method as well:

> What is at stake in the debate . . . is not whether rights are important but whether rights can be identified and justified in a way that does not presuppose any particular conception of the good life. At issue is not whether individual or communal claims should carry greater weight but whether the principles of justice that govern the basic structure of society can be neutral with respect to the competing moral and religious convictions its citizens espouse. The fundamental question, in other words, is whether the right is prior to the good.[65]

The Nature of Community

The ongoing discussion between liberal and communitarian social-political theorists offers a valuable perspective for our delineation of the nature and task of theology. The new communitarians have contributed to this conversation by retrieving an emphasis on the communal dimension of human existence. More importantly, we believe that the overarching focus of the biblical narrative is the person-in-relationship or the individual-in-community. This correspondence between the Bible and contemporary thought suggests that the concept of community ought to be the central theme or integrative motif in theology. Before we unpack our claim that theology must be communitarian, however, we must take a closer look at the concept of community as described by contemporary thinkers.

The Concept of Community

In recent years *community* has become a buzzword. Like all such terms, it defies any single, agreed-on definition. Even the new communitarians are not of one mind as to what they mean by *community*. After perusing the writings of the leading contemporary voices, Derek Phillips, in his 1993 critical appraisal of the movement, concludes that four central characteristics comprise the normative ideal of community in communitarian thought. He offers this summary: "A community is a group of people who live in a common territory, have a common history and shared values, participate together in various activities, and have a high degree of solidarity."[66]

Yet even Phillips's definition would not engender universal applause by communitarians. Especially questionable is his first characteristic. Contrary to Phillips's definition, communities do not necessarily need to be geographically concentrated.[67] Perhaps the most obvious counterexample is a religious

---

65. Sandel, *Liberalism and the Limits of Justice*, x.
66. Phillips, *Looking Backward*, 14.
67. Etzioni, "Introduction," xiv.

community, whose members might be widely dispersed while still maintaining an acute sense of constituting a single whole. Some thinkers suggest that scientists are another counterexample, in that they form a particular, worldwide community.[68]

At first glance the lack of uniformity of definition might suggest that the concept of community is too compromised to be of value. The difficulty of getting a handle on the idea is further complicated by the realization that people are members of several communities simultaneously[69] and therefore that community boundaries are fluid, overlapping, and even intertwined. Despite these potentially debilitating difficulties, we agree with those contemporary thinkers who maintain that the concept—if rightly understood—remains helpful. Three central aspects are endemic to our understanding of community.

First, a community consists of a group of people who are conscious that they share a similar frame of reference. This perspective is evident in Amitai Etzioni's assertion that, "communities are webs of social relations that encompass shared meanings and above all shared values."[70] Hence, members of a particular community tend to have a similar outlook toward life. They are inclined to view the world in a similar manner, to "read" the world through similar glasses. In Peter Berger's poignant description,

> every *Weltanschauung* is a conspiracy. The conspirators are those who construct a social situation in which the particular world view is taken for granted. The individual who finds himself in this situation becomes more prone every day to share its basic assumptions. That is, we change our world views (and thus our interpretations and reinterpretations of our biography) as we move from one social world to another.[71]

In addition, participants of a particular community construct the symbolic world they inhabit using similar linguistic and symbolic building materials, even if they are not of one mind as to the meaning of their world-constructing symbols.

Second, operative in all communities is a group focus. This dimension comes to the fore in what we might call the "standard definition" of community provided in the glossary in *Habits of the Heart*. Bellah et al. write that "a

---

68. Arthur Dyke claims that Michael Polanyi's "description of science provides a living example of a particular group, represented throughout the world, that pursues truth and can only do so as a community. Scientists constitute a community characterized by (1) a common tradition; (2) a common purpose; (3) an apprentice system of education; and (4) a network of publications, appointments, and research, all subject to peer review and well-represented in societally supported educational and research institutions." Dyke, *Rethinking Rights and Responsibilities*, 219.

69. Etzioni, "Introduction," xv.

70. Ibid., xv.

71. Peter L. Berger, *Invitation to Sociology: A Humanistic Perspective*, (Garden City, N.Y.: Doubleday, 1963), 63–64.

community is a group of people who are socially interdependent, who participate together in discussion and decision making, and who share certain *practices* . . . that both define the community and are nurtured by it."[72] The
group-centered aspect is likewise evident in Arthur J. Dyke's succinct statement: "A community is an affiliated and mutually beneficial network of interdependent human beings who, as human beings, share what is requisite for
forming and sustaining such a network."[73]

The group focus readily evokes a shared sense of group identity among the
members, whose attention in this sense is directed toward the group. One
important link in this chain of group identity is the belief that as participants
in the community they engage in a common task. Further, as Phillips noted,
the sense of group identity facilitates a type of solidarity among the members.
To borrow his informative description:

> [B]eing a member of a community involves interdependen-
> cies that impose nonvoluntary moral obligations and create
> relationships of reciprocity. Community members ought to
> share a general and diffuse sense of solidarity with everyone
> else in the community: from those with whom they are most
> intimate to those in circles most removed from them per-
> sonally. As members of the community, their responsibilities
> should run both to all other individual members and to the
> community as a whole.[74]

Contrary to what we might assume, a group focus does not necessitate
unanimity and uniformity of opinion among group members. Instead, what is
endemic to community is a shared interest in participating in an ongoing discussion about what constitutes the identity of the group. In an essay published
several years after the appearance of *Habits of the Heart*, Robert Bellah highlights the argumentative character of community life:

> A good community is one in which there is argument, even
> conflict, about the meaning of the shared values and goals,
> and certainly about how they will be actualized in everyday
> life. Community is not about silent consensus; it is a form of
> intelligent, reflective life, in which there is indeed consensus,
> but where the consensus can be challenged and changed—
> often gradually, sometimes radically—over time.

He then notes that what makes any kind of group a community and not just a
contractual association is the shared concern among its members with the question, "What will make this group a *good* group?" thereby indicating that the

---

72. Bellah et al., *Habits of the Heart*, 333.
73. Dyke, *Rethinking Rights and Responsibilities*, 126.
74. Phillips, *Looking Backward*, 17.

members share the goal of determining and attempting to create what in the case of this particular group they hold to be a good community.[75]

Third, the group orientation of a community is balanced by what we might call its "person focus." The members draw their personal identity from the community. In this manner, the group is a crucial factor in forming the identity of its members. This aspect of a community parallels Michael Sandel's "constitutive conception" of community. He writes,

> [T]o say that the members of a society are bound by a sense of community is not simply to say that a great many of them profess communitarian sentiments and pursue communitarian aims, but rather that they conceive their identity—the subject and not just the object of their feelings and aspirations—as defined to some extent by the community of which they are a part. For them, community describes not just what they *have* as fellow citizens but also what they *are*, not a relationship they choose (as in a voluntary association) but an attachment they discover, not merely an attribute but a constituent of their identity.[76]

Community and Identity

The "constitutive conception" of community leads to what for our purposes is the central function of community, its role in identity formation. In chapter 3, we drew from recent communitarian thinking the thesis that personal identity is socially produced and that religion plays a crucial role in the process. Our interest in this chapter is in the dynamic of identity formation within the context of community, for this will provide the strongest link between the idea of community and theological method.

Communitarian accounts of personal identity formation generally begin with a reminder of the self's dependency on the group. We noted in chapter 3 the work of George Herbert Mead, who asserted that meaning is no individual matter but rather is interpersonal or relational, that the mind is not only individual but also a social phenomenon,[77] and hence that the self—the maturing personality or one's personal identity—is socially produced.[78] According to Mead, rather than the individual being sui generis, human development is a product of the process of social interaction, for the mind, critical thinking, and a sense of self are facilitated by participation in the social group.

Another early voice in charting out the communal foundation for identity formation was the early twentieth-century philosopher, Josiah Royce

---

75. Bellah, "Community Properly Understood," 16.

76. Sandel, *Liberalism and the Limits of Justice*, 150.

77. George Herbert Mead, *Mind, Self and Society from the Standpoint of a Social Behaviorist*, ed. Charles W. Morris (1934; Chicago: University of Chicago Press, 1963), 118–25, 134.

78. For Mead's argument, see *Mind, Self and Society*, 144–64.

(1855–1916). Royce noted that we come to self-consciousness under the per-sistent influence of social others.[79] On this basis, he concluded, "My life means nothing, either theoretically or practically, unless I am a member of a community."[80]

More recently, thinkers such as Alasdair MacIntyre have linked communi-tarian understandings of the self, such as Mead and Royce propounded, with narrative theory. Like contemporary narrative thinkers, MacIntyre argues that humans are storytellers[81] and that our identity develops through the telling of a personal narrative, in accordance with which our lives "make sense."[82] These personal stories, MacIntyre quickly adds, are tied up with the larger group story, in that we enter human society "with one or more imputed characters—roles into which we have been drafted."[83] On this basis MacIntyre then concludes, "What I am . . . is in key part what I inherit, a specific past that is present to some degree in my present. I find myself part of a history and that is generally to say, whether I like it or not, whether I recognize it or not, one of the bearers of a tradition."[84]

George Stroup provides a fuller treatment of the narrative theory of personal identity and its relationship to community.[85] Stroup theorizes that identity is the pattern that memory retrieves from one's personal history and projects into the future; more specifically, identity emerges as individuals, through the exer-cise of memory, select certain events from the past and use them as a basis for interpreting the significance of the whole of their lives. Stroup's characterization at this point is reminiscent of Royce, who declared, "however a man may come by his idea of himself, the self is no mere datum, but is in its essence a life which is interpreted."[86] This identity, Stroup then adds, is not created merely from the "factual data," or "chronicle," of the events of one's life, but requires an "inter-pretive scheme" that provides the "plot" through which the chronicle of a per-son's life makes sense. The interpretive framework likewise cannot be derived from the data of one's own life; instead it arises from one's social context or "tra-dition."[87] For this reason, Stroup concludes, personal identity is never a private reality but has a communal element; it is shaped by the community of which the person is a participant. Such a community contributes to the formation of the "self" by mediating the communal narrative necessary for personal identity formation.

79. Josiah Royce, *The World and the Individual* (New York: Macmillan & Co., 1901), 261.

80. Josiah Royce, *The Problem of Christianity*, 2 vols. (New York: Macmillan & Co., 1913), 2: 313.

81. MacIntyre, *After Virtue*, 216.

82. On this point, see also, Bellah et al., *Habits of the Heart*, 81.

83. MacIntyre, *After Virtue*, 216.

84. Ibid., 221.

85. George W. Stroup, *The Promise of Narrative Theology* (Atlanta: John Knox Press, 1981), 101–98.

86. Royce, *Problem of Christianity*, 2: 50.

87. Here Stroup is in substantial agreement with social constructionist sociologists, such as Peter Berger. See, for example, Peter L. Berger, *The Sacred Canopy: Elements of a Sociological Theory of Religion*, Anchor Books ed. (Garden City, N.Y.: Doubleday & Co., 1969), 20.

The identity-conferring aspect of community leads to what sociologists label a "reference group."[88] According to Nisbet and Perrin, a person's reference group is

> the social group or category to which the individual "refers," consciously or unconsciously, in the shaping of his attitudes and beliefs and values on a given subject or in the formation of his conduct. It is the social entity toward which he orients his aspirations, judgments, tastes, and even at times his profoundest moral or social values.[89]

In this manner, "the reference group serves as both a standard for *comparison* of one's self with a set of norms, that is, for self-appraisal, and also as the *source* of the varied norms and values that operate in a given individual's life."[90] More important than geographic proximity, a community's role as a person's reference group is a function of—in the words of Nisbet and Perrin—"the degree of *symbolic* interaction that is involved."[91]

This suggests that whereas we are members of a variety of communities at any given time as well as throughout our lives, only a select few function as our reference group in the full sense of the term. Consequently, the community that functions (at least temporarily) as our ultimate reference group is the particular community from which we take our fundamental identity. Or turning the statement around, lying beneath the various competing conceptions we derive from the manifold communities in which we are members is a deeper sense of identity for which we are dependent on one such group (or at most a few select groups). This community functions as our primary reference group and is what we might call our "community of reference."

Communitarians point out that the role of a group as a community of reference is connected with its ability to forge a link to both the past and the future. One important early voice in articulating this theme was Josiah Royce. In *The Problem of Christianity*, Royce notes that through its orientation to both past and future, a social group functions as what he called a "community of memory" and a "community of hope." A community of memory emerges, Royce theorizes, as each member "accepts as part of his own individual life and self the same *past* events that each of his fellow-members accepts."[92] William Kluback offers a helpful clarification of what Royce has in mind:

> Memory is . . . more than a collective consciousness; it is the recognition that thought is the continuous retaking and reinterpretation of past categories forcing them to take new directions and to express in different ways perspectives that

---

88. Berger, *Invitation to Sociology*, 118.
89. Nisbet and Perrin, *Social Bond*, 100.
90. Ibid., 103.
91. Ibid., 103.
92. Royce, *Problem of Christianity*, 2:50.

had been developed in the past, but whose attitudes have not yet been realized. The development of new perspectives takes place within and in opposition to former ones.[93]

Equally important for Royce is the group's role as a "community of hope," which occurs as "each of its members accepts, as part of his own individual life and self, the same expected *future* events that each of his fellows accepts."[94]

This leads to Royce's most complete declaration of what "community" means:

> But let these selves be able to look beyond their present chaos of fleeting ideas and of warring desires, far away into the past whence they came, and into the future whither their hope lead them. As they thus look, let each one of them ideally enlarge his own individual life, extending himself into the past and future, so as to say of some far-off event . . . 'I view that event as a part of my own life.' . . .
>
> And further, let the various ideal extensions, forwards and backwards, include at least one common event, so that each of these selves regards that event as a part of his own life.
>
> Then, *with reference to the ideal common past and future in question, I say that these selves constitute a community.*[95]

In elaborating on this definition, Royce asserts that the existence of a community depends on three factors: "the power of an individual self to extend his life, in ideal fashion, so as to regard it as including past and future events which lie far away in time";[96] the presence in "the social world of a number of distinct selves capable of social communication";[97] and the inclusion in "the ideally extended past and future selves of the members . . . at least some events which are, for all these selves, identical."[98]

As this sketch of his proposal suggests, despite its far-reaching communal vision Royce's perspective still retains a strong sense of the primacy of the individual and an implicit foundationalist flavor. In the end, Royce's understanding of community—including its function as a community of memory and hope—emerges from his prior conception of the nature of the self. Recent communitarians have drawn from Royce's keen insight into the nature of community shorn of these typical early-nineteenth-century trappings. These theorists are interested in the role of a community in connecting the present with both past

---

93. William Kluback, "The Problem of Christianity," in *Josiah Royce: Selected Writings,* ed. John Edwin Smith and William Kluback (Mahwah, N.J.: Paulist Press, 1988), 43.
94. Royce, *Problem of Christianity,* 2:51.
95. Ibid., 2:59–60. Emphasis his.
96. Ibid., 2:61.
97. Ibid., 2:67.
98. Ibid., 2:68.

and future and thereby not only constituting the "self" of its members but also constituting the group as a whole.

As contemporary communitarians point out, a community has a history; in fact, it is in an important sense constituted by that history—a history that begins in the past and extends into the future. This "constitutive narrative" does not view time merely as a continuous flow of qualitatively meaningless sensations. Rather, in telling its story, a community punctuates the present—the day, the week, the season, the year—with a sense of the transcendent and thereby presents time as a meaningful whole.[99]

This constitutive narrative begins "in the beginning," with the primal event(s) that called the community into being. Rather than forgetting its past, a community retells the story of its genesis and of the crucial milestones that mark its subsequent trajectory, including accounts of shared suffering and even of past evils.[100] This narrative also calls to mind persons who have embodied or exemplified the meaning of the community and who thereby serve as models for life in the present.

More important than merely retelling past occurrences, recalling the narrative retrieves the constitutive past for the sake of personal and communal life in the present. Or stated more strongly, reciting the constitutive past narrative places the contemporary community within the primal events that constituted their forebears as this particular community. This act retrieves the past, bringing it into the present, and thereby reconstitutes the community in the present as the contemporary embodiment of a communal tradition that spans the years. By articulating the narrative in this identity-conferring manner, a community functions as a community of memory.

The communal history does not end in the past or even the present, however. Rather it extends into the future. As a result, a community turns the gaze of its members toward the future. It anticipates the continuation of, and even further development of, the community that awaits it in the future. The community senses that it is moving forward toward an ideal that lies yet before it. But above all, it expectantly looks to the ideal or "eschatological" future, when the purpose and goals—the *telos*—of the community will be fully actualized. This expectation of a glorious future serves as an ongoing admonition to its members to embody the communal vision in the present. They are to be, in the here and now, the anticipatory manifestation of the reality that will one day characterize their community in its fullness. In keeping this vision before its members, a community acts as a community of hope.

The community's constitutive narrative, then, stretches from the primal past to the ideal future. As this overarching, "cosmic" story, the narrative provides a transcendent vantage point for life in the here and now. It bestows a qualitative meaning on life, on time and space, and on community members as they inhabit their world. The recited narrative offers a plausible explanation of present existence, for

99. Bellah et al., *Habits of the Heart*, 282.
100. Ibid., 152–55.

it provides the overarching theme through which members of the community can view their lives and the present moment in history as a part of a stream of time that transcends every particular "now." Likewise, it supplies a context of meaning that allows community members to connect their personal aspirations with those of a larger whole and facilitates them in seeing their efforts as contributions to that whole. In this manner, as the community retells its constitutive narrative it functions as an "interpretive community," to borrow Royce's term.[101]

The telling of the constitutive narrative is accentuated through sacred practices of the type that anthropologists call "rites of intensification," rituals that "bring the community together, increase group solidarity, and reinforce commitment to the beliefs of the group."[102] Perhaps more descriptive is the designation "practices of commitment" offered by the Bellah group. These acts define the community way of life as well as the patterns of loyalty and obligation that keep the community alive.[103] Through their participation in these acts, a sense of community arises among the members, a community that emerges as—to cite Nisbet's succinct description—"a fusion of feeling and thought, of tradition and commitment, of membership and volition."[104]

Theology and Community

The insights that have emerged from the liberal-communitarian conversation offer a perspective from which to develop the second crucial dimension of a theological method in the postmodern context. By reminding us that our understandings of ourselves and our world are dependent on the community that nurtures us, communitarians indicate one aspect of the way beyond the foundationalism inherent in individualistic approaches to theology. We now turn our attention to the more explicit development of the communitarian focus of a nonfoundationalist theological method.

The line linking Christian theology and the concept of community runs through the church as a particular community, the fellowship of those who gather around the narrative of God at work through Christ. For this reason, en route to our delineation of a nonfoundationalist theological method we must ask whether—or in what manner—the church is a community.

The Church as Community

In chapter 5 we explored the question of whether we might appropriate the language of culture to speak of the church. In our response, we offered a sketch of the basis for viewing the church as a distinct social group, while remaining

101. Royce, *Problem of Christianity*, 2:211.
102. Stephen A. Grunlan and Marvin K. Mayers, *Cultural Anthropology: A Christian Perspective*, 2nd ed. (Grand Rapids: Zondervan, 1988), 222.
103. Bellah et al., *Habits of the Heart*, 152–54.
104. Nisbet, *Sociological Tradition*, 48.

cognizant of the limitations of such language.[105] We suggested that when viewed from the perspective of sociology, the church displays the basic hallmarks of a social group, such as unit awareness, common symbols, a common mission, and institutional structures. Our intention in that discussion was to set the context for talking about theology as a cultural practice. Now we must look more closely at the specifically *communal* character of the church. Setting out on this pathway brings us immediately to the central question of ecclesiology: What is the church? In the context of the present discussion this question takes the form, How is the church constituted? And this, in turn, lands us back in the individualist-communalist debate.

The Constitution of the Church

We noted above that individualism and social atomism gave birth to the modern conception of the political order. This conception views the state as the product of autonomous selves voluntarily entering into a "social contract" to gain certain personal advantages. Voluntarist contractualism in political theory finds its ecclesiological counterpart in the view that sees the church as the voluntary association of individual believers whose identity precedes their presence in the congregation, in that their identity is supposedly constituted prior to their joining together to form the church. According to this model, rather than constituting its members, the church is constituted *by* believers, who are deemed to be in a sense complete "spiritual selves" prior to, and apart from, their membership in the church. The church, in turn, is an aggregate of the individual Christians who "contract" with each other to form a spiritual society.[106]

The contractual view continues to typify much contemporary church life. This is borne out by the sociological study conducted by the Bellah group. They conclude, "Most Americans see religion as something individual, prior to any organizational involvement."[107]

To provide the theological rationale for the contractual view, some thinkers appeal to the idea of the church as an invisible company, the "fellowship" of all believers, in contrast to the visible church, understood as its local, institutional expression. Dispensationalist theologian Robert Lightner, to cite one example, asserts that membership in the invisible church comes through union with Christ accomplished solely through Spirit baptism (that is, apart from any institutional act such as water baptism).[108] Consequently the "company of the redeemed is called the church without consideration of whether or not those

105. For an example of rejection of the conclusion that the church forms a specific society, see Kathryn Tanner, *Theories of Culture: A New Agenda for Theology* (Minneapolis: Fortress Press, 1997), 93–102.

106. Bloesch is an example of those thinkers who bemoan the "appalling neglect" of ecclesiology in evangelicalism, which he believes is due in part to the emphasis on individual decision, as evangelicals give priority to the decision of faith rather than to nurture. Donald G. Bloesch, *The Future of Evangelical Christianity* (Garden City, N.Y.: Doubleday & Co., 1983), 127.

107. Bellah et al., *Habits of the Heart*, 226.

108. Robert P. Lightner, *Evangelical Theology* (Grand Rapids: Baker, 1986), 232.

who are a part of it are members of local churches."[109] Not only does such individualism reduce the local congregation to a voluntary society, it demotes participation in the visible community from an essential to an optional dimension of discipleship.

Contractual political theory has played an undeniably beneficial role in the development of Western democracy. Despite the important gains it has engendered, its link to modern individualism has had devastating effects, as the new communitarians point out. In a similar manner, contractual ecclesiology was a welcomed, positive innovation in the seventeenth century. Indeed, when properly understood as referring to the church as the covenanting community of committed disciples, a carefully nuanced contractual ecclesiology fosters a significant, beneficial advancement of the principle of the priesthood of all believers. Nevertheless, under the impulse of individualism, the contractual view all too easily devalues the church, reducing the community of Christ's disciples to little more than a lifestyle enclave, a society formed by persons united by their shared interest in certain religious practices or their belief that membership in a Christian group will contribute to their individual good. For this reason, "In what sense—if any—is the church a community?" emerges in our day as perhaps the central ecclesiological question.

Our intent in these pages is not to spell out a full-bodied ecclesiology but to indicate the communal nature of the church as a bridge to the communal focus of our theological method. To engage with the question of the church as community, we begin with the aspects of a community we delineated earlier in this chapter. We noted that a community is characterized by a shared frame of reference that includes shared meanings and values, a group focus that evokes a shared sense of group identity and group solidarity, and a person focus that leads the members to draw their identity from the community. Moreover, we indicated that in this process of personal and communal identity formation, the social group functions as a community of memory and hope, and thereby it connects the present with a transcendent narrative.

This sociological perspective provides a helpful vantage point from which to understand the church as community. We have repeatedly spoken of the church as the fellowship of those persons who gather around the narrative of God at work as inscripturated in the Bible. What must be emphasized in this context is that the God of this narrative is the one who constitutes the church. More specifically, the church is formed by the work of the Spirit who speaks through the biblical text and thereby creates a people who inhabit the world God is creating. This world, we noted in chapter 3, is a communal world, for it is a community of the Word. By speaking through scripture, centered as it is on the narrative of God acting on our behalf to fashion a new creation, the Spirit brings into being a new community—a fellowship of persons who gather

109. Ibid., 228.

around the name of Jesus the Christ, who is the Word. Consequently, the church is more than the aggregate of its members. It is a particular people imbued with a particular "constitutive narrative."

The Spirit-appropriated, community-fashioning biblical narrative spans the ages from the primordial past to the eschatological future. As the church retells this constitutive narrative it functions as a community of memory and hope. It provides the interpretive framework—the narrative plot—through which its members find meaning in their personal and communal stories. The church likewise links the present with the entire stream of God's action, a history that begins "in the beginning" (Gen. 1:1) and spans the ages, climaxing in "a new heaven and a new earth" (Rev. 21:1). Through their connection with this people, members of the community discover the connection between their personal lives and something greater—something transcendent—namely, the work of the biblical God in history.

As a consequence of this shared narrative, believers sense a special solidarity with one another. Within the context of the church, this solidarity works its way out in the practical dimensions of fellowship, support, and nurture that its members discover through their relationships as a communal people. And in this process, the church becomes what Daniel Migliore calls an "alternative community" that "gives the world reason to hope.[110] In short, as James McClendon succinctly states, the church is a community "understood not as privileged access to God or to sacred status, but as sharing together in a storied life of obedient service to and with Christ."[111]

The Theological Constitution of the Church

To this point we have spoken of the church as community by working from a sociological base.[112] We have briefly sketched how insights from sociology inform our understanding of the church as community, viewed not so much as an institution but as what some writers designate a *communitas*.[113] However, we must quickly add one crucial caveat. The appropriation of insights from sociology dare not deteriorate into a new foundationalism. Such degeneration occurs when speech about the church as community begins with some generic reality called "community," which can supposedly be discovered through objective observation of the world, and then proceeds to fit the church into this

---

110. Daniel Migliore, *Faith Seeking Understanding* (Grand Rapids: Wm. B. Eerdmans Publishing Co., 1991), 192.

111. James William McClendon Jr., *Ethics: Systematic Theology*, vol. 1 (Nashville: Abingdon Press, 1986), 28.

112. We have not, however, followed sociologists who look at particular ecclesiastical institutions. Instead, our focus has been on the church as "an abstract, universal institution," to cite Moberg's description. He then explains further, "Used in this way 'the church' refers to a generalized symbolic conception, including any and all aspects of organized religious practice, irrespective of denominational family." David O. Moberg, *The Church as a Social Institution: The Sociology of American Religion*, 2nd ed. (Grand Rapids: Baker, 1984), 17.

113. Victor Turner, for example, describes the relationship between community (i.e., *communitas*)

purportedly universal human phenomenon as if the community of Christ were a particular exemplar of some more general reality. This "sociological foundationalism of community" assumes the priority of sociology, viewed as an objective science that sets both the agenda and the methodological direction for theological reflection and construction.

Unfortunately, theologians routinely fall into the trap laid by foundationalist scientific positivism. Whether unwittingly or by design, many theologians look to some particular discipline within the corpus of science to provide what they accept as the fundamental, objective account of society or history. These theologians view their task, in turn, as that of determining what theological insights cohere with the supposedly "true" account provided by the particular science they idolize. But as John Milbank points out, "no such fundamental account, in the sense of something neutral, rational and universal, is really available." Or as George Pattison queries rhetorically, "If theologians are happy to redefine their work in terms of one or other human science . . . is it still *theology*?"[114]

Milbank, therefore, is surely on the right track when he unabashedly asserts, "It is theology itself that will have to provide its own account of the final causes at work in human history, on the basis of its own particular, and historically specific faith," for theology is "itself a social science, and the queen of the sciences for the inhabitants of the *altera civitas*, on pilgrimage through this temporary world."[115] Milbank then adds perceptively that Christian social theory

> is first and foremost an *ecclesiology*, and only an account of other human societies to the extent that the Church defines itself, in its practice, as in continuity and discontinuity with these societies. As the Church is *already*, necessarily, by virtue of its institution, a 'reading' of other human societies, it becomes possible to consider ecclesiology as also a 'sociology.'[116]

Theology, then, and not sociology as a scientific discipline, must emerge as our ultimate basis for speaking of the church as a community. More specifically, talk about the Christian church as a community takes its cue from the

---

and social structure. On the one hand, he notes that "Buber lays his finger on the spontaneous, immediate, concrete nature of communitas, as opposed to the norm-governed, institutionalized, abstract nature of social structure." On the other hand, he then adds, "Yet, communitas is made evident or accessible, so to speak, only through its juxtaposition to, or hybridization with, aspects of social structure." Victor W. Turner, *The Ritual Process: Structure and Anti-Structure* (Middlesex: Penguin Books, 1969), 114.

114. George Pattison, *The End of Theology—And the Task of Thinking about God* (London: SCM Press, 1998), 28.

115. John Milbank, *Theology and Social Theory: Beyond Secular Reason* (Oxford: Basil Blackwell Publishers, 1990), 380.

116. Milbank, *Theology and Social Theory*, 380.

particularly *Christian* conception of God that informs a specifically Christian ecclesiology. And as we outlined in chapter 6, at its core this conception speaks of God as the triune one whose goal includes bringing humankind, as the *imago dei*, to reflect the divine character, which is love.

Consequently, at the heart of our understanding of the church is the realization that our human calling is to reflect the character of God. Of course, there may well be a personal aspect to this human destiny. Nevertheless, because God is ultimately none other than the divine trinitarian persons-in-relationship, a relationship characterized by a mutuality that can only be described as love, the *imago dei* is ultimately human persons-in-loving-relationship as well. Only in relationship—as persons-in-community—are we able to reflect the fullness of the divine character.[117] And because the company of Jesus' disciples is called to be the divine image,[118] the church is essentially a community characterized by love, a people who reflect in relation to one another and to all creation the character of the Creator.

The grounding of the church as community in the Christian theological vision has another dimension as well. The Christian conception views God as the one who in grace shares the divine life with us. That is, ultimately we enjoy the fullness of community as, and only as, God graciously brings us to participate together in the fountainhead of community, namely, the life of the triune God. The agent of this participation is the Holy Spirit, through whom we become the children of God and through whom we thereby share in the love present within the eternal triune God. For this reason, the communal fellowship we have together as members of the church goes beyond what is generated by a common experience or even by a common narrative. The community we share is our shared participation, or participation together, in the perichoretic community of trinitarian persons. As J. M. R. Tillard declares,

> the ecclesial *koinonia* can be defined as the passing of the Trinitarian Communion into the fraternal relations of the disciples of Christ. . . . Seen from the human side, the ecclesial *koinonia* is none other than the fraternity of the disciples of Christ Jesus but in so far as it is caught up, seized by the Spirit who inserts it in the relation of the Father and the Son.[119]

117. For a discussion of the implications of the social Trinity for the concept of the image of God, see Cornelius Plantinga Jr., "Images of God," in *Christian Faith and Practice in the Modern World*, ed. Mark A. Noll and David F. Wells (Grand Rapids: Wm. B. Eerdmans Publishing Co., 1988), 59–67.

118. For a recent exploration of this theme, see Miroslav Volf, *After Our Likeness: The Church as the Image of the Trinity* (Grand Rapids: Wm. B. Eerdmans Publishing Co., 1998). See also, Miroslav Volf, "Kirche als Gemeinschaft: Ekklesiologische Überlegungen aus freikirchlicher Perspektiv," *Evangelische Theologie* 49/1 (1989): 70–76; Kilian McDonnell, "Vatican II (1962–1964), Puebla (1979), Synod (1985): *Koinonia/Communio* as an Integral Ecclesiology," *Journal of Ecumenical Studies* 25/3 (Summer 1988): 414.

119. J. M. R. Tillard, "What Is the Church of God?" *Mid-Stream* 23 (October 1984): 372–73.

Ecclesiology and Human Community

The Christian conception of God provides the perspective from which to speak about the church as community. But this, in turn, offers the touchstone for understanding the truly communal dimension in any human social group.

We noted above that a foundationalist perspective erroneously assumes that we have access to knowledge of some universal reality called "community," which knowledge then sits in judgment over every particular embodiment of community, including the church. This side of the demise of foundationalism, however, all we have are the specific claimants to community with their manifold—and sometimes differing—conceptions as to what community actually entails. Consequently, our understanding of community will always be particular, never generic. Indeed, a nonfoundationalist theological method will be the outworking of the particular, because it eschews the generically human to articulate, reflect on, and explicate the beliefs of a specific faith community. Hence, *Christian* theology will be concerned with and formed by the particularly *Christian* understanding of community.

As Christians, we maintain that in the end community entails participation in the perichoretic trinitarian life. This theological-ecclesiological perspective provides the lens through which to view all human social groups—all claimants to community—from the strictly informal to the highly institutional. It serves as the glasses through which we "read" all societies, as Milbank suggests. Nicholas Lash hints at a similar approach when he writes,

> From the standpoint of Christian theology, questions concerning the possibility of "true" community, of a state of affairs in which the appearance and reality of social relations wholly coincided, would appear as questions concerning the relationship between historical communities, secular or religious, political or sacramental, and God's "reign" or "Kingdom."[120]

Correcting the focus of Lash's characterization, we assert that all human relationships are to be measured from the perspective of the quest for true community (the establishment of which, as we will shortly indicate, is the content of the divine reign). This means that we seek to evaluate every social group on the basis of its potential for being a contribution to, prolepsis of, or signpost on the way toward the participation in the divine life that God destines us to enjoy.

Looking through the lens of a Christian theological ecclesiology enables us to see the world for what it is. It facilitates us in realizing that the various social groups in which people participate all fall short of the community God is fashioning. In comparison to the divine community, all human relationships are merely "splintered and tribal existence," to cite Stanley Hauerwas's description.[121]

---

120. Nicholas Lash, *A Matter of Hope: A Theologian's Reflections on the Thought of Karl Marx* (London: Darton, Longman & Todd, 1981), 75.

121. Stanley Hauerwas, *A Community of Character: Toward a Constructive Christian Ethic* (Notre Dame, Ind.: University of Notre Dame Press, 1981), 92.

The failure of community in the present leads us to realize that true community always remains an eschatological ideal, an "impossible possibility," to appropriate Niebuhr's well-known phrase. This realization ought to temper our expectations about the depth of community we will be able to experience in the present, and it ought to dissuade us from talking too glibly about our ability to construct true community in the present. Once again Lash offers an appropriate cautionary word:

> Christians continue, for the most part, to talk rather too easily about the fact or possibility of "true community," as if a situation in which the reality and appearance of social relationships wholly corresponded could be realized at almost any point in space and time, given a modicum of selflessness and goodwill.[122]

While we seek under the Spirit's guidance to be about the task of constructing community, we nevertheless wait expectantly for God to complete the divine work of bringing creation as a whole and the people of God in particular into the enjoyment of the fullness of community.

Theology and the Community

Understood from the perspective of a theological ecclesiology that takes its cue from the triune God, the church is a community. Indeed, community lies at the heart of the Christian concept of the church. Our task now is to draw out the implications of this assertion for theological method. At last we are in a position to delineate explicitly the communitarian focus of Christian theology.

Why Theology Must be Communitarian

Bubbling beneath the surface throughout this chapter has been an unexpressed but crucial question: Why must theology be communitarian? That is, In what sense is Christian theology by its very nature communitarian?

The context for our answer lies in the work of the proponents of what is sometimes referred to as "Reformed epistemology,"[123] especially Alvin Plantinga and Nicholas Wolterstorff. As we noted in chapter 2, these thinkers maintain against Enlightenment foundationalism that there is no universal human reason[124] but that reason is "person specific" and "situation specific."[125] Never-

---

122. Lash, *A Matter of Hope*, 75.

123. For this designation, see, for example, Nicholas Wolterstorff, "Introduction," in *Faith and Rationality: Faith and Belief in God*, ed. Alvin Plantinga and Nicholas Wolterstorff (Notre Dame, Ind.: University of Notre Dame Press, 1983), 7. See also Alvin Plantinga, "Reason and Belief in God," in *Faith and Rationality*, 73–74.

124. W. Jay Wood, *Epistemology: Becoming Intellectually Virtuous* (Downers Grove, Ill.: InterVarsity Press, 1998), 170.

125. Nicholas Wolterstorff, "Can Belief in God Be Rational If It Has No Foundations?" in *Faith and Rationality*, 155.

theless, Plantinga and Wolterstorff assert that certain beliefs are basic.[126] In response to the question of what—if anything—might be deemed basic for Christian theology, these philosophers, following the lead of other nonfoundationalists, point to the believing community. Plantinga and Wolterstorff assert that to be human means to be situated in a particular community, so that our respective communities (or traditions) play an indispensable role in shaping our conceptions of rationality, as well as the religious beliefs we deem basic and thus by appeal to which we test new claims. These aspects of Reformed epistemology provide the vantage point from which to see why theology is necessarily communitarian.

First, Reformed epistemology suggests that Christian theology must be communitarian because it is linked to a particular community, namely, the community of the disciples of Jesus the Christ. Classically, theology has been understood as faith seeking understanding. At the heart of faith is personal response to the good news. Yet this does not mean that theology is solely the faith of the individual believer seeking understanding. Rather, as the Reformed philosophers remind us, our beliefs—and hence our faith—is dependent on the community in which we are situated. More specifically, being a Christian entails membership in the fellowship of those who have come to know the God of the Bible through Jesus Christ by the Spirit. Theology, in turn, is the community seeking to understand the faith they share. Thus, McClendon declares, "[T]heology is always theology of the community, not just of the individual Christian."[127] As the shared faith of the community seeking understanding, Christian theology is necessarily communitarian.

This conclusion emerges as well from a parallel consideration. We noted in chapter 5 that a central task of theology is to express communal beliefs and values as well as the meaning of the symbols of the faith community. Theological construction has as its goal the setting forth of an understanding of the particular "web of significance," "matrix of meaning," or "mosaic of beliefs" that lies at the heart of a particular community. More specifically, the task of *Christian* theology includes the articulation of the cognitive mosaic of the Christian faith. This mosaic consists of the interlocking doctrines that together comprise the specifically Christian way of viewing the world. As a result, Christian theology is by its very nature "church dogmatics," to cite Karl Barth's description. As church dogmatics, as the faith of the community seeking understanding, theology is inherently communitarian.

Second, theology is communitarian because it is the explication of the Christian conception of God. In addition to being "faith seeking understanding," theology is "the study of God." This study, however, is never generic. Rather it is always specific; it is always the explication of the understanding set forth within a particular community. Hence, *Christian* theology speaks about

---

126. Merold Westphal, "A Reader's Guide to 'Reformed Epistemology,'" *Perspectives* 7/9 (November 1992): 11; Plantinga, "Reason and Belief in God," 73–78.

127. McClendon, *Ethics,* 36.

the God known in the Christian community. Christian theology is the explication of the God witnessed to by the community that has come to know God through Christ by the Spirit. As we pointed out in chapter 6, the God to whom the Christian community bears witness is the triune God. The only true God, Christians declare, is none other than the triune one, the fellowship of the trinitarian persons. Hence, God is social, communal . . . community. Christian theology is inherently communitarian, therefore, because it is the explication of the Christian understanding of God, and this God is the triune one.

This leads to yet a third reason as to why theology is inherently communitarian. As the explication of the faith of the Christian community, Christian theology is the study of the triune God. The community of Christ, however, is that people who find their identity through the Bible, for the Spirit speaking through scripture, constitutes them as God's children. The God of this community is the biblical God, the God whose activity is disclosed in the biblical narrative. Christian theology, in turn, is the study of the narrative of this God fulfilling the divine purposes as disclosed in the Bible. As we will delineate shortly, the biblical narrative presents as the ultimate goal of the biblical God the establishment of community. Theology, in turn, is the explication of this eschatological goal. For this reason, it is by its very nature communitarian.

The Basis of Theology

The communitarian nature of theology leads naturally to the concept of community as the integrative motif of Christian theology. Before turning our attention to this topic, however, we must give passing attention to one additional issue as to the connection between theology and community.

We noted above that according to the Reformed epistemologists the church is "basic" in theology. Similarly, Stanley Hauerwas recently quipped, "[I]n a world without foundations all we have is the church."[128] Yet viewing the church as "basic" to theology in this manner can lead to a debilitating problem. Perhaps against their own intentions, its proponents may be guilty of constructing a new foundationalism—an erroneous "foundationalism of the church," just as sociologically oriented theologians are tempted to fabricate a new foundationalism of community. This potential problem leads us to consider what actually is "basic" for Christian theology. More specifically, we ask, Is the *church* "basic"?

When seen in one light, the answer to this question can only be "No." At the heart of the Christian conception of faith is faith's connection to a saving encounter with the God of the Bible in Jesus Christ. This encounter is an identity-producing event, as the Spirit constitutes us as a community of believers and as individual members of that community. Therefore, this encounter with

---

128. Stanley Hauerwas, "The Church's One Foundation is Jesus Christ Her Lord; Or, In a World Without Foundations: All We Have Is the Church," in *Theology Without Foundations: Religious Practice and the Future of Theological Truth* (Nashville: Abingdon Press, 1994), 144.

the God of the Bible through Jesus is constitutive for Christian identity. We are children of God because the Holy Spirit has placed us in Christ.

Although Christians adhere to various understandings of what kind of event the divine-human encounter ultimately is, most Christian traditions view the encounter as somehow connected to an experience or a succession of experiences that believers have. In fact, the commonality of the experience of being encountered by God in Christ is a—arguably *the*—central feature that identifies participation in the Christian community.

Many contemporary philosophers point out that experience is closely connected to interpretation. In fact, experiences always come our way mediated by or filtered through a grid—an interpretive framework—that facilitates their occurrence.[129] Hence, religious experience is dependent on a cognitive framework that sets forth a specifically religious interpretation of the world. And any such interpretive framework is theological in nature, for it involves an understanding that sees the world in connection with the divine reality around which that tradition focuses. Christian experience is facilitated by the proclamation of the Christian gospel, inherent in which is a specifically Christian interpretive framework that views the world in connection with the God of the Bible, together with the biblical narrative of God at work bringing creation to its divinely destined goal.

Christian theology, in turn, is an intellectual enterprise by and for the Christian community. Theology is in part the ongoing conversation among those whom the God of the Bible has encountered in Jesus Christ, who are attempting together to articulate, delineate, and clarify the mosaic of beliefs that comprise the interpretive framework of the community that this encounter has called forth. Viewed from this perspective, what is "basic" for theology is not the church itself, but the specifically Christian-experience-facilitating interpretative framework, which in turn is connected to the biblical narrative.

At the same time, there is a sense in which the church *is* basic for theology. In fact, only by viewing the church as basic can we avoid the foundationalism of modern theology, in both its liberal and its conservative forms.

In chapter 2 we indicated how their common commitment to a foundationalist theological method has led liberals and conservatives alike to construct elaborate prolegomena to gain what they see as the sure foundation for engaging in theological construction. Seeking this foundation in universal religious experience, liberals tend to devote their prolegomena to a discussion of the nature of such experience in general and the supposedly Christian variety in particular. Conservatives, in contrast, generally elevate bibliology as prolegomenon. Consistent with this approach, conservative systematic theologies follow a stereotypical pattern. After explaining that theology is a science like the natural sciences, the authors routinely introduce revelation as the subject matter that they will explore. Then they argue that such revelation is inscripturated

---

129. See, for example, Owen C. Thomas, "Theology and Experience," *Harvard Theological Review* 78/1–2 (1985): 192.

in the Bible, which now functions as its inerrant repository. Only at this point can the actual theological construction get underway.

Viewing our question in the context of these alternative foundationalist approaches results in the conclusion that the church—and neither religious experience nor the Bible per se—is basic to theology. The church is basic in that our participation in the faith community calls forth theological reflection. Theology is faith seeking understanding. Therefore, the very existence of the faith community—the community in which faith is present—leads naturally to the reflection on faith that we call *theology*. For this reason, theological construction needs no elaborate, foundation-setting, certainty-gaining prolegomenon. Instead, it arises out of the life of the discipleship community who are joined together by the Spirit and who join together in living out the mandate they share. Therefore, it is our presence within the Christian community that leads us to engage in the theological task. And the existence of this community provides the only "foundation" necessary for launching into the process of explicating the mosaic of beliefs or the interpretive framework Christians share.

Community as Theology's Integrative Motif

The focus on the communal nature of theology as an activity of the faith community brings us finally to *community* as theology's integrative motif, that is, as the central, organizing concept of theological construction, the theme around which a systematic theology is structured. Community, we maintain, provides the integrative thematic perspective in light of which the various theological foci can be understood and the significant theological issues ought to be explored.[130]

Community and Kingdom Theology

Although theologians throughout the centuries have worked with a variety of integrative motifs, much of modern theology, whether liberal or conservative, has been oriented around the theme of the kingdom of God. Nevertheless, kingdom theology—theology oriented around *kingdom* as its integrative motif—is beset with certain debilitating shortcomings.

First, there is the seemingly contentlessness of the term. As the trajectory of biblical studies and the theological debates of the last hundred years have indicated, the term *the kingdom of God* is notoriously difficult to define. Without a clear understanding of the nature of the kingdom, kingdom theology is inadequate to the task of indicating what the world is like when it is transformed by the in-breaking of the divine rule.

---

130. For a discussion of the idea of the integrative motif in theology, see Gerhard Sauter and Alex Stock, *Arbeitswesen Systematischer Theologie: Eine Anleitung* (Munich: Chr. Kaiser Verlag, 1976), 18–19.

The fluidity of the concept leads to an even more problematic result. Because its integrative motif is devoid of content, kingdom theology is all too readily taken hostage to the individualism that characterizes the modern ethos. Kingdom theology easily degenerates into an individualistic theology—a theology that exalts and undergirds the radical individualist ideology of modernity. This tendency is evident in nineteenth-century liberalism. Although liberals defined the kingdom socially—as the ethical society of persons of good will founded by Jesus—their society of persons of good will was in the final analysis little more than an aggregate of individuals. The early-twentieth-century rediscovery of apocalyptic only exacerbated the problem, for its proponents simply opened the door for an individualistic "read" of the eschatological reign of God it claimed to find in the Bible.

More important than this first consideration, however, is a second. Kingdom does not lie at the heart of the biblical narrative. The kingdom of God is, of course, a pervasive biblical term. And God's purpose in history as set forth in the biblical narrative does include the demonstration of the divine rulership; it involves the establishment of the kingdom of God. This is preeminent, for example, in the central petition of the Lord's Prayer: "[Y]our kingdom come. Your will be done on earth as it is in heaven" (Matt. 6:10).

Yet as important as this theme is, in scripture it is superseded by another, more central motif, *community*. In fact, the concept of community forms the content of the kingdom of God. The divine reign consists of God at work redeeming, reconciling, and transforming creation into God's intended ideal and thereby constituting the world as God's realm. This reign both transcends history and works within history as the power effecting the new order. However, the new order God purposes for creation is communal in scope. When God's reign is present—that is, when God's will is done—community emerges. Or, stated in the opposite manner, the emergence of community marks the presence of God's rule and the accomplishing of God's will.

Community as the Biblical Motif

From the narratives of the primordial garden, with which the biblical drama begins, to the vision of white-robed multitudes inhabiting the new earth, which forms the drama's climax, the plot of scripture is community. Taken as a whole the Bible asserts that God's program is directed to the establishment of community in the highest sense of the word—a redeemed people, living within a redeemed creation, but above all enjoying the presence of the triune God.

The story of community as spelled out in the biblical drama begins "in the beginning." God's intent is articulated already in the Genesis 2 narrative, as God notes, "It is not good for the man to be alone." The divine activity from that point on is directed toward bringing into being the community envisioned by the Creator who noted the solitariness of the first human in the primordial Garden. As sociologist David Lyon notes, "It is clear from the creation account that sociality and interdependence are part of being human."[131]

At the heart of community as depicted throughout the biblical narrative is the idea of the presence of God among humans. Before the fall, God communed with Adam and Eve in the Garden. Then at various times and in various locations the patriarchs experienced God's presence and built landmarks, altars, and memorials to commemorate these encounters (e.g., Gen. 28: 13–17). With a view toward dwelling with humans, Israel's God delivered them from Egypt and constituted them as his covenant people (Ex. 20:2–3), in whose presence he himself would come to dwell. During the wilderness sojourn, Yahweh made his abode among them in the tabernacle; like theirs, his house would be a tent. So important for Israel was the presence of their God among them that when Yahweh proposed that the tabernacle not be built because of Israel's sin, Moses responded, "If your Presence does not go with us, do not send us up from here" (Ex. 33:15).[132] Later when Israel established fixed dwellings in the promised land, God also put the divine glory within a house, the temple in Jerusalem.

The Old Testament experience forms the context for the appearance of Jesus as Immanuel—God with us (Matt. 1:22–23). In Jesus, the divine Word became flesh and "tabernacled" among us (John 1:14); in him, God is present with humankind. Jesus promised that he and his Father would take up their dwelling with the disciples (John 14:23) through the sending of another Comforter who would be present among them (John 14:23). Jesus' promise forms the foundation for the work of the Spirit. Since his outpouring at Pentecost, the Holy Spirit facilitates the fulfilment of Jesus' assurance of his continual presence with his followers. The Spirit comprises us individually (1 Cor. 6:19) and corporately (1 Pet. 2:4–5) as the temple of God. Because of the finished work of Christ and the continuing work of the Spirit, therefore, God is truly among us, even though our experience of that presence is partial.

The biblical story does not end with Pentecost and hence not with the partial experience of God's presence Christ's disciples currently enjoy. The biblical drama reaches its climax only in the future, with the grand vision of the new heaven and new earth. The future new order will be characterized by community in the fullest sense. On that day, the peoples of the new earth will live together in peace. Nature will again fulfill its purpose of providing nourishment for all earthly inhabitants (Rev. 22:1–3a). Most glorious of all, however, God will dwell with humans, thereby bringing to completion the divine design for creation. The seer of the book of Revelation offers this glorious vision of God living with us in the eternal community: "And I heard a loud voice from the

---

131. David Lyon, *Sociology and the Human Image* (Downers Grove, Ill.: InterVarsity Press, 1983), 128.

132. For a discussion of the significance of this incident, see Edmund P. Clowney, "The Biblical Theology of the Church," in *The Church in the Bible and the World: An International Study*, ed. D. A. Carson (Exeter: Paternoster Press, 1987), 25–26.

throne saying, 'Now the dwelling of God is with human beings, and he will live with them, They will be his people, and God himself will be with them and be their God'" (Rev. 21:3, NIV ILE). In this new order, "The throne of God and of the Lamb will be in the city, and his servants will serve him. They will see his face, and his name will be on their foreheads" (Rev. 22:3b–4, NIV ILE).

This vision confirms our contention that the establishment of community lies at the heart of the biblical narrative. God's ultimate goal is not to transpose an aggregate of individual believers to an isolated realm "beyond the blue." Rather, God's program focuses on the corporate human story cast as it is within the story of all creation, and only in this context on individual humans as potential participants in the new creation. In fact, scripture consistently presents our eternal home in social rather than individual terms. It is a great city (Rev. 21:9–21); it encompasses many dwelling places or rooms (John 14:2); it is composed of a multitude of inhabitants (Rev. 7:9–10), etc. As Paul Hanson notes from his study of the theme of community in the Bible,

> God's future reign was not construed in terms of a blissful union of the elect with God that removed them from the world of humanity, but as a reign of justice and peace that repaired all wounds and restored righteousness as the standard among humans.[133]

The goal of community that lies at the heart of God's actions in history is displayed likewise in the focal point of salvation history, the Christ event. Thus, Jesus is the exemplar human being, the revelation of who we are to be, and the design Jesus reveals focuses on living in relationship with God and with others. Further, Jesus came as the Messiah—the fulfilment of the hopes and aspirations of the Hebrew people and, by extension, of all humankind (Luke 2:29–32). Jesus did not come to fulfill a private vocation of discovering God for his own sake but came to be obedient to the will of his Father for the sake of humankind. Thus, in his death he took upon himself the sins of all, and he rose from the grave to mediate to us eternal life through our union with him. David Fergusson draws out the implications of this observation:

> [T]he purpose of God's grace in the ministry and parables of Jesus is to include the marginalised individual within a community. . . . The individual must finally be understood in terms of his or her having an appointed place in the kingdom of God. The community under the rule of God is thus the goal of each individual life.[134]

---

133. Paul D. Hanson, *The People Called: The Growth of Community in the Bible* (San Francisco: Harper & Row, 1986), 510.

134. David Fergusson, *Community, Liberalism and Christian Ethics* (Cambridge: Cambridge University Press, 1998), 157.

The work of the Holy Spirit likewise has the establishment of community in view. His outpouring at Pentecost was directed toward the establishing of a new people composed of Jews and gentiles reconciled to each other (Eph. 2:11–22). During the present age the Holy Spirit is bringing together a people that transcends every human division—a people from every nation and every socioeconomic status, and consisting of both male and female (Gal. 3:28).

The completed work of Christ and the present work of the Spirit mean that the eschatological community that arrives in its fullness only at the consummation of human history is already present in a partial yet genuine manner. Although this present reality takes several forms, its focal point is the community of the followers of Christ. This observation returns to the concept of the divine reign. Above all, God comes to rulership in the community of Christ's disciples, in the fellowship of that people who by the Spirit have entered into covenant with the God of history and consequently live out their covenantal life through worship of the God revealed in Christ, through mutual care, and through mission in and for the world. The community of disciples is a laboratory of the kingdom insofar as it functions as a true community. As we embody the biblical vision of God's new community we reflect the character of God; thereby we are the *imago dei*.

To conclude: Josiah Royce declared, the "real world" means simply the "true interpretation" of our situation;[135] but "an interpretation is real only if the appropriate community is real, and is true only if that community reaches its goal."[136] Christian theology is the explication of the interpretation of God and the world around which the Christian community finds its identity. Theology engages in this task for the purpose of facilitating the fellowship of Christ's disciples in fulfilling their calling to be the image of God and thereby to be the biblical community God destines us to become. For this reason, theology is by its very nature communitarian.

135. Royce, *Problem of Christianity*, 2:264.
136. Ibid., 2:269.

Chapter Eight

Eschatology: Theology's Orienting Motif

From first to last, and not merely in the epilogue, Christianity is escha-
tology, is hope, forward looking and forward moving, and therefore
also revolutionizing and transforming the present. The eschatological
is not one element of Christianity, but it is the medium of Christian
faith as such, the key in which everything in it is set, the glow that suf-
fuses everything here in the dawn of an expected new day.

—Jürgen Moltmann[1]

Besides this, you know what time it is, how it is now the moment
for you to wake from sleep. For salvation is nearer to us now than
when we became believers; the night is far gone, the day is near. Let
us then lay aside the works of darkness and put on the armor of
light; let us live honorably as in the day . . .

—Romans 13:11–13 (NRSV)

In 1989, Francis Fukuyama boldly declared that liberal democracy marked the end of history understood in the Hegelian sense of "a single, coherent, evolutionary process" involving "the experience of all peoples in all times."[2] As this statement suggests and in contrast to the "incredulity toward metanarratives" that character-izes the "postmodern condition"—to cite Lyotard's well-known descriptors[3]—

1. Jürgen Moltmann, *Theology of Hope*, trans. James Leitch (New York: Harper & Row, 1967), 16.
2. Francis Fukuyama, "The End of History?" *The National Interest* (Summer 1989): 3–18.
3. Jean Francois Lyotard, *The Postmodern Condition: A Report on Knowledge*, trans. Geoff Bennington and Brian Massumi (Minneapolis: University of Minnesota Press, 1984), xxiv.

Fukuyama is convinced that we can continue to speak about a universal human history. In contrast as well to the widespread pessimism that characterizes our situation today, Fukuyama is optimistic about humankind attaining the goal of this history.[4]

In a sense, Fukuyama's thesis is a secularized version of Christian eschatology. Both embody a particular vision of the *telos,* or goal, of human life on earth. Both are convinced that ultimately human history is singular and unidirectional. And both are aware that the goal they envision cannot remain merely on the abstract, theoretical, and futurist level but has the capacity to inform— even transform—life in the present.

The life-transforming power potentially inherent in every eschatological vision leads to the third aspect of our proposal of what characterizes, or gives shape to, Christian theology. While being trinitarian and communitarian, theology must also be thoroughly eschatological. Stated more sharply, all theology is eschatology. But in what sense is this the case? What does a thoroughgoing eschatological theology look like? And how does eschatology shape theology? We contend that eschatology determines the content of theology insofar as eschatology serves to *orient* all theological reflection.[5] By this we mean that theology, with its trinitarian structure and communitarian focus, must likewise be at every turn directed toward and informed by a Christian understanding of creation's divinely given *telos.* The goal of this final chapter is to indicate why this is the case and to explicate how theology can be thoroughly eschatological.

What Is Eschatology?

In stating our thesis, we are immediately confronted with a difficulty. Christian theological history has witnessed the emergence of differing understandings of eschatology. How, then, is it possible for us to speak of eschatology as orienting theology? Which eschatological viewpoint ought to inform theology? This potentially debilitating problem requires that we clarify what we mean by eschatology, en route to our goal of setting forth the character of a thoroughgoing eschatological theology.

Eschatology as "Last Things"

The etymology of the term links eschatology with the concept of "last things." The word *eschatology* means literally the study of, the teaching about, or the doctrine of the last things.[6] But what "last things"?

---

4. For his fuller treatment of this thesis, see Francis Fukuyama, *The End of History and the Last Man* (New York: Avon Books, 1992).

5. This position has gained wide acceptance even among conservative theologians. Hence, Lewis and Demarest state, "Christian thought maintains that the whole of theology is eschatological in orientation." Gordon R. Lewis and Bruce A. Demarest, *Integrative Theology,* 3 vols. (Grand Rapids: Zondervan, 1987–1994), 3:369.

6. Hence, S. H. Travis, "Eschatology," in *New Dictionary of Theology,* ed. Sinclair B.

Some people interpret "last things" as referring to what is last *logically* (that is, last in importance), and hence eschatology is the study of those dimensions of Christian belief that are of least significance. More likely, however, "last things" is seen as referring to what is last *chronologically* (that is, what occurs last in history). In this view, eschatology is properly the delineation of the sequence of events marking the end of life as we know it and inaugurating eternity. Although admitting that it includes the climax of earthly life for each individual human, people are more likely to see as the particular focus of eschatology the climax of human history in its entirety. In this way, eschatology readily takes on a particularly futurist cast. And the study of last things tends to focus on the *eschata* rather than the *eschaton*, as Gerhard Sauter notes,[7] or on the future as *futurum* rather than *adventus*, to cite Jürgen Moltmann's appraisal.[8]

The Prevalence of the Viewpoint

Eschatology as the study of "last things" understood as the final events that will transpire in history is arguably the most widely held understanding among Christians today. It is especially prevalent among evangelicals, not only in the church but also in the academy. Thus, theologians in evangelical seminaries debate such issues as the time of the rapture in relation to the great tribulation[9] and whether what is transpiring in the Middle East carries prophetic significance.[10] In this task they are joined by pastors commanding a following within churches of various denominational affiliations[11] and by a variety of radio and television personalities eager to fill in the details.[12]

This viewpoint is not new. Rather, eschatology as "last things"—as the exploration of the final events of the age—has provided grist for the theological debate mill throughout the history of the church.[13] Already in the second century Christian leaders were divided over one crucial eschatological issue, namely, whether the inauguration of the new creation would be preceded by a

Ferguson, David F. Wright, and J. I. Packer (Downers Grove, Ill.: InterVarsity Press, 1988), 228; F. F. Bruce, "Eschatology," in *Evangelical Dictionary of Theology*, ed. Walter Elwell (Grand Rapids: Baker, 1984), 362.

7. For this distinction, see Gerhard Sauter, *Eschatological Rationality: Theological Issues in Focus*, (Grand Rapids: Baker, 1996), 146–47.

8. Jürgen Moltmann, *The Coming of God: Christian Eschatology*, trans. Margaret Kohl (Minneapolis: Fortress Press, 1996), 25.

9. Hence, Richard R. Reiter, *The Rapture: Pre-, Mid-, or Post-Tribulational?* (Grand Rapids: Zondervan, 1984).

10. For an example written on a more popular level, see John F. Walvoord, *Armageddon, Oil, and the Middle East Crisis*, rev. ed. (Grand Rapids: Zondervan, 1990). A "classical" scholarly treatment is Oswald T. Allis, *Prophecy and the Church* (Nutley, N.J.: Presbyterian and Reformed Publishing Co., 1972).

11. For an example, see Tim LaHaye, *No Fear of the Storm: Why Christians Will Escape All the Tribulation* (Sisters, Ore.: Multnomah, 1992).

12. See for example, Jack Van Impe, *Revelation Revealed Verse by Verse* (Troy, Mich.: Jack Van Impe Ministries, 1982).

13. For an overview of millenarianism in the church history, see Stanley J. Grenz, *The Millennial Maze: Sorting Out Evangelical Options* (Downers Grove, Ill.: InterVarsity Press, 1992).

thousand-year earthly reign of Christ. The apologist Justin Martyr, to cite one prominent example, defended premillennialism while acknowledging the presence of nonmillenarians in the church.[14] Although this issue receded into the background after the condemnation of premillennialism at the Council of Ephesus in 431 C.E., the millennium question resurfaced intermittently throughout the Middle Ages before emerging as a crucial theological topic in the post-Reformation era, especially in England and later in North America.

The Danger of the Futurist Viewpoint

The history of eschatological thinking in the church suggests that when viewed as "last things," a futurist eschatology tends either to generate an inordinate level of interest or to fade from view. As Thomas Finger notes, "In general, eschatology has suffered from two attitudes in the Church: neglect and overemphasis."[15] Hence, many Christians respond with disdain to the confusion they see emerging from the attempt to sort out the chronology of the future. Some even glibly call themselves "panmillennialists," for they are confident that—to cite the repeatedly voiced cliché—"everything will pan out in the end." Other Christians, in contrast, are consumed by the task of deciphering the exact details and timing of coming events. Eager to discern the "signs of the times," they are quick to link the latest geopolitical development, technological invention, or social crisis with biblical prophecy about the "end times."

Although at first glance neglect and overemphasis appear to be polar opposites, they so often lead to the same detrimental results.[16] Both all too readily separate eschatology from other topics of systematic theology, relegating it to merely one compartment within the corpus of Christian teaching. And both easily divorce eschatology from the life of the church, reducing it to simply the delineation of what will happen at some future time.

This-Worldly Eschatology

Not all theologians adhere to the futurist understanding of eschatology as "last things." In fact, its chief rival arose in the patristic era. As the church became an established and integral part of society, it lost much of its earlier anticipatory fervor. In this new context many theologians "spiritualized" the expectations of an end of the age found in the biblical texts and reinterpreted the kingdom of God as the church on earth.[17]

---

14. Justin (the) Martyr, *Dialogue with Trypho, A Jew*, in *The Ante-Nicene Fathers: Translation of the Fathers Down to A.D. 325*, American Edition, ed. A. Roberts and J. Donaldson (Grand Rapids: Wm. B. Eerdmans Publishing Co., 1975) 1:239.

15. Thomas N. Finger, *Christian Theology: An Eschatological Approach*, 2 vols. (Nashville: Thomas Nelson Publishers, 1985), 1:101.

16. For a similar critique, see ibid., 1:101.

17. Richard Kenneth Emmerson, *Antichrist in the Middle Ages* (Manchester: Manchester University Press, 1981), 51.

The Historical Trajectory

The rejection of the futurist approach dates to the Alexandrian church fathers, who were motivated by their preference for an allegorical, rather than a literal, exegesis of scripture. But the most influential critic was Augustine. In his monumental work *The City of God*, Augustine replaced the futurist interpretation with a view of eschatology as informing the character of the church in the here and now. More specifically, he characterized the church as the kingdom of Christ and spoke of it as sharing in Christ's rule.[18] To this end, Augustine drew from the work of the Donatist thinker Tyconius.[19] Following the more allegorical exegetical method of Alexandria that he helped adapt to the emerging Latin theology, Tyconius understood the book of Revelation as a picture of the history of the church in the world, rather than as a prophecy of the end of human history.

Under Augustine's influence, most medieval theologians moved completely away from the view of history that interprets it as a cosmic drama complete with plot and climax. In its stead they substituted the image of a pilgrim people of God seeking a destination beyond history, who through the rites of the church participate in God's kingdom. Although Luther used apocalyptic imagery to characterize his dispute with Rome, he nevertheless retained the Augustinian focus on the church as the kingdom of God[20] and bequeathed it to the mainstream Protestant tradition.

In the nineteenth century, the this-worldly eschatology of the Augustinian tradition lived on in the reigning liberal theology of the day. Yet liberal theologians shifted the focus from the church to the kingdom, which they viewed as a broader reality. Albrecht Ritschl, for example, set forth a this-worldly, ethical understanding of the divine reign. He spoke of the kingdom proclaimed by Jesus as the unity of humankind organized according to love,[21] which as our highest good and goal[22] progresses in the world. The this-worldly understanding of eschatology that typified Protestant liberalism reached its apex in the social gospel movement. Convinced that the kingdom of God was neither the realm of the afterlife nor a perfect social order inaugurated by Christ at his

---

18. Augustine, *The City of God* 20.9, trans. Marcens Dods, Modern Library ed. (New York: Random House, 1950), 725–27.

19. Peter Toon, "Introduction," in *Puritans, the Millennium and the Future of Israel: Puritan Eschatology 1600 to 1660*, ed. Peter Toon (Greenwood, S.C.: Attic Press, 1970), 13.

20. For an example of Luther's nonapocalyptic interpretation of scripture, see "Preface to the Revelation of St. John," trans. by H. E. Jacobs in *Works of Martin Luther*, 6 vols. (Philadelphia: A. J. Holman Co., 1932), 6: 480–88.

21. Ritschl's formal definition of the kingdom of God is rather lengthy and complicated: ". . . the uninterrupted reciprocation of action springing from the motive of love—a kingdom in which all are knit together in union with every one who can show the marks of a neighbour; further it is that union of men in which all goods are appropriated in their proper subordination to the highest good." Albrecht Ritschl, *The Christian Doctrine of Justification and Reconciliation* (Clifton, N.J.: Reference Books Publishers Inc., 1966), 334–335.

22. Ibid., 282. Here Ritschl refers to the kingdom of God as God's own glory and personal end.

second coming but an earthly society in which all humans live together in cooperation, love, and justice, social gospelers sought to cooperate with God in the construction of the ideal society.

Recent Reformulations

After World War I, the focus on ethics that characterized liberal eschatology was rejected in favor of other models. One critic of the liberal understanding of the kingdom of God and its embodiment in the social gospel was Reinhold Niebuhr, who throughout his career assailed what he saw as the two articles of liberalism, the idea of progress and the belief in the perfectability of humankind.[23] In response to its naive optimism, Niebuhr set forth what he considered a more balanced appraisal of the human situation in the world— "Christian realism." Regardless of our good intentions, he argued, because of our fallenness we will never reach perfection; the ideal always remains an "impossible possibility."[24] Niebuhr linked this ideal with Christian eschatology, especially the symbol of the kingdom of God.[25] As the ideal that always surpasses every historical reality, he argued, the kingdom forms a check on the human tendency toward self-assertion and pride. At the same time, according to Niebuhr, this symbol discloses the meaning of history in the present, a disclosure that, in turn, forms the basis for a positive Christian witness in the world.[26]

Another critique of the liberal portrait emerged from the work of Johannes Weiss[27] and Albert Schweitzer,[28] who argued convincingly that Jesus' message was thoroughly futuristic and apocalyptic in orientation. Schweitzer concluded that this discovery discredited the New Testament, in that its central content— the belief in an imminent end of the world—had been proven false.[29] One thinker who took up the challenge that this turn of events posed for Christian faith was Rudolf Bultmann.

Bultmann agreed that Jesus and the early Christian community anticipated the soon arrival of the kingdom of God and that their hope was not fulfilled.[30] Rather than being forced thereby to reject the biblical message as irrelevant, however, Bultmann solved the difficulty by reinterpreting the futurist eschatol-

23. See, for example, Reinhold Niebuhr, "Intellectual Autobiography," in *Reinhold Niebuhr: His Religious, Social and Political Thought*, vol. 2 of the Library of Living Theology, ed. Charles W. Kegley and Robert W. Bretall (New York: Macmillan Co., 1961), 15.

24. For example, Reinhold Niebuhr, *An Interpretation of Christian Ethics* (New York: Meridian Books, 1956), 97–123.

25. See, for example, his discussion in Reinhold Niebuhr, *The Nature and Destiny of Man*, Scribner Library ed. (New York: Charles Scribner's Sons, 1964), 2:287–98.

26. Niebuhr, *The Nature and Destiny of Man*, 2:320.

27. Johannes Weiss, *Jesus' Proclamation of the Kingdom of God*, trans. Richard H. Hiers and David L. Holland (Philadelphia: Fortress Press, 1971).

28. Albert Schweitzer, *The Quest of the Historical Jesus* (New York: Macmillan Co., 1954).

29. Ibid., 357–372.

30. Rudolf Bultmann, *Jesus Christ and Mythology* (New York: Charles Scribner's Sons, 1958), 14.

ogy of the New Testament. Taking his cue from Paul and John, who, according to Bultmann, spoke of the eternal life received in faith as a present, existential reality rather than a future, temporal hope,[31] he moved behind the temporal sense, in which the eschatological message had been given, to what Bultmann perceived to be its true *existential* meaning. Hence, he dehistoricized Jesus' proclamation of a catastrophic action of God marking the climax of history, and transformed Jesus' message from a word about the future of the world to a declaration about the private realm of the inner spirit of the individual believer. For Bultmann, then, "the end of the world" no longer referred to an event in human history but to the change from inauthentic existence to faith within the heart of the hearer of the proclamation.

Eschatology as Hope

Bultmann's program, with its complete loss of the future as a temporal reality, indicates the unhappy conclusion to which the wholesale rejection of biblical futurism can lead. In this sense, Bultmann stands at the end of a theological trajectory that began with the Alexandrians. In the wake of the dominance of Bultmann's existential reinterpretation of eschatology, a far-reaching proposal for the renewal of futurist eschatology and its significance for theology emerged in the 1960s in the work of several theologians who were initially grouped together under the designation "theology of hope." Perhaps the thinker most consistently associated with the retrieval of hope is Jürgen Moltmann. His approach, therefore, provides the paradigmatic eschatological theology.

Moltmann's Proposal

At the heart of Moltmann's contribution was his rediscovery that the Bible is oriented to history, or more specifically, to the future—to eschatology. Moltmann argues that modern theology (particularly Bultmann) misunderstood this central dimension of scripture. In contrast to the existentialists' focus on individual existence, Moltmann is convinced that the Bible proclaims a God who will do a new work on behalf of the world; indeed, the Bible is "the history book of God's promises."[32] This proclamation inspires hope in the present. Theology, in turn, arises out of hope in the promises of "the coming God."[33] Theology, Moltmann suggests, is the interpretation of the promissory history found in the Bible, articulated for the sake of providing an understanding of the present-day mission of the church in the world. In this sense, theology is by its very nature eschatological.

Central to his futurist, eschatologically oriented theology is Moltmann's understanding of the radical nature of Christian hope. He adamantly denies that the

---

31. Ibid., 32–34.
32. Jürgen Moltmann, *The Experiment Hope*, trans. M. Douglas Meeks (Philadelphia: Fortress Press, 1975), 45.
33. Ibid., 45.

future arises from possibilities already inherent in the here and now.[34] The future is not "that which is already pregnant in the present."[35] Hence, the future cannot be derived simply by extrapolating from current realities, for it comes to us as God's gift. And rather than being its fulfillment, the future contradicts the present; the kingdom of God comes from beyond and negates the present evil situation.

Moltmann draws this perspective from the idea of *promise*. "A promise," he writes, "is a pledge that proclaims a reality which is not yet at hand."[36] The promise about God's future is present as the proclaimed word about the future, a word that anticipates a new future and thereby commends us to seek that future.[37] This word announces as "future" the promise of the God who is present only as the "coming one," that is, the God who is present "in the way in which his future in promise and hope empowers the present."[38]

For Moltmann, this thoroughgoing futurist eschatological perspective informs the church's mission in the world. Rather than moving from the present to the future, our task is to look from the future to the present and to anticipate the future in the midst of our present existence. We do not simply wait passively for the arrival of the future, of course. Nevertheless Moltmann warns, we dare not confuse the glorious future of God with the fruit of our labors.[39] The promise of the future ought to motivate us to act in the present; yet in the final analysis the future does not come as the result of our doing, but must break into the present and transform it. Moltmann offers this description of our response to the promissory message:

> One does not move to another country to find freedom and God. One remains where one is in order to correspond to the conditions of the coming kingdom of God through the renewal of the heart and by practical transformation of social circumstances. The front line of the exodus is not emigration, but liberation through the transformation of the present. For in the present, where we always are, the powers of the past wrestle with the powers of the future, and fear and hope struggle for domination. By changing ourselves and the circumstances around us, by anticipating the future God, we emigrate out of the past into the future.[40]

Hope and Foundationalism

Moltmann is convinced that hope lies at the heart of eschatology. He writes, "In actual fact . . . eschatology means the doctrine of the Christian hope, which embraces both the object hoped for and also the hope inspired by it."[41] As a

34. Ibid., 49.
35. Ibid., 52.
36. Ibid., 49.
37. Ibid., 49.
38. Ibid., 51.
39. Jürgen Moltmann, "Hope and History," *Theology Today* 25/3 (Oct. 1968): 385.
40. Moltmann, *Experiment Hope*, 59.
41. Moltmann, *Theology of Hope*, 16.

consequence, for Moltmann Christian theology is by its very nature a theology of hope. At one point, however, this hope-filled, eschatologically oriented theological proposal risks falling into a potentially devastating difficulty.

In addition to the Bible, Moltmann derives his concept of hope from the revisionist Marxist philosopher, Ernst Bloch. For Bloch, hope for a perfect "homeland" where people overcome all alienation and are at one with themselves is a fundamental human instinct, and this instinct drives history through revolutionary change toward utopia. Consequently, Bloch developed an ontology of "not-yet-being" in which the as-yet-unrealized utopia exerts power over the present and past, giving rise to human "transcending without transcendence."[42] Although Moltmann rejects Bloch's "transcending without transcendence,"[43] Bloch nevertheless provides the stimulation and philosophical conceptuality for Moltmann's interpretation of hope.[44] Insofar as he is dependent on Bloch's ontology of the future, with its characterization of the human person as intrinsically hopeful, Moltmann hazards slipping into an anthropocentric foundationalism, which replaces the specificity of the biblical hope for hope as a structure of human existence.

The danger that lurks beneath the surface in Moltmann's theological proposal becomes explicit in certain contemporary practical theologians who introduce an anthropologically based hope into their work. Andrew Lester, for example, reappropriates hope by appeal to the nature of the human condition and the human person.[45] Following Moltmann's lead, he claims that to be human is to be a creature who hopes: "This ability to anticipate the future is an ontological given, perhaps the most authentic and distinctive characteristic of humanity."[46]

Contemporary practitioners of hope view hope as a basic human attitude toward life that looks to the future and its possibilities. Hence, Donald Capps asserts, "[H]ope becomes an attitude toward life and, as an attitude, it does not depend solely or even primarily on the attainment of specific hopes."[47] For Capps, hoping, therefore, is "the perception that what one wants to happen will happen, a perception that is fueled by desire and in response to felt deprivation," and hopes, in turn, are "projections that envision the realizable and thus involve risk."[48] Lester offers a similar explication: "When speaking of hope, I am addressing the configuration of cognitive and affective responses to life that believes the future is filled with possibilities and offers a blessing."[49]

---

42. Marcel Neusch, *The Sources of Modern Atheism: One Hundred Years of Debate Over God*, trans. Matthew J. O'Connell (New York: Paulist Press, 1982), 189.

43. Jürgen Moltmann, *God in Creation: A New Theology of Creation and the Spirit of God*, trans. Margaret Kohl (San Francisco: Harper & Row, 1985), 180.

44. M. Douglas Meeks, *Origins of the Theology of Hope* (Philadelphia: Fortress Press, 1974), 18.

45. Andrew D. Lester, *Hope in Pastoral Care and Counseling* (Minneapolis: Fortress Press, 1995), 3.

46. Ibid., 59.

47. Donald Capps, *Agents of Hope: A Pastoral Psychology* (Minneapolis: Fortress Press, 1995), 31.

48. Ibid., 53.

49. Lester, *Hope in Pastoral Care*, 62.

For the anthropological foundation on which hope is built, Lester appeals to the work of psychologist Erik Erikson, who places a high value on hope as a human attribute. Erikson defines hope as "the enduring belief in the attainability of fervent wishes, in spite of the dark urges and rages which mark the beginning of existence."[50] Such hope is the basic human virtue, Erikson maintains, the basic strength that sustains human life. It "is both the earliest and the most indispensable virtue inherent in the state of being alive," so that "if life is to be sustained hope must remain."[51]

The anthropological approach links our innate human hopefulness to personal identity. Proponents theorize that our sense of personal meaning is dependent on our ability to look beyond the present so as to anticipate our future. Viewed from this perspective, the future becomes an existential reality. The future is what gives meaning to our existence, in that it fosters our ability to transcend the present. Hope, in turn, is the means through which we lay hold of this identity-forming future.

Viewing the future as the realm of potentiality and seeing hope as the capacity that allows the emergence of meaningful existence in the present carries a potentially debilitating risk. It can easily lead to the "deactualizing" of the future and result in the demise of hope. In this anthropocentric schema, an actual, particular future is ultimately not crucial to the production of personal identity. What suffices in this process is merely the ability to anticipate a future—*any* future—so long as the anticipated future is able to generate the kind of hopeful response required for the construction of personal identity in the present. As the future loses its actuality, it no longer is definitive for the understanding of hope. Cut off from its grounding in a particular future, hope becomes merely a psychological tool—a powerful tool of course, but merely a tool nonetheless—in the task of forming one's own identity. In this way, the anthropologically focused, foundationalist approach reduces hope to wishful thinking.

Eschatology as *Telos*

The retrieval of hope and hence a futurist eschatology leading to a theology of hope is not itself misguided. Rather, it becomes problematic when hope—and with it eschatology itself—is grounded in some supposedly universal structure of human existence. An eschatological theology goes astray if it appeals to an experience of hope we supposedly all share. It errs, if it seeks to construct a Christian conception of hope—and hence a Christian eschatology—on a prior understanding of what is assumed to be universally human. In short, a hope-filled theology loses its way when it trots after the illusive foundationalist dream, seeking to secure its own certitude by appeal to a supposedly unassailable anthropological foundation.

50. Erik H. Erikson, *Insight and Responsibility* (New York: W. W. Norton & Co., 1964), 118.
51. Ibid., 115.

Our understanding of eschatology, and hence our delineation of a hope-filled theology, cannot follow the now-suspect foundationalist program. Rather, theological method must take seriously the nonfoundationalist turn. But what does this look like? What ought to characterize our understanding of hope, and hence, of eschatology?

A Particular Hope

At the heart of all foundationalist constructions, of course, is the appeal to a universal human experience of hope. Consequently, such constructions typically remain on the generic level. Although anticipating a future that is filled with possibilities is crucial to the construction of a healthy personal identity, every treatment of hope that looks to some supposedly universal human reality as its foundation can only leave us with a conception of hope that is too vague to be helpful.

Foundationalist conceptions are unhelpfully vague simply because human experiences of hope are always specific, never generic. By its very nature hope is always the anticipation of a specific something. The hoping person looks toward a future that offers (or forebodes) a particular reality or set of possibilities. In short, the generically human experience of hope cannot answer Immanuel Kant's question, "What can I hope for?"[52] It can only remind us that in order to survive we must be hopeful.

Consequently, our theology of hope must view hope as particular, not generic. Indeed, a nonfoundationalist theology of hope speaks about hope in the particular, because it eschews the generically human for the mosaic of beliefs of a particular faith community. Every nonfoundationalist theology explores the hope of the community to which it is linked, viewing the particular hope of the community as a dimension of the community's larger interpretive framework. Hence, *Christian* theology speaks of the particular hope *Christians* anticipate, which hope is articulated in the Bible.

Like human experiences of hope, hope in the Bible is always specific. Biblical hope is always directed toward, anticipates, and draws its life from a particular vision of the future. And the specific future that forms the object of biblical hope is not presented as a possibility, but as a certainty. Hence, viewed theologically, hope lays hold of a particular future that it sees as assured. Indeed, so certain is the anticipated future that the biblical writers present the Christian hope as more real than the context in which we now live, which is already passing away (e.g., 1 Cor. 7:31).

A Teleological Hope

But what is the particular Christian hope? And how can this hope be directed toward a particular future without degenerating into a hope directed merely

---

52. Immanuel Kant, *Critique of Pure Reason*, trans. Norman Kemp Smith (London: Macmillan & Co., 1933), A805/B833, 635.

toward the "last things" understood as the disheveled *eschata* characteristic of many futurist eschatologies?

According to Andrew Lester, there are two quite different horizons of hope: the finite and the transfinite.[53] Of course, all conceptions of eschatology that focus on the "last things" as the final events within the temporal sequence provide only a finite horizon for hope. But the same is true of anthropologically grounded concepts of hope. They too look to a horizon that is temporal and hence finite. This is especially evident in theologians who, despite all their lofty statements about a hope based in an absolute future, eventually revert to a basically therapeutic understanding of eschatology.

Daniel J. Louw is a case in point. He declares, "Eschatology is not about 'the end' of things, but about 'the essence' of creation, viewed from the perspective of grace, salvation, and justification."[54] Louw then asserts that Christians enjoy this essential reality in the present: "The believer already shares in the glory of the coming Kingdom of God in the mode of glorification. Gratitude thus becomes a metaphor for the reality of eschatology."[55]

If our theology of hope is to be anything more than therapeutic wishful thinking, it must realize that Christian hope is directed toward the future, understood as involving the longest horizon imaginable. From the perspective of the Bible this horizon is nothing less than the consummation of God's purposes for creation. In this sense, Christian hope is transfinite, to use Lester's category. Or perhaps stated more correctly, Christian hope is linked to our *telos*, to the goal, purpose, or end of our existence—not viewed in isolation, however, but within the context of the divine purpose for all creation. In short, hope is connected to the destiny of the entire universe, a destiny that we, in turn, share, and in which we have a crucial place. Consequently, eschatology is teleology, the teaching about the *telos* of creation.

Yet we must add one caveat. Ultimately, the object of Christian hope is not our destiny as such. Moltmann rightly intimates that hope arises out of, and is directed toward, the divine *promises*. We would add that more particularly our hope is generated by God's promises to bring creation to completion in the divine eternity, as articulated in the Bible. In the end, then, the object of Christian hope is not the future itself but the God of the future; not our creaturely destiny but the God who destines; not the *telos* of our existence but the God who is leading us toward that glorious goal. In short, our hope is in the God who declares, "I am making all things new" (Rev. 21:5).

By appropriating this biblical word of promise, the Spirit creates in our present a new community, the eschatological community of those whose personal identity finds its center in Jesus Christ. And in the final analysis only this vision of a concrete future awaiting us in the consummation of all things, with its

53. Lester, *Hope in Pastoral Care*, 67.
54. Daniel J. Louw, "Pastoral Care and the Therapeutic Dimension of Christian Hope," *Pastoral Sciences* 17 (1998): 89.
55. Ibid., 89.

identity-producing power in the present, can offer the basis for living in the present. When viewed theologically, therefore, Christian hope is teleological; in hope we lay hold of an eternal, transfinite horizon, the realization of that for which we are created.

A Pessimistic Hope

Yet we still have not arrived at a delineation of the content of the Christian hope. To bring us to this goal, we must introduce one final aspect of a non-foundationalist theology of hope: Such hope is pessimistic, not optimistic.

Because its beginning point lies in the universal experience of hope or with hope as a structure of human existence, the foundationalist approach is intrinsically optimistic. Foundationalist theologians view hope as a virtue we all possess, at least potentially. What is needed is simply the proper process or mechanism that can trigger this latent ability within the human psyche. As we noted earlier, the hope-triggering mechanism is a vision of a future—any future—so long as that future is filled with potential, so long as it holds out promise for human possibilities. In keeping with this optimistic stance, Capps asserts that hopes are "projections that envision the realizable."[56]

When compared to this optimistic stance, Christian hope appears hopelessly pessimistic. The Christian understanding does not look to what lies within the human person; it does not draw its understanding from our inherent human potential. Above all it has nothing to do with envisioning the realizable. Christian hope is pessimistic, because it is not based on what humans might potentially do but solely on what *God* will do. And when considered from the human perspective, what God promises to accomplish can only be dismissed as *un*realizable.

The unrealizable character of God's promise is illustrated in the story of Jesus and Jairus's daughter (Mark 5:35–42). What Jairus and his family needed in this dire situation was for Jesus to do what from their perspective was completely unrealizable—bring life from the dead. Indeed, for a couple who has lost a child, hope can only involve anticipating what is in fact completely beyond the realm of the realizable. It entails anticipating that their loss will one day be fully and completely overcome, an overcoming of loss that is of such magnitude that it cannot be expected, because it lies beyond what is humanly possible. In this situation, hope lays hold of what only God can do, but also what God promises to fulfill in the eschatological renewal, namely, give life to the dead.

In a sense, in every situation we need the one thing that lies beyond our human capability even to expect, namely, life from the dead—resurrection. Yet resurrection is precisely God's eschatological promise and hence the content of our hope, even when to grasp this promise means to hope against all hope. As Rubem Alves declared, "[T]here is but one truly theological problem, and that is the resurrection of the dead."[57]

---

56. Capps, *Agents of Hope*, 53.
57. Rubem Alves, *The Poet, the Warrior, the Prophet* (London: SCM Press, 1990), 137.

In focusing on the God who promises to bring life from the dead, the Christian vision does not naively minimize life's tragedies. Instead, it places the events of life in the only context in which they can take on any significance whatsoever, the context of the "impossible possibility," to cite Niebuhr's helpful phrase. The Christian vision places them within a new, humanly unrealizable narrative in which the tale of tragedy these events appear to be writing is recast within God's speaking a final No to evil and Yes to creation. Hence, the Christian vision places life's tragedies in the context of an unrealizable narrative that will nevertheless be eternally realized on that day when God, through the power of the Spirit and according to the pattern of the resurrected Christ, makes all things new.

Because it talks about this ultimate purpose of our existence, eschatology is not the study of "last things" as a conglomerate of future temporal occurrences—not the "last things" as disconnected *eschata*. Rather, eschatology is the study of "last things" as *telos*. Consequently, eschatology fosters a theology that becomes the teaching about the God who promises to bring creation to its divinely given *telos* in the eternal community that God will bring—and is already bringing—to pass. Viewed from this perspective we can see why all theology is eschatology and why eschatology orients theology. Ultimately, Christian theology—the study of God—is by its own nature at every stage and always eschatological, that is, *telic*. And Christian theology is always hopeful or hope-filled.

Theology and Christian Eschatology

In our discussion of the nature of eschatology we declared that Christian theology is inherently eschatological. Theology is the teaching about the promising God, the God who is bringing creation to an eternal *telos*. In this sense, theology finds its orientation in eschatology. As the teaching about the God of the Bible, theology is directed toward the teaching about the *telos* of creation as determined and effected by the God of creation. With this in view, we now turn our attention more closely to the intimate connection between eschatology and theology. Specifically, we explore what we see as the defining dimensions or crucial characteristics of an eschatological theology. In so doing, we also provide the basis for understanding the *manner* in which eschatology orients theology.

The Basis for an Eschatological Theology

To anticipate what follows, eschatology orients Christian theology because of the connection between eschatology and the narrative of God at work in creation disclosed in scripture. For this reason, an eschatological theology is linked to the biblical narrative, around which the Christian community gathers, with its focus on the divinely intended *telos* of creation.

In saying this, however, we immediately encounter a potential difficulty. For the content of eschatology, and consequently for any eschatological character that theology might contain, many theologians run immediately to texts that purportedly provide information about events that will transpire in the future. In this approach, eschatology becomes the systematic presentation of the details of the future as disclosed by particular verses of scripture. That is, the study of "last things" focuses on the compilation of what God has told us in scripture "about the major events yet to come in the history of the universe," to cite Wayne Grudem's characterization.[58]

Previously we rejected any approach that results in eschatology degenerating into the delineation of the *eschata* as disconnected facts about the future. In so doing, however, we are not denying that the eschatological orientation of theology has a definite futurist cast. Nor are we denigrating conversations about future events. On the contrary, we uphold the futurist and actual character of eschatology. Nevertheless, in contrast to theological methods that read the various texts merely to decipher some blueprint of the future hidden within the pages of the Bible, we maintain that the pathway into the eschatological orientation of theology travels through the biblical narrative, understood as the disclosure of the trajectory of God's action in history. It is in the context of this overarching narrative that all the various *genre* of scripture, in turn, find their appropriate meaning.

We maintain, therefore, that an eschatological theology is closely connected to the biblical narrative. But on what basis can we make this claim? Why must our theological method give primacy to narrative?

Narrative and Eschatology

Before stating explicitly our answer to this question, we must explore the eschatological character of the biblical narrative itself. The centrality of eschatology to the biblical narrative indicates why an eschatological theology must draw its life from that narrative, while providing a hint of what must characterize such a theology.

Taken as a whole, the biblical story is directed toward a *telos*. It speaks of the God who is bringing creation to its divinely intended goal. The development of a *telos*-directed narrative is among the most significant theological contributions of the biblical communities. While this development takes on its final canonical form in the documents of the early church, the genesis of the process lies in the Old Testament, in a far-reaching innovation in Israel's understanding of time. As we will sketch shortly, this innovation produced in Israel a *historical* consciousness that took on a *futurist* cast, gained an *eternal* focus, and finally came to be seen as *universal* in scope. The Old Testament faith community then bequeathed this understanding of time to the New Testament community and hence to the Christian church. Therefore, to understand the narrative basis for

58. Wayne Grudem, *Systematic Theology: An Introduction to Biblical Doctrine* (Grand Rapids: Zondervan, 1994), 1091.

an eschatological theology we must look more closely at this development, which, in turn, shapes so significantly our theological method.

The religious traditions of the ancient Near Eastern societies—from Egypt to Greece[59]—reflect a cyclical view of time. This conception sees life as following a rhythmic pattern, a circle of a finite number of events that occur repeatedly and with observable regularity. Canaanite worship rituals, which focused on two gods who were associated with the major seasons of the year, offer a prime example. As the coming drought began to dry out the vegetation in early summer, religious rituals lamented the death of the fertility god Baal and the triumph of Mot the god of death. Then as the winter rains brought the promise of good crops, the Canaanites celebrated Baal's rebirth.[60]

One of the greatest achievements of Israel,[61] one that set them apart from the surrounding peoples,[62] was the understanding of time as a linear historical span,[63] that is, the development of a *historical* consciousness. The basis for this development lay in neither philosophical speculation nor mythology[64] but in Israel's theological understanding.

The idea of the linearity of time arose initially out of Israel's sense that Yahweh had acted savingly in the experiences of the patriarchs and later of the nation itself. These experiences formed a sequence of events, a whole that was greater than simply the sum of its various parts. Israel concluded that Yahweh had a definite plan for the nation and that the God who journeys with people[65] had been traveling with them since the days of the patriarchs—a journey that marked their identity as a nation.[66] Consequently, the linear, historical nature of time was dependent on the God who acts in time. Gerhard von Rad offers this lucid explanation:

> Thus, Israel's history existed only in so far as God accompanied her, and it is only this time-span which can properly be described as her history. It was God who established the continuity between the various separate events and who ordained their direction as they followed one another in time.[67]

As a result, time—and history—became a narrative, the story of God at work in Israel's experiences.

---

59. For a comparison of the Greek outlook with that of the biblical communities, see Karl Loewith, *Meaning in History* (Chicago: University of Chicago Press, 1950), 4–10.

60. Hans-Joachim Kraus, *Worship in Israel: A Cultic History of the Old Testament*, trans. G. Bushwell (Richmond: John Knox Press, 1966), 38–43.

61. Gerhard von Rad, *Old Testament Theology*, trans. D. M. G. Stalker, 2 vols. (New York: Harper & Row, 1965), 2:107.

62. Ibid., 2:110.

63. Loewith, *Meaning in History*, 19.

64. von Rad, *Old Testament Theology*, 2:106.

65. Werner H. Schmidt, *The Faith of the Old Testament: A History*, trans. John Sturdy (Philadelphia: Westminster Press, 1983), 52.

66. von Rad, *Old Testament Theology*, 2:106.

67. Ibid.

Israel's concept of time as linear, as the narrative of God acting savingly on their behalf, led secondly to the development of a *future* consciousness. The impetus in this direction lay largely with the prophets, who did not retell the stories of former days simply as past events but as pointers foreshadowing the future. In their depictions, the stories of Israelite history become "pregnant with future," to cite Moltmann's description.[68] Or as Werner Schmidt describes the phenomenon, "What was already realized becomes future again, in order to retain its present significance for later generations."[69]

On this basis, Old Testament scholars from Gerhard von Rad[70] to John Sailhammer[71] speak about the prophetic engagement with the historical narratives as an "eschatological reading." Yet what made this use of past stories truly eschatological was the conclusion that dawned in the minds of the prophets that God's new historical action would—in von Rad's words—"surpass and therefore to a certain extent supersede" the "old basic events of the canonical history." In this, he adds, the prophets were motivated by "their conviction that Jahweh was bringing about a new era for his people."[72]

Anticipating that God would do a new thing in Israel, the prophets came to expect that some future event would mark the decisive factor in Israel's entire existence. Nevertheless, for them, the new was tied to the past narrative—at least initially—in that God's new act would come about in a way somewhat analogous to God's former saving work.[73] From this, it was a short step to a dualistic conception of history as divided into two "aeons" separated by God's great act. Eventually the prophets viewed this act as marking such a deep breech with the present that the future era is totally distinct from and not merely the continuation of this age.[74] In this way, the narrative gained a decidedly futurist cast.

The prophets in the later Persian period added an *eternal* consciousness to this developing narrative perspective. They concluded that the eschatological reality that one day will come on earth is already present in heaven. The events that will precede the advent of God's reign on earth, they asserted, are already accomplished in the realm above, so that the heavenly events anticipate the course of history on earth,[75] thereby forming in a certain sense a double or parallel narrative.

The move in this direction was accompanied by a growing pessimism toward the present world. Divine salvation would come not as part of the ongoing history of the nation but only through a divine act that would establish a new

---

68. Moltmann, *Theology of Hope*, 108.
69. Schmidt, *Faith of the Old Testament*, 22.
70. von Rad, *Old Testament Theology*, 2:113
71. John H. Sailhammer, *Introduction to Old Testament Theology: A Canonical Approach* (Grand Rapids: Zondervan, 1995), 212.
72. von Rad, *Old Testament Theology*, 2:112–13.
73. Ibid., 2:117.
74. Ibid., 2:115.
75. Ibid., 2:288.

creation. This shift in mood gave birth to a new outlook to the drama of human history, a radical, eternal-focused futurism known as *apocalypticism*.[76] According to the apocalyptic view, the outcome of the earthly narrative is the outworking of the set, eternal purposes of God, who is ultimately in control of history.[77] These divine purposes are fixed already in heaven.[78] Paul D. Hanson summarizes the apocalyptic ethos well: "The security and repose of a timeless realm of the vision of myth established itself as the hope of a people made weary by an overly harsh world."[79]

The apocalyptic style[80] flourished between 200 B.C.E. and 100 C.E., first within Jewish and later within Jewish-Christian circles. It focused on world history as the stage on which a cosmic drama is being played out.[81] The climax of world history brings the replacement of all earthly empires, which are in the service of Satan, with the eternal kingdom of God.[82] Although they viewed God's kingdom as a future reality, the apocalypticists declared that it is present, albeit in concealed form, as a hidden power currently at work in bringing the end to pass. And even more strongly than their forebears among the prophets they saw the anticipated future as forming a contradiction to rather than merely a continuation of the present.[83] The apocalypticists were certain that this climactic moment in the narrative would arrive because the end of the story was eternally present with God in heaven.

Finally, the prophets came to see that the eschatological narrative must be *universal* in scope. The universality of Israel's eschatological expectation arose in part out of the anticipation of a final display of divine justice. Central to the prophetic message was the belief in a God who was just and therefore who desired justice. When neither the exodus nor the monarchy established justice

---

76. Paul D. Hanson, "Old Testament Apocalyptic Reexamined," in *Visionaries and Their Apocalypses*, ed. Paul D. Hanson (Philadelphia: Fortress Press, 1983), 58. This discussion assumes that the basis for the rise of apocalypticism lay within the Old Testament itself, rather than to outside influences, and more particularly in the prophetic movement. See Jonathan Z. Smith, "Wisdom and Apocalyptic," reprinted in *Visionaries and Their Apocalypses*, 115; Michael E. Stone, "New Light on the Third Century," reprinted in *Visionaries and Their Apocalypses*, 99; Paul D. Hanson, "Introduction," in *Visionaries and Their Apocalypses*, 5; R. H. Charles, *Eschatology: The Doctrine of a Future Life in Israel, Judaism and Christianity*, rev. ed. (1913; New York: Schocken, 1963), 173–206; H. H. Rowley, *The Relevance of Apocalyptic*, 2nd ed. (London: Lutterworth, 1947), 13–14, 35.

77. Rowley, *Relevance of Apocalyptic*, 151.

78. For some writers, the major content or characteristics of each of the ages was determined from the days of creation. See, for example, the *Book of the Secrets of Enoch*, a Egyptian-Jewish apocalyptic writing of the first century C.E., as discussed in Charles, *Eschatology*, 315.

79. Hanson, "Old Testament Apocalyptic Reexamined," 58.

80. For a summary of the characteristics of the apocalyptic writings, see Klaus Koch, *The Rediscovery of Apocalyptic* (London: SCM Press, 1972), 18–35. This chapter is reprinted as Klaus Koch, "What Is Apocalyptic? An Attempt as a Preliminary Definition," in *Visionaries and Their Apocalypses*, ed. Paul Hanson (Philadelphia: Fortress Press, 1983), 16–36. See also von Rad, *Old Testament Theology*, 2:301–304.

81. For a recent discussion of these and other common apocalyptic themes, see Klaus Koch, *Rediscovery of Apocalyptic*, 28–33.

82. Rowley, *Relevance of Apocalyptic*, 165.

83. Ibid., 35.

in Israel, the prophets increasingly directed their hopes away from the present and toward a future that stood as a contradiction to the injustice of the present.[84] The prophets declared that God would vindicate himself by sending a righteous king who would come in the name and power of Yahweh. But they concluded that God's act of self-vindication could not be an isolated, national event. As early as the call of Abraham, God had promised that this nation would be the means of blessing to the entire world (Gen. 12:1–3). Consequently, the prophets concluded, the demonstration of the divine glory must be universal in scope; it must occur in the presence of all nations.

The universal scope of Israel's eschatological consciousness arose from another crucial theological innovation as well, namely, the universalizing of Israel's understanding of God (i.e., monotheism).[85] Prophets such as Ezekiel and Isaiah declared that Yahweh—and not the deities worshiped by Israel's neighbors—is the only God. As the only God, Yahweh is not merely a tribal deity but the God of all humankind. On this basis, the prophets came to see history as the activity of the one God asserting his rulership over all the nations. They believed this divine work, which constitutes the linearity of time, had begun in the past and would continue until the day when "the earth will be filled with the knowledge of the glory of the LORD, as the waters cover the sea" (Hab. 2:14; see also, Ps. 102:15; Isa. 66:18–19).

Monotheism in Israel led to an even wider understanding of the universal scope of history, however. The One whom Israel worshiped was not only the God of the nations but also the God of all creation. As the only God, Yahweh was the Creator—the *sole* Creator—of the world. For Israel, Yahweh's creative work was not limited to some initial act in the primordial past. Rather, it was ongoing and ultimately still future, for the Creator was actively bringing creation to its divinely intended goal. Consequently, as Werner Schmidt notes, belief in God as Creator meant that "creation is not only the remembered past, but also the expected future."[86] In Israel, then, creation became eschatology.[87]

Just as the apocalyptic vision brought human history into a universal whole, so also through Israel's acknowledgment of Yahweh as Creator the entire universe became a unity. In this manner the idea of God as Creator led to an all-encompassing understanding of history as traversing the whole of time from the primordial past to the future consummation. And this universal scope gave the historical narrative its ultimate meaning; it is the story of God actively bringing to pass the divine purpose for creation.

Jesus and the disciples shared the linear understanding of time that developed in Israel. And Israel's eschatological narrative provided both the context and the categories for the earliest formulation of the gospel message. Imbued

84. Schmidt, *Faith of the Old Testament*, 216.
85. Wolfhart Pannenberg, *Systematic Theology*, trans. Geoffrey W. Bromiley, 3 vols. (Grand Rapids: Wm. B. Eerdmans Publishing Co., 1991–1998), 3:246.
86. Schmidt, *Faith of the Old Testament*, 177.
87. Ibid.

with hope born out of faith in the God of the future, the New Testament writers handed on to the church and to Christian theology the Old Testament vision of God's grand action in bringing history—and hence all creation—to its purposeful end. The New Testament added one important feature to this story, however. The apostles declared that the event that will mark the climax of human history is the return of the crucified and risen Jesus. For the first Christians, this vision of a consummation centered in the return of Christ did not remain merely a set of beliefs about the future but functioned as a central aspect of their faith in the living, active God, a faith that led to hopeful engagement in the world.

Theology and Narrative

The eschatological perspective that developed within the biblical communities provides the basis for our assertion that the biblical narrative is formative for an eschatological theology. We must now tie what emerged from our overview of this process to the points we developed in the previous section, so as to draw out the implications for Christian theology understood as the "teaching about God."

Several contemporary theologians have pointed out that theology is linked to the biblical narrative simply because in this narrative we see God acting, and from God's acting we know who God is and what God is like.[88] The actual connection, however, is more complex. To understand this we must return to the two central conclusions that emerged from our previous discussions.

First, we noted that theology cannot look to some generic eschatology as the foundation for its uniquely Christian vision. Rather, the turn to a nonfoundationalist method means that theology can only orient itself toward the particular eschatology of the community in which it is embedded. Second, we asserted that the biblical faith communities came to see time as a linear process connected to the purpose, goal, or *telos* of creation and humans as embedded in creation. At the heart of this understanding is the idea that time is connected to the creative work of God. The divine work is not confined to a solitary act occurring at a single point in the primordial past but is an ongoing process that comes to completion only in the future. Viewed from this perspective, time takes the form of a narrative. It is the account of God bringing creation from inception to consummation.

Putting the two points together leads to the realization that the particular eschatology of the Christian community is integrally related to the narrative of God's creative work. More specifically, eschatology is not simply the compilation of the various events that mark the termination of history; instead it speaks about the goal[89] of a narrative that spans the ages. Eschatology is not merely the listing of what comes last in the temporal time line; instead, it is

---

88. For an example, see Finger, *Christian Theology*, 1:105.
89. Ibid.

the explication of the *meaning* of the entire narrative of God at work throughout the ages.

The biblical narrative, then, is thoroughly eschatological. And this eschatological narrative forms the Christian community. But if, as we have suggested, Christian theology explicates the faith of the Christian community and hence is the teaching about the God whose activity is disclosed in the biblical narrative, then theology must be attentive to the biblical narrative from start to finish. And if theology is attentive to the biblical narrative, it will as a matter of course be thoroughly eschatological.

Viewed from this perspective, all *genre* of scripture inform our eschatology and consequently our eschatological theology, but always within the context of the overarching biblical narrative. Even the didactic texts find their significance in relationship to the story of God at work bringing creation to its goal. These texts comprise the biblical faith community's ongoing reflection on and explication of the significance of the narrative of the God who journeys with us. Hence, the texts provide insight into the manner in which the Holy Spirit led that community to apply the one story of God to particular historical situations so as to live as an eschatological people in the world and thereby experience the actions of God in their midst, which experiences served to augment the narrative itself. These community reflections—like all scripture—remain paradigmatic for believers in all ages, for the Spirit continually speaks through the biblical text, illuminating subsequent generations to understand their present in the light of the grand, *telic* narrative of God and guiding them in the task of living out in their own contexts the vocation all Christians share, namely, that of being the community of Christ in the contemporary world.

The Character of an Eschatological Theology

We have argued that as the teaching about the promising God at work bringing creation to its *telos*, Christian theology is inherently eschatological. We have outlined as well the basis for the claim that the way toward an eschatological theology leads through the biblical narrative, the story of God's action in history, which cradles the Christian community. Now we must sketch more explicitly the methodological considerations that follow from this understanding of the orienting role of eschatology in theology. That is, we now set forth the central features of a theological method that leads to an eschatological theology.

Thoroughly Theological

First, an eschatological theology must be thoroughly theological. A method in which the eschatological trajectory of the biblical narrative is central leads to a theology that is theocentric, not anthropocentric as in much foundationalist theology.

To explicate this assertion, we must return to the concept of time we charted previously. Now, however, our interest is not in the contrast between Israel's understanding and that of other ancient peoples. Rather, we want to note how history in the biblical narrative differs radically from the concept that has emerged in Western thought.

For the first thousand years after Constantine, under the influence of Christianity the eschatological vision of the biblical narrative pervaded the Western understanding of time and history. As we observed already, this narrative views God as the acting subject of history. Consequently, Christian thinkers looked to the God of the Bible as the one who unites the diverse moments of time into one universal story.

Eventually, however, the revival of the humanistic impulse led thinkers to divorce the biblical idea of history as a linear movement encompassing both "the beginning" and "the end" from its theological moorage. These "revisionist" accounts of history exchanged the God-centeredness of the biblical vision for a human-centered portrayal.[90] Nevertheless, the resultant secularized history retained the eschatological orientation that had characterized the biblical drama. Historians simply depicted humankind as a whole (or one specific nation in particular) as moving through linear time toward some ultimate fulfillment.[91]

In the modern era, the anthropocentric shift reached its zenith. "Man" deposed the biblical God as the subject of the historical narrative, and the idea of inevitable human progress supplanted the story of God working in the world as the plot of the narrative of the one universal history. What formerly had been the account of God bringing creation to its *telos* became the story of the rise and advance of "civilization."

Further, the modern story focused on the role of science in fostering human progress. Jean-Francois Lyotard notes that this narrative took two basic forms—a political and a philosophical variant.[92] According to the first story, all peoples have a right to knowledge but are hindered by priests and tyrants. Through science humanity rises up in freedom and dignity to emancipate itself by assaulting the bastions of ignorance and oppression. In the second expose, the subject engaging in the quest for knowledge is not humanity but knowledge itself (or the Spirit or Life), and the scientific enterprise facilitates the growth of Knowledge. In either case, Lyotard adds, the narrative of the progress of Science unites the variegated events of this history into a unified whole.

Modern theology, in turn, routinely took its cue from the progressivist mind-set of modernity. The most striking example, of course, is classical Protestant liberalism. The anthropocentric orientation of liberalism came from the link liberals forged between Christian faith and what they saw as universal human nature. Liberals portrayed the Christian faith in general and Jesus' life and teaching in particular as the fulfillment of humankind's highest religious

---

90. For a discussion of the development of this historical shift, see Hans Schwarz, *On the Way to the Future*, rev. ed. (Minneapolis: Augsburg Publishing House, 1979), 19–23.

91. von Rad, *Old Testament Theology*, 2:101.

92. Lyotard, *Postmodern Condition*, 31–36.

(or moral) aspirations, aspirations that these thinkers thought they found engraved—albeit perhaps only in embryonic form—in human nature. This connection required, however, "a demythologizing within theology, whereby theological assertions take on new kinds of meaning,"[93] to cite Claude Welch's characterization.

Under the onslaught of the postmodern critique the modern narrative in both its forms is losing credibility. In fact, many scholars define the postmodern condition as the demise of the modern myth of progress through human scientific achievement.[94] While some thinkers bemoan this turn of events, postmoderns celebrate it.[95] Terry Eagleton, for example, offers this characterization of the postmodern mood:

> Post-modernism signals the death of such "metanarratives" whose secretly terroristic function is to ground and legitimate the illusion of a "universal" human history. We are now in the process of awakening from the nightmare of modernity, with its manipulative reason and fetish of the totality, into the laid-back pluralism of the post-modern, that heterogeneous range of life-styles and language games which has renounced the nostalgic urge to totalize and legitimate itself. . . . Science and philosophy must jettison their grandiose metaphysical claims and view themselves more modestly as just another set of narratives.[96]

Viewed from a Christian perspective postmodernism has simply laid bare the bankruptcy of the modern narrative with its anthropocentric orientation. The postmodern "incredulity toward metanarratives" strikes at the heart of any purported universal narrative that begins and ends with humankind. The postmodern condition indicates that "humanity" cannot function as the subject of an all-encompassing history, for any anthropocentric narrative eventually dissipates into a plethora of competing stories.

The narrative Israel passed on to the church provides a clear contrast to the myth of secular progressivism that reigned in the modern era and has become the target of the postmodern critique. According to the eschatologically oriented biblical narrative, history is not *our* story—it is not the story of Man or the tale of the progress of humankind. Further, while agreeing with the modern narrative that history is going somewhere, the biblical story denies that this "somewhere" is a humanly devised utopia. Rather, history's goal is nothing less than the realization of God's purposes for creation. And the grand culmination

---

93. Claude Welch, "Dispelling Some Myths about the Split between Theology and Science in the Nineteenth Century," in *Religion and Science*, ed. W. Mark Richardson and Wesley J. Wildman (New York: Routledge & Kegan Paul, 1996), 37.
94. Lyotard, *Postmodern Condition*, 37.
95. Ibid., xxv, 81.
96. Terry Eagleton, "Awakening from Modernity," *Times Literary Supplement* (February 20, 1987): 194.

of history arrives only because the God who stands at the end of the human story is already in grace ordering the cosmic story toward its intended goal.

The debate between modern progressivists and their postmodern detractors provides Christian theology with an opportunity to present a third way. Theology can only do so, however, if it jettisons its flirtation with the anthropocentricism of modernity and recaptures is moorings in the theocentric narrative of scripture with its eschatological orientation. But in thereby becoming thoroughly theological, Christian theology is simply reclaiming its own identity as *Christian* theology.

As we noted earlier, Christian theology is by definition the teaching about the understanding of God of the Christian community, the community that finds its identity through the biblical narrative. According to the Bible, this God is the subject of history and the unity of history. More specifically, Christian theology is the teaching about the God who is bringing creation to its *telos*. Hence, Christian theology speaks about God from the perspective of the fulfillment of the divine work, that is, from the perspective of the goal of the biblical narrative, which is the consummation of creation. As Christian theology rejects the siren call of the modernist myth of Man progressing toward utopia and instead orients itself around the culmination of the story of God bringing creation to its *telos*, it becomes an eschatological theology that is thoroughly theocentric.

Thoroughly Eschatological

Not only is an eschatological theology thoroughly theological, it will also be thoroughly eschatological. A method in which the eschatological trajectory of the biblical narrative is central leads to a theology that is oriented toward the consummation, that is, toward eternity future and not eternity past. We can best elaborate this characteristic by noting what we do *not* mean by the phrase.

A thoroughly eschatological theology does not merely consist of a systematic presentation of Christian doctrine in which the traditional order of theological foci is reversed or scrambled.[97] An eschatological theology is not one in which eschatology becomes the first topic that appears in our systematic-theological construction. Placing eschatology first does not guarantee that theology itself will be eschatological. In fact, it may do little more than open the door for the theologian conveniently to abandon eschatology once it has been explicated in the opening sections. Nor is the likelihood that the treatment of eschatology will remain no more than a delineation of disconnected *eschata* reduced significantly if it is placed first rather than coming last. Actually, eschatology ought not to be treated first, for doing so gives primacy to what in fact cannot be primary in theology, for as we argued in chapter 6 primacy can belong only to the triune God, who alone is the intrinsic content of theology.

---

97. For an example of a theology that reverses and scrambles the theological foci, see Finger, *Christian Theology*, 1:103–7.

A theology is not thoroughly eschatological because eschatology appears first but because it is oriented toward eschatology at every turn. Yet we do not accomplish this by making eschatology in general or one aspect of eschatology the integrating motif for our systematic construction. We noted in chapter 7 that in the twentieth century the eschatological concept of the kingdom of God emerged as the integrating motif of many theologies. As we concluded from that discussion, however, theology's integrative motif is "community."

What, then, makes a theology eschatological? Theology is thoroughly eschatological when at every turn the theological construction finds its orientation from the perspective of our human *telos* together with the *telos* of creation as a whole. Hence, a method that fosters a thoroughly eschatological theology engages all theological questions from the perspective of the future consummation. It looks to the completion of God's creative work—that is to the biblical narrative in its eschatological culmination—for the revelation not only of who God is but also of who we are and of what creation is, as well as the revelation of God's purposes for all creation including humankind. It engages in theological reflection and construction from this *telic* vantage point.

This approach forms a distinct contrast to those theologies that are oriented toward the past. More specifically, it provides a counterpoint to any theological method that takes its cue from the task of discerning what supposedly went on in the mind of God before the creation of the universe.

The attempt to raise theological questions and engage in theological construction from the perspective of God's eternal past is especially pronounced in Reformed scholasticism. Similar to the method we have spelled out in these pages and in keeping with the definition of theology itself, the Reformed theological tradition is centered on the doctrine of God.[98] In its scholastic expression, this proper elevation of God became focused on one dimension of the divine being, namely, God's sovereignty, which many Reformed thinkers viewed in an all-encompassing, deterministic manner. Louis Berkhof provides a typical articulation of this characteristic of much of Reformed scholasticism: "Reformed theology stresses the sovereignty of God in virtue of which He has sovereignly determined from all eternity whatsoever will come to pass, and works His sovereign will in His entire creation, both natural and spiritual, according to His pre-determined plan."[99]

Reformed scholastic theologians took this emphasis one additional step. The concern to maintain divine sovereignty led them to orient their theological considerations around the idea of God's eternal decrees. So central is this theological distinctive that Berkhof can claim, "Reformed theology stands practically alone in its emphasis on the doctrine of the decrees."[100]

---

98. R. W. A. Letham, "Reformed Theology," in *New Dictionary of Theology*, ed. Sinclair B. Ferguson, David F. Wright, and J. I. Packer (Downers Grove, Ill.: InterVarsity Press, 1988), 569.

99. Louis Berkhof, *Systematic Theology*, rev. and enl. ed. (Grand Rapids: Wm. B. Eerdmans Publishing Co., 1953), 100.

100. Ibid., 100.

According to Reformed scholastic thinkers, the divine decrees are eternal, having been fixed in God's mind before time. For this reason they look to God's decrees as the basis for all that happens in history, so that the divine decrees become the theological or logical intermediary between belief in God's sovereignty and historical occurrences. The nineteenth-century Calvinist Charles Hodge offers this telling statement: "The decrees of God are his eternal purpose, according to the counsel of his own will, whereby for his own glory He hath foreordained whatsoever comes to pass."[101] Hodge then explains that

> from the infinite number of systems, or series of possible events, present to the divine mind, God determined on the futurition or actual occurrence of the existing order of things, with all its changes, minute as well as great, from the beginning of time to all eternity. The reason, therefore, why any event occurs, or, that it passes from the category of the possible into that of the actual, is that God has so decreed.[102]

Hodge's contemporary disciples concur with the basic picture that he, following the earlier Reformed scholastics, painted. Hence, Millard Erickson writes, "God manifests his purpose within history . . . but his decisions have been made long before. They have always been God's plan, from all eternity, from before the beginning of time."[103] Similarly, Lewis and Demarest assert, "The decrees were also *eternal decisions* giving direction to dynamic action in time. Before the creation of the world the Father envisioned creation's goals. His settled determinations secure the direction of his dynamic acts in history."[104]

We should note in passing that while not being the thoroughgoing determinists that the strict Calvinist thinkers are, Arminian scholastic theologians follow the same basic approach. They too often orient their theological constructions around eternity past, differing in substance with their opponents only in the exact content of the eternal decrees. This is evident in the first point of controversy presented by the Remonstrants, which H. Orton Wiley describes as follows: "That God, from all eternity, determined to bestow salvation on those who, as He foresaw, would persevere unto the end in their faith in Jesus Christ, and to inflict everlasting punishment on those who should continue in their unbelief, and resist, to the end of life, His divine succors."[105] In a typical Reformed scholastic manner, Wiley speaks of the "order of the decrees," even though as an Arminian he proposes a quite different list of the exact decisions that comprise those decrees.[106]

---

101. Charles Hodge, *Systematic Theology*, 3 vols. (New York: Scribner, Armstrong, & Co., 1872), 1:535.
102. Ibid., 1:537–38.
103. Millard J. Erickson, *Christian Theology*, 3 vols. (Grand Rapids: Baker Book House Co., 1983), 1:351.
104. Lewis and Demarest, *Integrative Theology*, 1:312.
105. H. Orton Wiley, *Christian Theology*, vol. 2 (Kansas City, Mo.: Beacon Hill, 1952), 351.
106. Ibid., 108.

Because Reformed scholastic theologians look to God's decrees for the foundation for all that God does and the basis for all that happens in history, it is not surprising that they routinely place the discussion of the divine decrees before their systematic treatments of God's action in creation and redemption. The reason is obvious. As Hodge declares, "[T]he vast scheme of creation, providence, and redemption, lies in the divine mind as one simple purpose."[107]

In short, Reformed scholastic theologians tend to engage central theological questions from the perspective of eternity past, that is, from the vantage point of God's sovereign decisions that occurred before the universe was created and that subsequently come into view in, or are revealed through, the historical processes. Hence, Lewis and Demarest effectively summarize their entire theological orientation when they declare, "The overarching *great idea* of divine revelation focuses on the *Father's* eternal purposes revealed in *promises* to do gracious things for *his redeemed people* and *through them* individually and collectively for the *whole world*."[108]

Despite its wide influence, the Reformed scholastic approach suffers from a debilitating weakness. As an abstraction from the scriptural witness, it all too readily becomes disconnected from the biblical narrative with its eschatological goal. In contrast to that narrative, with its close connection to history, the attempt to decipher what allegedly went on in the mind of God before creation simply does not take history seriously. Rather than the story of God at work bringing creation to its *telos* in the eternal new community, in the hands of the Reformed scholastic theologians history becomes merely the appendage to the preordaining divine decree. Events in time have no raison d'etre except to reveal sovereign decisions made in eternity past. Even the *eschaton* becomes little more than the final event in a vast chain of happenings known already to God before the beginning of time. No wonder eschatology can be relegated to the category of "last things"; by the time the theologian gets to this section of the systematic-theological corpus its content has long since been previewed in what forms the "real" matter of theology, namely, the task of determining the content of the divine decree.

Rather than understanding the present and projecting the future on the basis of what can supposedly be deduced from the perspective of eternity past, a thoroughly eschatological theology moves from the future to the present. It views its task of speaking about the past and the present as they find not only their fulfillment but also their very meaning in the story of God bringing history to its consummation. In this manner, an eschatological theology anticipates the future within the present. Being oriented toward the eschatological completion of history in God's future *telos*, an eschatological theology speaks about the *not-yet* within the context of the *already*. It finds our human identity, as well as the identity of all creation, in the God who promises to make everything new (Rev. 21:5). And it speaks about the in-breaking of this new creation (2 Cor. 5:17) in our lives in the here and now.

107. Hodge, *Systematic Theology,* 1:537.
108. Lewis and Demarest, *Integrative Theology,* 1:26.

One question remains, however. What are the implications of this *telic* focus, this orientation toward the new creation, for our understanding of reality?

Eschatological Theology and the "Real" World

We have argued for a theological method that leads to an eschatologically oriented theology. Such a theology, we said, does not view eschatology as the teaching about the *eschata*; it is not the delineation of a set of disconnected facts about the future. Taking our cue from Moltmann over against Bultmann, we quickly added that we are not denying the futurist cast of theology's eschatological orientation. But then, parting company with Moltmann, we suggested that there is also a place for speaking about future events as actual events. In short, we stated that our call for a *telic* theology upholds what we might call the *actual* character of eschatology. Our final task in this chapter is to build on what we said earlier about the content of the Christian hope to indicate what we mean by the actuality of the future.

Eschatological Ontology

Raising the question of *actuality* lands us immediately in the realm of metaphysics. Like many philosophical terms, there is no unanimity as to what comprises this intellectual discipline. Nevertheless, a typical definition speaks of it as the "philosophical study whose object it is to determine the real nature of things—to determine the meaning, structure, and principles of whatever is insofar as it is."[109] Following in the footsteps of Aristotle, philosopher Michael Loux adds that metaphysics is more particularly "the science of being *qua* being,"[110] thereby linking this division of the philosophical enterprise with what other philosophers call *ontology*. Similarly, Stroll and Popkin suggest that the basic question of metaphysics is, "What is the ultimate nature of reality?" a question that they note is related to the distinction between appearance and reality.[111]

Although some philosophers surmise that the postmodern situation has made ontology passe, we agree with feminist theologian Rebecca Chopp that "the refusal to continue foundationalism does not let us beg off the metaphysical question."[112] But how can we continue to speak about ontology and actuality? And, more importantly, what perspective determines the ontological nature of things?

109. Bruce Withington Wilshire, "Metaphysics," *The New Encyclopedia Britannica*, 30 vols. (Chicago: Encyclopedia Britannica, Inc., 1998), 24:1–25. See also, Archie J. Bahm, *Metaphysics: An Introduction* (Albuquerque, N.M.: World Books, 1974), 19.

110. Michael J. Loux, *Metaphysics: A Contemporary Introduction* (London: Routledge & Kegan Paul, 1998), 12.

111. Avrum Stroll and Richard H. Popkin, *Introduction to Philosophy*, 3rd ed. (New York: Holt, Rinehart & Winston, 1979), 98.

112. Rebecca S. Chopp, "Feminist Queries and Metaphysical Musings," in *Rethinking Metaphysics*, ed. L. Gregory Jones and Stephen E. Fowl (Oxford: Basil Blackwell, 1995), 46.

From "Being" to "Becoming"

The dominant approach to ontology throughout much of Western history views the "real" fundamentally as what persists through time. Hence, identity is linked to, or determined by constancy. And the focus of determining the real lies in the present: the real is what remains constant in every present moment. The roots of this outlook lie in the decision made by the ancient Greek philosophers to accept Parmenides rather than Heraclitus, that is to elevate Being, rather than Becoming, as the basic metaphysical concept. Parmenides (c. 515–450) argued that what is truly real is what remains the same despite the appearance of change in the realm of sense experience,[113] in contrast to Heraclitus (c. 540–475), who asserted that reality entails incessant change.[114]

Parmenides's position ruled almost unchallenged in Western philosophy until the nineteenth century, when developments in philosophy and science reintroduced the idea of change into the conception of reality. This led in the twentieth century to several new theories of ontology.

One influential proposal was the process philosophy of Alfred North Whitehead (1861–1947).[115] According to Whitehead, the fundamental building blocks of reality are not permanently enduring things. Rather, reality consists of "actual occasions," each of which is an activity or a "becoming" that comes into existence and then quickly disappears.[116] Occasions, in turn, form "societies of occasions,"[117] of which the human person comprises a unique exemplar. As a society of occasions, the human person can remember the past, anticipate the future and weave the two together. God is the final "repository" of each occasion once it perishes.[118] By remembering all experiences and envisioning all possibilities, God weaves past and future together in a never-ending process. In so doing, God forms the world into a unity and, in contrast to humans who are finite societies of occasions, becomes the unbounded society.[119]

---

113. "Parmenides," in William L. Reese, *Dictionary of Philosophy and Religion* (Atlantic Highlands, N.J.: Humanities Press, 1980), 412–13.

114. Eduard Zeller, *Outlines of the History of Greek Philosophy*, 13th ed., rev. Wilhelm Nestle, trans. L. R. Palmer (New York: Meridian Books, 1957), 61. Some historians, however, have questioned this interpretation of Heraclitus. "Can Heraclitus really have thought that a rock or a bronze cauldron, for example, was invariably undergoing invisible changes of material?" ask G. S. Kirk and J. E. Raven, *The Presocratic Philosophers*, corrected reprint (Cambridge: Cambridge University Press, 1963), 197.

115. A succinct summarization of Whitehead's philosophy is offered by Rosemary T. Curran, "Whitehead's Notion of the Person and the Saving of the Past," *Scottish Journal of Theology* 36/3 (1983): 363–85.

116. Alfred North Whitehead, *Process and Reality* (New York: Harper & Row, 1960), 28.

117. Ibid., 30; Alfred North Whitehead, *Adventures of Ideas* (New York: Mentor Books, 1955), 204.

118. The immortality of every actual entity is required by Whitehead's "ontological principle," for "everything in the actual world is referable to some actual entity." God functions as the ontological principle that fulfills this necessity. Whitehead, *Process and Reality*, 373.

119. Whether Whitehead thought of God as an unbounded society or an actual entity has been debated by subsequent process thinkers. See Gene Reeves and Delwin Brown, "The Development of Process Theology," in Delwin Brown, Ralph E. James Jr. and Gene Reeves, eds. *Process Philosophy and Christian Thought* (Indianapolis: Bobbs-Merrill Co., 1971), 39–40.

Although process philosophy offers an innovative ontology of becoming, it nevertheless retains the more traditional view of time as moving from present to future, with ontological primacy placed on the present. It is not surprising, therefore, that eschatology plays only a minor role in process thought. In this aspect, process has been superseded by another metaphysical proposal, the eschatological ontology articulated by several thinkers but most notably by Wolfhart Pannenberg.

The Future and Essence

The way toward Pannenberg's eschatological ontology was paved by those twentieth-century philosophers who, under impulses from the scientific method, underscored the anticipatory or future character of knowing. The acquisition of knowledge, they observed, routinely moves through a procedure that involves the formation, testing, and subsequent revising of hypotheses.[120]

For Pannenberg, however, this future orientation is not only epistemological but also operative in the realm of ontology. Hence, he declares, "Not only our knowing but also the identity of things themselves are not yet completely present in the process of time."[121] Similar to process thought, Pannenberg envisions a "new definition of the concept of substance, one that would consider the viewpoint of time and becoming as the medium that constitutes the whatness of things." Yet unlike Whitehead's proposal, Pannenberg maintains that in this new understanding, things are "what they are, substances, retroactively from the outcome of their becoming on the one hand, and on the other in the sense of anticipating the completion of their process of becoming, their history."[122] Hence, Pannenberg is arguing for what we might call "the ontological priority of the future," which looks to the future for the determination of ontological reality.

According to Pannenberg, this eschatological ontology is the result of a long philosophical trajectory. At its genesis stands Plotinus, who realized that eternity is the source of time, in that the eternal is the future whole of what to the soul are the separate temporal moments.[123] The real breakthrough, however, came with Dilthey's analysis of the historicity of experience. Pannenberg explains: "Like the historicists, Dilthey sought the final decision concerning the meaning of the individual's life—and the meaning of the other details that are linked to them—in the broader context of history,"[124] which led to "the retroactive constitution of the essence of a thing that is becoming from its end."[125]

Pannenberg is not content merely to argue for an eschatological ontology on the basis of philosophy. Rather, he sees a close affinity between the philosophi-

---

120. Wolfhart Pannenberg, *Metaphysics and the Idea of God*, trans. Philip Clayton (Grand Rapids: Wm. B. Eerdmans Publishing Co., 1990), 94.
121. Ibid., 104.
122. Ibid., 107.
123. For his expose on Plotinus, see ibid., 76–77.
124. Ibid., 109.
125. Ibid., 107.

cal development he traces and the apocalyptic movement. At the heart of apoc-alypticism, he declares, is the idea that "the end of worldly history will bring fully to light all of its events and the life of each individual human being."[126] Bringing philosophy and biblical theology together, Pannenberg then adds that the end of history is not nothingness, but eternity. And this leads to an escha-tological ontology, which Pannenberg summarizes in this succinct statement: "It is from the standpoint of this end that the essence of each individual thing, the manner in which it has anticipated eternity, will be decided."[127]

The Future and Identity

Pannenberg was not the first modern thinker to propose an eschatological ontology. This honor belongs to Martin Heidegger. Like Pannenberg, Heidegger drew from Dilthey to link the future to the self, albeit in a manner somewhat different from Pannenberg's proposal. Heidegger looked to human existence (*Dasein*) as the horizon for time and concluded that the possibility for becoming a whole being lies in the anticipation of—that is, the "running for-ward" to (German: *verlaufen*)—one's own death,[128] because, according to Heidegger, the knowledge of one's death discloses the whole of *Dasein* as a finite being. This thesis, in turn, implies the priority of the future in defining personal identity.[129]

Heidegger's fellow existentialist philosophers applied his conclusion to the psychology of the self in the process of identity formation. According to the existentialist proposal, the authentic self is the becoming self, the self-who-is-becoming and hence the self who is "potentiality" or "possibility." Jean-Paul Sartre, to cite one prominent example, declared that the future tense provides the clues to a person's identity, in that the future is linked to human potential-ity or to the capacity for choosing from among possibilities.[130] Our sense of per-sonal meaning is dependent on our ability to look beyond the present and anticipate our future. Hence, our human awareness of the future, connected with the capacity for hope, is what allows us to construct purposes for our lives and thereby create a meaningful existence in the present. The future, then, is an existential reality; that is, it gives meaning to our existence as it fosters our abil-ity to transcend the present.

More recently the existentialist understanding of personal identity forma-tion has been augmented by appeal to narrative. Narrative thinkers point out

---

126. Ibid., 109.

127. Ibid., 109.

128. See, for example, the extended discussion in Martin Heidegger, *Being and Time*, trans. John Macquarrie and Edward Robinson (New York: Harper & Row, 1962), 279–311, 356–58. This edition translates the German *verlaufen* as "anticipation."

129. Heidegger speaks of the "priority of the future," declaring, for example, that "the future has a priority in the ecstatical unity of primordial and authentic temporality." Heidegger, *Being and Time*, 378.

130. Jean-Paul Sartre, *Being and Nothingness: An Essay on Phenomenological Ontology*, trans. Hazel E. Barnes (New York: Philosophical Library, 1956), 128–29, 184–86.

that a sense of identity develops through the telling of a personal narrative. Finding ourselves entails finding the story or narrative in terms of which our lives make sense.[131]

George Stroup,[132] for example, theorizes that through memory an individual selects certain events from one's past (i.e., from one's personal history) and uses them as a basis for interpreting the significance of the whole of one's life. Personal identity, then, is the pattern that memory retrieves from one's personal history and projects into the future. Stroup adds, however, that a person's identity is not created from the "factual data," or "chronicle," of the events of one's life alone. Crucial in this process is an "interpretive scheme," apart from which the chronicle of a person's life—the events and experiences of one's personal history—is meaningless, in that it lacks a "plot." Hence, it is the interpretation that makes a personal narrative "history" and thus gives rise to personal identity. This opens the door for a determinative role for the future perspective.

This step, however, requires that we add an insight from the communitarians we delineated in chapter 7. As Stroup himself notes, the interpretive framework cannot be derived from the data of one's life. Rather it emerges from one's social context or "tradition."[133] Hence, personal identity is never a private reality but has a communal element, for it is shaped by the community of which the person is a participant. Such a community contributes toward the formation of the "self" by mediating a communal narrative—a history. This narrative includes the community's past,[134] of course, but, more important, it gazes toward the future, speaking about the ideal that lies yet before the community and toward which it is moving.

In this manner, the future becomes a narrative reality. Our lives are ultimately oriented toward a communal future from which our identity—our essential nature—is derived. Consequently, that future comprises the ultimate defining moment in one's ongoing personal narrative.

As participants in the community of Christ, our identity is bound up with a particular vision, the eschatological horizon of the biblical narrative, which speaks about our joining Christ in his resurrection and participating in God's eternal community in the new creation. Our ongoing task, therefore, is to construct our personal identities in the present according to the paradigmatic narrative of the Christian faith community, with its expectant anticipation of the eschatological future. Indeed, our true identity is *in Christ*, to cite Paul's favorite description. And as those who are in Christ we already are a new creation (2 Cor. 5:17); yet this new creation is an *eschatological* reality. We are, in other

---

131. Robert N. Bellah et al., *Habits of the Heart: Individualism and Commitment in American Life* (Berkeley, Calif.: University of California Press, 1985), 81.

132. George W. Stroup, *The Promise of Narrative Theology* (Atlanta: John Knox Press, 1981), 101–98.

133. Here he is in substantial agreement with social constructionist sociologists, such as Peter Berger. See, for example, Peter L. Berger, *The Sacred Canopy: Elements of a Sociological Theory of Religion* (Garden City, N.Y.: Doubleday & Co., 1969), 20.

134. For a helpful discussion of this point, see Bellah, *Habits of the Heart*, 152–55.

words, the community of risen and glorified saints (Eph. 2:4–7) that we one day will be (1 John 3:1–3).

Eschatological Realism

The Christian vision with its eschatological ontology does not apply only to the human person. Rather, it is cosmic in scope. In fact, ultimately it is directed to a new heaven and a new earth—that is, a new cosmos. We, in turn, participate in the eschatological reality insofar as the new creation encompasses redeemed humans. What does this say about the ontology of reality as a whole? From what perspective does the cosmos gain its actuality?

In previous chapters we drew from the social constructionists who assert that the world we inhabit is not simply given; it is not merely prefabricated for us. On the contrary, we are world-builders. We live in a world of our own construal.[135] More particularly, we live in a social-cultural world of our own creation; we inhabit a "socially constituted reality," to cite Berger and Luckmann's phrase.[136] Of course, the constructed world attains for us the character of objectivity, for it seems to be external to our personal consciousness, and we appear to experience the world with others.[137] Nevertheless, as the demise of naive realism[138] has led scholars from a variety of disciplines to conclude, we do not live in a universe that is simply a given, external reality.[139] We do not inhabit the *world-in-itself.*

Does this insight require that we give up all sense of an objective universe existing "out there"? Are we left with nothing but our socially constructed worlds? Is there no actuality to the world? Not necessarily.[140] There is a certain undeniable givenness to the universe, as critical realists point out.[141] But the question is, Where does its givenness lie? Wherein is its actuality?

We acknowledge that there is indeed a certain objective actuality to the world. But the objectivity we can attribute to the universe is not that of a static actuality existing outside of, and cotemporally with, our socially and linguistically constructed reality. It is not the objectivity of what some might call "the

135. See, for example, Norwood Russell Hanson, *Patterns of Discovery: An Inquiry into the Conceptual Foundations of Science* (Cambridge: Cambridge University Press, 1958), 23–24.

136. Peter L. Berger and Thomas Luckmann, "Sociology of Religion and Sociology of Knowledge," *Sociology and Social Research* 47 (1963):423.

137. Berger, *Sacred Canopy,* 3–13.

138. For a critique, see David Elton Trueblood, *General Philosophy* (New York: Harper & Row, 1963), 29–33.

139. Hence, scientists now generally view their proposed theories and models as "candidates for reality," to cite Arthur Peacocke's descriptor, rather than as simply reflections of reality itself. See Arthur Peacocke, *Intimations of Reality: Critical Realism in Science and Religion* (Notre Dame, Ind.: University of Notre Dame Press, 1989), 25.

140. For a theological appraisal, see J. Wentzel van Huyssteen, "Postfoundationalism in Theology and Science: Beyond Conflict and Consonance," in *Rethinking Theology and Science: Six Models for the Current Dialogue,* ed. Niels Henrik Gregersen and J. Wentzel van Huyssteen (Grand Rapids: Wm. B. Eerdmans Publishing Co., 1998), 39.

141. See, for example, Trueblood, *General Philosophy,* 38–45. See also, Arthur Peacocke, *Theology for a Scientific Age: Being and Becoming—Natural, Divine, and Human,* enl. ed. (Minneapolis: Fortress Press, 1993), 21.

world as it is." Here we can take our cue from the Bible itself. The objectivity set forth in the biblical narrative is the objectivity of the world as God wills it. Hence, Jesus taught his disciples to pray, "Your will be done on earth as it is in heaven" (Matt. 6:10, NIV).

The universe as God wills it, however—the realm in which the divine will is actualized in keeping with the petition of the Lord's Prayer—is not a present reality.[142] Rather, it lies in the eschatological future (e.g., Isa. 65:17–19; Rev. 21:5). Therefore, the "objectivity of the world" about which we can truly speak is an objectivity of a *future*, eschatological world. The "actual" universe is the universe as it one day will be. And this eschatological universe is nothing short of a *new* creation. Because this future reality is God's determined will for creation, as that which cannot be shaken (Heb. 12:26–28), it is far more real—and hence far more objective, far more actual—than the present world, which is even now passing away (1 Cor. 7:31).

In this manner, the biblical perspective leads to what we might call an "eschatological realism." There is a real universe "out there," we readily acknowledge. But this reality—this "out there"—lies "before," rather than "beneath" or "around" us. Ours is a universe that is in the process of being created, as many scientists acknowledge.[143] Therefore, rather than merely being discovered via experimentation, the new creation toward which our world is developing is experienced through anticipation.[144]

We must take eschatological realism one step further, however. We must bring it together with the insights from the social constructionists we noted earlier. As God's image bearers, we have a divinely given mandate to participate in God's work of constructing a world in the present that reflects God's own eschatological will for creation. Because of the role of language in the world-constructing task, this mandate has a strongly linguistic dimension. We particip ipate with God, for through the constructive power of language we inhabit a present linguistic world that sees all reality from the perspective of the future, real world that God is bringing to pass. Further, the divine eschatological world that stands at the climax of the biblical narrative is a realm in which all creation finds its connectedness in Jesus Christ (Col. 1:17), who is the *logos* or the Word (John 1:1), that is, the ordering principle of the cosmos as God intends it to be. This eschatological realm breaks into the here and now as the Holy Spirit fashions our present in the light of God's future. And as culture-constructing beings, we participate in the Spirit's world-fashioning process.

142. For a delineation of the nature of prayer as viewed from an eschatological perspective, see Stanley J. Grenz, *Prayer: The Cry for the Kingdom* (Peabody, Mass.: Hendrickson, 1988).

143. For an example of a theological appropriation of this contemporary understanding, see Karl Schmitz-Moormann, *The Theology of Creation in an Evolutionary World* (Cleveland: Pilgrim Press, 1997), 27–49.

144. It is for this reason that scientific eschatology needs the counterbalance of theological eschatology. For a summary of eschatology as a topic of conversation—and divergence—between theology and science, see Mark William Worthing, *God, Creation, and Contemporary Physics* (Minneapolis: Fortress Press, 1996), 159–98.

***

Eschatological realism carries significant implications for theological method and our understanding of theology. Through the use of linguistic models[145] and under the guidance of the Holy Spirit, the Christian community constructs a particular world for human habitation. For its part, theology explores the world-constructing, knowledge-producing, identity-forming "language" of the Christian community. The goal of this enterprise is to show how the Christian mosaic of beliefs offers a transcendent vision of the glorious eschatological community God wills for creation and how this vision provides a coherent foundation for life-in-relationship in this penultimate age as we anticipate the glorious fullness of the eschatological new creation. In fulfilling this role, theology assists the community of Christ in its mandate of being the sign of the age to come.

In short, then, theologians assist the church in the world-construction business we share. The specific task of theology within this overarching vocation is to draw from the unique grammar of the biblical narrative to build a linguistic world for human habitation in the present, a world whose basis lies in the new creation that God is already bringing to pass. Hence, the ultimate purpose of theology is to speak about the actual world for the sake of the mission of the church in the present, anticipatory era. And for this to occur, theology must be oriented toward the future; it must be eschatological.

145. For a helpful summary of the contemporary discussion of models in both science and theology, see Peacocke, *Intimations of Reality,* 29–34, 40–44; Ian Barbour, *Religion in an Age of Science,* vol. 1 of The Gifford Lectures, 1989–1991 (San Francisco: HarperSanFrancisco, 1990), 41–51.

Works Cited

Abraham, William J. *The Divine Inspiration of Holy Scripture.* Oxford: Oxford University Press, 1981.

Achtemeier, Paul J. *The Inspiration of Scripture.* Philadelphia: Westminster Press, 1980.

Aichele, George, et al. *The Postmodern Bible.* New Haven, Conn.: Yale University Press, 1995.

Allen, Diogenes. "The End of the Modern World." *Christian Scholar's Review* 22, no. 4 (June 1993): 339–47.

Allis, Oswald T. *Prophecy and the Church.* Nutley, N.J.: Presbyterian and Reformed Publishing Co., 1972.

Alves, Rubem. *The Poet, the Warrior, the Prophet.* London: SCM Press, 1990.

Andersen, Francis I. "We speak . . . in the words . . . which the Holy Ghost Teacheth." *Westminster Theological Journal* 22 (May 1960): 113–32.

Anderson, Walter Truett. *Reality Isn't What It Used to Be: Theatrical Politics, Ready-to-Wear Religion, Global Myths, Primitive Chic, and Other Wonders of the Postmodern World.* San Francisco: Harper & Row, 1990.

Athanasius. *Contra Gentes.* Oxford: Clarendon Press, 1971.

Augustine. *The City of God.* Translated by Marcens Dods, Modern Library ed. New York: Random House, 1950.

———. *Confessions.* Translated by Henry Chadwick. Oxford: Oxford University Press, 1992.

———. *On the Trinity.* Translated by Arthur West Haddon. Vol. 3. First series of The Nicene and Post-Nicene Fathers. Reprint Grand Rapids: Wm. B. Eerdmans Publishing Co., 1980.

Austin, J. L. *How to Do Things with Words.* Edited by J. O. Urmson and Marian Sbisa. 2nd ed. Cambridge: Harvard University Press, 1975.

Bahm, Archie J. *Metaphysics: An Introduction.* Albuquerque, N.M.: World Books, 1974.

Barbour, Ian G. *Religion in an Age of Science.* San Francisco: HarperSanFrancisco, 1990.

Barr, James. *The Scope and Authority of the Bible.* Philadelphia: Westminster Press, 1980.

Barth, Karl. *Church Dogmatics,* I/1, Translated by G. W. Bromiley. 2nd ed. Edinburgh: T. & T. Clark, 1975.

Basil the Great, Saint. *De Spiritu Sancto.* In *Patrologia Graeca.* Edited by J. P. Migne. Paris: Migne, 1857–1912.

———. *On the Holy Spirit.* Crestwood, N.Y.: St. Vladimir's Seminary Press, 1980.

Baudrillard, Jean. "The Ecstasy of Communication." In *The Anti-Aesthetic.* Edited by Hal Foster. Port Townsend, Wash.: Bay Press, 1983.

Bauer, Walter. *Orthodoxy and Heresy in Earliest Christianity.* Edited by Robert A. Kraft and Gerhard Krodel. Philadelphia: Fortress Press, 1971.

Bauman, Michael. *Pilgrim Theology: Taking the Path of Theological Discovery.* Grand Rapids: Zondervan, 1992.

Bayles, Martha. "Immunity Not Surgery: Why It Is Better to Exert Cultural Authority than to Impose Censorship." In *Toward the Renewal of Civilization: Political Order and Culture.* Edited by T. William Boxx and Gary M. Quinlivan. Grand Rapids: Wm. B. Eerdmans Publishing Co., 1998.

Beaudoin, Tom. *Virtual Faith: The Irreverent Spiritual Quest of Generation X.* San Francisco: Jossey-Bass, 1998.

Beegle, Dewey M. *Scripture, Tradition and Infallibility.* Grand Rapids: Wm. B. Eerdmans Publishing Co., 1973.

Bell, Daniel. *Communitarianism and Its Critics.* Oxford: Clarendon Press, 1993.

Bellah, Robert N. "Community Properly Understood: A Defense of 'Democratic Communitarianism.'" In *The Essential Communitarian Reader.* Edited by Amitai Etzioni. Lanham, Md.: Rowman & Littlefield, 1998.

Bellah, Robert N. et al. *Habits of the Heart: Individualism and Commitment in American Life.* Berkeley, Calif.: University of California Press, 1985/Perennial Library ed. New York: Harper & Row, 1986.

Benhabib, Seyla. *Situating the Self: Gender, Community and Postmodernism in Contemporary Ethics.* New York: Routledge & Kegan Paul, 1992.

Bennett, John W. and Melvin M. Tumin. *Social Life.* New York: Alfred A. Knopf, 1948.

Berger, Peter L. *Invitation to Sociology: A Humanistic Perspective.* Anchor Books ed. Garden City, N.Y.: Doubleday, 1963.

———. *The Sacred Canopy: Elements of a Sociological Theory of Religion.* Anchor Books ed. Garden City, N.Y.: Doubleday, 1969.

Berger, Peter L. and Brigitte Berger. *Sociology: A Biographical Approach.* New York: Basic Books, 1972.

Berger, Peter L. and Thomas Luckmann. *The Social Construction of Reality: A Treatise in the Sociology of Knowledge.* New York: Anchor Books, 1967.

———. "Sociology of Religion and Sociology of Knowledge." *Sociology and Social Research* 47 (1963): 417–27.

Berkhof, Louis. *Systematic Theology.* Grand Rapids: Wm. B. Eerdmans Publishing Co., 1953.

Berkouwer, G. C. *Holy Scripture.* Grand Rapids: Wm. B. Eerdmans Publishing Co., 1975.

Bettenson, Henry, ed. *Documents of the Christian Church.* 2nd ed. London: Oxford University Press, 1963.

Bevans, Stephen B. *Models of Contextual Theology.* Maryknoll, N.Y.: Orbis Books, 1992.

Bird, Phyllis A. "'Male and Female He Created Them': Gen. 1:27b in the Context of the Priestly Account of Creation." *Harvard Theological Review* 74 (April 1981): 129–59.

Blocher, Henri. *In the Beginning: The Opening Chapters of Genesis.* Translated by David G. Preston. Downer's Grove, Ill.: Leicester, England: InterVarsity Press, 1984.

Bloesch, Donald G. *Essentials of Evangelical Theology.* 2 vols. San Francisco: HarperCollins, 1978.

———. *The Future of Evangelical Christianity: A Call for Unity Amid Diversity.* Garden City, N.Y.: Doubleday, 1983.

———. *Holy Scripture: Revelation, Inspiration & Interpretation.* Downers Grove, Ill.: InterVarsity Press, 1994.

————. *A Theology of Word and Spirit*. Downers Grove, Ill.: InterVarsity Press, 1992.

Boff, Leonardo. *Trinity and Society*. Translated by Paul Burns. Maryknoll, N.Y.: Orbis Books, 1988.

Bourdieu, Pierre. *Outline of a Theory of Practice*. Translated by Richard Nice. Cambridge: Cambridge University Press, 1977.

Braaten, Carl E. "Prolegomena to Christian Dogmatics." In *Christian Dogmatics*. Edited by Carl E. Braaten and Robert W. Jenson. 2 vols. Philadelphia: Fortress Press, 1984.

Bruce, F. F. "Eschatology." In *Evangelical Dictionary of Theology*. Edited by Walter Elwell. Grand Rapids: Baker, 1984.

Brunner, Emil. *The Christian Doctrine of Creation and Redemption*. Translated by Olive Wyon. Philadelphia: Westminster Press, 1953.

————. *The Christian Doctrine of God*. Translated by Olive Wyon. Philadelphia: Westminster Press, 1950.

Buckley, Michael J., S. J. *At the Origins of Modern Atheism*. New Haven, Conn.: Yale University Press, 1987.

Bultmann, Rudolf. *Jesus Christ and Mythology*. New York: Charles Scribner's Sons, 1958.

Calvin, John. "Reply to Sadolet." In *Calvin: Theological Treatises*. Edited by J. K. S. Reid. Philadelphia: Westminster Press, 1954.

Campbell, Charles A. *Scepticism and Construction*. London: George Allen & Unwin, Ltd., 1931.

Capps, Donald. *Agents of Hope: A Pastoral Psychology*. Minneapolis: Fortress Press, 1995.

Chadwick, Owen. *From Bossuet to Newman: The Idea of Doctrinal Development*. London: Cambridge University Press, 1957.

Charles, R. H. *Eschatology: The Doctrine of a Future Life in Israel, Judaism and Christianity*. Rev. ed. 1913; New York: Schocken, 1963.

Charry, Ellen T. *By the Renewing of Your Minds: The Pastoral Function of Christian Doctrine*. New York: Oxford University Press, 1997.

Chopp, Rebecca S. "Feminist Queries and Metaphysical Musings." In *Rethinking Metaphysics*. Edited by L. Gregory Jones and Stephen E. Fowl. Oxford: Basil Blackwell Publisher, 1995.

Cicero. *Tusculan Disputations*. In *Cicero in Twenty-eight Volumes*. Translated by J. E. King. Rev. ed. Cambridge, Mass.: Harvard University Press, 1971.

Clapp, Rodney. "How Firm a Foundation: Can Evangelicals be Nonfoundationalists?" In *The Nature of Confession: Evangelicals and Postliberals in Conversation*. Edited by Dennis L. Okholm and Timothy R. Phillips. Downers Grove, Ill.: InterVarsity Press, 1996.

Clark, Gordon H. *Karl Barth's Theological Method*. Philadelphia: Presbyterian and Reformed Publishing Co., 1963.

Clement of Alexandria. *The Stromata*. In The Ante-Nicene Fathers. 10 vols. Edited by Alexander Roberts and James Donaldson. Grand Rapids: Wm. B. Eerdmans Publishing Co., 1986.

Clifford, James. *The Predicament of Culture: Twentieth Century Ethnography, Literature, and Art*. Cambridge, Mass.: Harvard University Press, 1988.

Clowney, Edmund P. "The Biblical Theology of the Church." In *The Church in the Bible and the World: An International Study*. Edited by D. A. Carson. Exeter: Paternoster Press, 1987.

Cohen, Anthony P. *Self Consciousness: An Alternative Anthropology of Identity*. London: Routledge & Kegan Paul, 1994.

Cole, Stewart Grant. *The History of Fundamentalism*. New York: R. R. Smith, 1931.

Coleman, Richard J. *Issues of Theological Conflict*. Grand Rapids: Wm. B. Eerdmans Publishing Co., 1980.

Congar, Yves. *Tradition and Traditions*. New York: Macmillan & Co., 1967.

Cousins, Ewert. "A Theology of Interpersonal Relations." *Thought* 45 (1970): 56–82.

Csikszentmihalyi, Mihaly. "Why We Need Things." In *History from Things: Essays on Material Culture*. Edited by Steven Lubar and W. David Kingery. Washington, D.C.: Smithsonian Institution Press, 1993.

Csikszentmihalyi, Mihaly and Eugene Rochberg-Halton. *The Meaning of Things: Domestic Symbols and the Self*. New York: Cambridge University Press, 1981.

Cunningham, David S. *These Three Are One: The Practice of Trinitarian Theology*. Malden, Mass.: Blackwell Publishers, 1998.

Curran, Rosemary T. "Whitehead's Notion of the Person and the Saving of the Past." *Scottish Journal of Theology* 36, no. 3 (1983): 363–85.

Dancy, Jonathan. "Epistemology, Problems of." In *The Oxford Companion to Philosophy*. Edited by Ted Honderich. New York: Oxford University Press, 1995.

D'Andrade, Roy G. *The Development of Cognitive Anthropology*. Cambridge: Cambridge University Press,1995.

Davidson, Donald. "On the Very Idea of a Conceptual Scheme." Reprinted in *Relativism: Cognitive and Moral*. Edited by Jack W. Meiland and Michael Krausz. Notre Dame, Ind.: University of Notre Dame Press, 1982.

Davis, Charles. "Religion and the Sense of the Sacred." *Proceedings of the Catholic Theological Society of America* 31 (1976): 87–105.

Davis, John Jefferson. *Foundations of Evangelical Theology*. Grand Rapids: Baker, 1984.

Davis, Kingsley. *Human Society*. New York: Macmillan & Co., 1948.

Dawson, David. *Literary Theory*. Minneapolis: Fortress Press, 1995.

Denzinger, H. and A. Schonmetzer, eds. *Enchiridion Symbolorum*. 33rd ed. Freiburg: Herder, 1965.

Descartes, René. "Discourse on Method." In *Philosophical Works of Descartes*. Translated by Elizabeth Haldane and G. R. T. Ross. New York: Dover Publications, 1955.

———. *Selected Philosophical Writings*. Translated by John Cottingham, Robert Stoothoff, and Dugald Murdoch. New York: Cambridge University Press, 1988.

DeWolf, L. Harold. *The Case for Theology in Liberal Perspective*. Philadelphia: Westminster Press, 1959.

Dhavamony, Mariasusai. "The Christian Theology of Inculturation." *Studia Missionalia* 44 (1995): 1–43.

Dilthey, Wilhelm. *Dilthey: Selected Writings*. Edited by H. P. Rickman. Cambridge: Cambridge University Press, 1976.

Driedger, Sharon Doyle. "On a Higher Plane." *Maclean's* 108, no. 52 (Dec. 25, 1995–Jan. 1, 1996): 23.

Driver, Tom F. *The Magic of Ritual: Our Need for Liberating Rites that Transform Our Lives and Our Communities*. San Francisco: HarperSanFrancisco, 1991.

Dulles, Avery. *The Craft of Theology: From Symbol to System*. New York: Crossroad, 1992.

———. "Scripture: Recent Protestant and Catholic Views." In *The Authoritative Word*. Edited by Donald McKim. Grand Rapids: Wm. B. Eerdmans Publishing Co., 1983.

Dworkin, Ronald. "Liberal Community." In *Communitarianism and Individualism*. Edited by Shlomo Avineri and Avner De-Shalit. New York: Oxford University Press, 1992.

Dyke, Arthur J. *Rethinking Rights and Responsibilities: The Moral Bonds of Community*. Cleveland: Pilgrim Press, 1992.

Dyrness, William. *Learning about Theology from the Third World*. Grand Rapids: Zondervan, 1989.

Eagleton, Terry. "Awakening from Modernity." *Times Literary Supplement* (February 20, 1987): 194.

Eliot, T. S. *Notes Towards the Definition of Culture*. London: Faber & Faber, 1948.

Emmerson, Richard Kenneth. *Antichrist in the Middle Ages*. Manchester: Manchester University Press, 1981.

Ericksen, Robert P. *Theologians Under Hitler: Gerhard Kittel, Paul Althaus and Emanuel Hirsch*. New Haven, Conn.: Yale University Press, 1985.

Erickson, Millard J. *Christian Theology*. 3 vols. Grand Rapids: Baker, 1983.

———. *The Evangelical Left*. Grand Rapids: Baker, 1997.

———. *Postmodernizing the Faith*. Grand Rapids: Baker, 1998.

Erikson, Erik H. *Insight and Responsibility*. New York: W. W. Norton & Co., 1964.

Estep, William R. *The Anabaptist Story: An Introduction to Sixteenth-Century Anabaptism*. 3rd ed. Grand Rapids: Wm. B. Eerdmans Publishing Co., 1996.

Etzioni, Amitai. "Introduction: A Matter of Balance, Rights and Responsibilities." In *The Essential Communitarian Reader*. Edited by Amitai Etzioni. Lanham, Md.: Rowman & Littlefield, 1998.

Fackre, Gabriel. *The Christian Story: A Narrative Interpretation of Basic Christian Doctrine*. 3rd ed. Grand Rapids: Wm. B. Eerdmans Publishing Co., 1996.

Farley, Edward and Peter C. Hodgson. "Scripture and Tradition." In *Christian Theology: An Introduction to Its Traditions and Tasks*. Edited by Peter C. Hodgson and Robert H. King. 2nd ed. Philadelphia: Fortress Press, 1985.

Fergusson, David. *Community, Liberalism and Christian Ethics*. Cambridge: Cambridge University Press, 1998.

Fillmore, Charles J. "An Alternative to Checklist Theories of Meaning." In *Proceedings of the First Annual Meeting of the Berkeley Linguistics Society*. Edited by Cathy Cogen et al. Berkeley, Calif.: Berkeley Linguistics Society, 1975.

Finger, Thomas N. *Christian Theology: An Eschatological Approach*. 2 vols. Nashville: Thomas Nelson & Publishers, 1985.

Fiorenza, Francis Schüssler. "The Crisis of Scriptural Authority: Interpretation and Reception." *Interpretation* 44 (October 1990): 353–68.

———. *Foundational Theology: Jesus and the Church*. New York: Crossroad, 1984.

Ford, David. *Barth and God's Story*. Frankfurt: Perter Lang, 1985.

Fortman, Edmund. *The Triune God: A Historical Study of the Doctrine of the Trinity*. Philadelphia: Westminster Press, 1972.

Fosdick, Harry Emerson. *The Modern Use of the Bible*. New York: Macmillan & Co., 1924.

Fowler, Robert M. "Postmodern Biblical Criticism." *Eastern Great Lakes & Midwest Bible Society Proceedings* 8 (September 1989): 1–22.

Frank, Douglas W. *Less Than Conquerors: How Evangelicals Entered the Twentieth Century*. Grand Rapids: Wm. B. Eerdmans Publishing Co., 1986.

Frei, Hans W. *The Eclipse of Biblical Narrative: A Study in Eighteenth and Nineteenth Century Hermeneutics*. New Haven, Conn.: Yale University Press, 1974.

———. "Response to 'Narrative Theology: An Evangelical Appraisal.'" *Trinity Journal* 8 (Spring 1987): 21–24.

———. *Types of Modern Theology*. Edited by George Hunsinger and William C. Placher. New Haven, Conn.: Yale University Press, 1992.

Friedman, Marilyn. "Feminism and Modern Friendship: Dislocating the Community." In *Communitarianism and Individualism*. Edited by Shlomo Avineri and Avner De-Shalit. New York: Oxford University Press, 1992.

Frohnen, Bruce. *The New Communitarians and the Crisis of Modern Liberalism*. Lawrence, Kans.: University Press of Kansas, 1996.

Frye, Northrop. *The Great Code: The Bible and Literature*. New York: Harcourt Brace Jovanovich, 1982.

Fukuyama, Francis. "The End of History?" *The National Interest* (Summer 1989): 3–18.

———. *The End of History and the Last Man.* New York: Avon Books, 1992.

Funk, Robert W., ed. *The Acts of Jesus: The Search for the Authentic Deeds of Jesus.* San Francisco: HarperSanFrancisco, 1998.

———. *The Five Gospels: The Search for the Authentic Words of Jesus.* New York: Macmillan Publishing, 1993.

Gadamer, Hans-Georg. *Truth and Method.* Translation edited by Garrett Barden and John Cumming. New York: Crossroad, 1984.

Geertz, Clifford. *The Interpretation of Cultures.* New York: Basic Books, 1973.

Gelpi, Donald L. "Conversion: Beyond the Impasses of Individualism." In *Beyond Individualism: Toward a Retrieval of Moral Disclosure in America.* Edited by Donald L. Gelpi. Notre Dame, Ind.: University of Notre Dame Press, 1989.

George, Timothy. *Theology of the Reformers.* Nashville: Broadman Press, 1988.

Gerrish, B. A. *Tradition and the Modern World: Reformed Theology in the Nineteenth Century.* Chicago: University of Chicago Press, 1978.

Goldingay, John. *Models for Scripture.* Grand Rapids: Wm. B. Eerdmans Publishing Co., 1994.

González, Justo L. *Out of Every Tribe and Nation: Christian Theology at the Ethnic Roundtable.* Nashville: Abingdon Press, 1992.

———. *The Story of Christianity.* San Francisco: HarperSanFrancisco, 1984.

Goodrick, Edward W. "Let's Put 2 Timothy 3:16 Back in the Bible." *Journal of the Evangelical Theological Society* 25, no. 4 (December 1982): 479–87.

Grant, Robert M. *Greek Apologists of the Second Century.* Philadelphia: Westminster Press, 1988.

Green, Garrett. *Imagining God: Theology & the Religious Imagination.* San Francisco: Harper & Row, 1989.

Grenz, Stanley J. "Belonging to God: The Quest for a Communal Spirituality in the Postmodern World." *Asbury Theological Journal* 54, no. 2 (Fall 1999): 41–52.

———. "Beyond Foundationalism: Is a Nonfoundationalist Evangelical Theory Possible?" *Christian Scholar's Review* 30, no. 1 (Fall 2000).

———. *The Millennial Maze: Sorting Out Evangelical Options.* Downers Grove, Ill.: InterVarsity Press, 1992.

———. *Prayer: The Cry for the Kingdom.* Peabody, Mass.: Hendrickson & Publishers, 1988.

———. *A Primer on Postmodernism.* Grand Rapids: Wm. B. Eerdmans Publishing Co., 1996.

———. *Reason for Hope: The Systematic Theology of Wolfhart Pannenberg.* New York: Oxford University Press, 1990.

———. *Renewing the Center: Evangelical Theory in a Post-Theological Era.* Grand Rapids: Baker, 2000.

———. *Revisioning Evangelical Theology: A Fresh Agenda for the 21st Century.* Downers Grove, Ill.: InterVarsity Press, 1993.

———. "The Spirit and the World: The World—Creating Function of the Text." *Theology Today* 57, no. 3 (2000).

———. *Theology for the Community of God.* Grand Rapids: Wm. B. Eerdmans Publishing Co., 2000.

Grudem, Wayne. *Systematic Theology: An Introduction to Biblical Doctrine.* Grand Rapids: Zondervan, 1994.

Grunlan, Stephen A. and Marvin K. Mayers. *Cultural Anthropology: A Christian Perspective.* 2nd ed. Grand Rapids: Zondervan, 1988.

Gundry, Stanley N. "Evangelical Theology: Where Should We Be Going?" *Journal of the Evangelical Theological Society* 22 (March 1979): 3–13.

Gunton, Colin E. *The One, the Three and the Many: God, Creation and the Culture of Modernity.* Cambridge: Cambridge University Press, 1993.

———. *The Promise of Trinitarian Theology.* 2nd ed. Edinburgh: T. & T. Clark, 1997.

———. "Using and Being Used: Scripture and Systematic Theology." *Theology Today* 47, no. 3 (October 1990): 248–59.

Gustafson, James M. "The Sectarian Temptation: Reflections on Theology, the Church, and the University." *Proceedings of the Catholic Theological Society of America* 40 (1985): 83–94.

Gutmann, Amy. "Communitarian Critics of Liberalism." In *Communitarianism and Individualism.* Edited by Shlomo Avineri and Avner De-Shalit. New York: Oxford University Press, 1992.

Hall, Douglas J. *Thinking the Faith: Christian Theology in a North American Context.* Minneapolis: Augsburg, 1989.

Hannerz, Ulf. *Cultural Complexity: Studies in the Social Organization of Meaning.* New York: Columbia University Press, 1992.

Hanson, Norwood Russell. *Patterns of Discovery: An Inquiry into the Conceptual Foundations of Science.* Cambridge: Cambridge University Press, 1958.

Hanson, Paul D. "Introduction." In *Visionaries and Their Apocalypses.* Edited by Paul D. Hanson. Philadelphia: Fortress Press, 1983.

———. "Old Testament Apocalyptic Reexamined." In *Visionaries and Their Apocalypses.* Edited by Paul D. Hanson. Philadelphia: Fortress Press, 1983.

———. *The People Called: The Growth of Community in the Bible.* San Francisco: Harper & Row, 1986.

Hardin, Michael. "The Authority of Scripture: A Pietist Perspective." *Covenant Quarterly* 49, no. 1 (February 1991): 3–12.

Harrington, Daniel J. "The Reception of Walter Bauer's Orthodoxy and Heresy in Earliest Christianity During the Last Decade." *Harvard Theological Review* 73, nos. 1–2 (1980): 289–98.

Harrisville, Roy A. and Walter Sundberg. *The Bible in Modern Culture: Theology and Historical-Critical Method from Spinoza to Käsemann.* Grand Rapids: Wm. B. Eerdmans Publishing Co., 1995.

Hart, Trevor. *Faith Thinking: The Dynamics of Christian Theology.* Downers Grove, Ill.: InterVarsity Press, 1995.

Hauerwas, Stanley. *A Community of Character: Toward a Constructive Christian Ethic.* Notre Dame, Ind.: University of Notre Dame Press, 1981.

———. *The Peaceable Kingdom: A Primer in Christian Ethics.* Notre Dame, Ind.: University of Notre Dame Press, 1983.

Hauerwas, Stanley, Nancey Murphy, and Mark Nation, eds. *Theology Without Foundations: Religious Practice & the Future of Theological Truth.* Nashville: Abingdon Press, 1994.

Heard, Gerry C. *Basic Values and Ethical Decisions: An Examination of Individualism and Community in American Society.* Malabar, Fla.: Robert E. Krieger, 1990.

Hegel, G. W. F. *The Phenomenology of Mind.* Translated by J. B. Ballie. New York: Harper & Row, 1967.

Heidegger, Martin. *Being and Time.* Translated by John Macquarrie and Edward Robinson. New York: Harper & Row, 1962.

Helminiak, Daniel A. "Human Solidarity and Collective Union in Christ." *Anglican Theological Review* 70, no. 1 (January 1988): 34–59.

Henry, Carl F. H. *God, Revelation, and Authority.* 6 vols. Waco, Tex.: Word Publishing, 1976–1983.

———. "Narrative Theology: An Evangelical Appraisal." *Trinity Journal* 8 (Spring 1987): 3–19.

Hensley, Jeffrey. "Are Postliberals Necessarily Antirealists? Reexamining the Metaphysics of Lindbeck's Postliberal Theology." In *The Nature of*

Confession: Evangelicals and Postliberals in Conversation. Edited by Dennis L. Okholm and Timothy R. Phillips. Downers Grove, Ill.: InterVarsity Press, 1996.

Herder, J.G. *Ideen zur Philosophie der Geschichte der Menschheit,* Berlin: G. Hempel, 1879.

Herskovitz, Melvin. *Man and His Works.* New York: Alfred A. Knopf, 1948.

Hick, John. *God Has Many Names.* Philadelphia: Westminster Press, 1982.

Hiebert, Paul G. *Cultural Anthropology.* 2nd ed. Grand Rapids: Baker, 1983.

Hodge, A. A. and B. B. Warfield. "Inspiration." *Presbyterian Review* (1881): 237.

Hodge, Charles. *Systematic Theology.* 3 vols. New York: Scribner's, Armstrong, & Co., 1872.

———. "The Theology of the Intellect and That of Feelings." In *Essays and Reviews.* New York: Robert Carter & Bros., 1857.

Hodges, H. A. *The Philosophy of Wilhelm Dilthey.* 1952. Reprint, Westport, Conn.: Greenwood Press, 1974.

Hoffman, Thomas A. "Inspiration, Normativeness, Canonicity, and the Unique Sacred Character of the Bible." *Catholic Biblical Quarterly* 44 (July 1982): 447–469.

Holdcroft, David. *Saussure: Signs, System and Arbitrariness.* Cambridge: Cambridge University Press, 1991.

Holmer, Paul L. *The Grammar of Faith.* New York: Harper & Row, 1978.

Huizinga, Johan. *Homo Ludens: A Study of the Play-Element in Culture.* London: Paladin, 1970.

Irenaeus, Saint. *Adversus Haereses.* Edited by W. W. Harvey. Cambridge, 1857.

———. *Against the Heresies: Book 1.* Translated and Annotated by Dominic C. Unger. Further revised by John J. Dillon. New York: Paulist Press, 1992.

Ivo of Chartres. *Patrologia Latina.* Edited by J. P. Migne. Paris: Migne, 1844–1890.

Jacobs, H. E., trans. "Preface to the Revelation of St. John." In *Works of Martin Luther.* 6 vols. Philadelphia: A. J. Holman Co., 1932.

James, William. *Pragmatism: A New Name for Some Old Ways of Thinking.* Reprint, New York: Longmans, Green & Co., 1928.

Jameson, Fredric. *Postmodernism, or the Cultural Logic of Late Capitalism.* Durham, N.C.: Duke University Press, 1995.

Jenson, Robert W. *Systematic Theology: Vol. 1, The Triune God.* New York: Oxford University Press, 1997.

———. *The Triune Identity: God According to the Gospel.* Philadelphia: Fortress Press, 1982.

Joachim, Harold H. *The Nature of Truth.* London: Oxford University Press, 1906, 1939.

Jodock, Darrell. "The Reciprocity between Scripture and Theology: The Role of Scripture in Contemporary Theological Reflection." *Interpretation* 44, no. 4 (October 1990): 369–82.

Johnson, Elizabeth A. *She Who Is: The Mystery of God in Feminist Theological Discourse.* New York: Crossroad, 1992.

Johnson, William Stacy. *The Mystery of God: Karl Barth and the Postmodern Foundations of Theology.* Louisville, Ky.: Westminster John Knox Press, 1997.

Justin the Martyr. *Dialogue with Trypho, A Jew.* In *The Ante-Nicene Fathers: Translation of the Fathers Down to A.D. 325.* 10 vols. Edited by A. Roberts and J. Donaldson. Grand Rapids: Wm. B. Eerdmans Publishing Co., 1975.

Kant, Immanuel. *Critique of Pure Reason.* Translated by Norman Kemp Smith. London: Macmillan & Co. 1933.

Kasper, Walter. *The God of Jesus Christ.* Translated by Matthew J. O'Connell. London: SCM Press, 1983.

Kaufman, Gordon. *An Essay on Theological Method.* Rev. ed. Missoula, Mont.: Scholars Press, 1979.

————. *In Face of Mystery.* Cambridge, Mass.: Harvard University Press, 1993.

Kelly, J. N. D. *Early Christian Doctrines.* 5th rev. ed. London: Adam & Charles Black, 1977/San Francisco: Harper & Row, 1978.

Kelsey, David H. "Church Discourse and Public Realm." In *Theology and Dialogue: Essays in Conversation with George Lindbeck.* Edited by Bruce D. Marshall. Notre Dame, Ind.: University of Notre Dame Press, 1990.

————. *The Uses of Scripture in Recent Theology.* Philadelphia: Fortress Press, 1975.

Kirk, G. S. and J. E. Raven. *The Presocratic Philosophers.* Corrected reprint. Cambridge: Cambridge University Press, 1963.

Klaassen, Walter. "Anabaptist Hermeneutics: Presuppositions, Principles and Practice." In *Essays on Biblical Interpretation: Anabaptist-Mennonite Perspective.* Edited by Willard M. Swartley. Elkhart, Ind.: Institute of Mennonite Studies, 1984.

Kluback, William. "The Problem of Christianity." In *Josiah Royce: Selected Writings.* Edited by John Edwin Smith and William Kluback. Mahwah, N.J.: Paulist Press, 1988.

Koch, Klaus. *The Rediscovery of Apocalyptic.* London: SCM Press, 1972.

————. "What Is Apocalyptic? An Attempt as a Preliminary Definition." In *Visionaries and Their Apocalypse.* Edited by Paul Hanson. Philadelphia: Fortress Press, 1983.

Koester, Helmut. "Gnomai Diaphorai: The Origin and Nature of Diversification in the History of Early Christianity." In *Trajectories through Early Christianity.* Edited by James M. Robinson and Helmut Koester. Philadelphia: Fortress Press, 1971.

Kort, Wesley A. *Take, Read: Scripture, Textuality, and Cultural Practice.* University Park, Penn.: Pennsylvania State University Press, 1996.

Kraft, Charles H. *Christianity in Culture: A Study in Dynamic Biblical Theologizing in Cross-Cultural Perspective.* Maryknoll, N.Y.: Orbis Books, 1979.

Kraus, Hans-Joachim. *Worship in Israel: A Cultic History of the Old Testament.* Translated by G. Bushwell. Richmond: John Knox Press, 1966.

Kroeber, Alfred L. *Style and Civilizations.* Ithaca, N.Y.: Cornell University Press, 1957.

Kroker, Arthur and David Cook. *The Postmodern Scene: Excremental Culture and Hyper-Aesthetics.* New York: St. Martin's Press, 1986.

Kuhn, Thomas. *The Structure of Scientific Revolutions.* 2nd ed. Chicago: University of Chicago Press, 1970.

LaCugna, Catherine Mowry. "Current Trends in Trinitarian Theology." *Religious Studies Review* 13, no. 2 (April 1987): 141–7.

————. *God for Us: The Trinity and the Christian Life.* San Francisco: HarperCollins, 1991.

————. "Philosophers and Theologians on the Trinity." *Modern Theology* 2, no. 3 (April 1986): 169–81.

LaHaye, Tim. *No Fear of the Storm: Why Christians Will Escape All the Tribulation.* Sisters, Ore.: Multnomah, 1992.

Lakeland, Paul. *Postmodernity: Christian Identity in a Fragmented Age.* Minneapolis: Fortress Press, 1997.

Lane, Anthony N. S. "Calvin's Use of the Fathers and the Medievals." *Calvin Theological Journal* 16 (November 1981): 149–205.

Lash, Nicholas. *A Matter of Hope: A Theologian's Reflections on the Thought of Karl Marx.* London: Darton, Longman & Todd, 1981.

Lawson, Hilary. "Stories about Stories." In *Dismantling Truth: Reality in the Post-Modern World.* Edited by Hilary Lawson and Lisa Appignanesi. New York: St. Martin's Press, 1989.

Leith, John H., ed. *Creeds of the Churches: A Reader in Christian Doctrine from the Bible to the Present.* 3rd ed. Philadelphia: John Knox Press, 1982.

Lester, Andrew D. *Hope in Pastoral Care and Counseling*. Minneapolis: Fortress Press, 1995.

Letham, R. W. A. "Reformed Theology." In *New Dictionary of Theology*. Edited by Sinclair B. Ferguson, David F. Wright, and J. I. Packer. Downers Grove, Ill.: InterVarsity Press, 1988.

Lewis, Gordon R. and Bruce A. Demarest. *Integrative Theology*. 3 vols. Grand Rapids: Zondervan, 1987–1994.

Lightner, Robert P. *Evangelical Theology*. Grand Rapids: Baker, 1986.

Lindbeck, George A. "Confession and Community: How My Mind Has Changed." *Christian Century* 107, no. 16 (May 9, 1990): 492–6.

————. *The Nature of Doctrine: Religion and Theology in a Postliberal Age*. Philadelphia: Westminster Press, 1984.

Lints, Richard. *The Fabric of Theology: A Prolegomenon to Evangelical Theology*. Grand Rapids: Wm. B. Eerdmans Publishing Co., 1993.

Loewith, Karl. *Meaning in History*. Chicago: University of Chicago Press, 1950.

Lossky, Vladimir. *The Mystical Theology of the Eastern Church*. Translated by Fellowship of St. Alban and St. Sergius. Cambridge: James Clark & Co., 1957; reprint, Crestwood, N.Y.: St. Vladimir's Seminary Press, 1976.

Louw, Daniel J. "Pastoral Care and the Therapeutic Dimension of Christian Hope." *Pastoral Sciences* 17 (1998): 89.

Loux, Michael J. *Metaphysics: A Contemporary Introduction*. London: Routledge & Kegan Paul, 1998.

Lubar, Steven and W. David Kingery, eds. *History from Things: Essays on Material Culture*. Washington, D.C.: Smithsonian Institution Press, 1993.

Luther, Martin. *Lectures on Genesis* in *Luther's Works*. Edited by Jaroslav Pelikan. Translated by George V. Schick. American ed. St. Louis: Concordia Publishing House, 1958.

Lyon, David. *Sociology and the Human Image*. Downers Grove, Ill.: InterVarsity Press, 1983.

Lyotard, Jean-Francois. *The Postmodern Condition: A Report on Knowledge*. Translated by Geoff Bennington and Brian Massumi. Minneapolis: University of Minnesota Press, 1984.

MacIntyre, Alasdair. *After Virtue*. 2nd ed. Notre Dame, Ind.: University of Notre Dame Press, 1984.

————. "The Spectre of Communitarianism." *Radical Philosophy* 70 (March/April 1995): 34–35.

————. *Three Rival Versions of Moral Enquiry: Encyclopaedia, Genealogy, and Tradition*. Notre Dame, Ind.: University of Notre Dame Press, 1990.

————. *Whose Justice? Which Rationality?* Notre Dame, Ind.: University of Notre Dame Press, 1988.

Mackey, James P. *The Modern Theology of Tradition*. New York: Herder & Herder, 1963.

————. *Tradition and Change in the Church*. Dayton, Ohio: Pflaum Press, 1968.

Marsden, George. "The Collapse of American Evangelical Academia" In *Faith and Rationality: Reason and Belief in God*. Edited by Alvin Plantinga and Nicholas Wolterstorff. Notre Dame, Ind.: University of Notre Dame Press, 1983.

————. *Fundamentalism and American Culture: The Shaping of Twentieth-Century Evangelicalism, 1870–1925*. New York: Oxford University Press, 1980.

————. *Reforming Fundamentalism: Fuller Seminary and the New Evangelicalism*. Grand Rapids: Wm. B. Eerdmans Publishing Co., 1987.

Marshall, Bruce D. "Absorbing the World: Christianity and the Universe of Truths." In *Theology and Dialogue: Essays in Conversation with George Lindbeck*. Edited by Bruce D. Marshall. Notre Dame, Ind.: University of Notre Dame Press, 1990.

Mathews, Shailer. *The Faith of Modernism*. New York: Macmillan Co., 1924.
McClendon, James William Jr. *Systematic Theology: Ethics*. Nashville: Abingdon Press, 1986.
McCracken, Grant. *Culture and Consumption: New Approaches to the Symbolic Character of Consumer Goods and Activities*. Bloomington, Ind.: University of Indiana Press, 1990.
McDonnell, Kilian. "Vatican II (1962–1964), Puebla (1979), Synod (1985): *Koinonia/Communio* as an Integral Ecclesiology." *Journal of Ecumenical Studies* 25, no. 3 (Summer 1988): 399–427.
McFadyen, Alistair I. *The Call to Personhood: A Christian Theory of the Individual in Social Relationships*. Cambridge: Cambridge University Press, 1990.
McGiffert, Arthur C. *A History of Christian Thought*. 2 vols. New York: Charles Scribner's Sons, 1932–33.
———. *Protestant Thought Before Kant*. London: Duckworth, 1911.
McGrath, Alister E. "An Evangelical Evaluation of Postliberalism." In *The Nature of Confession: Evangelicals and Postliberals in Conversation*. Edited by Timothy R. Phillips and Dennis L. Okholm. Downers Grove, Ill.: Intervaristy Press, 1996.
———. *The Intellectual Origins of the European Reformation*. Oxford: Basil Blackwell Publisher, 1987.
McKnight, Edgar V. *Postmodern Use of the Bible: The Emergence of Reader-Oriented Criticism*. Nashville: Abingdon Press, 1988.
McLeod, Mark S. "Making God Dance: Postmodern Theorizing and the Christian College." *Christian Scholar's Review* 21, no. 3 (March 1992): 275–92.
McRay, J. R. "Bible, Canon of." In *The Evangelical Dictionary of Theology*. Edited by Walter A. Elwell, 140–1. Grand Rapids: Baker, 1984.
Mead, George Herbert. *Mind, Self and Society from the Standpoint of a Social Behaviorist*. Edited by Charles W. Morris. Chicago: University of Chicago Press, 1934, 1963.
Meeks, M. Douglas. *Origins of the Theology of Hope*. Philadelphia: Fortress Press, 1974.
Meiland, Jack W. and Michael Krausz, eds. *Relativism: Cognitive and Moral*. Notre Dame, Ind.: University of Notre Dame Press, 1982.
Meland, Bernard E. *Faith and Culture*. Carbondale, Ill.: Southern Illinois University Press, 1953.
———. *Fallible Forms and Symbols: Discourses of Method in a Theology of Culture*. Philadelphia: Fortress Press, 1976.
Migliore, Daniel L. *Faith Seeking Understanding: An Introduction to Christian Theology*. Grand Rapids: Wm. B. Eerdmans Publishing Co., 1991.
Milbank, John. *Theology and Social Theory: Beyond Secular Reason*. Oxford: Basil Blackwell Publisher, 1990.
Mill, John Stuart. *On Liberty*. Edited by Curran V. Shields. 1859. Reprint, Indianapolis: Bobbs-Merrill Co., 1956.
Miller, Daniel. *Material Culture and Mass Consumption*. Oxford: Basil Blackwell Publisher, 1987.
Miller, Donald E. *The Case for Liberal Christianity*. San Francisco: Harper & Row, 1981.
Moberg, David O. *The Church as a Social Institution: The Sociology of American Religion*. 2nd ed. Grand Rapids: Baker, 1984.
Moltmann, Jürgen. *The Coming of God: Christian Eschatology*. Translated by Margaret Kohl. Minneapolis: Fortress Press, 1996.
———. *The Experiment Hope*. Translated by M. Douglas Meeks. Philadelphia: Fortress Press, 1975.
———. *God in Creation: A New Theology of Creation and the Spirit of God*. Translated by Margaret Kohl. San Francisco: Harper & Row, 1985.

————. "Hope and History." *Theology Today* 25, no. 3 (October 1968): 369–86.

————. *Theology of Hope.* Translated by James Leitch. New York: Harper & Row, 1967.

————. *The Trinity and the Kingdom of God.* Translated by Margaret Kohl. London: SCM Press, 1981.

Morgan, David. *Visual Piety: A History and Theory of Popular Images.* Berkeley, Calif.: University of California Press, 1998.

Mouw, Richard J. "The Bible in Twentieth-Century Protestantism: A Preliminary Taxonomy." In *The Bible in America: Essays in Cultural History.* Edited by Nathan O. Hatch and Mark A. Noll. New York: Oxford University Press, 1982.

Muller, Richard A. *Post-Reformation Reformed Dogmatics, Vol. 1: Prolegomena.* Grand Rapids: Baker, 1987.

————. *Post-Reformation Reformed Dogmatics, Vol. 2: Holy Scripture: The Cognitive Foundation of Theology.* Grand Rapids: Baker, 1993.

Mullins, Edgar Young. *The Christian Religion in Its Doctrinal Expression.* Philadelphia: Roger Williams Press, 1917.

Murphy, Arthur E. *The Uses of Reason.* New York: Macmillan & Co., 1943.

Murphy, Nancey. *Anglo-American Postmodernity: Philosophical Perspectives on Science, Religion, and Ethics.* Boulder, Colo.: Westview Press, 1997.

————. *Beyond Liberalism and Fundamentalism: How Modern and Postmodern Philosophy Set the Theological Agenda.* Valley Forge, Penn.: Trinity Press International, 1996.

————. "Philosophical Resources for Postmodern Evangelical Theology." *Christian Scholar's Review* 26, no. 2 (Winter 1996):184–205.

Naegele, Kaspar D. "The Institutionalization of Action." In *Theories of Society: Foundation of Modern Sociological Theory.* 2 vols. Edited by Talcott Parsons et al. New York: Free Press, 1961.

Naisbitt, John and Patricia Aburdene. *Megatrends 2000: Ten New Directions for the 1990s.* New York: Avon Books, 1990.

Neuhaus, Richard John. "A Voice in the Relativistic Wilderness." *Christianity Today* 38 (February 7, 1994): 33–5.

Neusch, Marcel. *The Sources of Modern Atheism: One Hundred Years of Debate Over God.* Translated by Matthew J. O'Connell. New York: Paulist Press, 1982.

Newbigin, Lesslie. *The Gospel in a Pluralist Society.* Grand Rapids: Wm. B. Eerdmans Publishing Co., 1989.

Nichols, Aidan. *The Shape of Catholic Theology.* Edinburgh: T. & T. Clark, 1991.

Niebuhr, Reinhold. "Intellectual Autobiography." In *Reinhold Niebuhr: His Religious, Social and Political Thought.* Edited by Charles W. Kegley and Robert W. Bretall. New York: Macmillan & Co., 1961.

————. *An Interpretation of Christian Ethics.* New York: Meridian Books, 1956.

————. *The Nature and Destiny of Man.* Scribner Library ed. New York: Charles Scribner's Sons, 1964.

Nisbet, Robert A. *The Quest for Community: A Study in the Ethics of Order and Freedom.* New York: Oxford University Press, 1953.

————. *The Sociological Tradition.* New York: Basic Books, 1966.

Nisbet, Robert and Robert G. Perrin. *The Social Bond.* 2nd ed. New York: Alfred A. Knopf, 1977.

Noll, Mark A. *The Scandal of the Evangelical Mind.* Grand Rapids: Wm. B. Eerdmans Publishing Co., 1994.

Nygren, Anders. *The Significance of the Bible for the Church.* Translated by Carl C. Rasmussen. Philadelphia: Fortress Press, 1963.

Oberman, Heiko. *The Harvest of Medieval Theology: Gabriel Biel and Late Medieval Nominalism.* Rev. ed. Grand Rapids: Wm. B. Eerdmans Publishing Co., 1967.

———. "Quo Vadis, Petre? The History of Tradition from Irenaeus to Humani Generis." *Scottish Journal of Theology* 16 (September 1963): 225–55.

O'Dea, Thomas F. *The Sociology of Religion.* Englewood Cliffs, N.J.: Prentice-Hall, 1966.

Oden, Thomas C. *After Modernity . . . What? Agenda for Theology.* Grand Rapids: Zondervan, 1990.

———. *Systematic Theology: The Living God.* San Francisco: Harper & Row, 1987.

Olson, Roger E. "The Future of Evangelical Theology." *Christianity Today* 42 (February 9, 1998): 40–48.

———. *The Story of Christian Theology: Twenty Centuries of Tradition and Reform.* Downers Grove, Ill.: InterVarsity Press, 1999.

———. "Whales and Elephants: Both God's Creatures But Can They Meet? Evangelicals and Liberals in Dialogue." *Pro Ecclesia* 4, no. 2 (Spring 1995): 165–89.

Pannenberg, Wolfhart. *Basic Questions in Theology,* Translated by George H. Kehm. 2 vols. Philadelphia: Fortress Press, 1971.

———. "The Christian Vision of God: The New Discussion on the Trinitarian Doctrine." *Trinity Seminary Review* 13, no. 2 (Fall 1991): 53–60.

———. *Metaphysics and the Idea of God.* Translated by Philip Clayton. Grand Rapids: Wm. B. Eerdmans Publishing Co., 1990.

———. "The Nature of a Theological Statement." *Zygon* 7, no. 1 (March 1972): 6–19.

———. *Systematic Theology.* Translated by Geoffrey W. Bromiley. 3 vols. Grand Rapids: Wm. B. Eerdmans Publishing Co., 1991–1998.

Pattison, George. *The End of Theology—And the Task of Thinking about God.* London: SCM Press, 1998.

Peacocke, Arthur. *Intimations of Reality: Critical Realism in Science and Religion.* Notre Dame, Ind.: University of Notre Dame Press, 1989.

———. *Theology for a Scientific Age: Being and Becoming—Natural, Divine, and Human.* Enl. ed. Minneapolis: Fortress Press, 1993.

Peirce, Charles Sanders. "How to Make Our Ideas Clear." In Charles S. Peirce, *Selected Writings (Values in a Universe of Chance).* Edited by Philip P. Wiener. New York: Dover Publications, 1958.

Pelikan, Jaroslav. *The Emergence of the Catholic Tradition (100–600).* Chicago: University of Chicago Press, 1971.

———. *From Luther to Kierkegaard.* St. Louis: Concordia Publishing House, 1950.

———. *Historical Theology: Continuity and Change in Christian Doctrine.* New York: Corpus Publishers, 1971.

———. *The Melody of Theology: A Philosophical Dictionary.* Cambridge: Harvard University Press, 1988.

———. *The Spirit of Eastern Christendom (600–1700).* Chicago: University of Chicago Press, 1974.

———. *The Vindication of Tradition.* New Haven, Conn.: Yale University Press, 1984.

Peters, Ted. *GOD as Trinity: Relationality and Temporality in Divine Life.* Louisville, Ky.: Westminster/John Knox Press, 1993.

———. *God—the World's Future: Systematic Theology for a Postmodern Era.* Minneapolis: Fortress Press, 1992.

Phillips, Derek L. *Looking Backward: A Critical Appraisal of Communitarian Thought.* Princeton, N.J.: Princeton University Press, 1993.

Phillips, Timothy R. and Dennis Okholm, eds. *The Nature of Confession: Evangelicals and Postliberals in Conversation.* Downers Grove, Ill.: InterVarsity Press, 1996.

Pike, James A. "The Bible, God's Inspired Word." In *Spectrum of Protestant Beliefs.* Edited by Robert Campbell. Milwaukee: Bruce Publishing Co., 1968.

Pinnock, Clark H. *Biblical Revelation—The Foundation of Christian Theology*. Chicago: Moody Press, 1971.
———. *The Scripture Principle*. San Francisco: Harper & Row, 1984.
———. *Tracking the Maze: Finding Our Way through Modern Theology from an Evangelical Perspective*. San Francisco: Harper & Row, 1990.
Placher, William C. *A History of Christian Theology: An Introduction*. Philadelphia: Westminster Press, 1983.
———. *Unapologetic Theology: A Christian Voice in a Pluralistic Conversation*. Louisville, Ky.: Westminster/John Knox Press, 1989.
Plant, Raymond. *Community and Ideology: An Essay in Applied Social Philosophy*. London: Routledge & Kegan Paul, 1974.
Plantinga, Alvin. "Reason and Belief in God." In *Faith and Rationality: Faith and Belief in God*. Edited by Alvin Plantinga and Nicholas Wolterstorff. Notre Dame, Ind.: University of Notre Dame Press, 1983.
Plantinga, Alvin and Nicholas Wolterstorff, eds. *Faith and Rationality: Reason and Belief in God*. Notre Dame, Ind.: University of Notre Dame Press, 1983.
Plantinga, Cornelius Jr. "Images of God." In *Christian Faith and Practice in the Modern World*. Edited by Mark A. Noll and David F. Wells. Grand Rapids: Wm. B. Eerdmans Publishing Co., 1988.
Polanyi, Michael. *Personal Knowledge: Towards a Post-Critical Philosophy*. Chicago: University of Chicago Press, 1958.
Preus, James Samuel. *From Shadow to Promise: Old Testament Interpretation from Augustine to the Young Luther*. Cambridge, Mass.: Harvard University Press, 1969.
Putnam, Hilary. *Reason, Truth, and History*. Cambridge: Cambridge University Press, 1981.
Quine, W. V. and J. S. Ullian. *The Web of Belief*. New York: Random House, 1970.
Quinn, Naomi and Dorothy Holland. "Culture and Cognition." In *Cultural Models in Language and Thought*. Edited by Dorothy Holland and Naomi Quinn. Cambridge: Cambridge University Press, 1987.
Rahner, Karl. *The Trinity*. New York: Herder & Herder, 1970.
Rainbow, Paul. "On Hearing the Word of God." Unpublished convocation address, North American Baptist Seminary, 1990.
Ramm, Bernard. *The Pattern of Religious Authority*. Grand Rapids: Wm. B. Eerdmans Publishing Co., 1959.
Rappaport, Roy. *Ecology, Meaning, and Religion*. Richmond, Calif.: North Atlantic Books, 1979.
Ratzinger, Joseph. "On the Interpretation of the Tridentine Decree on Tradition." In *Revelation and Tradition*. Edited by Karl Rahner and Joseph Ratzinger. New York: Herder & Herder, 1966.
Rawls, John. *A Theory of Justice*. Cambridge, Mass.: Harvard University Press, 1971.
Reardon, Bernard M. G., ed. *Liberal Protestantism*. Stanford, Calif.: Stanford University Press, 1968.
Reese, William L. "Parmenides." In *Dictionary of Philosophy and Religion*, 412–13. Atlantic Highlands, N.J.: Humanities Press, 1980.
Reeves, Gene. and Delwin Brown. "The Development of Process Theology." In Delwin Brown, Ralph E. James Jr., and Gene Reeves, eds. *Process Philosophy and Christian Thought*. Indianapolis: Bobbs-Merrill, 1971.
Reiter, Richard R. *The Rapture: Pre-, Mid-, or Post-Tribulational?* Grand Rapids: Zondervan, 1984.
Reumann, John. "The New Testament Concept of the Word: Forms of the Word." *Consensus: A Canadian Lutheran Journal of Theology* 4, no. 3 (July 1978): 15–24.
———. "The New Testament Concept of the Word: Function of the Word."

Consensus: A Canadian Lutheran Journal of Theology 5, no. 1 (January 1979): 15–22.

Richardson, Cyril C.. *The Doctrine of the Trinity.* New York: Abingdon Press, 1958.

———. "The Enigma of the Trinity." In *A Companion to the Study of St. Augustine.* Edited by Roy Battenhouse. Oxford: Oxford University Press, 1955.

Ricoeur, Paul. *Hermeneutics and the Human Sciences: Essays on Language, Action, and Interpretation.* Edited and translated by John B. Thompson. Cambridge: Cambridge University Press, 1981.

———. *Interpretation Theory: Discourse and the Surplus of Meaning.* Fort Worth, Tex.: Texas Christian University Press, 1976.

Ritschl, Albrecht. *The Christian Doctrine of Justification and Reconciliation.* Clifton, N.J.: Reference Books Publishers, 1966.

Rogers, Arthur Kenyon. *What Is Truth?* New Haven, Conn.: Yale University Press, 1923.

Rohls, Jan. *Reformed Confessions: Theology from Zurich to Barmen.* Louisville, Ky.: Westminster John Knox Press, 1998.

Roten, Johann G. "The Marian Counterpoint of Postmodern Spirituality." In *Divine Representations: Postmodernism and Spirituality.* Edited by Ann W. Astell. New York: Paulist Press, 1994.

Rowley, H. H. *The Relevance of Apocalyptic.* 2nd ed. London: Lutterworth, 1947.

Royce, Josiah. *The Problem of Christianity.* 2 vols. New York: Macmillan & Co., 1913.

———. *The World and the Individual.* New York: Macmillan & Co., 1901.

Rundle, Bede. "Correspondence Theory of Truth." In *The Oxford Companion to Philosophy.* Edited by Ted Honderich. New York: Oxford University Press, 1995.

Sailhammer, John H. *Introduction to Old Testament Theology: A Canonical Approach.* Grand Rapids: Zondervan, 1995.

Sandel, Michael J. *Liberalism and the Limits of Justice.* 2d ed. Cambridge: Cambridge University Press, 1998.

———. "The Procedural Republic and the Unencumbered Self." In *Communitarianism and Individualism.* Edited by Shlomo Avineri and Avner De-Shalit. New York: Oxford University Press, 1992.

Santmire, H. Paul. "The Genesis Creation Narratives Revisited: Themes for a Global Age." *Interpretation* 45, no. 4 (October 1991): 366–79.

Sartre, Jean-Paul. *Being and Nothingness: An Essay on Phenomenological Ontology.* Translated by Hazel E. Barnes. New York: Philosophical Library, 1956.

Sauter, Gerhard. *Eschatological Rationality: Theological Issues in Focus.* Grand Rapids: Baker, 1996.

Sauter, Gerhard and Alex Stock. *Arbeitswesen Systematischer Theologie: Eine Anleitung.* Munich: Chr. Kaiser Verlag, 1976.

Sayers, Dorothy. *Creed or Chaos.* New York: Harcourt, Brace & Co., 1949.

Scalise, Charles J. *From Scripture to Theology: A Canonical Journey into Hermeneutics.* Downers Grove, Ill.: InterVarsity Press, 1996.

Schaeffer, Francis A. *The God Who Is There.* Downers Grove, Ill.: InterVarsity Press, 1968.

Schleiermacher, Friedrich. *The Christian Faith.* Edited by H. R. Mackintosh and J. S. Stewart. Edinburgh: T. & T. Clark, 1928.

———. *Hermeneutics: The Handwritten Manuscripts.* Edited by Heinz Kimmerle. Translated by James Duke and Jack Forstman. American Academy of Religion Texts and Translation Series, no. 1. Atlanta: Scholars Press, 1977.

Schmidt, Werner H. *The Faith of the Old Testament: A History.* Translated by John Sturdy. Philadelphia: Westminster Press, 1983.

Schmitz-Moormann, Karl. *The Theology of Creation in an Evolutionary World.* Cleveland: Pilgrim Press, 1997.

Schott, Faye E. "God is Love: The Contemporary Theological Movement of Interpreting the Trinity as God's Relational Being." Th.D. dissertation, Lutheran School of Theology at Chicago, 1990.

Schreiter, Robert. "Inculturation of Faith or Identification with Culture?" In *Christianity and Cultures: A Mutual Enrichment.* Edited by Norbert Greinacher and Norbert Mette. London: SCM Press, 1994.

Schwarz, Hans. *On the Way to the Future.* Rev. ed. Minneapolis: Augsburg Publishing House, 1979.

Schweitzer, Albert. *The Quest for the Historical Jesus.* New York: Macmillan & Co., 1954.

Segovia, Fernando F. "The Text as Other: Towards a Hispanic American Hermeneutic." In *Text and Experience: Towards a Cultural Exegesis of the Bible.* Edited by Daniel Smith-Christopher. Sheffield: Sheffield Academic Press, 1995.

Shults, F. LeRon. *The Postfoundationalist Task of Theology: Wolfhart Pannenberg and the New Theological Rationality.* Grand Rapids: Wm. B. Eerdmans Publishing Co., 1999.

Smalley, Beryl. *The Study of the Bible in the Middle Ages.* 2d ed. Oxford: Oxford University Press, 1952.

Smith, Jonathan Z. "Wisdom and Apocalyptic." In *Visionaries and Their Apocalypses.* Edited by Paul D. Hanson. Philadelphia: Fortress Press, 1983.

Solomon, Robert C. *Continental Philosophy since 1750: The Rise and Fall of the Self.* Oxford: Oxford University Press, 1988.

Spiro, Melford E. *Culture and Human Nature: Theoretical Papers of Melford E. Spiro,* Edited by Benjamin Kilborne and L. L. Langness. Chicago: University of Chicago Press, 1987.

Steiner, George. *Real Presences.* Chicago: University of Chicago Press, 1989.

Stiver, Dan R. "The Uneasy Alliance between Evangelicalism and Postmodernism: A Reply to Anthony Thiselton." In *The Challenge of Postmodernism: An Evangelical Engagement.* Edited by David Dockery. Wheaton, Ill.: Bridge Point, 1995.

Stocking, George. *Race, Culture and Evolution.* Chicago: University of Chicago Press, 1982.

Stone, Michael E. "New Light on the Third Century." In *Visionaries and Their Apocalypses.* Edited by Paul D. Hanson. Philadelphia: Fortress Press, 1983.

Stotts, Jack L. "Introduction: Confessing after Barmen." In Jan Rohls, *Reformed Confessions: Theology from Zurich to Barmen.* Translated by John Hoffmeyer. Louisville, Ky.: Westminster John Knox Press, 1998.

Stout, Jeffrey. *Ethics After Babel: The Languages of Morals and Their Discontents.* Boston: Beacon Press, 1988.

———. *Flight from Authority: Religion, Morality, and the Quest for Autonomy.* Notre Dame, Ind.: University of Notre Dame Press, 1981.

Strauss, Claudia and Naomi Quinn. *A Cognitive Theory of Cultural Meaning.* Cambridge: Cambridge University Press, 1997.

Stroll, Avrum and Richard H. Popkin. *Introduction to Philosophy.* 3rd ed. New York: Holt, Rinehart & Winston, 1979.

Stroup, George W. *The Promise of Narrative Theology.* Atlanta: John Knox Press, 1981.

Sumner, William Graham. *Folkways.* Boston: Ginn & Company Publishers, 1906.

Tanner, Kathryn. *Theories of Culture: A New Agenda for Theology.* Minneapolis: Augsburg, 1997.

Tavard, George H. *Holy Writ or Holy Church: The Crisis of the Protestant Reformation.* New York: Harper & Brothers, 1959.

Taylor, Charles. "Cross-Purposes: The Liberal-Communitarian Debate." In *Liberalism and the Moral Life.* Edited by Nancy L. Rosenblum. Cambridge, Mass.: Harvard University Press, 1989.

————. *Human Agency and Language: Philosophical Papers, Vol. 1.* Cambridge: Cambridge University Press, 1985.

————. *Philosophy and the Human Sciences: Philosophical Papers, Vol. 2.* Cambridge: Cambridge University Press, 1985.

————. *Sources of the Self: The Making of Modern Identity.* Cambridge, Mass.: Harvard University Press, 1989.

Taylor, H. F. *Balance in Small Groups.* New York: Van Nostrand Reinhold Co., 1970.

Tertullian. *The Prescription Against Heretics.* In *The Ante-Nicene Fathers.* 10 vols. Edited by Alexander Roberts and James Donaldson. Grand Rapids: Wm. B. Eerdmans Publishing Co., 1986.

Thiel, John E. *Nonfoundationalism.* Minneapolis: Fortress Press, 1994.

Thiemann, Ronald F. *Revelation and Theology: The Gospel as Narrated Promise.* Notre Dame, Ind.: University of Notre Dame Press, 1985.

Thomas, George F. "The Method and Structure of Tillich's Theology." In *The Theology of Paul Tillich.* Edited by Charles W. Kegley. New York: Pilgrim Press, 1982.

Thomas, Owen C. "Theology and Experience." *Harvard Theological Review* 78, nos. 1–2 (January–April 1985): 179–201.

Thompson, John. *Modern Trinitarian Perspectives.* New York: Oxford University Press, 1994.

Tickle, Phyllis A. *God-Talk in America.* New York: Crossroad, 1997.

Tillard, J. M. R. "What Is the Church of God?" *Mid-stream* 23 (October 1984): 363–80.

Tilley, Terrence W. *Postmodern Theologies: The Challenge of Religious Diversity.* Maryknoll, N.Y.: Orbis Books, 1995.

Tillich, Paul. *A History of Christian Thought.* New York: Harper & Row, 1968.

————. *The Shaking of the Foundations.* New York: Charles Scribner's Sons, 1948.

————. *Systematic Theology.* 3 vols. Chicago: University of Chicago Press, 1951.

————. *Theology of Culture.* Edited by Robert C. Kimball. New York: Oxford University Press, 1959.

Tocqueville, Alexis de. *Democracy in America.* Translated by Henry Reeve, Francis Bowen, and Phillips Bradley. Vintage Books ed. 2 vols. New York: Alfred A. Knopf, 1945.

Toennies, Ferdinand. *Community and Society.* Translated by Charles P. Loomis. East Lansing, Mich.: Michigan State University Press, 1957.

Toon, Peter. "Introduction." In *Puritans, the Millennium and the Future of Israel: Puritan Eschatology 1600 to 1660.* Edited by Peter Toon. Greenwood, S.C.: Attic Press, 1970.

Torrance, Alan J. *Persons in Communion: Trinitarian Description and Human Participation.* Edinburgh: T. & T. Clark, 1995.

Toulmin, Stephen. *Cosmopolis: The Hidden Agenda of Modernity.* Chicago: University of Chicago Press, 1990.

————. *The Uses of Argument.* Cambridge: Cambridge University Press, 1958.

Touraine, Alain. *Return of the Actor.* Translated by Myrna Godzich. Minneapolis: University of Minnesota Press, 1988.

Tracy, David. *The Analogical Imagination: Christian Theology and the Culture of Pluralism.* New York: Crossroad, 1981.

————. *Blessed Rage for Order: The New Pluralism in Theology.* New York: Seabury Press, 1975.

————. "Defending the Public Character of Theology." *The Christian Century* 98 (April 1, 1981): 350–6.

Travis, S. H. "Eschatology." In *New Dictionary of Theology.* Edited by Sinclair B. Ferguson, David F. Wright, and J. I. Packer. Downers Grove, Ill.: InterVarsity Press, 1988, 228–231.

Trueblood, David Elton. *General Philosophy.* New York: Harper & Row, 1963.

Turner, Victor W. *The Ritual Process: Structure and Anti-Structure.* Middlesex: Penguin Books, 1969.

Tylor, Edward Burnett. *Primitive Culture.* London: J. Murray, 1871.

van Dusen, H. P. *The Vindication of Liberal Theology.* New York: Charles Scribner's Sons, 1963.

Vanhoozer, Kevin J. *The Cambridge Companion to Postmodern Theology.* Cambridge: Cambridge University Press, forthcoming.

———. "The Semantics of Biblical Literature: Truth and Scripture's Diverse Literary Forms." In *Hermeneutics, Authority, and Canon.* Edited by D. A. Carson and John D. Woodbridge. Grand Rapids: Zondervan, 1986.

van Huyssteen, J. Wentzel. *Essays in Postfoundationalist Theology.* Grand Rapids: Wm. B. Eerdmans Publishing Co., 1997.

———. "Postfoundationalism in Theology and Science: Beyond Conflict and Consonance." In *Rethinking Theology and Science: Six Models for the Current Dialogue.* Edited by Niels Henrik Gregersen and J. Wentzel van Huyssteen. Grand Rapids: Wm. B. Eerdmans Publishing Co., 1998.

———. "Tradition and the Task of Theology." *Theology Today* 55, no. 2 (July 1998): 213–28.

Van Impe, Jack. *Revelation Revealed Verse by Verse.* Troy, Mich.: Jack Van Impe Ministries, 1982.

Volf, Miroslav. *After Our Likeness: The Church As the Image of the Trinity.* Grand Rapids: Wm. B. Eerdmans Publishing Co., 1998.

———. "Kirche als Gemeinschaft: Ekklesiologische Überlegungen aus freikirchlicher Perspektiv." *Evangelische Theologie* 49, no. 1 (1989): 52–76.

———. "Theology, Meaning & Power: A Conversation with George Lindbeck on Theology & the Nature of Christian Difference." In *The Nature of Confession: Evangelicals and Postliberals in Conversation.* Edited by Timothy R. Phillips and Dennis L. Okholm. Downers Grove, Ill.: InterVarsity Press, 1996.

von Rad, Gerhard. "*Eikon.*" In the *Theological Dictionary of the New Testament.* Edited by Gerhard Kittel. Translated by Geoffrey W. Bromiley. Grand Rapids: Wm. B. Eerdmans Publishing Co., 1964.

———. *Genesis.* Translated by John H. Marks, in the Old Testament Library. Edited by G. Ernest Wright. Philadelphia: Westminster Press, 1972.

———. *Old Testament Theology.* Translated by D. M. G. Stalker. 2 vols. New York: Harper & Row, 1965.

Wainwright, Geoffrey. *Doxology: The Praise of God in Worship, Doctrine and Life.* New York: Oxford University Press, 1980.

Walvoord, John F. *Armageddon, Oil, and the Middle East Crisis.* Rev. ed. Grand Rapids: Zondervan, 1990.

Walzer, Michael. *Spheres of Justice: A Defense of Pluralism and Equality.* New York: Basic Books, 1983.

Warren, Michael. *Seeing Through the Media: A Religious View of Communications and Cultural Analysis.* Philadelphia: Trinity Press International, 1997.

Watson, Francis. *Text, Church and World: Biblical Interpretation in Theological Perspective.* Edinburgh: T. & T. Clark, 1994.

Webber, Robert. *Common Roots: A Call to Evangelical Maturity.* Grand Rapids: Zondervan, 1979.

Weborg, John. "Pietism: Theology in Service of Living Toward God." In *The Variety of American Evangelicalism.* Edited by Donald W. Dayton and Robert K. Johnston. Downers Grove, Ill.: InterVarsity Press, 1991.

Weiss, Johannes. *Jesus' Proclamation of the Kingdom of God.* Translated by Richard H. Hiers and David L. Holland. Philadelphia: Fortress Press, 1971.

Welch, Claude. "Dispelling Some Myths about the Split between Theology and Science in the Nineteenth Century." In *Religion and Science*. Edited by W. Mark Richardson and Wesley J. Wildman. New York: Routledge & Kegan Paul, 1996.

————. *In This Name: The Doctrine of the Trinity in Contemporary Theology*. New York: Charles Scribner's Sons, 1952.

————. *Protestant Thought in the Nineteenth Century, Vol. I, 1799–1870*. New Haven and London: Yale University Press, 1972.

Wells, David. *No Place For Truth; or, Whatever Happened to Evangelical Theology?* Grand Rapids: Wm. B. Eerdmans Publishing Co., 1993.

West, Cornel. *Prophetic Thought in Postmodern Times*. Monroe, Minn.: Common Courage, 1993.

Westphal, Merold. "A Reader's Guide to 'Reformed Epistemology.'" *Perspectives* 7, no. 9 (November 1992): 10–13.

Whitehead, Alfred North. *Adventures of Ideas*. New York: Mentor Books, 1955.

————. *Process and Reality*. Harper Torchbook ed. New York: Harper & Row, 1960.

Wiley, H. Orton. *Christian Theology*. 3 vols. Kansas City, Mo.: Beacon Hill, 1952.

Williams, Raymond. *The Sociology of Culture*. New York: Schocken Books, 1982.

Wilshire, Bruce Withington. "Metaphysics." In *New Encyclopedia Britannica*. 30 vols. 15th ed. Chicago: Encyclopedia Britannica, Inc. 1998, 24:1–25.

Wittgenstein, Ludwig. *Philosophical Investigations*. Translated by G. E. M. Anscombe. Oxford: Basil Blackwell Publisher, 1953.

Wolin, Sheldon S. *Politics and Vision: Continuity and Innovation in Western Political Thought*. Boston, Mass.: Little, Brown & Co., 1960.

Wolterstorff, Nicholas. "Can Belief in God Be Rational If It Has No Foundations?" In *Faith and Rationality: Faith and Belief in God*. Edited by Alvin Plantinga and Nicholas Wolterstorff. Notre Dame, Ind.: University of Notre Dame Press, 1983.

————. *Divine Discourse: Philosophical Reflections on the Claim that God Speaks*. Cambridge: Cambridge University Press, 1995.

————. "The Importance of Hermeneutics for a Christian Worldview." In *Disciplining Hermeneutics: Interpretation in Christian Perspective*. Edited by Roger Lundin. Grand Rapids: Wm. B. Eerdmans Publishing Co., 1997.

————. "Introduction." In *Faith and Rationality: Faith and Belief in God*. Edited by Alvin Plantinga and Nicholas Wolterstorff. Notre Dame, Ind.: University of Notre Dame Press, 1983.

————. *Reason Within the Bounds of Religion*. Grand Rapids: Wm. B. Eerdmans Publishing Co., 1976.

————. *What New Haven and Grand Rapids Have to Say to Each Other*. Grand Rapids: Calvin College, 1993.

Wood, W. Jay. *Epistemology: Becoming Intellectually Virtuous*. Downers Grove, Ill.: InterVarsity Press, 1998.

Worthing, Mark William. *God, Creation, and Contemporary Physics*. Minneapolis: Fortress Press, 1996.

Wright, N. T. "How Can the Bible Be Authoritative?" *Vox Evangelica* 21 (1991): 7–32.

————. *The New Testament and the People of God*. Minneapolis: Fortress Press, 1992.

Wroe, Martin. "American Pie in the Sky." *Third Way* 18, no. 7 (September 1995): 13.

Wuthnow, Robert. *Rediscovering the Sacred: Perspectives on Religion in Contemporary Society*. Grand Rapids: Wm. B. Eerdmans Publishing Co., 1992.

Yoder, John Howard. "Hermeneutics of the Anabaptists." *Mennonite Quarterly Review* 41 (October 1967): 291–308.

————. "The Use of the Bible in Theology." In *The Use of the Bible in Theology: Evangelical Options*. Edited by Robert K. Johnston. Atlanta: John Knox Press, 1985.

Young, Alexander. *Chronicles of the Pilgrim Fathers of the Colony of Plymouth, from 1602 to 1625.* Boston: Little & Brown, 1841.

Young, Frances. *The Art of Performance: Towards a Theology of Holy Scripture.* London: Darton, Longman & Todd, 1990.

Zeller, Eduard. *Outlines of the History of Greek Philosophy.* 13th ed. Revised by Wilhelm Nestle. Translated by L. R. Palmer. New York: Meridian Books, 1957.

Zinn, Grover A., ed. *Richard of St. Victor.* New York: Paulist Press, 1979.

Zizioulas, John D. *Being as Communion: Studies in Personhood and the Church.* Crestwood, N.Y.: St. Vladimir's Seminary Press, 1985.

Index